The Right to Know One's Origins

Assisted Human Reproduction
and the Best Interests of Children

Juliet R. Guichon, Ian Mitchell, Michelle Giroux (eds.)

The Right to Know One's Origins

Assisted Human Reproduction
and the Best Interests of Children

ASP

Cover design: Maarten Deckers
Cover image: *Painting of Family Tree*, by Mary-Claire Verbeke and Kelly Wilson
Print: Wilco, Amersfoort

© 2012 ASP nv (Academic and Scientific Publishers nv)
Ravensteingalerij 28
B-1000 Brussels
Tel. + 32 (0)2 289 26 50
Fax + 32 (0)2 289 26 59
E-mail info@aspeditions.be
www.aspeditions.be

ISBN 978 90 5718 235 8
NUR 883 / 740 / 770
Legal deposit D/2012/11.161/169

All rights reserved. No parts of this book may be reproduced or transmitted in any form or by any means, electronic, mechanical, photocopying, recording, or otherwise, without the prior written permission of the publisher.

Recognition

The editors are grateful for the financial support of the
Alberta Law Foundation

Alberta LAW FOUNDATION

Many contributors are members of the
Alberta Children's Hospital Research Institute

Dedication

*In memory of Urban Guichon and Mary McCormick Guichon,
and to Alain Verbeke and our children,
Raymond-Laurent, Mary-Claire and Sophie-Charlotte*

J.R.G.

To Anne

I.M.

To Eric, Julien and Paul

M.G.

Epigraph

As I never saw my father or my mother [...] my first fancies regarding what they were like, were unreasonably derived from their tombstones. The shape of the letters on my father's gave me an odd idea that he was a square, stout, dark man, with curly black hair.

Charles Dickens, *Great Expectations*, 1861

Current AID [assisted insemination by donor] practices are based primarily on consideration of protecting the interests of practitioners and donors rather than recipients and children. [...] Obsessive concern with self-protection must give way to concern for the child.

George J. Annas, Fathers Anonymous:
Beyond the Best Interests of the Sperm Donor, 1980

The Parliament of Canada recognizes and declares that [...] the health and well-being of children born through the application of assisted human reproductive technologies must be given priority in all decisions respecting their use.

Assisted Human Reproduction Act (Canada) 2004, c. 2, s. 2.

The evidence in this case, including the evidence of current practices that are designed to avoid cutting off donor offspring from their roots compels me to the conclusion that cutting off a child from half of his or her biological origins is not in that child's best interests.

Pratten v. Attorney General of British Columbia,
British Columbia Supreme Court, 2011, per Adair, J.

Table of Contents

Recognition	5
Dedication	6
Epigraph	7
Table of Contents	9
Preface	13
Acknowledgements	20
Foreword by Professor Paul De Knop, Rector of the VUB	21
Foreword by Professor Emeritus Paul Devroey	23

Chapter One: Introduction   25
Juliet Guichon, Ian Mitchell, Michelle Giroux

PART ONE: WHAT DO SOME DONOR-CONCEIVED PEOPLE SAY ABOUT THE IMPORTANCE OF THE RIGHT TO KNOW ONE'S ORIGIN?
    Introduction to Part One   29

Chapter Two: Who I Come From   31
Barry Stevens

Chapter Three: Everyone Is Here for a Reason   36
'Naomi Williams', Age 12

Chapter Four: How I Learned the Truth and What Else I'd Like to Know   38
J.S., Age 13

Chapter Five: Does the Right to Know Matter?   40
Bill Cordray

Chapter Six: Attempting to Learn My Biological Father's Identity
A Canadian Tale of Frustration and Eventually Litigation   49
Olivia Pratten

Chapter Seven: Seeking Answers in the Ether: Longing to Know One's Origins Is Evident from Donor Conception Websites   57
Rhonda E. Harris and Laura Shanner

PART TWO: WHAT IS THE HISTORY AND MEDICAL REGULATION OF THIS PRACTICE AND WHAT HAVE WE LEARNED FROM ADOPTION?

    Introduction to Part Two   73

Chapter Eight: Historical Aspects of Advanced Reproductive Technology   75
    Ian Mitchell

Chapter Nine: Canadian Medical Codes of Ethics and the Issue of Gamete Provider Anonymity   91
    Ian Mitchell and Juliet Guichon

Chapter Ten: Identity Harm: Lessons from Adoption for Donor Conception   106
    Joanna Rose

PART THREE: WHAT DO COMMUNITY HEALTH, SOCIAL SCIENCE AND MEDICAL RESEARCH SUGGEST IS KNOWN ABOUT THE HEALTH AND WELL-BEING INTEREST OF THE DONOR-CONCEIVED?

    Introduction to Part Three   121

Chapter Eleven: A Review of Studies that Have Considered Family Functioning and Psychosocial Outcomes for Donor-Conceived Offspring   124
    Stacey A. Page

Chapter Twelve: The Effect of Disclosure or Non-Disclosure on the Psychosocial Development of Donor-Conceived People: A Review and Synthesis of the Literature   151
    W. Ben Gibbard

Chapter Thirteen: Identity Development in the Donor-Conceived   166
    Jean Benward

Chapter Fourteen: The Health Benefits to Children Having their Genetic Information
The Importance of Constructing Family Trees   192
    Julie L. Lauzon

Table of Contents

PART FOUR: COMPETING ARGUMENTS FOR DONOR ANONYMITY: LEGISLATIVE EFFECTS AND ETHICAL ASSESSMENT
    Introduction to Part Four   215

Chapter Fifteen: Donor Anonymity in the *Assisted Human Reproduction Act*: The Back Story   217
    Alison Motluk

Chapter Sixteen: When Is a Secret Justified? Ethics and Donor Anonymity   233
    Laura Shanner

PART FIVE: THE CURRENT STATE OF THE LAW: INTERNATIONAL LAW AND ANALOGOUS DOMESTIC LAW
    Introduction to Part Five   249

Chapter Seventeen: *This Is Not Baby Talk:* Canadian International Human Rights Obligations Regarding the Rights to Health, Identity and Family Relations   251
    Verónica B. Piñero

Chapter Eighteen: A Comparison of the Law in Canada Related to the Disclosure of Information Regarding Biological Parents of Adoptees and the Donor-Conceived   276
    Juliet R. Guichon

Chapter Nineteen: A Tale of Two Embryos: Record Keeping after Gamete or Embryo Donation in Cattle and Humans   299
    Alison Motluk

PART SIX: WHAT CHANGES WOULD BE NECESSARY IN PROVINCIAL LAW TO FACILITATE A BAN ON ANONYMITY?
    Introduction to Part Six   309

Chapter Twenty: The Recognition of the Right to Identity of Children Born of Assisted Procreation: A Provincial Responsibility   310
    Michelle Giroux and Mariana De Lorenzi

Chapter Twenty-One: How Canadian Common Law Might Change
to Facilitate Legislation to Permit the Donor-Conceived to Access
Information Regarding Their Progenitors   319
   Juliet R. Guichon

PART SEVEN: WHAT CAN WE CONCLUDE?
   Introduction to Part Seven   339

Chapter Twenty-Two: Time to Stop Lying   340
   David Gollancz

Chapter Twenty-Three: Conclusion   344
   Juliet Guichon, Ian Mitchell, Michelle Giroux

List of Contributors   347

Preface

Juliet Guichon

1. History

This book was conceived in the West Block of Canada's Parliament Buildings. There, in June 2002, the House of Commons Health Standing Committee was conducting hearings on the then-proposed *Assisted Human Reproduction Act*.[1] The assembled Parliamentarians had called expert witnesses to decide if people created by donated sperm or eggs should have the right to learn the identities of their biological parents and to obtain their medical, social and cultural histories. I observed as the testimony became heated and dramatic.

Our nation had trod a long and challenging path to that Parliamentary moment in the history of Canadian attempts to regulate assisted human reproduction. A 1985 report of the Ontario Law Reform Commission[2] provided the impetus and background for the federal Royal Commission on New Reproductive Technologies which spent $28 million on hearings throughout the country and commissioned volumes of original academic research.[3] In 1993, that Commission recommended urgent federal legislation to regulate the practices of clinics which aim to create children.[4]

Despite this recommendation and the cost and effort of the Royal Commission, nine years passed before the Commons Health Standing Committee meeting in June 2002 where Members of Parliament reviewed the proposed legislation. Before them was a draft statute granting permission for sperm and egg providers to remain anonymous to their children. But this legislative proposal flew in the face of the same Committee's recommendation, only six months earlier, that the interests of the donor-conceived should be given priority.[5] And so the Committee reconvened on that early summer day to seek advice from experts.

The stakes were high. Among the experts called were a representative from a sperm bank, and an obstetrician gynaecologist who specializes in reproductive endocrinology and infertility.

The sperm bank spokesperson, Heather Brooks of Xytex Corporation, argued that sperm providers (called "donors") should continue to be paid and to be anonymous. Although the corporation agreed that there should be a registry to hold pertinent medical information, it maintained that general non-identifying information was sufficient. Ms Brooks said:[6]

> Our supplemental profiles provide far more information than would likely be required by regulations, including a donor personal essay, personality evaluation, and a three- to four-generation detailed social and medical history. Since 1994, many of our donors voluntarily provide childhood and adult photographs, and since 2000 some of our donors voluntarily sign identity release agreements.

Ms. Brooks justified her company's "progressive" approach by asserting that the "patients" – the women who receive the semen – are pleased to receive the information the company offers about the men with whom they have a child.

Ms. Brooks cautioned against a government requirement of identity disclosure because it would cause a decline in supply. "A mandatory identity release policy would reduce the number of available donors in our program from about 45 to 10," she said.[7] Ms. Brooks concluded by pleading with the Commons Committee to be pragmatic:[8]

> We ask and implore you to balance the consideration of children's rights with those of patients across Canada, from Newfoundland to British Columbia, who desperately want a family but are handicapped by male factor infertility or genetic illnesses. Please balance idealism with pragmatism and enact legislation that addresses tomorrow's hopes with today's realities.

Fertility specialist, Dr. Clifford Librach, supported the position that gamete providers should continue to be paid and to be anonymous. Dr. Librach testified,[9]

> Regarding donor anonymity, I am pleased to see that the most recent draft of this bill allows those who donate their ova or sperm to protect their right to remain anonymous if they so choose. All of those who donate eggs in our program are asked if they prefer to remain anonymous or are open to contact after the child reaches the age of 18. Approximately 50% of donors choose each option.

Dr. Librach expressed concern about the decline in egg and semen supply if adults were obligated to be known to their offspring and suggested that the information provided to egg and sperm recipients was otherwise sufficient.[10]

> I am certain that if we do not allow anonymity for sperm and egg donors, the pool of donors would be dramatically reduced. [...] The prospective parents are given a full, though non-identifying, medical and social profile on the donor and their extended family.

Preface

Dr. Librach concluded by stressing the importance of personal experience in informing how assisted human reproduction is regulated. He said,[11]

> I feel it is essential that one or more parents who have had a child through egg donation or surrogacy be on this committee, as it is only they who really know what it is like to be in this situation and who have experienced this method of creating the family.

When Dr. Librach completed his testimony in that neo-Gothic chamber, I looked around for who would speak about the personal experience of the donor-conceived. How much information about their biological parents did they need and want? Was there also a paediatrician in the room to address the question of the medical needs of donor-conceived people to know their progenitors? A specialist in developmental psychology? A donor-conceived person?

Two people were present to speak against donor anonymity, including an employee of an infertility clinic, a social worker, Jean Haase, who observed that:[12]

> The concept of providing choice about identity disclosure to the donor is in direct conflict with the principle [...] that the health and well-being of children must be given priority in all decisions. It is also in contradiction [with the clause that] speaks about promoting and protecting the health, safety, human dignity, and human rights of Canadians.

Also testifying was Shirley Pratten, a mother of a donor-conceived person, and founding member of the first Canadian support group for donor-conceived families. Ms. Pratten lamented that the draft legislation seemed "to be paying lip-service to the rights, needs, health, and welfare of the children being conceived through these technologies."[13] Ms. Pratten took issue with statements made by the then Minister of Health, Anne McLellan: "She's saying it's acceptable for us to decide before these children are even born that they will never know or have access to their biological identities. How ethical is that?"[14]

But the words of these soft-spoken women did not have the dramatic ring of the medical fertility specialist who had announced at the outset of his testimony that he was speaking in a representative capacity for people whose suffering merited concern:[15]

> I would like to express my own thoughts [...] But even more importantly, I will be relating to you the views, of virtually every patient I have ever seen in consultation for egg donation or gestational surrogacy, on the implications that will follow should Bill C-56 and your recommendations become law.

He said,[16]

> My patients are devastated and enraged that the proposed legislation will prevent them from being able to have children through this currently available technology. Are we really going to subject these people to huge fines or put them in jail? Where's the justice, the morality, or the dignity in all of this, as mentioned in the preamble to the bill? Bill C-56 and your recommendations will, in effect, deny many Canadians the fundamental human right and freedom of choice to have a biologically related child, and will prevent thousands of Canadian couples from knowing the extraordinary joy and wonder of having a child.

The authority of his metaphorical white coat gave gravity to his words in a manner that seemed almost decisive. People in his profession had set the terms of sperm donation since its inception when donor anonymity had been established as the custom by infertility practitioners.

The donor-conceived themselves and physicians and health scientists, who support and study their health and well-being, were not present to inform the legislators. Their absence was particularly surprising because the donor-conceived are the vulnerable and involuntary outcome of a profitable semen, ova and embryo supply industry, and a medical speciality.

The legislators who convened that afternoon in the West Block were doing their best to address the complex ethical, sociological, medical and legal issues to which gamete and embryo donation give rise. In the bill that eventually became law in March 2004 as the *Assisted Human Reproduction Act*,[17] it was recognized and declared that "the health and well-being of children born through the application of assisted human reproductive technologies must be given priority in all decisions respecting their use."[18] Yet the same statute endorsed donor anonymity by stipulating that, unless gamete donors agree in writing, their offspring may not know their identities.[19] To many, it appeared that Parliament had adopted a contradictory position within the same statute.

Since the enactment of the *Assisted Human Reproduction Act*, the Supreme Court of Canada's ruling[20] in December 2010 that much of that statute is unconstitutional,[21] and the Province of British Columbia's appeal of a judgement that recognized the rights of the donor-conceived,[22] the important question remains unresolved. In the constellation of professional, commercial and profoundly personal interests, can Canadian lawmakers and judges discern the correct balance between the rights of those wishing to be parents, and the rights of the children of families formed using gamete and embryo donation?

2. Purpose

The public debate about the proper regulation of reproductive technology will continue. This edited volume aims to enhance that debate by presenting the opinion and research of some donor-conceived people and some of those who study their health and well-being, and the ethical and legal implications of the practice.

3. Scope

This work considers the legislative matter of donor anonymity following the point at which it was codified in 2004. To answer the question whether donor anonymity is consistent with the health and well-being of the donor-conceived, the book begins by considering what some donor-conceived people say is in their interest and examines other evidence that the right to know matters. The work then considers the history and medical regulation of this practice and what we have learned from adoption.

The book also considers the issue of secrecy – where rearing parents do not tell donor-conceived children about the circumstances of their conception. Because donor insemination is increasingly used by single women and women in same-sex partnerships, there is no male to protect, and so secrecy is less often practiced. Nevertheless, it remains an important matter.

The book offers new research into the very question at issue: What does research in the fields of community health science, social science and medicine claim is known about the health and well-being interests of the donor-conceived regarding secrecy and anonymity? Because such research tends to suggest that neither secrecy nor anonymity is in the interests of the donor-conceived, the work then asks whether there are important barriers to granting a right to know. Examining and deciding that there is no moral theory to justify donor anonymity, the book considers whether international and Canadian law require state recognition of the right to know one's origins and summarizes the judicial ruling that the *Canadian Charter of Rights and Freedoms* protects such a right. Finding templates for legislative action in adoption disclosure law and in federal law that requires record keeping in the use of donor gametes of other mammalian species, the book suggests what changes must be made in provincial civil and common law to make a ban on anonymity viable. The book concludes where it began with the words of a donor-conceived person who asserts that the stories of our origins are an entitlement and among our most precious goods; while we cannot prevent individuals from lying to us, the state must not connive.

4. Conclusion

This book takes seriously Parliament's statement (which is still in force) that the health and well-being interests of the offspring come first and, therefore, aims to understand better what those interests are and to help the legislative process give effect to their interests. This work recommends active discouragement of secrecy and a ban on donor anonymity and because, even though much research is preliminary, the evidence to date suggests that state recognition and protection of the right and opportunity to learn the identities and medical, social and cultural history of their biological parents is almost certainly in the health and well-being interests of the donor-conceived.

This work is an international collaborative effort to address the Canadian context of ethical, medical and legal questions that now confront policy makers in many domestic and international jurisdictions. As an interdisciplinary exploration of the health and well-being interests of the donor-conceived and of the public policy and legislative implications of placing priority on those interests, this volume will advance and continue the necessary debate about how society should regulate the use of the reproductive technologies available in our time.

Notes

1. Bill C-56: Assisted Human Reproduction, 49-50-51 Elizabeth II, 2001-2002 House of Commons of Canada.
2. Ontario Law Reform Commission, Report on human artificial reproduction and related matters, Ministry of the Attorney General, 1985.
3. Anonymous, *A short history of the Royal Commission on New Reproductive Technologies*; *The Hamilton Spectator*, Hamilton, Ont.: 1 December 1993 at A.9.
4. *Proceed with Care*, Final Report of the Royal Commission on New Reproductive Technologies, (Ottawa: Minister of Government Services Canada, 1993).
5. *Assisted Human Reproduction: Building Families*, Report by the Commons Standing Committee on Health, Bonnie Brown, Chair, (Ottawa: Public Works and Government Services Canada, December 2001).
6. Evidence, Standing Committee on Health, 37th Parliament, 1st Session, Wednesday, June 12, 2002 at 16:55.
7. *Ibid.*, at 17:00.
8. *Ibid.*
9. *Ibid.*, at 15:45.
10. *Ibid.*
11. *Ibid.*
12. *Ibid.*, at 16:45.
13. *Ibid.*, at 16:25.
14. *Ibid.*, at 16:30.
15. *Ibid.*, at 15:35.
16. *Ibid.*, at 15:40.

17 *Assisted Human Reproduction Act* S.C. 2004, c.2.
18 *Ibid.*, s.2(a).
19 *Ibid.*, s.18(2).
20 Reference re *Assisted Human Reproduction Act*, 2010 SCC 61.
21 On December 22, 2010, the Supreme Court of Canada, in an advisory opinion, ruled that sections 10-11, 13-18, 40(2), 40(3), 40(3.1), 40(4), 40(5), and section 44(2) and 44(3) of the Act exceeded the legislative jurisdiction of the Parliament of Canada pursuant to the *Constitution Act*, 1867.
22 Neal Hall, B.C. government appeals landmark sperm donor ruling, *Vancouver Sun*, June 17, 2011 http://www.vancouversun.com/health/government+appeals+landmark+sperm+donor+ruling/4966861/story.html#ixzz1RkQK527L.

Acknowledgements

This book has been aided by the wisdom, work and steadfast support of Professor of Pediatrics, Dr. Ian Mitchell, and Professor of Civil Law, Michelle Giroux.

I acknowledge with gratitude the generous support of the Alberta Law Foundation, which funded both the research in this book and a Calgary meeting of collaborators. I thank Ivan Whitehall and Judith Parisien of the firm Heenan Blaikie, Ottawa; the law firm May, Jensen, Shawa, Calgary; and Laura Snowball, Barrister and Solicitor in Calgary, for their insight and encouragement.

In particular, I am grateful to two prominent Canadian advocates for the interests of the donor-conceived – Diane Allen of the Infertility Network, Toronto, and Joe Arvay of Arvay Finlay Barristers, Vancouver – for their generous responses to inquiry and for their example.

Juliet R. Guichon
November 15, 2012
Calgary, Canada

Foreword

Professor Paul De Knop, Rector of the VUB (Free University of Brussels)

The Right to Know One's Origins represents an impressive collection of essays describing the vulnerability of children conceived through assisted human reproduction. Assisted human reproduction includes a variety of technologies and practices that allow infertile people to realize their dream of raising a child. Advances in medical science that allow alleviating adult suffering are unequivocally welcome. But scientists and policy makers should also reflect carefully on any new vulnerability, created when infusing novel technologies and medical practices in human society.

Assisted human reproduction should always put first protecting vulnerable children. They are entitled to the truth about their origins, even if sperm donors, some members of the medical establishment, and the infertile adults who gain the status of parent, may find it more appropriate to hide what they consider an 'inconvenient truth'. Secrecy and anonymity of donors have no place in the realm of assisted reproduction. When ignoring the importance of children's genetic origins, individuals are denied any knowledge about the medical history of their family. Many dangers loom, including the medical dangers of incest, when two individuals share a genetic parent without knowing and without the possibility of knowing.

From a humanistic perspective, it is simply unacceptable that individuals would be denied the very same information that we systematically gather about animals raised for purposes of professional sports such as racehorses, or for purposes of human consumption such as cattle. I am proud that the Free University of Brussels has decided to publish this book as it is consistent with our founding principle: 'Scientia Vincere Tenebras', meaning that scientific knowledge will conquer the dark ages. Paradoxically, in this case the dark ages do not result from the absence of science *per se* but rather from the ill-conceived social component of assisted human reproduction.

This book thankfully does not seek to strike a mundane 'faux-intellectual' balance between the arguments of the proponents and the opponents of formal, systematic registration of gamete donors. The book convincingly demonstrates that advances in medical science must go hand in hand with full disclosure of the truth to those who would not have been created without this science.

The Right to Know One's Origins

I sincerely hope that this volume may incite jurisdictions around the world to guarantee to all donor-conceived children full access to their medical, social and cultural histories. It is time to defeat the dark-age aspects of assisted human reproduction and to tell the truth to those who most deserve to know.

Professor Paul De Knop, Rector of the Free University of Brussels

Foreword

Professor Emeritus Paul Devroey

This volume discusses one of the most important features of what it means to be a human being, namely to have actionable knowledge of one's own genetic history. The absence of gametes in a female or a male individual creates a fundamental barrier to human reproduction. The subsequent decision to be made by the individual(s) involved, is not an easy one. The fundamental question is whether to introduce a foreign gamete in order to obtain a viable pregnancy. Clinical experience tells us that many individuals and couples go through a long process of reflection before deciding to move ahead. However, once the decision has been reached to initiate a pregnancy through donor gametes, a cascade of new decision-making challenges arises. These challenges relate to questions such as: what information should be given to the child? What information should be accessible regarding the donor? To what extent should there be protection of donor anonymity vis-à-vis some parties?

From a humanistic perspective, it is clear to me that transparency is of paramount importance. There is no doubt in my mind that every child has a fundamental right to know the truth concerning her or his origin. Honest and transparent information on what happened should be shared with the child as soon as possible, and preferably in the early stages of childhood. It is undoubtedly difficult for many parents to explain to their child that either the female or the male had deficient sperm or oocytes, but once this information has been disclosed, the child will find it easy to understand that the only way to reproduce was through the use of donor gametes.

What information on the donor should be disclosed? The most critical information on the donor is related to health matters, for example to anticipate or mitigate genetic disease in the offspring. The medical laboratory and clinic where the procedure was performed must have full information on file, so that potentially serious disease of the offspring can be dealt with appropriately. If information on genetic diseases is known in advance, the health workers should inform the potential donor *ex ante* about the risks of initiating a pregnancy.

Another fundamental question is related to the rights of the child to know the donor. From a conceptual, ethics-based perspective the importance of this right is almost self-evident, as highlighted in this book. However, in practice full disclosure is not always easy to achieve, since some potential donors may be unwilling intellectually and emotionally to do the right thing. Here, the role of health care workers, especially counsellors and psychologists should not be neglected. They play a crucial role in the decision-making processes of both the infertile couples seeking gametes and the potential donors of such gametes.

The key lesson always to be remembered by parents and donors alike is the need to be transparent, because transparency will fundamentally affect the wellbeing of the offspring.

Dr. Paul Devroey
Professor Emeritus of Reproductive Medicine, Free University of Brussels
Chairman of the Belgian National Committee for Bioethics, Past Chairman of the European Society for Human Reproduction and Embryology and Past President of the Belgian Society of Reproductive Medicine
Director of Medical Education of the International Federation of Fertility Societies

Chapter One

Introduction

Juliet Guichon, Ian Mitchell, Michelle Giroux

Since at least 1884, physicians have circumvented male infertility by obtaining human sperm and inserting it in the wives of infertile men.[1] The technique, known as "donor insemination", has more recently been employed to create pregnancies in women who do not have a male partner or do not wish to have one. To circumvent female infertility or childlessness, human eggs have, since the 1980's, been extracted from women, fertilized in a petri dish and then the resulting embryo transferred to a second woman. In both sperm and egg 'donation', the goal is to conceive a child who will not be reared by the gamete provider. Many people conceived by these methods have argued that they should be told about their unusual conception and that gamete providers should not be anonymous to their offspring. In other words, many offspring argue that secrecy and anonymity are morally objectionable.

To be sure, secrecy is not the issue it once was. People born to a single woman or a woman with a female partner are likely to know, or at least to be alerted to the possibility that, they were donor-conceived. Nevertheless, many people are not told the truth about their conception by their rearing parents.[2]

This book considers whether people in Canada ought to have the right and opportunity to know of their donor conception and to access identifying and medical, cultural and social information about their progenitors when they are created by third party gametes with the assistance of healthcare professionals. What law would be in the best interests of the health and well being of those conceived by the practice of donor conception?

Regulatory history and social change

Canada has had a difficult time regulating the field of assisted human reproduction. In 1989, the federal government, responding to public outcry, created the Royal Commission on New Reproductive Technologies.[3] Four years and $28 million later, and after hearing from over 40,000 Canadians, that body recommended that the federal government legislate immediately.[4] Nevertheless, it took 11 more years before the *Assisted Human Reproduction Act* was finally enacted in 2004.[5] Then, in 2010, the Supreme Court of Canada held that most sections of the Act, including those that concern the creation, preservation and disclosure of gamete donor records, are within provincial jurisdiction.

This ruling, which struck down major sections of the federal statute, has left Canada's most important aspects of human reproductive technology virtually unregulated, and marked a new chapter in Canada's beleaguered attempt to regulate the emotionally-sensitive field. As of the date of this publication, only Quebec has legislation regulating assisted reproduction activities. That legislation did not, however, amend the Civil Code of Quebec, to ban donor anonymity. Consequently, the Code still prevents donor-conceived people from knowing the identity of their progenitors.[6]

While our federal governmental system has responded slowly, the challenges of reproductive technology have grown rapidly. From one private reproductive Canadian clinic in 1989, there are now about 28,[7] in an estimated $4 billion international industry.[8] In vitro fertilization and egg, sperm and embryo provision have become regular clinic-based interventions with little long-term data on the physical and psychological outcomes for all, especially the offspring.

Likewise, a social revolution has occurred in which there is less questioning of the deliberate separation of genetic, gestational and social parenting. Accelerating this change has been the lobbying of public and government opinion. So-called "infertility patient groups", funded by fertility clinics, lobby to change public policy in Canada and elsewhere.[9] Clinics and the pharmaceutical industry can profit from an unregulated market.

Government mandate

Now that the provincial legislatures clearly have jurisdiction to regulate the practice of gamete donation, legislatures from Newfoundland to British Columbia must consider what policy to adopt regarding practices that create other humans outside the body and can put maternity in doubt. Despite the complexity of the issues, urgent action is required. To quote the Royal Commission, "The field is developing too rapidly, the consequences of inaction are too great and the potential for harm to individuals and to society is too serious to allow Canada's response to be delayed [...]".[10]

Guiding principle and book's focus

As provincial governments consider how best to govern assisted human reproduction, they might adopt the preamble to the federal *Assisted Human Reproduction Act*:[11]

> The health and well-being of children born through the application of assisted human reproductive technologies must be given priority in all decisions respecting their use.

In an attempt to advance discussion and to assist provincial legislators, this book considers seriously the question of what is in the health and well-being interests of the donor-conceived. It adopts an interdisciplinary approach exploring the significance of the right to know one's origins, why other interests have been allowed to take precedence, the health and wellbeing implications of the right to know and how protecting this right might be achieved provincially. By commissioning new health science and medical research, this work has come to the preliminary conclusion that the creation, preservation, updating and disclosure of gamete donor records is in the health and well-being interest of the donor-conceived. This conclusion is consistent with international law and can be relatively easily achieved by specified reform of civil and common law.

The existing and considerable medical and sociological literature tends to focus on adult interests, which can coincide also with commercial interests. Therefore, it is easy to justify this child-centered contribution to the literature. The interests of children are not only under-represented but the children of assisted reproduction are the most affected by the technologies for the longest time; children need adult protection and their interests are unlikely to attract a commercial spokesperson.

This work aims to bring new perspective to a wide and varied audience regarding an issue that will continue to affect an increasing number of Canadians. We hope also that this book will help governments in Canada in their decisions to act urgently to protect the children of reproductive technology whose conceptions have, for decades, been challenging us to focus on what it means to be human in an increasingly complex world.

November 15, 2012

Notes

1 A.T. Gregoire and R.C. Mayer, The Impregnators. *Fertility and Sterility*, 1965; 16 (1):130-134.
2 See, for example, Jadva, Vasanti, Tabitha Freeman, Wendy Kramer and Susan Golombok. "The Experiences of Adolescents and Adults Conceived by Sperm Donation: Comparisons by Age of Disclosure and Family Type." *Human Reproduction*, 2009; 24: 1909-19; Owen, L. and S. Golombok. "Families Created by Assisted Reproduction: Parent-Child Relationships in Late Adolescence." *Journal of Adolescence*, 2009; 32: 835-48.
3 Decret 1989-2150, 25 October 1989. p. 3, Volume 1.

4 Royal Commission on New Reproductive Technologies, Ottawa, Minister of Supply and Services Canada, 1993.
5 SC 2004, c 2.
6 *An Act respecting clinical and research activities relating to assisted procreation*, R.S.Q., c. A-5.01; see also section 542 Civil Code of Québec, L.Q. 1991, c. 64.
7 Canadian Fertility and Andrology Society, Human Assisted Reproduction 2011 Live Birth Rates for Canada, September 25, 2011, http://www.cfas.ca/index.php?option=com_content&view=article&id=1130:2010-cartr-results&catid=1012:cartr&Itemid=670.
8 TMC news, U.S. "Baby Business" (Infertility Services) Worth $4 Billion, August 17, 2009 quoting a study conducted by Marketdata Enterprises, Inc. entitled, U.S. Fertility Clinics & Infertility Services: An Industry Analysis, http://www.tmcnet.com/usubmit/2009/08/17/4326513.htm.
9 Infertility Awareness Association of Canada, http://www.iaac.ca/front.
10 Royal Commission on New Reproductive Technologies, Ottawa, Minister of Supply and Services Canada, 1993, volume 1, page 405.
11 S. 2(a) [*AHRA*].

PART ONE

WHAT DO SOME DONOR-CONCEIVED PEOPLE SAY ABOUT THE IMPORTANCE OF THE RIGHT TO KNOW ONE'S ORIGIN?

The book begins with accounts by donor-conceived people of their own experiences and their statements about what they claim they need.

One of the most prominent donor-conceived persons in Canada is filmmaker, *Barry Stevens*. After seven years of following clues and tracing DNA, he learned the identity of his donor father. Though the man was by then deceased, Barry Stevens describes the experience of learning his identity as granting him "a great sense of confidence" and a feeling of being "more grounded".

More common, however, are the stories of people who do not know and cannot know their donors' identity. A 12-year-old contributing under the pseudonym, "*Naomi Williams*" laments, "I will never know; I'll never quite get to know how I came to be, or who he really is." A second child, "*J.S.*" aged 13 years, responds with anger at the law that prevents her from knowing the identity of her father. She writes, "Imagine, you can never meet your birth father, it's like a chunk of you has been torn out, is missing."

Struggling with this problem for a much longer period is 64-year-old architect, *Bill Cordray*, who learned that he was donor-conceived when he was 37 years old. Cordray offers a historical perspective and states that more parents would tell the truth about the conception if they could also tell their children the identity of their genetic parent. He decries the pernicious words of the gynaecologist to his parents telling them to keep the fact of his donor conception secret, even from him. Impatient with people who ask him why he wants to know the identity of his sperm donor father, Cordray wonders why anyone believes that an adult would not want to know, and not be entitled to know, his or her identity.

The desire for such knowledge led donor-conceived person, *Olivia Pratten*, as a last resort, to sue the Province of British Columbia and the Provincial College of Physicians and Surgeons for their failure to create, preserve and disclose records regarding genetic parentage. Initially successful in her argument that the province denies her constitutional right to equality, Olivia was the Respondent to an appeal by the Attorney General of British Columbia. We await the judgement.

Seeking knowledge about one's genetic parents and siblings is not uncommon. Social scientist, Rhonda Harris and philosopher, Laura Shanner, have described the many ways people are using the worldwide web to gain such information. The consequences of learning the identity of the donor are described as creating powerful moments of self-recognition and sometimes representing unique challenges.

Chapter Two
Who I Come From

Barry Stevens

It is rare to know the actual minute when some great chapter of one's life began. But I do remember the precise moment when I started to search for the identity of an anonymous man who sired me. It was a beautiful day in 1998, in a Canadian prairie city. My mother and I were sitting in the comfortable living room of a family friend and his wife whom we were visiting. Nervously, I waited for a certain subject I expected would come up.

My sister, Janice, had earlier written to ask this friend, our host, to help put her in contact with his father. The father had referred our parents to a physician in London more than a half century before who had twice used what was then called "Artificial Insemination by Donor" to give my mother two babies: my sister and me.

My mother's recollections of the identity of the physician were not good. She remembered that she was a woman, and that her office was near Harley Street. My sister wanted to know the physician's name as a first clue and thought maybe our host's father could tell her. But when our host finally raised the subject, there was a sudden tension in the room. Janice's query had violated the secrecy that still often surrounds what we now call donor insemination.

Only a few months before, Janice had announced to me that she would attempt to get more information about our biological origin. I was surprised. By then, we had known of our unusual conception for more than 25 years. In 1970, our father, a physician, had died in an accident. To help deal with his sudden death, our mother had visited a psychiatrist who told her that we certainly would have sensed the great family secret and that telling us the truth about our origins would be the healthy thing to do. So, that Christmas in Montreal, as the snow softly fell outside Jan's little apartment, our mother nervously and gently told us the truth: that Dad had been infertile and that we had both been conceived artificially from another man's sperm.

A sort of bubble of silence descended around me; my world seemed to shift quietly beneath me like the plates that slide under continents. I remember being worried for our mother, who, in that moment, looked very shaky. But I think she was relieved: telling the truth helped her feel less alone. My first thought was about my father: keeping that secret all those years must have been isolating for him, too. His distance and reluctance to inhabit the role of father now made sense.

My next thought was to wonder who the mysterious 'donor' could have been. But our mother made it clear that we could never know anything more about our progenitor. The procedure was secret, the 'donor' anonymous. The absolute and final nature of that secrecy and anonymity seem to me now characteristic of the Britain that shaped us. But when we were conceived, it made sense: in the 1940's, the practice was widely condemned by everyone from the House of Lords (who owed their political authority to knowing where sperm comes from) to the Archbishop of Canterbury (who, oddly, was my father's patient for a time.) In British society, my mother could have been seen as an adulteress, and my sister and I, illegitimate: bastards. Hence, secrecy.

In the years that followed, I liked feeling there was something special about me, but I also felt oddly alone – in some sense, lacking a mirror. I also realized with some anxiety that we were part of the first wave of a movement that might one day turn into something like Huxley's *Brave New World*. I confided only in very close friends or girlfriends. Janice and I would sometimes speculate, sometimes joke about our origins. The empty space in our story allowed us to fill it with fantasy. We pretended that our mystery masturbator was a film star (I favoured Dirk Bogarde, my sister, Prince Philip). But discovering any more seemed so impossible as to halt any further contemplation of a quest. And Janice and I were building our lives. Even though I wanted to know, I thought it pointless to worry about searching for something that could not be found.

Janice felt the same way until three events coincided. In mid-life, she had a health scare. She was fine, but when her doctor needed more information about her family history, she realized that she had major gaps in her knowledge. Her daughter's development into young adulthood helped Janice recognize that she felt unable to give her a proper account of where she came from. And by some strange coincidence, at a Toronto bed and breakfast, Janice met two adults also conceived by artificial insemination. Of course, we knew, in theory, that there must be others like us, but somehow meeting two other people made the way we were was still a shock, and brought that aspect of our lives out of fantasy and into reality. These two – Bill Cordray and Lynne Spencer – were in Toronto to address a conference on 'donor' insemination organized by the *Infertility Network*. Not only did others like us exist, they were actually speaking publicly about their conceptions!

All of these developments inspired Janice to do some research about the sperm 'donor's' identity. I thought her effort was doomed to failure and therefore foolish. (I had always been the pessimist and she the optimist.) But despite my misgivings, she wrote to that family friend – in whose living room I now sat with my mother.

The family friend, annoyed at the prospect of intruding upon his 90-something father, told my mother and me that it was ridiculous that Janice wanted to uncover these secrets. He said that Janice had had a perfectly good father and asked what possible purpose could be served by digging up the past? "She doesn't need to know who this man was," he said. His wife concurred. And my mother, embarrassed that her daughter's letter had caused her host difficulty, strongly agreed. She said that Janice was being silly. And then, at the same moment, all their heads turned to me. They wanted my agreement. And I, sitting on the couch in this sunny living room, a china teacup in my hand, was about to join them by repeating, "That's right, Janice is being silly."

But the words didn't come out. They were blocked by something that had risen up inside my chest and stopped me. It was anger. The feeling was accompanied by two questions for them all: "How do *you* know what people in our position need or don't need? You cannot know, and therefore have no right to tell us what we need." And second: "What is it about this question that makes it so important to you that we not ask it?" I stammered something probably quite inarticulate, in my sister's defense. But in that moment, I realized I had joined Janice's quest.

After we began to search, that initial anger was replaced with determination, curiosity, the realization that I had always wanted to know the truth, and excitement as we approached it. But my conviction remains that it is not for others to tell the offspring of 'donor' conception that they do not need to know who they come from. We want to know for reasons of personal identity, for reasons of health, because secrecy in families is corrosive – and because we all have a right to our own stories. My indignation in that moment is still there: nobody has the right to withhold from us essential information about ourselves.

Our search for our biological father took the better part of a decade, from 1998 to 2007. The search for half-siblings continues to this day. To the first quest, I was able to take over from Janice and devote a lot more time and energy. It helped, too, when I started to make a film about the process (called *Offspring*, which was seen around the world in 2001-2002.) The search generated its own momentum – once in the grip of it, I became obsessed and did not stop until we had solved the mystery.

It proved, of course, very difficult to learn anything about our biological paternity, given that our conceptions happened in 1947 and 1951 respectively; most of the key players were dead, and all records had been destroyed. But those who hid the secrets had not anticipated the development of two technologies: the internet and DNA testing. Our family tree is written in the nucleus of every one of our body's cells, and we are learning how to read it.

Our first leap was to identify that London physician, Dr. Mary Barton, and her husband, Bertold Wiesner, the man who recruited the sperm providers. The next stage was to identify the men in Wiesner's circle who had contributed to their project, find their children, and approach them for DNA. We were lucky enough to find quite quickly a genetic half-brother, David Gollancz, who shared the same biological father with me (and who is a contributor to this book.) It was one of the great meetings of my life. But when my documentary *Offspring* was released, we had still not been able to identify the man from whose loins we had sprung. I did, however, discover that I myself was the biological father (through traditional means) of a daughter I had never known was mine. This unexpected paternity gave me additional respect for, and insight into, the meaning and power of the genetic link between father and child.

After more years of searching, we did finally solve the central mystery. I now know who my biological progenitor was, and Janice also identified hers. David's and my bio-dad was Bertold Wiesner, the husband of the physician who treated my mother. Janice's bio-dad was Wiesner's star sperm provider, Derek Richter. She has found five half-siblings. Last time I counted, there were thirteen in my clan, as well as numerous extended family members. It is probable that there are several hundred more whom we shall never know – or perhaps we shall. But I have met many of those, whom I do know of, and some of us have met as a group several times now and finding this extended family has brought deep satisfaction. It's very hard to say what the genetic tie means or how much it matters. But it does mean something. It does matter.

The search itself was the greatest journey of my life so far. I documented the last chapter in it in a second film, called *Bio-Dad*, which also takes an anxious look at the future of reproductive and genetic technologies, and follows the emerging movement of offspring to have the right to their personal information recognized.

Even if governments in Canada choose not to recognise that right, future offspring of assisted conception will demand to know their origins and their connections just as we did, and they will have success more quickly. If we were able to solve a half-century-old mystery with only primitive DNA testing, how much easier is it going to be for the coming generation to uncover *their* truths, with all the advances coming in genetic testing? Secrecy and anonymity are weak barriers indeed.

My pleasure in knowing who I come from is not to diminish the memory of my father. He became my father when he decided to have children. My connection to him did not depend on DNA. The search has given me a deeper and more compassionate understanding of him, and he remains my father.

But I still needed to search for Bertold Wiesner, that man I never call 'father.' Because he belongs to me, too. It is useful, of course, to know the weaknesses in his health. But I also deserve the dignity of knowing the identity of the man whose body gave me life. I would have liked to have heard his voice, to have learned whether he believed that love conquers all, to know if he feared death, to hear what advice he had on women, or just to have watched the way he tied his shoelaces. But knowing who he was is still powerful. It yields, for some reason, a sense of being more grounded, of a surer confidence. Now I can see glimpses of him in my new family's faces. I can see him in me, as I can see me in Sarah, my bio-daughter. There is a sense of membership. And now I can thank both my twin fathers for the gift of my life.

Chapter Three
Everyone Is Here for a Reason

'Naomi Williams', Age 12[1]

Whatever it is, I know that everyone is here for a reason. Every person's reason might be different, but it's a reason nonetheless. In the end, though, we're all trying to accomplish one thing; we're trying to find out why we're here. And, to find out why we're here, we have to know how we got here.

I was born using the help of sperm insemination – the sperm of an anonymous sperm donor was donated to be fertilized with my mother's egg in order for my parents to have a child. But, because the donor is anonymous, this means that it is very likely that I will never know who my biological father is.

When I was at an age just old enough to understand, my parents explained to me how I was made – that a man donated a sperm to my parents so that they could have a family. Of course I had many questions, as I still do, but not many of my questions were answered. The amount of information that I know about my sperm donor is very limited. I've always been looking for answers that aren't available to me.

Now that I'm older – 12 years old, I can better understand information about such things as the anonymity of sperm donors, the disputes between donor-conceived people and their parents, and the constant demand for more information about the sperm donors. This leaves me with a lot to think about. I'm not angry at my parents for choosing to make me how I was made, although I am upset about the lack of information that we've received about our sperm donor.

The curiosity is always there, as to who my sperm donor is. As I walk down the street, I could be walking past him. I could have a dozen half-siblings that I don't even know about. And, I will probably never know, because of the fact that a sperm donor's identity is kept confidential.

Sometimes, I think about (if I ever did get a chance to meet my sperm donor) what I would say, and what I would want to know, if I met my sperm donor. Sometimes, I wonder why I want to know who he is, but, I can't really explain it myself. Mainly, I'm simply curious, but I would also want to thank him. I remember when I was a little girl, and how I used to write little letters to God, thanking him for the sperm that the sperm donor had given to my parents.

There are other reasons too – like knowledge of family health and medical conditions, that aren't as important to me now, but they will be.

Maybe I've passed by him on the street a million times before. I will never know; I'll never quite get to know how I came to be, or who he really is. So, I guess I can't quite figure out why I'm here just yet. Someday I'll know for sure, but for now, I'll have to wait and see. And until then, you can be sure that I'll be waiting.

Note

1 "Naomi Williams" is a pseudonym chosen by the 12-year-old author to protect her identity.

Chapter Four
How I Learned the Truth and What Else I'd Like to Know

J.S.,[1] Age 13

Ever since I can remember, maybe three times a year, I would ask my Mom, "Am I adopted?" And my mother would reply "No, you are not adopted." I can see some resemblances with my Mom: dark brown eyes, brown hair, tall, same shaped legs, same hair line and forehead. On the other hand, when I look over to my Dad – well, we don't have many physical looks that are the same. We're both tall and we both have brown hair (at least he used to but his was a lighter tone than mine – now he has white hair). He has blue eyes and I have brown eyes, he has thin scruffy eyebrows and I have thicker definitely not scruffy eyebrows. He has a big Adam's apple and mine is not that noticeable. I'm 13 and I have the same size feet as his – there's definitely something wrong with this picture.

In the summer of 2007, my father, my mother and I decided to visit Québec City where my mother was born. We were having a great time, we visited my great aunt's house which is now a museum, we shopped and we explored pretty much everything inside the walls of old Québec.

It was about the fifth day we had been in Québec. It was dark out and my parents and I were just roaming around the legislative buildings. I was right in front of my parents happily walking along. I had just finished walking across a little bridge, when my Dad stopped. "Come over here," he said.

I walked over to him wondering what was so important that he had to tell me at, I don't know, 10:00 pm? He was grasping the railing of the bridge, didn't look me in the eyes but watched the water tumble, fall and splash everywhere.

"We're in Québec City where your mother's side of the family came from and so I would like to tell you more about your history." At the time I was thinking "Oh, what is he going to tell me – some boring old story of how my grandparents settled in Québec or something?"

"You were artificially inseminated," he told me. As soon as I heard "artificially" I thought, "I'm fake?"

"Do you know what that means?" my father asked.

"No," I replied.

"Well, it means that I couldn't produce sperm so your mother and I had to go to use a donor." When I asked about my biological father, my parents told me that as a condition of this process the donor remains anonymous. "Do you understand?"

I nodded and walked far enough ahead that you wouldn't think I was with them. I'M ARTIFICIALLY INSEMINATED??? ONE PART OF ME IS WORTH 20 BUCKS? THAT'S ALL?? THIS "DAD" OF MINE IS NOT ACTUALLY HIM. WELL WHO IS HE? SOME RANDOM GUY THAT JUST MOVED IN THE FAMILY! WHO IS HE? GET OUT OF MY LIFE! GO AWAY! YOU'RE PROBABLY JUST SOME STALKER IN MY LIFE. WHERE'S MY REAL DAD? WHERE IS HE? I CAN'T MEET HIM…. I can't meet him… I can't know him…

All this rage was gathered up; it's kind of like snot. I guess it all builds up and then it comes out as one loud disaster. We got back to the hotel and I hid under my covers, tears streaming down my cheeks. By now, my parents were asleep so I walked over to the bathroom under the sink with uncountable thoughts bursting into my head. Guess what? It is, in fact, illegal to meet your birth father! YOU CAN NEVER MEET HIM. I gulped so it didn't come out as a loud cry. Even as I write this story I gulp, I still feel the pain. Imagine, you can never meet your birth father, it's like a chunk of you has been torn out, is missing. Some of the reasons given for why I cannot meet my birth father are:

1. He might think my mother and I would be looking for him to support our family.
2. He might want to take me away because I am, in fact, his daughter.
3. He might be some bad guy and could hurt me.

Well, I say that it's still my story, and I don't care what the consequences are. You still shouldn't take him away from me. Look, if he's such a bad guy then there's something called prison. Even then, I could go visit him and talk to him. It should not be the government or the law saying whether you can meet your father or not. It's between my birth father and me to decide. If he doesn't want to meet me, fine. That's where it ends for me.

My parents are fine with what I'm deciding; they have given permission so I could meet my birth father. I would appreciate if the government gave me permission to meet my birth father and not be against it. As I said, my father was the one to tell me I was artificially inseminated so he has no problem with the fact that he is not my birth father, sometimes he says he even forgets that we aren't blood related, but to him it doesn't matter. If I could wave a magic wand, and change the law any way I wanted, I would allow permission to meet my birth father. One thing I would not do is I would not stop the process of artificial insemination. I wish I could meet my birth daddy.

Note

1 J.S. are the initials of a minor conceived by assisted insemination.

Chapter Five
Does the Right to Know Matter?

Bill Cordray

Why do I want to know my identity, my family genealogy, my heritage? Ever since I began speaking in public about my donor conception, I have been asked this question countless times. And each time, I'm astounded. My right to know my genetic father is so crucial to my sense of identity that I'm shocked that anyone should ask such a question. Why wouldn't I want to know? Wouldn't anyone else want to know?

In fact, I'm outraged that I'm in this position. How can a physician withhold from me my history? No legislature or court gave a gynaecologist the power to deny me my basic identity. He and thousands of other fertility physicians and clinic directors have simply presumed to sever the genealogical connections of millions of people before they are even conceived, making it impossible for these same people, when they become autonomous adults, to gain access to these important ties. This arrogation of power without democratic due process is illegitimate, immoral and outrageous.

I developed my impassioned view about my rights to know my origins over a twenty-six year period in which I have conversed with hundreds of donor-conceived adults, conducted a major study of the experiences of 104 donor-conceived adults,[1] and engaged in extended research on the history of donor conception and how it has affected countless people. The expertise I have thus developed is, however, grounded in the personal story of my parents, three brothers and me.

1. My Origins

This story was based on a lie. For 37 years, I did not even know that I was conceived through donor insemination. A physician interfered with even this basic right to the truth by insisting that my parents never tell me about the circumstances of my conception.

My parents' participation in this deception must be understood in context. They were desperate for their first natural child. They had suffered ten years of infertility, three attempts at adoption (only one successful), my father's shame at contracting the gonorrhoea that eliminated his ability to create sperm, and the unhelpful comments from family members and friends. In this emotional context of grief, shame, suffering, social stigma and isolation, my parents in 1944 visited a gynaecologist whom they believed would help them. Such gynaecologists could create the miracle of birth and change adults' sadness into joy. And the initial joy was evident: after adopting my brother, my mother gave birth to me and, later, two more boys, each with a different genetic father.

My parents' joy was to come at a price. They were instructed not only to hide the truth from me but also never to seek to learn the identity of my genetic father. The gynaecologist even required them to sign a document to this effect, causing them to believe that they were contractually bound. Although my parents complied with the doctor's stipulations, it would be wrong to say that they freely consented; their emotions and social isolation put them in a very weak bargaining position.

2. Effects of Gynaecologist's Imposition of Secrecy

How did the doctor's command that my parents hide the truth actually work out for my family? In short, it poisoned my relationship with my parents and brothers, and confounded my developing identity. The gynaecologist's stipulations were unjustly imposed and completely misguided.

My parents' only source of guidance was the gynaecologist. There was no social support, internet discussion groups, or insightful writings about the psychological impact of secrecy within the family. They had no idea. The gynaecologist's instructions were based merely on conjecture and his own unexamined assumptions that things would work out just fine if they kept everything a secret, especially from the child.

My mother did her best to preserve the illusion of normalcy, deflecting any conversation about family traits and our genealogy, often joking about why I looked and acted so differently from my brothers and my cousins.

Although my mother managed to deceive me, she did so only rarely with outright lies. Our bond was strong. We had a common, great love for literature and had many long talks. But I felt her secret as a palpable presence without guessing what it could be. She seemed to be smothering something within herself. As I grew older, my connection with her lessened because, even though we shared many traits, I had interests that bored her, making me feel that I had to create an artificial identity to please her. I also felt she was withholding something from me. Much later, when she finally disclosed the truth, she explained that the secrecy had been a burden when we were children and created even more agony for her when I married and had my own children.

My father was a naturally introverted man with his own history of father abandonment at age 2. With few personal skills to express his pain or his love, he was nevertheless a deeply devoted father. After all, he agreed to two more children through donor insemination and worked hard to make his home secure, moving to an upscale neighbourhood beyond his economic means to ensure that his four boys would have decent education. I believe his remoteness was due to the terms imposed by the agreements he signed with the doctor. Hundreds of other donor-conceived people have told me that their fathers were remote.

In post-war United States, parents of unusually-created families feared telling their children the truth about their conceptions. At that time, even my parents' adopted son was not told that he was adopted because most people accepted adoption experts' beliefs that the truth was too painful for adopted children to know. Unfortunately, my adopted brother learned the truth by accident and in a particularly damaging way. Because he had more obviously disparate traits than the rest of us, some of my mother's close friends learned he was adopted. When my brother was nine, another boy taunted him for being so bad that his mother gave him away. This information shocked and alarmed me, too. Immediately, I wanted to know whether I was also adopted. My mother tried to reassure me that I was "her" child. Even at age five, I knew her answer was evasive.

As I reached puberty, I grew aware of my differences from my father and three brothers. I knew I was connected to my mother but I seemed to share no traits at all with my father. Perhaps I was more sensitive to these disparities because I had learned that my older brother was adopted, but I could not resolve them. My teenage years at home became a private torment that festered beneath the surface of an otherwise happy family. I was absolutely certain that my father could not have been genetically-related to me and that I could not have been adopted. It is difficult to convey the intensity of the emotions that resulted. I found it impossible to speak about any of this with my mother. Consumed by anxiety, I was unable to express myself without choking up. I would have preferred to approach my dad but he was remote and uncomfortable in speaking about feelings. I knew that his hard exterior hid an inner personal struggle. I felt more empathy for him than for my mother even though I was sure he wasn't my "father." This is all too complex to put into mere words.

Some of my emotion stemmed from a feeling of failure. I had desperately tried to be the kind of son my father would be proud to claim but I was never athletic enough to match my older brother's local fame, which I knew made my father very proud. I loved many things that my father had no interest in. Even my mother could not comprehend at all why I would care about classical music, ballet, fine art and drama. Even though we shared a mutual love of world literature, she did not appreciate Shakespeare or modern drama as I did. I wanted to be like my father – more aggressive, more athletic and stronger. I came to despise myself because I failed. No longer able to live with the artificial identity

I had tried to forge, I began to explore my other interests – yet I felt guilty about these pursuits. I blamed myself for feeling like a stranger within my own family. I thought something must be wrong with me, not them.

Knowing nothing about sperm donation, I came to the only logical conclusion available: my mother conceived me through an extra-marital affair. Worse still, I concluded that she must have had affairs with a total of three men because my two younger brothers were so radically different from me – and my father, of course – that even their friends were often surprised to learn we were brothers. This incorrect conclusion about my mother caused me deep shame.

I had lost confidence in my mother's love and good character. I could not accept that she would be so unfaithful to my father. Nor could I understand why he accepted this infidelity. I wondered whether my mother's apparent past behaviour explained why my father seemed to resent me as I matured into someone he could not understand.

The emotions I describe might seem extreme but hundreds of donor-conceived adults have expressed to me similar emotions. Like me, many other donor-conceived adults eventually suppress these feelings to preserve their sanity.

3. The Gift of the Truth

After twenty years during which I suppressed dark feelings, I sought and eventually found clarity with the unexpected gift of the truth. When I was 37 years old in 1983, my younger brother suddenly died from an acute respiratory disorder (probably caused by the Hantavirus). This death occurred one year and four days after the death of my father from late-onset diabetes and kidney failure. We were all devastated by the death of my father and brother. One afternoon, I visited my mother to share our grief together. Much to my surprise, the long burden of carrying the secret finally gave way and she dramatically revealed my donor conception, simply blurting it out while I was speaking about the differences between my brother and I, between both of us and our father.

Her sudden disclosure aroused in me a tornado of varying and strong feelings: elation, anger, confusion and intense curiosity. Her story explained so much but, at first, I didn't believe it. I had been aware of donor insemination only for a few years, after a *Life Magazine* article about the *Repository for Germinal Choice*, the so-called "Nobel Prize Sperm Bank". I couldn't believe that donor insemination existed back in 1945. My mother affirmed that indeed I had been conceived by the practice.[2]

4. Loneliness

In the months that followed this revelation, I experienced total isolation; I knew of no one who could help me understand donor conception or even how I should feel about it. My mother wanted neither to discuss my feelings, nor to entertain my curiosity about my genetic father. Soon after, my mother suffered a series of strokes, deteriorated mentally and died a few years later. Ultimately, I was alone with my personal crisis. Library research about donor conception was vague and focused entirely on the plight of infertile couples. As the AIDS crisis loomed and semen was shown to transmit HIV, sperm banks replaced the highly secretive individual gynaecologists as the only providers who could warrant the safety of their semen supply. HIV and AIDS forced donor conception into the public arena; soon there were many new books, radio programs and magazine articles about the practice. Yet all such sources of information were directed to addressing the needs of the infertile. If the issues of children were discussed at all, the commentary was limited to helping the infertile husband relate to the child. The minimal discussion about truth telling was limited to the opinion that parents should not tell children the truth. Ironically, these 'experts,' who knew little about our lives, suggested that the donor-conceived people would never suspect the truth about their conception.

I became angry that such ignorant statements about people like me were so blatantly repeated and accepted as wise advice. It took over four years – not until 1987 – before I found anyone else, besides my youngest brother, who was also donor-conceived. And finally in 1989, a couple of books appeared which offered encouragement. One of these books was written by two veteran adoption experts;[3] the other author is a woman who used a male friend to help her become pregnant.[4] As I read these books today, I'm surprised by their insight; they still offer the best advice I've read. Critics, especially infertility experts and the infertile public, however, dismissed the books' recommendation of truth-telling and their assertion that donor-conceived people have the right to know the identity of our genetic fathers.

5. Finding a Community

This was a conclusion I had already reached. I had joined an adoption support group because adoptees shared the same experiences of being deprived of the truth by a system that focused on adults' interests and accepted no sense of obligation to the children whose lives the system profoundly affected.

Once the internet became ubiquitous, I began to use it to communicate directly with infertile people free of the many edits that came with media interviews. Such direct communication finally drew other donor-conceived adults into my life. Because of the benefits I experienced in sharing a common experience, I have created a web site restricted to people conceived through donor conception that has well over 200 members. This number represents a small fraction of the donor-conceived population because most are still living unaware of the truth. Nevertheless, the site has proven useful to many. One person found my site the day after she learned the truth about her conception and instantly connected with those veterans who could give her empathy and advice on how to understand what feelings she would be likely to encounter. Fortunately, she did not suffer the years of bewilderment I experienced after my mother finally told me the truth.

6. Pernicious Role of Professionals in Causing Unnecessary Suffering

I now understand that this suffering was unnecessary. The passage of time and the growth of information and ease of communication have revealed that much of the suffering engendered by secrecy and anonymity was and is still unknown to the public. Nor can it be justified as inevitable or properly blamed on the parents. Despite my many years of anger at my parents during my young adulthood, I have come to understand that they were not the ultimate source of my predicament.

Such insight is not encouraged by professionals. They often propound a theory that adoption and donor conception are practices that inevitably engender a conflict of rights among a triad. In adoption, the triad consists of adoptive parents, relinquishing natural parents, and the adopted person. In donor conception, the triad is said to involve gamete donors, recipient parents, and the people conceived through donor conception. The theory is that each member of the triad has rights that are difficult to reconcile. But note that, by this analysis, the role of adoption placement officers and the gynaecologist, clinic or broker is not apparent.

Such absence is significant. Michael Grand, a Psychology Professor at the University of Guelph, and an adopted person, claims that it is a myth that conflict is inevitable. The myth was created by adoption professionals to deflect legitimate criticism of their policies. The same conflict occurs in donor conception, or so the theory goes.

But conflict does *not* stem from the fact of a triad. Conflict stems from secrecy about the facts of conception and from the anonymity of the donor. It is created because vital information is hidden rather than disclosed to people whose human dignity and welfare requires them to know it. Conflict exists not because parents or donors necessarily want anonymity but because physicians have believed, from the outset of the practice of donor insemination, that they needed control to protect their practice. They sought control using means to prevent the complications of dissatisfied parents, curious donors, and the demands for information from the people whom they helped to create. Infertility physicians, sperm banks and brokers seek also to avoid public criticism and legal regulation.

Secrecy and anonymity have served the profession well but at the cost of great individual suffering, some of which I have recounted here. Secrecy has insulated this medicalized social experiment for years from receiving the rigorous biomedical analysis and public scrutiny to which other such innovations are ordinarily subjected. Anonymity has enabled physicians to use medical language and euphemisms effectively to disguise and discount the social and psychological impact on families.

7. The Harms of Anonymity

Anonymity permits the humanity of sperm donors – who are really genetic fathers – to be reduced to "sperm", a mere medical product, treated like a magic dose of some drug that "cures" infertility – which of course, it does not. Sperm is not a product, medical or otherwise; it is part of the essence of life. Its profound nature and generative force in creating new people cannot be altered by anonymity.

The arguments against disclosing the truth about donor conception and the identity of the donor are weak. If the information about my genetic father still exists after sixty-four years – and I have been reliably informed that it does – then why can't I have it? If I sued to get this information, I would have few resources to pursue a long legal battle against a profession with unlimited resources and significant prestige. I believe that they could merely claim that the records no longer exist or that no one would have any right to examine their private medical records. Doubtless, if the gynaecologist were living, he would claim that he is protecting the privacy of my genetic father. Yet how could this man – if he is still alive – feel threatened by the curiosity of his own son? I don't want his money; to be accused of such a motive is both profoundly insensitive and insulting. Nor would I wish to force a relationship. Nevertheless, his connection to me is sacred. Of course, I owe him respect for the privacy of his personal life but that life is also part of me. Laws exist to protect him from any true violation of his privacy but my knowledge of who he is would not violate his privacy because our genetic connection is a private matter we share together, something I feel I should be able to pass to my own children and grandchildren as their birthright. My legitimate demands upon him are clearly limited. But his duty must be acknowledged. All men have a moral obligation to meet the children they create and to answer their questions about their paternal heritage. No doctor can absolve anyone of this duty.

The gynaecologist might also claim that he is protecting the parental rights of his one-time patient, my mother. It is not justice to be bound by an agreement requiring anonymity of the donor, which my parents signed under constrained emotional circumstances, and to which I was not even a party, especially now that I am an adult and my parents are both deceased.

The secrecy required by the gynaecologist is not just poisonous, it fails. When parents are forced to deceive the very people who completely rely on them for honesty – their children, shame begins to infect the parents' dignity. When one parent can no longer live with the deception while the other is too threatened or embarrassed to reveal the truth, then marriages lose the cords of love that bind them together. When revelation comes late, the accumulated damage may prevent a restoration of trust. Too much of a carefully constructed artificial identity must be demolished to rebuild a better structure based on truth.

8. Secrecy is Poisonous but Anonymity Can Encourage It

As I have implied throughout, secrecy is only one problem with the current practice of donor conception. Perhaps there will always be parents who will never reveal the circumstances of the conception because they don't want the child to know. Yet many parents *would* tell the truth about the conception if they could then go on to tell the child the whole truth. But the absolute dead end that anonymity creates is deeply discouraging. Some parents ask themselves, "How can I tell my son he was created by assisted insemination, when I cannot tell him the identity of his genetic father?"

I fundamentally disagree with this parental choice to hide the truth about donor conception. Secrecy is much more harmful than the inability to learn one's genetic history. As an advocate for openness over the last twenty years, I advise couples to reveal the truth no matter what other consequences may occur. The many donor-conceived adults whom I've interviewed almost never tell me that they regret being told the truth. Even though the inability to know one's heritage causes lifelong pain, such pain is nothing like growing up with secrecy's harmful consequences that confuse children and sap family strength. Late disclosure may destroy trust in one's parents but it is more likely that donor-conceived adults, like me, have already lost faith in our mothers and fathers because we have already guessed that our parents are wrongly keeping vital information from us.

Indeed, my long-term survey of donor-conceived adults confirms that openness does not harm; in fact it heals. Only 7% of respondents wished they hadn't been told the truth, and this feeling tends to be short-lived. The great majority believed the disclosure was beneficial, even though tainted by the troubling new mystery about their unresolved identity. Nevertheless, they are glad that the secret is gone. Over 85% of the donor-conceived adults who responded believe they have a right to know their identity.

9. Conclusion

The adoption triad myth wrongly presents the situation as merely a static interplay between adopted persons, adoptive parents and birth parents; as Michel Grande points out the interplay consists of "black holes of silence, restricted communication and closed records." Yet adoption and donor conception are much more than that. The constellation of actors are much greater and includes "legislators, policy analysts, social theorists and the media" that will lead to reshaping the form of adoption (and donor conception) and opening up "possibilities of new ways of thinking about adoption." I feel the same reformation will happen for donor conception.

Should donor-conceived people have a right to know the circumstances of their conception and their identity? No child of assisted reproduction should be asked such a question. The profession should not have the power to say that our identity does not matter to us, to usurp our fundamental natural right without our consent. We should have the power to assert our dignity. We are the only authority who can define our own values. No one else can decide for us what we need. We need the central truth that tells us who we are.

Bibliography

Baran, Annette and Reuben Pannor. *Lethal Secrets: The Shocking Consequences and Unsolved Problems of Artificial Insemination.* New York: Warner Books Inc, 1989.
Noble, Elizabeth. *Having your Baby by Donor Insemination: A Complete Resource Guide.* Boston: Houghton Mifflin Company, 1987.
Addison Hard, M.D, letter to the editor, *Medical World.* April, 1909.
Cordray, A. William and Joanna Scheib. "A Survey of DI Adults about Secrecy, Disclosure and Access to Information", *Mimeo.*

Notes

1 Cordray and Scheib, "A Survey of Attitudes of DI Adults", (forthcoming).
2 Addison Hard, M.D, letter to the editor, *Medical World.* April, 1909.
3 Baran and Pannor, *Lethal Secrets.*
4 Noble, *Having Your Baby by Donor Insemination.*

Chapter Six

Attempting to Learn My Biological Father's Identity
A Canadian Tale of Frustration and Eventually Litigation

Olivia Pratten

1. Introduction

In June 1981, a Caucasian man with A positive blood type walked into a clinic along Vancouver's West Broadway and donated his sperm. He received $50 for his time and, with that exchange, he sold any connection or obligation to that semen and to any resulting biological ties. His semen facilitated a conception; nine months later, I was born. Even though more than 30 years have now passed, I often wonder whether that man realizes that he has a biological daughter who walks down that same street. Does he know that, having exhausted all other avenues, I won a class action lawsuit to try to learn his identity? Does he care?

2. My Parents and My Beginnings

To explain what led me to file the lawsuit in the autumn of 2008, it is important first to understand who my parents are and what they did.

My parents never thought they would need to use donor sperm to become parents. They met, fell in love, married and figured children would soon follow even though my father had fertility problems. They were adventurous. Simply to consider sperm donation requires a certain kind of person and a certain kind of couple. My parents were not put off by the taboo about donor insemination perhaps because they are unconventional, albeit in different ways. They had married in England and then immigrated to Canada, breaking free of family expectations. They think for themselves. My mother, who trained and practiced as a registered nurse, did not accept that doctors are always right or that their views must necessarily be followed unquestionably. Thankfully, my parents raised me to think for myself and to make my own decisions, independently of what I was told and even of my parents' opinion.

After two years of attempting to conceive and a couple of attempts at assisted insemination, my parents were told by a urologist to "Go see Dr. Korn; he uses donor sperm" as though there were no difference between using my Dad's sperm and that of a stranger. Eventually my mother became pregnant with donor sperm. When my mom asked Dr. Korn what she and my dad should tell me, he replied, "Most people don't say anything and it's probably best you don't say anything either." With this, my parents began to question the authority of those who purported to know the best policies of donor conception. The seeds were (quite literally) sown and questioning begun, which would eventually lead to me filing a lawsuit 27 years later.

I remember clearly the moment when my mother told me about my donor conception, at the age of five. My mom told me a simple story of a sperm and egg and explained that "Daddy didn't have enough seeds, so a nice man who the doctor knew, gave us extra so we could have you." I remember thinking this unusual beginning was cool and that it made me different from everyone – different in a positive way. This happy reaction almost certainly occurred because I was told in a loving positive way.

3. Why I Would Like to Know My Biological Father

My donor conception is my reality; it is all I have ever known. Being conceived from an anonymous sperm donor is not all of my identity, but it is a significant part of who I am. At age five, I didn't fully appreciate what I was told, but as I grew older, I began to take my parents' story and to make it mine. Even though to my parents, he was always the "donor", I knew instinctively that he was not just the "donor" to me because I received no sperm. Rather, he was my biological father; he had helped create me.

Saying that this anonymous man is my biological father is powerful; it expresses my reality. It is true for me. No amount of euphemisms can change this truth. I do have a dad, and the term "Dad" to me is familiar and represents my family. "Biological father" reflects my reality, but I understand that term to connote a formal distance and lack of a personal relationship. My dad is the one who was there for me growing up, who took me to Disneyland, whom I fought with as a teenager and to whom I am much closer as an adult. He's my dad. He and my mom raised me and continue to love me. Yet, the fact I have a dad who loves me is separate and distinct from the fact that I don't know the identify of my biological father. I seek this not because I want a relationship with him, want more family or want another dad – I already have all of that with my family and parents. What I seek and what the love of my parents cannot give me is the full knowledge of my biological origins.

We each choose to construct our identities in different ways. Some people embrace identity through their families and through their biological ties. For some, identity is constructed solely from a cultural group affiliation or from other non-blood relationships. For many more, it's a combination of both. Our identities are not fixed; they change as we grow and find our paths in the world. But those who have full knowledge of their biological origins are free to accept or reject nature's influence on their personhood and how they see themselves. Those who, like me, are donor-conceived by anonymous people, are left to wonder how much, if at all, the unknown person's genetic legacy and social history relate to who we are. Knowledge would be empowerment. To know who my biological father is would allow me the control to accept or reject him, and thus nature, as part of my identity. Not knowing means that the clinical, paternalistic system of reproduction will permeate my very existence for the rest of my life.

I filed the lawsuit to take control from the hands of the medical establishment and to learn my full biological origins. Having experienced the nurturing of my parents and with better knowledge of my genetic nature as the outcome of the litigation, I aim to gain control of how I choose to construct my identity.

What continues to give me fire and to speak out, including filing the lawsuit, is the fact that I want the entire power structure of artificial conception dismantled and removed from my life. It exhausts me and frustrates me. I've had enough. I want to know my biological father's identity, and then incorporate it into my sense of self.

4. Donors' "Right to Anonymity"

People often ask me whether I have considered the interests of my biological father: "What about his 'right to anonymity'? Isn't this lawsuit going to violate the guarantee of anonymity he received from the physician?"

In response, I always reply that I have sympathy for him. It is highly likely that he was young when he surrendered his semen, probably under the age of 25 and relatively unaware of the significance of what he was doing. Perhaps he thought it was great that he was being paid for something he did anyway.

But my sympathy for him is countered by the fact that the very terms used to describe the practice – sperm donation – defy the truth and deny my reality. Technically, he gave sperm but he was paid so this contribution was not a 'donation'. The exchange was for semen, not only for one part of semen, sperm. Moreover, the sperm doesn't remain sperm. The whole point of the contribution is to unite the sperm with an egg so that it can become a person. Therefore, "sperm donation" is really the sale of one's biological ties.

The euphemism of "sperm donation" might have been deliberately chosen to prevent my biological father from being in a position to give informed consent. The physician had a responsibility to fully inform the young man so that he could freely consent to trading his biological ties for cash. And yet it is unlikely that anyone spent time with him to explain that he was helping to create a family and, in an unusual and insufficiently appreciated away, to become a type of family member. The physician should have asked, "Do you understand? Do you agree?" The physician should have explained the potential long-term consequences for him.

To the extent that this man was not fully informed, I have great sympathy for him. Yet more than 30 years have now passed. Perhaps he now has children whom he has raised. Maybe he is more mature, understands the full effect of what he did and wants to meet his offspring as many donors do.

Even assuming that my biological father is among those who don't want to know the identity of their offspring, I still reject the premise that he has the right to his anonymity. Anonymity is not a right; privacy is. He has the right that I not interfere in his life, that I not ever ask him for money, or make a claim on his estate. But it is absurd to cite privacy as a reason to deny me the knowledge of his identity, which is all I want. Knowledge of the identity of my biological father is information relevant to my health and well-being and that of any children I might have. This information cannot justly be withheld. His identity is not something that belongs exclusively to him. His identity is part of my lineage. The identity of my paternal grandparents and great uncles and aunts can be known only through learning his identity. It is offensive to suggest that my biological father may hide behind laws created to protect banking and personal information from falling into corporate or criminal hands, when what is really going on is that a biological father is denying information relevant to the health and well-being of his own biological children.

Moreover, our genetic connection goes beyond him. His mother and father, brothers and sisters might still be alive and want to meet me: I am their grandchild and niece.

Again, I appreciate that my biological father might regret what he did and that he might not want me or the remembrance of what he did in his life now. But the fact is he did trade his semen for cash, he did sell his biological ties; his choices have had consequences. I'm not asking for a relationship if he doesn't want to have one with me. But I'm asking to know who he is, his name, and the biography of his life because, as I've said, knowing his identity is the key to me constructing my full identity.

5. Steps My Parents and I took to Learn My Identity

In the time between learning about my origins and actually commencing litigation, lie over 20 years of frustrating lobby and advocacy work by my parents and me. My parents felt isolated as patients when they underwent the procedure and were told not to tell me the truth. They had no one to turn to in an age before the internet and before any sort of literature or counseling were available. The isolation all changed one day when my mom saw two adult donor offspring speaking on a television program called, *The Phil Donahue Show*. Listening to the donor offspring speak, my mom worried that I might one day experience the same distress about not knowing my biological father's identity and about having no medical history. She decided to contact these adult donor offspring.

Through the *Phil Donahue Show,* my parents made contact with Canadian sociologist, Rona Achilles, who was conducting research on participants of donor conception. In 1987, when I was five, my parents and Vancouver lawyer, Carey Linde, called a press conference to draw attention to the lack of laws and protection of medical files in donor conception practices. Consequently, my parents met other parents and formed the *New Reproductive Alternatives Society*, Canada's first support and lobby group for donor-conceived families. There were regular meetings and picnics for the families where adults gathered to share frustration and compare notes about feeling isolated, worried about preservation and access to their children's health records, and the need for new policies and laws that would protect them.

My parents thought it would all be simple: bring the practice of gamete donation out of the closet, show how secrecy and anonymity were detrimental to the health and well being of the resulting children, and surely, the government and medical profession would be happy to help quickly change these practices. My mother now tells me they were naïve to believe the system would work for them. Eventually we realized the medical profession would not voluntarily submit to regulation. They were not comfortable with the thought of giving up control.

6. Obstacles Arose

I became fully aware of this fact when I was 16 and attended North American gatherings of physicians, biologists, nurses, counselors and suppliers of the reproductive technology equipment. The annual meetings of the Canadian Fertility and Andrology Society (the CFAS) and the American Society for Reproductive Medicine (the ASRM) are the largest gatherings of the fertility industry, which aims to make babies. During the breaks in proceedings, I would speak with some of these doctors and representatives from the industry. Inevitably, they would ask me, "Where do you work? Are you a counselor? An intended parent?" I would reply, "No, I'm a result of their procedures. I am the product of the procedures you spend your days promoting or perfecting." You would think these people would have been curious to speak to me, to ask what I think of what they do. But they weren't. At least not in my experience. In fact, the announcement of who I was often left them speechless and uncomfortable; they would quickly excuse themselves to speak to other people. I soon got the message. I wasn't supposed to be there. I was supposed to be happy and off enjoying my life, either ignorant or indifferent to the circumstances of my conception and my inability to learn the identity of my biological father.

7. Why I Resorted to Litigation

Isn't it curious that lobbying attempts to make the rights of children a priority in reproductive technologies would involve over 20 years of letters, debates, press conferences, a Royal Commission, four health ministers, a federal statute which was not enforced and has now been declared in large part unconstitutional? It would be 15 years of numerous donor offspring conferences, rounds of interviews with the media and consultations with Health Canada. I even spoke before both the Canadian Senate and Commons Standing Committees of Health.

While my mother and I were working toward contributing to future policy, my own situation that required the protection of medical files remained secondary. I thought surely, once there is a federal authority, they will do what is right and seize the past files. Health Canada promised that the new Assisted Reproduction Agency would protect the past files. But when we wrote to Dr. Elinor Wilson, the President of Assisted Human Reproduction Canada, to ask her to intervene to require that the medical file be transferred to her Agency, she replied that the federal Agency had no jurisdiction to do so.

These efforts ended when we received what we regarded as a threat by the B.C. College of Physicians and Surgeons that my records could be shredded or incinerated. We came to understand that, despite all the lobbying efforts, it would only be through an actual legal trial that the issue of the health and wellbeing of people born through the technologies would be addressed. On learning from others that some files had already been destroyed, we saw the lawsuit as the only possibility to preserve the records that name my biological father and contain my medical and social history.

It was at this point, when we received the letter from the College of Physicians and Surgeons and understood that the Government was not going to protect my records, that we sought the advice of constitutional lawyer, Joseph Arvay Q.C. In October 2008, Mr. Arvay and his co-counsel, Sean Hern, filed the lawsuit. But even proceeding to trial was not easy. Just weeks before the trial was due to begin on 25 October 2010, the Province of British Columbia sought to dismiss or to delay the trial. Fortunately, the court denied that application and we did have an eight-day trial as scheduled.

8. Judgement of British Columbia Supreme Court

Madame Justice Adair, who heard the case, found in my favour on the grounds of equality. In May 2011, her judgement was released. She held that the Province of British Columbia does not treat donor-conceived people equally to adopted people even though we are alike in being reared by one or more genetically related people. Like adopted people, the donor-conceived need access to records of their identity and medical, social and cultural history. The Province tried to argue that it had not discriminated against donor-conceived people because it treated all adopted people equally and the donor-conceived are not adopted. But this was ridiculous. The *Charter of Rights and Freedoms* grants substantive equality: likes should be treated alike – and we are like adoptees in having the same needs and desires to know about our progenitors.

Because I was in new legal territory fighting for rights for the donor-conceived, this case required a legal team that was tenacious, creative and fearless in challenging the status quo. Thankfully, just the right team argued the case.

Yet in late June 2011, the Province of British Columbia announced that it would appeal the British Columbia Supreme Court's decision. This means that the long, winding road of advocacy, activism and litigation is not over. Because of the Province's decision, we must go to the Court of Appeal, and we now have to raise more money to fight on.

All of this has given me invaluable insight into how our legislative and policy process works in Canada, or at least how it's supposed to work to regulate this issue. To witness the politics of passivity considering the number of failed bills that predate the federal Act, the finding that the Act is unconstitutional and the resulting delays have been very frustrating and totally shameful, because these delays have sacrificed the health and well-being of children born without access to information about their progenitors.

9. Significance of this Litigation

As a figurehead of sorts for others, I have received many messages from donor-conceived people across Canada, the United States, UK, France and Australia, all in support of what I am doing and expressing gratitude for my courage. I feel fortunate; many offspring do not have supportive parents, knowledge of previous policy discussions and access to people who might help further their cause. I feel a responsibility not only to other donor-conceived people, but also to future people who will be conceived this way. The industry is increasingly commercial and announces new ways of baby-making regularly. Mine is the first North American litigation brought by a "product" of reproductive technology. I am told that the fertility industry is paying attention. Hopefully, this litigation will send the very important message: that the implications of donor conception do not end with a pregnancy. The ramifications of what a physician does in his or her office are inherited by the child who grows up and who might have big issues with the terms of their conception – terms that were stipulated without thought to their needs or rights.

10. My Hopes for Future: Putting Children's Interests First

The use of assisted reproductive technologies is rising because of delayed childbearing, declining sperm counts and increasing societal acceptance of non-traditional family structures. As the number of children of assisted reproduction rise and the stigma diminishes, so does the percentage of parents who tell their children about their assisted conception. If the industry does not change its practices and policy makers continue to ignore us, then I predict that there will be an army of litigants like me in the future.

Of course, I hope people will not need to resort to litigation. This was not my first choice to learn the identity of my biological father. Yet it proved an extraordinary experience. After all the years of fruitless advocacy, it was empowering to have a lawyer listen to me and take seriously what I was saying. And then to have a judge listen to the effects that donor anonymity has on me and people like me was even more empowering. With Justice Adair's ruling, I felt vindicated. The law is on our side now. The ruling validated what people like me and my family have been saying for decades. However, I'm disappointed that I must continue now to defend the Province's appeal.

But I will not give up. Donor anonymity is unethical and treats the resulting children like commodities. Those of us conceived with donated gametes are entitled to be treated like everyone else. We are entitled to records of our identity and our medical, social and cultural history.

Chapter Seven

Seeking Answers in the Ether: Longing to Know One's Origins Is Evident from Donor Conception Websites

Rhonda E. Harris and Laura Shanner

1. Introduction

Rapidly evolving Internet technology has revolutionized searching for genetic relatives over the past two decades, particularly for people conceived via donated sperm, eggs or embryos. Under the traditional veil of secrecy and shame that had long shrouded infertility, those few who learned that donors had been involved in their conception were limited to lonely (and usually futile) tasks of writing letters to infertility clinicians and scouring university yearbooks for photos of possible donors.

As the stigma of infertility gradually eased through the 1990's and 2000's, parallel advances in Internet capacities for information sharing, coalition building and global networking enabled donor-conceived individuals ("Offspring") to challenge the lack of information that continues to surround their origins under policies protecting anonymous gamete donation. Some online resources are able to bypass official policies of anonymous donation by linking half-siblings and allowing donors to make themselves available to their genetic progeny. Perhaps most important, the Internet enables individuals to feel less lonely while dealing with the complex social and emotional issues involved in donor conception.

This chapter reviews two categories of English-language websites[1] commonly used by DC offspring, families and donors. The first group includes infertility, adoption and donor conception networks for support, information and advocacy (Table 1). Individual blogs, Facebook and MySpace pages, and personal web pages posted by donor-conceived people supplement the first group, and are not reviewed here. Sites in the second group facilitate connections among genetically related donor offspring and/or gamete donors (Table 2). Together, these online resources provide evidence of the profound questions and frustrations that donor-conceived people can experience when their genetic origins are obscured.

2. Websites for Information, Support and Advocacy – Table 1

> When I first discovered the truth about my DI [donor insemination] conception I didn't know of a single person in my situation. I felt like freak of the week. Some of my best support comes from the other side of the world… I didn't know it was normal to feel angry at being cheated out of knowing my biological family.[2]

> Hi, My name is Daniel and I recently found out I am a donor baby. I am a bit confused, and definitely lost. I know some info. I also have a "half" sister … Any help or suggestions are welcome. Thanks![3]

A very wide range of responses are common when older children and adults learn that donors were involved in their conception, but feelings of confusion are understandably a typical component. Parents of Offspring who are young children may feel equally adrift while trying to answer their children's questions. Where does one even begin to find others in similar circumstances, to find advice and support, or to figure out what to do next?

Typing "donor conception" into an Internet search engine quickly leads to the major donor conception, infertility and adoption support network sites around the world. Many of these organizations began as local, self-help support groups for patients and parents. As awareness of the concerns of donor-conceived people has increased, many infertility support groups expanded to embrace the offspring as well as the adults involved in their birth, while groups uniquely dedicated to donor conception issues also formed. In the 1990's, web pages for these support groups were often little more than simple listings of meeting schedules and "how to contact us" information, rarely accessed by people beyond the core membership. Over time, these sites expanded to serve critical roles in public education and reshaping societal attitudes toward infertility, adoption, and the perspectives of donor-conceived individuals.

Today, the major sites are extensively hyper-linked repositories of background scientific and psychological information, legal updates, academic studies, cases in the news, personal stories and global networking opportunities. Many have online bookstores, downloadable documents and videos, and links to additional resources for patients, families, prospective patients or donors, health care professionals, counsellors, researchers, policy makers and others. Many continue their original support-group functions of facilitating individual connections and responding to confidential inquiries, while providing electronic newsletters to members and moderating discussion boards.

The major support groups are non-profit, volunteer-run resources, sometimes with nominal membership fees requested to offset expenses. Perhaps unsurprisingly, given the effort required to create and update such comprehensive online resources, only one or two major websites tend to be available in each country, although there may be numerous local support groups and additional private web pages.

Canada's most extensive donor conception resource is the *Infertility Network*, a registered charity founded in 1990 to provide "information, support and referral on issues related to infertility, miscarriage, donor conception, adoption and reproductive & genetic technologies."[4] Operated by Diane Allen of Toronto, the Network creates newsletters and distributes email news feeds summarizing legal, media, advocacy and related fertility news from around the world to a mailing list of approximately 6000. The *Donor Sibling Registry* is the primary resource in the U.S.; it is discussed in the section 3, below, with registries.

The *Donor Conception Support Group of Australia* (DCSG) and *Donor Conception Network* (DCNetwork or DCN) in the United Kingdom, both founded in 1993, focus their energies on donor offspring, their parents, prospective users of donor conception, and donors. DCSG is a volunteer support group founded by the Hewitt family, whose daughter Geraldine was conceived via donor sperm. *DCNetwork* grew from 1,000 families or individuals in the membership database in December 2006,[5] to over 1600 families in 2012.[6] Both groups advocate ending policies of anonymous donation.

Several online discussion groups enable direct mutual support and information sharing, with varying degrees of public accessibility to comments posted by members. *People Conceived via Artificial Insemination (PCVAI)*, a Yahoo! Group with 233 members in 2012, is an online support group restricted to persons conceived through DI, with few comments accessible by the general public. This group restricts access to create a place for donor-conceived people to express their feelings without social censure and to provide "a haven for those who do not care to defend their feelings, attitudes or opinions."[7] Other discussion groups, such as *Donor Misconception Open Forum*,[8] the Yahoo! Group *Donor Offspring Health*,[9] and the *Australian Donor Conception Forum*[10] allow general public access to the moderated postings.

While the support and information group sites continue to expand their reach steadily, many of the discussion boards showed a peak of activity around 2006-2009.[11] Further inquiry is needed to confirm the reasons for this shift, but it appears that many of the discussion groups have coalesced into the larger sites, while Facebook and other social networking sites may have replaced others.

Several networks promote legal activism to end anonymous gamete donation. *TangledWebs* originated in Victoria, Australia, to promote use of the state *Infertility Treatment Authority*'s Voluntary Registers, and to push for full identity release.[12] *TangledWebs UK*, a British offshoot, likewise "advocates equal rights and protection for all DC people, as defined in the UN Convention on the Rights of the Child...." [and] that future legislation be enacted to provide all DC adults with retrospective access to information concerning their biological/genealogical parentage.[13] The *International Donor Offspring Alliance* (IDOA) advocates legislation to require recording the identity of a child's genetic and biological parents as well as their social parents on birth certificates, in two-part documents that would ensure accuracy while also protecting "the legitimate privacy of everyone involved."[14] *Canadian Donor Offspring* went online in 2009 to share information and to raise funds for Olivia Pratten's legal fight to protect donor records from destruction and to reverse Canada's legislated requirement of donor anonymity.[15]

3. Registries and Websites that Focus on Facilitating Relationships – Table 2

Whether and when individuals involved with donor conception begin to search for genetic relatives varies widely. Parents of young children may search for half-siblings so that their child can have a sense of kinship and extended family while growing up. Parents may also assist a young child or teen to seek answers to the child's questions about the donor. Dating and marriage often prompt Offspring to begin searching, in order to prevent accidental consanguinity, while having children of one's own frames questions of one's roots, connections and relations in a different light.

> Being that Saskatoon is such a small city, there could be multiple brothers/sisters here that I don't even know. The donor should be rest-assured that I do not want to disrupt his life if he is scared that I might do that [...][16]

Although donors are often presumed to favour anonymity, increasing numbers are choosing to make themselves available for contact.

> It was at the point of parenthood for myself, long after the money was gone, that the whole meaning of what it was to be a parent made sense. [...] I think we owe it to them to let them learn. [...] I think there are many reasons a donor father might want to get involved with a genetic offspring. I think though that those reasons change over time as we grow older and wiser.[17]

> I would love to know the outcome, give you more medical history if needed or God forbid, if there is ANYTHING your child may need in the future such as bone marrow or something I could be a match for, I have no issues with being contacted for this. [...] I'd hate to think a child could be dying because of court protected anonymity. Even if the child(ren) want to meet me or know my reasons for donating, I have no issues with that.[18]

Health matters remain a key area of concern for Offspring who do not know their genetic relatives and are frequent explanations for "seeking information" posts.

> I was 34 years old when my mother told me my father was not my actual father… I have four children, my two youngest were [diagnosed] with leukemia. There is no history of childhood cancers on my mother's side. If anyone has any idea on how I might possibly find information please let me know. My mother now has early dementia. There is [no] way to get more information from her. Thank you.[19]

> I'm looking for any information I can find about my donor father … I have all the symptoms of aspergers syndrome but have not been diagnosed [...][20]

> My mom doesn't remember much about my donor, but I know that he was tall…[and] possibly was a medical student at UCLA. … I also have synesthesia, which is a possibly inherited condition in which a person's senses are cross-wired. I associate sounds, numbers, and letters with colors.[21]

The non-profit *Donor Offspring Health* registry (separate from the discussion forum of the same name) allowed donor-conceived individuals and donors to post their own health-related information, and enabled infertility patients to look for health information about potential donors. Launched in 2006, this project is no longer online.[22]

The most important non-governmental, voluntary registry and matching service in the world is the *Donor Sibling Registry* ("DSR"), which uses sophisticated computer technology to find connections among half-siblings and/or donors.[23] This non-profit organization charges an annual membership fee of US$75, or a lifetime fee of $175, to access its database, and it automatically sends email messages to registrants when the computer identifies a potential match. Created in 2000 by Wendy Kramer and her donor-conceived son, Ryan, the DSR has emerged as a powerful global resource.

Activity at the *Donor Sibling Registry* has exploded: in 2005, the DSR reported 4,000 families registered, with over 600 matches;[24] in 2006, over 7,000 registrants;[25] in 2009, over 24,000 registrants and almost 6,500 matches;[26] and in July 2011, 31,248 registrants and almost 8,400 matches.[27] By November 2012, DSR reports over 38,300 registrants and over 9,688 matches.[28] The DSR website receives over 10,000 unique visitors every month.

Several governments around the world have established voluntary contact registries for people involved in donor conception prior to the enactment of relevant mandatory reporting legislation. For example, the government-supported *UK DonorLink* offers DNA testing and data-banking of submitted samples, and facilitates voluntary contacts for "the exclusive purpose of matching donor-conceived adults, donors and genetically related half or full siblings"[29] involving conception prior to 1991. However, funding and the registry's future beyond 2012 is uncertain. The U.K.'s official *Human Fertilisation and Embryology Registry* includes all gamete donors, recipient parents and offspring conceived after August 1, 1991;[30] offspring conceived after April 1, 2005 are entitled to the donor's identifying information when they turn 18, but those involved in conceptions between 1991 and 2005 may re-register with HFEA to facilitate voluntary contact.

The situation in Australia is much more complicated than in the UK because each state is responsible for creating its own assisted reproduction legislation, and maintaining its own registries as required. The *Donor Conception Support Group* offers a flow chart to keep track of the options according to location and date of conception.[31] As of 2012, the states of Victoria, Western Australia and New South Wales allow access to donor identity through mandatory donor conception databases for those conceived after the relevant legislation took effect (respectively, 1998, 2004 and 2010), with voluntary registries in each state for those involved in donor conception at earlier dates. In other Australian states, the only option for Offspring is to contact the infertility clinics and to hope for the best.

Unfortunately, people who use the voluntary registries must rely on faulty memories and incomplete or missing paperwork, often leading to heartbreak when potential matches are proved through genetic testing to be inaccurate. The Cayman Biomedical Research Institute (CaBRI), an offshoot of Cayman Chemical established in the U.S. in 2005, is a non-profit, tax-exempt organization that supports research into rare genetic defects[32] CaBRI maintains a Donor Gamete Archive that "provides comprehensive services to clients seeking genetic analysis. Through our programs and database, CaBRI can analyze genetic markers, compare genetic profiles, assess potential genetic relationships, or confirm previously obtained genetic results."[33] Half-sibling relationships can be identified both through analyzing submitted samples and via database matching, and tests are available for several specific genetic diseases. However, approximately 80% of Offspring DNA samples submitted to CaBRI as suspected matches prove not to be related after all.[34]

4. Back to the Support Groups

Starting a web search can raise complex emotional challenges, such as how to call a support group, "What would I say? 'Hello I am donor-conceived, can we chat?' I was freaking out. I didn't know these people."[35]

When Offspring succeed in learning the identity of their donors or half-siblings, their experiences can be life altering.

> "[I]t is almost impossible to describe the explosively powerful effect that this had on me. In one moment everything changed. I felt more solid, and the shame slid off me. No longer did I feel apologetic about my appearance, or the workings of my mind."[36]

Another writes, "Now when I look in the mirror I tell myself, 'I am W's daughter', and I smile."[37]

Strong relationships may develop between half-siblings and/or donors and offspring, enriching the lives of extended family members. But meeting each other can also create unexpected challenges. "Becky" articulates several unique challenges that DC offspring with new-found relatives may face:

> She is our donor's first child – his "full," or "real" daughter. He has a "real" son, too. That feels odd, including them in our group at all – they are not donor-conceived, and yet they are no more related to their dad than I am. […] The youngest is one year younger than me – and how pissed off I was when she turned up, and I was not the youngest any more. […] What had once been an empty space – the anonymous donor – was now full of people: I had a story and I had characters. […] We are in uncharted territory without a map, and sometimes we get lost … We are part-family, part self-help group, and I think we have a duty to help one another if we can. […]There is a certainly a real bond between us, and an intimacy, and yet no shared history.[38]

For others, however, the search process can be long, frustrating, and ultimately unfruitful even when it appears to succeed.

> [T]his whole process however … might be compared to slow torture … I find out [I am donor-conceived] when [I] am 15, get a few non-identifying bits

of information [...] another year and [I] find out [I] have many more siblings than [I] had ever imagined [...] There is a voice inside of me screaming like an impatient child "I want it all [and I] want it NOW!"[39]

5. Conclusions

The explosion in donor conception support groups and registries since 2000, reveals the great need for support, connection and answers among donor-conceived individuals. There is a very wide range of "typical" reactions to the news of donor parentage, with feelings of confusion and isolation extremely common. Finding others conceived in the same way provides genuine relief, regardless of whether or when the Offspring searches for genetic relatives. Those who are actively searching may merely be curious about their progenitors (or their offspring), may seek to establish relationships with an extended family, or may feel desperate to make sense of missing pieces in their lives.

It might be argued that because relatively few donor-conceived individuals have become prominent voices in the public discourse, the objections to donor anonymity merely reflect the views of a few malcontents. Yet perhaps the opposite is true. Comments and stories posted to the Internet discussion boards and search networks frequently reveal deeply personal medical information, painful emotional perspectives, and pleas for assistance. In the general public, most people are uncomfortable sharing such difficult details of their lives with strangers. Indeed, the emotional challenges of publicly voicing one's deep concerns and frustrations might also explain why a minority of donor-conceived people are currently speaking openly about their search for the truth about their origins. Given that most Offspring do not know of their status,[40] and that many who have been told are still young, those who are currently speaking out and initiating searches probably represent only the first ripple of a wave to come which could be huge.

It is clear that large, coordinated voluntary donor conception databases must be established – with secure long-term funding, and ideally the resources to include DNA testing – to enable donor-conceived individuals, donors, and families to find each other in the absence of policies that ban anonymity. "Seeking information" postings to Offspring discussion boards, personal web page appeals, and smaller database programs simply cannot achieve the critical mass to enable matches to be made; such attempts are usually just shots in the dark, and may subject searchers to painful public scrutiny. Large-scale databases, such as the *UK Donor Link*, the *Donor Sibling Registry*, and the Australian voluntary registries are much more likely to succeed in finding matches. Given the international trade of donated sperm and the growing practice of reproductive tourism, it would, however, be ideal if various national databases could cross-reference each other.

The visibility and successes of this first generation of online searchers will no doubt inspire many more to come forward, because it is likely that many Offspring have simply assumed it would be impossible to obtain information about their donors, had no idea how to start, or lacked the support they needed to undertake the quest. In any event, the recent emergence of DNA testing through private genealogy services[41] may eventually make donor anonymity obsolete. For those Offspring who ache to know their roots and relatives, the answers probably do not come soon enough.

TABLE 1: DONOR CONCEPTION SUPPORT, INFORMATION AND ADVOCACY
All sites accessed in November, 2012 unless noted otherwise

		Year Est.	2012 Members	Comments
Australian Donor Conception Forum http://www.ausdcf.org/	Aus.		337	Multiple discussion threads on DC topics, including "searching for information" posts
Australian Donor Conception Network www.australiandonorconceptionnetwork.org	Aus.	2012		Free, members-only online discussion forum social activities, links
Canadian Donor Offspring www.canadiandonoroffspring.ca	Canada	2009		Information and fundraising site to support legal challenges to donor anonymity in Canada
Donor Conception Network (DCNetwork, DCN) www.dcnetwork.org	UK	1993	1,600+ families	Members-only online discussion group; activities throughout the UK Online bookstore
Donor Conception Support Group (DCSG) www.dcsg.org.au	Aus.	1993	1,000+	Free membership for families and donors. Legislative updates, flow chart for Australian DC offspring registries by state; consumer/ patient advocacy, newsletter, links 2012 membership: 450

Name	Location	Year	Members	Description
Donor Misconception Open Forum http://health.groups.yahoo.com/group/DonorMisconception-Open/	Yahoo! Group	2006	47	Open online discussion group, minimal moderation (ads deleted) Cross posting of Infertility Network news items
Donor Offspring Health http://groups.yahoo.com/group/donoroffspringhealth/	Yahoo! Group	2006	84	Discussion group for issues related to health concerns that may be related to a donor's DNA. Greatest activity 2008-09, but still active in 2012
Infertility Network (IN) www.infertilitynetwork.org	Canada	1990	6000+	Primary Canadian network. Advocacy, news, links, online bookstore, resources for all areas of infertility and adoption. Initially a chapter of the Infertility 1700 subscribers to email newsletter; international mailing list incl. approx. 5000 current/former infertility patients, 400 DC parents, 100 DC adults, 450 counsellors, 2500 others (professionals, organizations)
International Donor Offspring Alliance (IDOA) http://www.idoalliance.org	Int'l	2007	51	International legal advocacy for accurate, detailed birth certificates listing donors as well as social parents 2009 membership: 26
Parents via Egg Donation http://www.parentsviaeggdonation.org/	USA	2004		Resources, discussion forums and blogs related to ovum donation.
People Conceived via Artificial Insemination (PCVAI) http://groups.yahoo.com/group/pcvai	USA	2000	233	Discussion group limited to persons conceived via donor insemination. Moderated by Bill Cordray and Shelley Kreutz
TangledWebs Australia www.tangledwebs.org.au	Aus.	2006	Unknown	Promotes Victoria's Voluntary Registries; human rights and legal advocacy to end donor anonymity

Seeking Answers in the Ether: Longing to Know One's Origins is Evident

TangledWebs UK www.tangledwebs.org.uk/tw	UK	2006	Unknown	Human rights and legal advocacy to end donor anonymity; offshoot from Australian TW
VANISH (Victorian Adoption Network for Information and Self-Help) http://www.vanish.org.au	Aus.	1989	Unknown	State-funded for adoption search and reunion, expanded for anyone separated from family of origin through adoption, institutional or foster care, or donor conception
Donor-Conceived People	USA	2007	53*	Discussion group membership in 2009; no longer in service 2012
We Are Donor-Conceived People http://community.livejournal.com/we_are_dcp/profile	Aus.	2004	20*	Discussion group, last updated in 2008

TABLE 2: VOLUNTARY DONOR OFFSPRING REGISTRIES
All sites accessed in November, 2012 unless otherwise noted

		Year Est.	2012 Members	Comments
Americans For Open Records (AmFOR) http://www.amfor.net/DonorOffspring	USA	2001	1,957 entries	Free worldwide registry. Self-reported information available openly
Australian Donor Conception Forum http://www.ausdcf.org/	Aus.		87 posts	"Searching for information" threads in discussion forum; "Searching for past donors" lists 68 posts, "searching for offspring" lists 19 posts as of Nov. 8, 2012
Australian Donor Conception Registry http://health.groups.yahoo.com/group/AustralianDonorConceptionRegistry	Aus.	2006	57	Free Yahoo! Group posts information from Australian donors, parents and donor-conceived persons seeking contact, to members-only, moderated site

67

Cayman Biomedical Research Institute (Cabrimed) http://www.cabrimed.org	USA	2005		Non-profit research company specializing in rare genetic diseases and cancers; maintains Donor Gamete Archive, provides DNA testing, and identifies DC-relation matches in its database
Donor Connections https://www.donorconnections.com/tmp/	USA	2012	new	Formerly "Donor Offspring Matches" (2008-2012). Site under construction at press time
Donor Sibling Groups www.donorsiblinggroups.com	USA	2007	20 groups	Free umbrella site for multiple Yahoo! Groups for people connected to specific donors (e.g. Fairfax Donor 401; CCB donor 3311). No database for individual matching.
Donor Sibling Link www.hfea.gov.uk/donor-sibling-link.html	UK	2010	25	HFEA-sponsored registry to enable voluntary contact among relatives for persons conceived after 1991 in the UK, who have already learned the identity of their donor under the Human Fertilisation and Embryology Authority Act. All registrants are DC adults, as donors and parents are not included. No matches have been made as of Nov., 2012
Donor Sibling Registry (DSR) www.donorsiblingregistry.com	USA	2000	38,298	Largest North American database, with matching technology to enable mutually desired contact among half-siblings and/or gamete donors. 9,688 familial connections facilitated to Nov. 8, 2012. US$75/year to access the registry; $175 lifetime membership

Scandinavian Seed Siblings www.seedsibling.org	Swe.	2009	100	Registry and discussion forum for offspring, parents and donors from clinics in Sweden, Norway, Denmark, Finland, Iceland and the Faroe Islands, with some info on Nordic donors in clinics elsewhere around the world. One-time membership fee of 350 SEK. Membership includes approx. 5% sperm donors, 10% DC adults, and 85% parents of underage children. Approximately 10 matches made to date
UK Donor Link www.ukdonorlink.org	UK	2004	346	DNA testing, database and contact register for persons conceived in the UK prior to the Human Fertilisation and Embryology Act of 1991. Originally a pilot project of the Dept. of Health, funding beyond 2012 is uncertain. Also see *Donor Sibling Link*, above, for those born after 1991. Registered members include 145 DC adults, 81 donors and 91 biological parents, as well as approximately 200 inquiries that may go on to register; as of 2012, 6 donor-offspring and 38 half-sibling matches have been made

Notes

1 All websites referred to in this chapter were accessed November 6-12, 2012, unless otherwise noted.
2 "C", on Donor Conception Support Group, http://www.dcsg.org.au/membership/offspring.html.
3 Americans for Open Records (AFMOR) http://www.amfor.net/DonorOffspring/viewregistry.cgi. Posted December 27, 2011.
4 Infertility Network, www.infertilitynetwork.org.
5 Donor Conception Network, "Annual Report 2007," http://www.donor-conception-network.org/DCN_ANNUAL_REPORT_2007.pdf. Accessed June 28, 2009.
6 Donor Conception Network www.dcnetwork.org.

7. NPCVAI, group description, http://groups.yahoo.com/group/PCVAI.
8. Donor Misconception Open Forum http://health.groups.yahoo.com/group/DonorMisconception-Open.
9. Donor Offspring Health http://groups.yahoo.com/group/donoroffspringhealth.
10. Australian Donor Conception Forum http://www.ausdcf.org/Accessed.
11. Yahoo! Groups pages, for example, show a usage calendar listing the number of postings per month over the past several years. The *Donor-Conceived People* site had disappeared by 2012, while *We are Donor-Conceived People,* http://community.livejournal.com/we_are_dcp/profile was last updated in 2008.
12. TangledWebs Australia, http://www.tangledwebs.org.au/index.php.
13. Tangled Webs UK www.tangledwebs.org.uk/tw.
14. IDOA, home page, http://www.idoalliance.org.
15. Canadian Donor Offspring http://www.canadiandonoroffspring.ca.
16. Pamela Pierlot on AMFOR http://www.amfor.net/DonorOffspring/viewregistry.cgi. Posted November 22, 2011.
17. Donor Sibling Registry, "A parent asks, a donor responds," December 23, 2007, Donor Sibling Registry Blog, http://www.donorsiblingregistry.com/DSRblog/?m=200712 Accessed July 20, 2009.
18. "Shelby" on AMFOR http://www.amfor.net/DonorOffspring/viewregistry.cgi. Posted March 22, 2011.
19. "Gresh" on AMFOR http://www.amfor.net/DonorOffspring/viewregistry.cgi. Posted November 20, 2011.
20. Stephen Hawton on AMFOR http://www.amfor.net/DonorOffspring/viewregistry.cgi. Posted June 18, 2012.
21. "Ickybana5" on AMFOR http://www.amfor.net/DonorOffspring/viewregistry.cgi. Posted November 16, 2010.
22. Donor Offspring Health, www.donoroffspringhealth.com. Last accessed May 29, 2009.
23. Donor Sibling Registry, home page, http://www.donorsiblingregistry.com/index.php. Matches have been made among people in the U.S., Denmark, England, Canada, Australia, Bolivia, Brazil, Finland, France, Germany, Hong Kong, Israel, Korea, New Zealand, Norway, South Africa, Sweden and Switzerland.
24. "Looking for blood relatives: Web site offers answers to some donor offspring," Early Show, CBS News, January 26, 2005, http://www.cbsnews.com/stories/2005/01/18/earlyshow/living/caught/main667531.shtml.
25. "Sperm donor siblings find family ties: Children, moms using the web to find anonymous relatives," 60 Minutes, CBS News, June 24, 2007, http://www.cbsnews.com/stories/2006/03/17/60minutes/main1414965_page2.shtml.
26. Donor Sibling Registry home page, www.donorsiblingregistry.com May 29, 2009.
27. Donor Sibling Registry, home page, http://www.donorsiblingregistry.com/index.php. Accessed July 29, 2011.
28. Donor Sibling Registry home page www.donorsiblingregistry.com, accessed, November 10, 2012.
29. UK DonorLink, "Donor Conception: Find the missing piece," http://www.ukdonorlink.org.uk/assets/documents/leaflet.pdf, accessed June 6, 2009.
30. Human Fertilisation and Embryology Act, 1990.
31. Human Fertilisation and Embryology Authority, "For donor-conceived people; what you can find out" http://www.hfea.gov.uk/112.html.
32. CaBRI, "About Us," http://www.cabrimed.org/about.jsp.
33. CaBRI, "Donor-Conceived Testing Services," http://www.cabrimed.org/donorconceivedservices.jsp.
34. Kirk Maxey, MD, President and CEO, CaBRIMed, personal communication, November 9, 2012.
35. 'Rel', "Connecting with others who are disconnected," March 18, 2006, T5's Daughter Blog, http://t5sdaughter.blogspot.com/2006_03_01_archive.html, accessed July 27, 2009.
36. "Louise's story," Tangled Webs UK, http://www.tangledwebs.org.uk/tw/Stories/Louise, Accessed July 27, 2009.

37 "Shirley's story," UK DonorLink, http://www.ukdonorlink.org.uk/story4.asp. Accessed July 27, 2009.
38 Becky's Story http://www.donor-conception-network.org/beckys_talk.htm. Accessed July 27, 2009.
39 'Rel', "Reclaiming a part of my heritage," August 18, 2006, T5's Daughter Blog, http://t5sdaughter.blogspot.com/2006_08_01_archive.html.
40 Ken Daniels, "Donor gametes: anonymous or identified", *art.cit.*,113-128.
41 See, for example, the International Society of Genetic Genealogy, http://isogg.org; Family Tree DNA, http://www.familytreedna.com/Default.aspx?c=1; The Ultimate Family Historians, http://www.theultimatefamilyhistorians.com; Ancient Roots Research, http://www.ancientrootsresearch.com/ARR_Consulting_Services.html; GenealogyByDNA.com, http://groups.yahoo.com/group/genbydna/; "Brick Wall" DNA/Genealogy Consulting, http://home.comcast.net/~philgoff/dnagenealogy.htm; the Short Tandem Repeat DNA Internet DataBase, http://www.cstl.nist.gov/div831/strbase/index.htm; and Genealogy-DNA-L mailing list, http://lists.rootsweb.ancestry.com/index/other/DNA/GENEALOGY-DNA.html.

PART TWO

WHAT IS THE HISTORY AND MEDICAL REGULATION OF THIS PRACTICE AND WHAT HAVE WE LEARNED FROM ADOPTION?

Ian Mitchell traces the history of the development of assisted human reproduction from a period when human reproduction was not understood, into the 21st century. The first recorded use of donor sperm in the 19th century was accompanied by secrecy and deception. To address infertility in women, a number of research groups in the 20th century tried artificially to fertilize eggs and sperm outside the body, re-implant the fertilized zygote in the uterus and achieve a successful pregnancy. Mitchell describes the revolutionary work of Edwards and Steptoe in achieving the first live birth from *in vitro* fertilization and Edwards' concerns about the ethical issues their techniques raised. Their basic techniques, which were recognized by the award of the Nobel Prize in 2010, have been refined and new treatment modalities added. For example, it is now possible to obtain sperm directly from the testis and inject a single sperm directly into the ovum, a process known as intra-cytoplasmic sperm injection (ICSI). Ova are also obtained from third parties for use by infertile couples. The process of obtaining ova is much more complicated than obtaining sperm, is uncomfortable to the woman providing ova, and has a definite incidence of complications, and a low, but real risk of mortality. Studies of the outcome of assisted reproductive technology (ART) suggest very high morbidity in the offspring related to prematurity, which is largely related to multiple births which, in turn, is related to the implantation of a large number of embryos at one time. Regulation in Canada is, to date, ineffective because the Supreme Court of Canada ruled that the *Assisted Human Reproduction Act* is to a large extent invalid. In most jurisdictions, ART is regulated by professional bodies.

How Canadian professional bodies regulate ART is the subject of the next chapter. *Ian Mitchell* and *Juliet Guichon* report that Canadian medical ethics codes do not require Canadian physicians to enable donor-conceived persons to know their progenitors' identity. The authors argue that Canadian medical ethics codes ought to be amended because: (1) the Canadian Medical Association itself recommended that accurate records be kept for at least 40 years and a registry be created; (2) understandings of moral obligation have changed permitting those affected by physicians' actions to be entitled to a greater consideration in physician ethics codes; (3) the values that underpin existing Canadian medical codes – compassion, trustworthiness, competence and integrity – support changes to the codes to require that physicians' actions be directed to ensuring the best interests of the children whom they help to create. Physicians engaged in reproductive medicine have a strong duty to the children whom they aim to create, to maintain detailed records, to make them available to the donor-conceived when they reach the age of majority, and to carry out research particularly when engaged in a novel practice.

History demonstrates that we sometimes choose to reinvent the wheel. Academic and donor offspring, *Joanna Rose*, has studied the effect of adoption on many adoptees and argues that the lessons learned in adoption are not being applied in donor conception even though the two practices involve the deliberate decision to rear a child by one or more genetically unrelated persons. As was true in adoption, the loss people suffer is simply denied. Rose criticizes the failure of government and society to offer reasons that adoptees are encouraged to search and are legally supported in their search for their kin, whilst the donor-conceived do not receive the same treatment despite being similarly situated. She argues that the practice of donor conception has been created to address the needs and desires of adults and does not attend to the interests of the children that the practice deliberately aims to bring into being. Rose laments the secrecy, adult-centric openness and anonymity that characterise the practice. These have facilitated a naïve or wilfully blind 'wait and see' approach to the rupturing and replacement of kinship and identity which, as we know from adoption, is highly problematic. Rose advances the argument that whereas adoption is perhaps an unfortunate solution to an unintended problem (typically the accidental conception of a child), donor conception deliberately brings children into being to separate them from one or both of their progenitors and their kin. The consequent identity loss and burdens are systemically created and yet avoidable. Rose argues that we would be wrong to fail to learn from adoption and that we should "do what is right, not what is easy" by making prior the best interests of the child in reproductive technology. She concludes that donor conception, with its intentional loss, should neither be regarded as an ethical solution to childlessness nor institutionally supported.

Chapter Eight

Historical Aspects of Advanced Reproductive Technology

Ian Mitchell

1. Introduction

Assisted Reproductive Technology (ART) is the creation of new human life other than by sexual intercourse. This historical overview provides an outline of reproductive anatomy and physiology (knowledge of which were essential precursors to the development of ART); and describes how the practice has evolved, the beginnings of ART and current concerns regarding the use of the technology.

2. Current Understanding of Human Reproduction

In all the cells of the human body, except in the gamete (the egg in females and sperm in males), there are 46 chromosomes containing genetic material arranged in 23 pairs. In the gametes, there are 23 chromosomes. At conception, the 23 chromosomes in the egg and sperm unite. In females, there are cyclical hormonal changes involving follicle-stimulating hormone (FSH), estrogen and luteinizing hormone (LH). The egg is released approximately mid-menstrual cycle; it is viable for 12-24 hours and if fertilization does not occur, the lining of the uterus is shed.

In males, sperm are produced continuously in the testes and are mixed with fluid from the testes and the prostate gland. When ejaculation occurs during intercourse, the sperm pass from the vagina, through the uterus and into the fallopian tubes that go towards the ovary where the sperm remain viable for 48-72 hours inside the female reproductive tract.

Fertizilation normally occurs in the Fallopian tube. The "zygote" (it is soon called an "embryo") passes down the Fallopian tube into the uterus. Implantation takes place about 7-10 days after fertilization.

3. Development of Assisted Reproductive Technology

The first form of Assisted Reproductive Technology (ART) used was artificial insemination (AI) which entails the nonsexual insertion of sperm into the cervix or uterus to achieve a pregnancy. The sperm used might be from the future social father. If donor[1] sperm is used, then the practice is known as "assisted insemination by donor", "donor insemination" or "DI".

Physicians, cell biologists and other health-care professionals collaborate to use ART to help infertile heterosexual couples or individuals who do not or choose not to have a heterosexual partner, to have a child by non-sexual means. The development of ART has led to many controversies regarding its application.[2,3]

The next three sections deal separately with the use of sperm, *in vitro* fertilization and eggs in ART. These divisions are arbitrary but convenient. In reality, developments in these three areas overlapped in time, and developments in one area often depended on changes in another.

3.1 Use of Sperm in ART

Spermatic fluid was used as an aid to conception before the precise role of sperm within the fluid was recognized. John Hunter in the 18th century[4] experimented with spermatic fluid and artificially inseminated silkworms. Later he applied his knowledge to help a couple who were having problems conceiving. Hunter collected the man's semen in a warmed syringe and injected it into his wife's vagina. Successful pregnancy resulted.

The first insemination with donor sperm seems to have taken place in Philadelphia in 1884.[5] A woman whose husband was azoospermic was anesthetized with chloroform. Sperm was obtained from one of the students in the audience and inserted into her uterus with a syringe, then the cervix plugged temporarily. Pregnancy followed, and an infant delivered at term. The husband knew the details of the conception but was advised not to tell his wife. Following the publication of this case in 1909, there was a flurry of letters to the editor claiming, among other things, that there had been previous cases.

Three articles in the 1970s[6,7,8] gave similar explanations for the rise in DI: the common use of effective birth control, abortion, and acceptance of single motherhood. Each article raised the same concerns and shared uncertainties that focused on the number of children who might be conceived from one sperm donor (five suggested) and the role of the physician in deciding who might be eligible to receive the donation. One article mentioned that many donors were medical students,[9] which raises the possibility some IVF physicians in practice today have been donors. The articles expressed anxiety about the legal parentage of the child born after DI, and accepted that the male partner of the woman impregnated would be the social father.

Donor sperm remains an important part of ART. Donors are screened by history and physical examination, and tested for sexually transmitted diseases and genetics. Sperm undergoes trial freeze and thaw to assess for quality. The successful use of cryopreserved semen in infertility was described in 1953.[9] Over the next 20 or so years, the procedure became "common in several centres across Canada" and was available "in 22 centres in Britain", although accurate figures of individual cases are difficult to find.[10] When accepted, sperm is frozen in nitrogen vapour and, when required, thawed and then placed in the uterus, at a time when spontaneous or induced ovulation has just occurred.[11]

The use of cryopreserved sperm had its supporters and detractors, but became the norm for donated sperm with the onset of the HIV epidemic.[12] Donors (and sperm) can be screened for infectious diseases, and the donor retested 6 months later before the sperm is used. The testing required to screen donors and sperm for a number of infectious diseases and for genetic diseases, and the expenses of recruiting donors has made it difficult for small sperm banks to continue. Daniels and Golden claim that at present in the United States there may be less than 30, mainly commercial, sperm banks supplying sperm worldwide. It is unclear how many donations may come from one sperm donor. Because the banks supply a wide geographical area in the United States and other countries, they may believe that the risk of inadvertent incest is unlikely. Given the cost of recruiting donors and testing sperm, the banks go to considerable lengths to ensure that repeat donors are who they say they are, even using biometric markers. However, it may be difficult for outsiders to identify donors who are paid in cash by the sperm banks.

Cryopreserved sperm held by sperm banks is described in catalogues, with "a dazzling array of seminal products available for purchase" listing the "race, ethnicity, height, weight, hair color, hair texture, skin tone, facial structure, IQ, hobbies, talents and interest."[13] In the early days of sperm donation, physicians decided which women had access to sperm donation. If a woman was accepted into a sperm donation program, then the physician decided whose sperm would be used. Now, most women have access to sperm donations, and the woman, not the physician, chooses the donor sperm from a catalogue.

3.2 Development of *in vitro* Fertilization.

Fertilization outside the body known as "*in vitro* fertilization" or "IVF", developed much later. Physicians extract eggs from women and cell biologists mix the egg with sperm in a petri dish to achieve fertilization. Once normal early development is confirmed, an embryo (2-3 days) or blastocyst (about 5 days) is inserted into the cervix or uterus of the woman. The woman may be the person from whom the egg was extracted, or a second woman. One or both of these women, or a third woman may intend to rear the child. A child may, because of the combination of donated gametes and IVF, have a variety of parents – genetically-related, gestational and social.

The first recorded human child conceived by IVF and carried to term was Louise Brown, born 25 July 1978.[14] A number of research groups in the 1960s and 1970s sought to understand reproduction in great detail and to use this knowledge to develop an approach to infertility. The first IVF birth resulted from collaboration between a basic scientist (John Edwards) and an innovative physician (gynaecologist, Bob Steptoe). Louise was conceived *in vitro* with an egg from her mother (who had blocked Fallopian tubes) and sperm from her father; Mr. and Mrs. Brown were committed to rearing Louise. One year later, another woman who conceived by the same technology gave birth. By 1982, approximately 30 IVF children had been born worldwide. There followed a growth in medical knowledge of the practice such that, by 2008, more than three million infants worldwide had been born after IVF.[15]

Edwards and Steptoe identified one another as appropriate collaborators. Steptoe had the surgical skill and the desire to solve the clinical problem of infertility and Edwards had the training in basic science. Edwards had heard about the laparoscope and Steptoe's adeptness in using it. The two men developed a tiny research laboratory in Oldham to which Edwards frequently undertook the six hour drive from there to Cambridge, leaving at 6 a.m. if there was a mid-morning operation.

Edwards and Steptoe reported experiments with human eggs being reliably fertilized with human sperm in a test tube, in the prestigious journal, *Nature,* in 1969.[16] *Nature* itself counselled caution, especially as public opinion would not uniformly favour these advances.[17]

Edwards and Steptoe applied for funding from the Medical Research Council (MRC) to have a clinical unit in the Cambridge area but were denied because the funding body thought they should work on other primates. Edwards and Steptoe were both angry and very upset[16]. It was already known that the fertility drugs used successfully in women did not work with female monkeys, and eggs obtained from monkeys could not be fertilized *in vitro*.

Edwards and Steptoe obtained private funding. By 1972, Edwards and Steptoe had reimplanted an eight-cell embryo into a woman's uterus but pregnancy did not occur – perhaps because the fertility drugs shortened the menstrual cycle. The next step in the research is still used today. They fertilized eggs *in vitro* and then froze the embryos until the fertility drugs were no longer in the woman and the menstrual cycle had returned to normality. Even with this technique, Edwards and Steptoe still did not achieve a successful pregnancy. They decided that they needed to know exactly when the surge of luteinising hormone (LH) occurred in the woman.

Their efforts were eventually successful. Edwards and Steptoe reported the medical details of Louise Brown's birth in the Lancet.[18] The *Daily Mail* revealed the news to the world after buying exclusive rights to the story from the Browns for a reported £300,000. Because of public and political pressure, the Medical Research Council now agreed to fund IVF research.

Following Louise Brown's birth, further births using similar techniques occurred in many different centres. The next several births, including the first twins, occurred in Australia. The first Canadian test tube births were twins, Colin and Greg Rankin, and were the seventh and eighth such infants ever born. In the Rankin case, *in vitro* fertilization was performed in England by Steptoe and the birth was in Ontario's Oakville-Trafalgar Memorial Hospital.[19] The first American infant born in 1981 was the world's fifteenth.

IVF is now regarded as a routine medical procedure. Physicians still follow the same general principles used by Steptoe but of course, many of the details are different. The 2010 Nobel Prize in Physiology or Medicine was awarded to Edwards, rather a belated recognition of his great scientific achievements and many years after the death in 1988 of his colleague, Steptoe.[20] One of Edwards graduate students, Professor Martin Johnson, described the animosity towards Edwards in the scientific community in the 1960s and 1970s and how strongly he himself was discouraged from working with Edwards.[21] Johnson emphasized Edwards's lifelong concern about the ethical implications of his research. Now the only hostile voice about the Nobel Prize came from a religious source, Vatican Bishop Ignacio Carrasco de Paula, who seemed "to hold Bob personally responsible for all the perceived ills of assisted reproductive therapies", and an "authoritarian desire to prohibit any thought, word or deed that may challenge dogma or lead to risky discoveries."

The story behind the birth of Louise Brown illustrates many of the basic scientific questions that had to be resolved.[22] It is the story of *in vitro* fertilization using eggs from the wife (the biological and rearing mother), sperm from the husband (the biological and rearing father), and the uterus of the wife (thus also the gestational mother).

3.3 Use of Eggs in ART

In the early days of *in vitro* fertilization, a child's gestation would be in the uterus of the nurturing mother and with a genetic connection to both social parents. In some cases, the sperm was from a male who was not the life-partner. By 1983, the egg might be acquired from one female and, after fertilization, implanted into the uterus of another. There have been many further developments in the use of sperm and eggs in ART that are more easily understood by describing them after *in vitro* fertilization itself has been described.

Usually a woman will ovulate one egg per month. When eggs are required for IVF, timing is important and hormones (HCG) must be administered 36 hours before the procedure to mature the eggs before retrieval. Acquiring only one egg and mixing with sperm *in vitro,* watching for fertilisation and cell division, and reinserting the embryo can work as it did for Louise Brown. But the chances of success are less, and now several eggs are used to ensure at least one will be fertilised and can be reinserted into the uterus. If more than one embryo is reinserted, there is a risk of multiple pregnancies. Not every egg will be mature and able to be fertilized and among those that are fertilized not all can result in a completed pregnancy.

The clinician's aim is to achieve super ovulation, that is, maturation of a number of oocytes. Early regimens used gonadotrophins alone or combined with clomiphene but this process required careful monitoring and even then oocyte collection might be required at night or weekends – which is inconvenient to the health-care providers. Now combinations of gonadotrophin releasing hormone agonists with low dose gonadotrophin have resulted in greater ease of planning. The oocyte retrieval can be precisely timed. Ultrasound is used to confirm the ovary has been successfully stimulated and, with the help of anesthesia or sedation, a long needle is then passed through the vagina, guided by ultrasound, towards the ovary and eggs aspirated.

In most cases of ART today, eggs may be removed from the ovary, inseminated with sperm in the laboratory and the resulting embryo inserted into the uterus of the same woman who is therefore both the genetic and gestational mother and responsible for the upbringing of the child, the rearing mother. But eggs may now also be acquired from "donors", a development that makes possible for the first time in human history the separation of genetic and gestational motherhood.

Egg provision has a number of recognized complications, such as vaginal bleeding. While egg provision is said to be relatively safe and most complications can be readily addressed, women have died after this procedure.[23] Somewhere between 0.5 and 5% have had significant complications such as renal or respiratory failure but it is difficult to know the frequency of complications. Gynaecologists suspect that complications have become less frequent with a shift away from laparoscopy to transvaginal ultrasound guided oocyte aspiration. Also, women undergoing IVF (or acting as egg donors) are likely to be healthier than the general population, and hence less likely to have significant complications. However, deaths do occur. In a study in the Netherlands (1984-

2008),[24] there were 31 deaths, six related to IVF, 17 directly related to the IVF pregnancy and eight related neither to IVF nor the IVF pregnancy. The authors went to great lengths to gather this information and suspect there is "worldwide under-reporting of IVF-related mortality."

Many of the side effects of egg extraction are related to discomfort secondary to the use of hormones and there is a definite but small risk of infection or bleeding. A few women have a specific syndrome, Ovarian Hyperstimulation Syndrome (OHSS). These women have a series of uncomfortable symptoms such as abdominal distension, bloating and pain, vomiting and diarrhea but can have more serious complications such as fluid in the abdomen, in the lung cavities and coagulation abnormalities.

The use of eggs from other than the gestational mother was first reported from Australia in 1983.[25] The recipient had premature ovarian failure, meaning her ovaries had no functional follicles. The increasing incidence of age-related infertility has led to an increased incidence of use of eggs from donors. It is reported that in 2003 at least 5767 babies were born after being conceived with "donated" eggs.[26]

The development of egg donation raises many of the ethical questions that had been discussed with sperm provision, including the use of the word "Donor" and the nature of "altruism". Steinberg[27] cites the Ethics Committee of the American Society for Reproductive Medicine as advocating payment of up to $10,000 for women providing eggs and claiming that this payment does not affect the altruistic nature of the act. The reality in the USA is that there are egg brokers who advertise for specific characteristics and offer payments in the range $35,000-$50,000. Steinberg characterizes provision of eggs for reproduction as a "commercial transaction". Payment for egg donors is forbidden in some jurisdictions and permitted or encouraged in others.

A new technique, vitrification, has widened the possibilities of egg donation. In early forms of egg freezing, ice crystals formed, often damaging the ovum and raising anxieties about the resulting children. Such problems are said to have been largely overcome by vitrification, which is the rapid freezing of eggs without formation of crystals.[28] Specifically, the process was developed primarily for professional women who wish to defer childbearing, and for the smaller numbers who require chemotherapy or radiation therapy. The goal is to permit eggs to be stored for future use, of course using IVF. Motluk quotes the American Society for Reproductive Medicine as stating that "all egg freezing should be regarded as experimental and should be performed as part of a research project."[29] Reproductive specialists do not seem to believe that the procedure is experimental.[30]There are few studies of successful use of previously vitrified eggs, and while no major problems have been noted conclusions are cautious; Wennerholm and colleagues write, "properly controlled follow-up studies of neonatal outcome are needed" and "child long term studies for all cryopreservation techniques are essential."[31]

3.4 Embryo Transfer

Embryo transfer is an essential part of IVF. The fertilized embryo is transferred from the petri dish to the uterus of the gestational mother. The biological possibility of this manoeuvre in mammalian species was described in the 19th century by Heape.[32,33,34] In the case reported, a woman (A) was artificially inseminated by sperm from the husband (B) of a second woman (C). Fertilization took place in the body of A, and as the embryo developed but before it was implanted it was transferred from A to the uterus of C. The pregnancy went to term. In this case, the genetic father (B) was the rearing father (B), the gestational mother (C) was his wife and the rearing mother (C) but not the genetic mother (A). Current trends in egg and embryo donation are best considered together. A 2006[35] report mentioned that 100,000 treatment cycles had already occurred in the United States, and that the procedures involved, including rigorous screening, were already "mainstream". Now the cycles of the donor and recipient are commonly synchronized using oral contraceptives. The donor is stimulated with gonadotrophin hormone, at the same time using some gonadotrophin releasing hormone (GnRH) agonist to prevent luteinizing hormone surge. The recipient is given GnRH, estradiol and progesterone to prepare the endometrium. If everything is favourable, then the embryo is transferred, and a pregnancy test conducted two weeks after the transfer. The recipient usually remains on exogenous estrogen and progesterone for 10 weeks. The procedure of egg and/or embryo donation is used in a variety of conditions, such as premature ovarian failure, advanced reproductive age, unexplained recurrent implantation failure and inherited conditions. For several years after this intervention was described, it was performed only on women under the age of 40, but since 1990 it has increasingly been used in women over 40 including postmenopausal women. However, this is becoming less popular because, as noted above, many women wish to keep the eggs frozen in case they themselves need them later.

3.5 Intra-cytoplasmic Sperm Injection (ICSI)

In natural sexual reproduction and in conventional IVF, one egg is exposed to many sperm. Only one spermatozoan penetrates the egg and fertilization occurs. At that moment, the egg changes and no more sperm can enter. In some men, there may be very few sperm and those that are present may lack full motility.

Historical Aspects of Advanced Reproductive Technology

In such circumstances, an individual sperm may be injected directly into the egg. This procedure is "intra-cytoplasmic sperm injection – ICSI".[36] Sperm may be obtained by testicular biopsy for direct injection into an egg. (It is from this means, that sperm are extracted from cadavers.) Following injection of sperm into the ovum, the ovum is placed in cell culture. Fertilization will be obvious within 24 hours or so. ICSI has been associated with the specific congenital anomalies such as Beckwith-Wiedemann Syndrome[37], Angelman Syndrome and sex chromosomal anomalies. These seem to be specific to ICSI, although a slight increase in the incidence of congenital anomalies with all forms of ART has been noted.[38]

4. Legislative History

The sorry tale of the failure to develop a legislative framework in Canada, including an effective oversight body can be briefly described.[39]

Eleven years after a Royal Commission on New Reproductive Technologies called in 1993 for the urgent establishment of a national oversight agency, the Federal Government passed legislation creating that regulatory authority in 2004. The legislation prohibited a number of activities including:

> Paying, offering to pay, or advertising payment for sperm, eggs or *in vitro* embryos from donors or for the services of surrogate mothers (including payment to a third party for arranging for the services of a surrogate mother)

Other activities were to be regulated under the authority of Assisted Human Reproduction Canada. These included:

- *In vitro* fertilization (IVF)
- Intra-cytoplasmic sperm injection (ICSI)
- Intrauterine insemination (IUI)
- Egg donation
- Transfer of an *in vitro* embryo

However, Health Canada produced only one regulation before the Province of Québec successfully challenged the power of the Federal Government to regulate reproductive technology.[40] In a divided decision, the Supreme Court of Canada upheld parts of the law involving criminal sanction but stated that most activities were to be regulated by the Provinces. The practical implications are not yet clear. The possibilities range from a total lack of any regulation, to widely differing arrangements among provinces, to inter-provincial collaboration producing standard national guidelines. The last possibility, while perhaps best for patients and offspring appears unlikely.

5. Situation, Outcomes and Possible Developments

In Canada, ART including IVF is accepted and widely practiced. Worldwide there has been acceptance of the technique of *in vitro* fertilization, various degrees of legal oversight and of course refinements and changes in the medical techniques used. The International Committee for Monitoring Assisted Reproductive Technology (ICMART) collects information, and recently produced its eighth report, for the year 2002.[41] The information used by ICMART is gathered from national registries or from individual ART units; 1563 clinics in 53 countries. Overall, there was poor reporting of congenital anomalies. Approximately 2291 Canadian children were born after IVF in 2002. World wide, 219,000 to 246,000 babies were born after IVF in 2002, an increase of 12% compared with 2000, from an estimated 911,000 to 1,025,000 cycles. Pregnancy and delivery rates increased for fresh and frozen embryo cycles despite a drop in the number of embryos transferred. More than 601,250 cycles worldwide resulted in delivery rates per aspiration or attempt at egg retrieval of 22% after *in vitro* fertilization. Intracytoplasmic sperm injection increased in use between 2000 and 2002, 54% to 61% in North America and from 46% to 54% in Europe. Intracytoplasmic sperm injection had successful delivery rates of 21%.

Over the many years since Louise Brown was born, concern has been raised about the number of embryos transferred in any given time and the linked outcome of twin and triplet pregnancies. The ICMART 2002 Report noted that the percentage of four or more embryo transfers had decreased from 15.4% in 2000 to 13.7% in 2002 and that the proportion of twin pregnancies dropped from 26.5% to 25.7% and triplet pregnancies from 2.9% to 2.5%. In Canada, four or more embryo transfers occurred in 9.6% of transfers, 31.9% of births were twins and 2.7% triplets.

Only a minority of treatment cycles results in a live birth[42] with little evidence of improvement over time, and, with respect to IVF, "we are still not very good at it." The ICMART report suggests that most implanted embryos did not result in successful pregnancy. The rates would seem to vary from round about 10% to just under half, but it is not clear whether all centers and countries use the same criteria for reporting. Also, it is stated that "success of a cycle of infertility treatment is counted as a live birth after twenty weeks' gestation."[43] This of course means that there is a considerable morbidity in infants born after IVF. This is largely related to prematurity, which in turn is related to the number of multiples born, which in turn is related to the number of embryos implanted.

The effects of IVF on low birth weight, preterm delivery and multiple births are considerable. In Alberta, Canada, in the years 1994 to 1996,[44] 17.8% of infants <2500 g at birth, were born after IVF. 43.5% of very small infants, those <1500g at birth, were conceived by IVF. Strikingly, of all infants in the province, 1.2% are born <30 weeks' gestation, but of IVF births nearly 8% are born at this extreme degree of prematurity. However, it is not just multiples that are at risk for morbidity. In a review of published studies of 12,283 IVF and 1.9 million spontaneously conceived singletons, there was still an increased morbidity.[45] The adverse perinatal outcomes related to IVF were an increased incidence of singletons after IVF, perinatal mortality, preterm delivery whether low birth weight or very low birth weight, and small for gestational age. Some of these adverse outcomes may be related to increased maternal age, which by itself is associated with pregnancy and perinatal complications, in combination with the IVF conception.[46] In addition to the morbidity due to premature delivery, there is a small increase in congenital anomalies. It is not clear whether this is associated with the infertility itself, or the IVF treatment.[47]

There seems to be a poor understanding of some of the risks of IVF in the general public. In telephone interviews of more than 1500 randomly selected individuals,[48] most (70%) knew that there may be conception difficulties with increased maternal age. The reason cited for delaying childbearing were financial security and partnership ability to parent. Unfortunately, less than half knew about the increased risk of stillbirth, caesarean delivery, multiple birth and preterm delivery.

Johnson[49] noted that society is increasingly market led. This leads to considerable "demands being made on scientists and doctors by the 'consumers' in our clinics." Some advances are considered, such as further development of ICSI, to include spermatocyte injection (with limited success). While cryo-storage of spermatozoa and pre-implantation conceptuses is routine, this is now being used for immature oocytes or spermatozoon stem cells. Improvements are being made in culture media to improve conceptus viability. This author believes that having regulation in the UK protects the patient from "unduly enthusiastic innovating doctors." The regulations allow the creation of life, mandate research before treatment is attempted and require licensing of new approaches to treatment.

6. History of ART – Persistent Concerns

Reproduction is an intensely emotional topic. Infertility has caused distress throughout recorded history. Many solutions have been sought, but an effective, scientifically-based response in the 20th century depended upon discoveries achieved during the preceding 300 years. That both sperm and egg contribute genes to the child was not recognised until the 19th century. Understanding of the hormonal and biochemical changes of reproduction came in stages throughout the 20th century. Manipulation of the embryo at an early stage is now possible, given recent advances in molecular genetics.

These scientific advances have been accompanied by ethical unease. The first recorded cases of DI were conducted in an atmosphere of secrecy and deception. In many respects the situation has not changed. In Canada, although payment for sperm is not allowed, there are no regulations on how many children can come from one sperm supplier and the sperm supplier may remain anonymous. The international trend is toward banning payment, limiting donations and identifying the sperm provider. In Canada, litigation is underway challenging government and medical practice of denying children knowledge of their genetic origins in gamete donation.[50]

In vitro fertilization likewise has raised ethical issues. Although IVF is widely used, the number of children resulting is unclear. Centres express results differently, some by a number of cycles, and some by ultimate success after many attempts which is rather colloquially referred to as the "take home baby rate." Only recently have there been follow up studies on infant health; there is a small increase in congenital anomalies and a larger morbidity related to the high incidence of prematurity, particularly when multiple embryos are implanted creating twins and triplets.

The extraction of eggs for transfer to be used by other women raises ethical issues concerning the long term health implications for so-called 'egg donors' and issues similar to those raised with semen donation: the possibility of consanguinity and the right to know the identity of the donor. Egg donation can raise concern also when it is used to create pregnancies in older and sometimes normally post-menopausal women and when multiple embryos are implanted creating pregnancies of multiples which have poorer outcomes.

In summary, many scientific discoveries have been driven by curiosity about the details of reproduction. Scientific approaches to infertility followed concerns for people who are unable to be parents and compassion for their situation. Concern for the best interest of the offspring has rarely been prominent. Even those closely involved in the process are troubled by some of the excesses, such as implanting so many embryos that multiple pregnancies are inevitable. However, Canada does not have an effective regulatory body to deal with this and other issues such as whether offspring should have access to their genetic identity.

Bibliography

AFP. 'Octomom' doctor accused again of 'gross negligence', 14 July 2010, http://www.vancouversun.com/health/Octomom+doctor+accused+again+gross+negligence/3277116/story.html.

Anonymous. Safety of egg donation 'unclear'. BBC News, 30 June 2005. http://news.bbc.co.uk/2/hi/health/4634625.stm.

Biggers, D. and Walter Heape, FRS: a pioneer in reproductive biology. Centenary of his embryo transfer experiments. *J Reprod Fert* 1991, 93: 173-186.

Blakeslee, Sandra. Infertile Woman Has Baby Through Embryo Transfer, 4 February 1984, http://www.nytimes.com/1984/02/04/us/infertile-woman-has-baby-through-embryo-transfer.html?sec=health.

Braat, D.D.M. and others. Maternal death related to IVF in the Netherlands, 1984-2008. *Human Reproduction* 2010; 25 (7): 1782-1786.

Burnett, Thane. Canada's first test-tube babies turning 25. Sun Media, 18 March 2007, http://cnews.canoe.ca/CNEWS/Features/2007/03/15/3756633-sun.html.

Bustillo, M., J.E. Buster, S.W. Cohen, F. Hamilton, I.H. Thorneycroft, J.A. Simon, I.A. Rodi, S.P. Boyers, J.R. Marshall, J.A. Louw, et al. Delivery of a healthy infant following nonsurgical ovum transfer. *JAMA*, 17 February 1984, 251(7):889.

Canada: The Long Road to Regulation, Jean Haase in Third-Party Assisted Conception across Cultures: Social, Legal and Ethical Perspectives. Eric Blyth and Ruth Landau eds., Jessica Kingsley Publishers, Philadelphia 2003.

Coutts, Matthew. National Post, Wednesday, 4 February 2009, http://www.nationalpost.com/story.html?id=1256913.

DeBaun, M.R. and others. Association of In Vitro Fertilization with Beckwith-Wiedemann Syndrome and Epigenetic Alterations of LIT1 H19. *Am J Hum Genet*, 2003; 72:156-160.

Delpisheh, A. and others. Pregnancy Late in Life: A Hospital-Based Study of Birth Outcomes. *Journal of Women's Health*, 2008; 17:1-6.

De Mouzon, J. and others. World Collaborative Report on Assisted Reproductive Technology, 2002. *Human Reproduction* 2009, May 27, doi,10.1093/humrep/dep098.

Edwards, R.G., Bavister, B.D. and Steptoe P.C. Early Stages of Fertilization *in vitro* of Human Oocytes Matured *in vitro. Nature*, 15 February 1969; 221: 632-635.

Edwards, Robert and Patrick Steptoe. *A Matter of Life,* Hutchison and Co., Ltd., Great Britain, 1980.

Farhi, J. and B. Fisch. Risk of Major Congenital Malformations Associated with Infertility and its Treatment by Extent of Iatrogenic Intervention. *Pediatric Endocrinology Reviews*, 2007; 4: 352-357).

Frankel M.S. Cryobanking of human sperm. *J Med Ethics*. 1975 Apr;1(1):36-8.

Garner P.R. Artificial insemination. *CMAJ*, 1979, 120:11-12.

Gregoire A.T. and R.C. Mayer. The Impregnators. *Fertility and Sterility*, 1965; 16 (1):130-134.

Jackson, R. and others. Perinatal outcomes in Singletons Following in Vitro Fertilization: A Meta-Analysis. *Obstetrics and Gynecology*, 2004; 103:551-563.

Janvier, A. Jumping to premature conclusions. Virtual Mentor. *American Medical Association Journal of Ethics*, 2008; 10: 659-664.

Johnson, M. Reproduction in the Noughties: will the scientists have all the fun? *J Anat*, 2001; 198: 385-398.

Johnson, M.H. Elusive Nobel prize finally lands! *BioNews*, http://www.bionews.org.uk/page 71897.asp?print=1.

Kerr M.G. and C. Rogers. Donor insemination. *J Med Ethics*, 1975, 1; 30-33.

Kirby T. Profile. Robert Edwards: Nobel Prize for father of in-vitro fertilisation. *Lancet* 376 (9749); 16)ct 20101: 1293.

Millán, L Federal government overstepped its authority, says Quebec Court of Appeal. Law in Quebec,17/03/2009, http://lawinquebec.wordpress.com/2009/03/17/federal-government-overstepped-its-authority-says-quebec-court-of-appeal/. Accessed 17 November, 2010.

Moore, Wendy. *The Knife Man: The Extraordinary Life and Times of John Hunter, Father of Modern Surgery*. 2005 Bantam Press, ISBN 0593 052099.

Orenstein, Peggy. In Vitro We Trust, *New York Times*, 20 July 2008, http://www.nytimes.com/2008/07/20/magazine/20wwln-lede-t.html?ref=assisted_reproductive_technology.

Palermo, G., H. Joris, P. Devroey and Van Steirteghem. Pregnancies after intracytoplasmic injection of single spermatozoon into an oocytes. *Lancet,* 4 July 1992; 340(8810):17-8.

Sauer, M.V. and S.M. Kavic. Oocyte and embryo donation 2006: reviewing two decades of innovation and controversy. *Reproductive Biomedicine Online*, 2006; 12 (2): 151-162.

Spar, D. The Egg Trade – Making Sense of the Market for Human Oocytes. *New England Journal of Medicine*, 2007; 356:1289-1291.

Steinberg, D. "Altruism in Medicine: Its Definition, Nature, and Dilemmas", *Cambridge Quarterly of Healthcare Ethics*, 2010; 19; 249-257.

Steptoe, P.C. and R.G. Edwards. Birth after the Reimplanation of a Human Embryo, *Lancet*, 12 August 1978; 366.

Tomlinson, M. and C. Barrat. *Donor Insemination in Good Clinical Practice in Assisted Reproduction*, Paul Serhal and Caroline Overton eds., Cambridge University Press, 2004.

Tough, S.C. and others. Effects of in vitro fertilization on low birth weight, preterm delivery, and multiple births. *Journal of Pediatrics*, 2000; 136: 618-622.

-- and others, Factors Influencing Childbearing Decisions and Knowledge of Perinatal Risks among Canadian Men and Women. *Maternal and Child Health Journal*, 2007; 11:189-198.

"What comes after Fertilization?", Editorial. *Nature*; 221, 15 February 1969: 613.

Notes

1. In this chapter, this book, and elsewhere, the term 'donor' is used despite knowledge of the fact that gamete providers are usually paid.
2. Matthew Coutts, National Post, Wednesday, 4 February 2009, http://www.nationalpost.com/story.html?id=1256913.
3. AFP, 'Octomom' doctor accused again of 'gross negligence', 14 July 2010, http://www.vancouversun.com/health/Octomom+doctor+accused+again+gross+negligence/3277116/story.html.
4. Wendy Moore, *The Knife Man: The Extraordinary Life and Times of John Hunter, Father of Modern Surgery*. 2005 Bantam Press, ISBN 0593 052099.
5. A.T. Gregoire and R.C. Mayer, The Impregnators. *Fertility and Sterility*, 1965; 16 (1):130-134.
6. M.G. Kerr and C. Rogers, Donor insemination. *J Med Ethics*, 1975, 1; 30-33.
7. P.R. Garner, Artificial insemination. *CMAJ*, 1979, 120:11-12.
8. Lord Feversham (chmn): *Report of the Departmental Committee on Human Artificial Insemination, Presented to Parliament by the Secretary of Stat for the Home Department and the Secretary of State for Scotland*, July 1960, HMSO, London, 1960. Quoted by Garner.
9. M.S. Frankel, Cryobanking of human sperm. J Med Ethics. 1975 Apr;1(1):36-8.
10. P.R. Garner, Artificial insemination. *CMAJ*, 1979, 120:11-12.
11. M. Tomlinson and C. Barrat, *Donor Insemination in Good Clinical Practice in Assisted Reproduction*, Paul Serhal and Caroline Overton eds., Cambridge University Press, 2004.
12. Daniels CR and Golden J. Procreative compounds: popular eugenics, artificial insemination and the rise of the American sperm banking industry. Journal of Social History, 2004; 38 (1): 5 – 27.
13. Daniels and Golden p 5.
14. P.C. Steptoe and R.G. Edwards, Birth after the Reimplanation of a Human Embryo, *Lancet*, 12 August 1978, 366.
15. Peggy Orenstein, In Vitro We Trust, *New York Times*, 20 July 2008, http://www.nytimes.com/2008/07/20/magazine/20wwln-lede-t.html?ref=assisted_reproductive_technology.
16. R.G. Edwards, B.D. Bavister and P.C. Steptoe, Early Stages of Fertilization *in vitro* of Human Oocytes Matured *in vitro*. *Nature*, 221; 15 February 1969, 632-635.
    Editorial, What comes after Fertilization? *Nature*, 221, 15 February 1969:613.
17. Robert Edwards and Patrick Steptoe, *A Matter of Life*. Hutchison and Co, Ltd, Great Britain, 1980.
18. Steptoe and Edwards, *Lancet*, 1978.
19. Thane Burnett, Canada's first test-tube babies turning 25. Sun Media, 18 March 2007, http://cnews.canoe.ca/CNEWS/Features/2007/03/15/3756633-sun.html.
20. Kirby T. Profile. Robert Edwards: Nobel Prize for father of in-vitro fertilisation. *Lancet* 376 (9749); 16)ct 20101: 1293.
21. M.H. Johnson, Elusive Nobel prize finally lands! *BioNews*, http://www.bionews.org.uk/page71897.asp?print=1.
22. R. Edwards and P. Steptoe, *A Matter of Life*.
23. Anonymous. Safety of egg donation 'unclear'. BBC News, 30 June 2005. http://news.bbc.co.uk/2/hi/health/4634625.stm Accessed 17 November, 2010.
24. D.D.M. Braat and others, Maternal death related to IVF in the Netherlands, 1984-2008. *Human Reproduction* 2010; 25 (7): 1782-1786.
25. M.V. Sauer and S.M. Kavic, Oocyte and embryo donation 2006: reviewing two decades of innovation and controversy. Reproductive Biomedicine Online, 2006, 12 (2): 151-162.
26. D. Spar, The Egg Trade – Making Sense of the Market for Human Oocytes. *New England Journal of Medicine* 2007, 356:1289-1291.
27. D. Steinberg, "Altruism in Medicine: Its Definition, Nature, and Dilemmas", Cambridge Quarterly of Healthcare Ethics, 2010, 19; 249-257.
28. Harwood K, Egg Freezing: a breakthrough for reproductive autonomy? Bioethics, 2009; 23 (1); 39 – 46.
29. Motluk A. Growth of egg freezing blurs 'experimental' label. Nature, 2011; 476: 382-3.
30. *Ibid*.

31 Wennerholm U-B. Children born after cryopreservation of embryos or oocytes: a systematic review of outcome data. Hum Reprod. 2009 Sep;24(9):2158-72].
32 J.D. Biggers and. Walter Heape, FRS: a pioneer in reproductive biology. Centenary of his embryo transfer experiments. *J Reprod Fert* 1991, 93: 173-186.
33 Sandra Blakeslee, Infertile Woman Has Baby Through Embryo Transfer, 4 February 1984, http://www.nytimes.com/1984/02/04/us/infertile-woman-has-baby-through-embryo-transfer.html?sec=health.
34 M. Bustillo, J.E. Buster, S.W. Cohen, F. Hamilton, I.H. Thorneycroft, J.A. Simon, I.A. Rodi, S.P. Boyers, J.R. Marshall, J.A. Louw, et al. Delivery of a healthy infant following nonsurgical ovum transfer. JAMA, 17 February 1984, 251(7):889.
35 M.V. Sauer and S.M. Kavic, Oocyte and embryo donation 2006: reviewing two decades of innovation and controversy. Reproductive BioMedicine Online 2006;12:153-162.
36 G. Palermo, H. Joris, P. Devroey, Van Steirteghem, Pregnancies after intracytoplasmic injection of single spermatozoon into an oocytes. *Lancet*, 4 July 1992 Jul 4;340(8810):17-8.
37 M.R. DeBaun and others, Association of In Vitro Fertilization with Beckwith-Wiedemann Syndrome and Epigenetic Alterations of LIT1 H19. *Am J Hum Genet*, 2003;72:156-160.
38 J. Farhi and B. Fisch, Risk of Major Congenital Malformations Associated with Infertility and its Treatment by Extent of Iatrogenic Intervention. *Pediatric Endocrinology Reviews*, 2007;4: 352-357.
39 Canada: The Long Road to Regulation, Jean Haase in Third-Party Assisted Conception across Cultures: Social, Legal and Ethical Perspectives. Eric Blyth and Ruth Landau eds., Jessica Kingsley Publishers, Philadelphia 2003.
40 Millán, L Federal government overstepped its authority, says Quebec Court of Appeal. Law in Quebec, 17/03/2009, http://lawinquebec.wordpress.com/2009/03/17/federal-government-overstepped-its-authority-says-quebec-court-of-appeal/. Accessed 17 November, 2010.
41 J. De Mouzon and others, World Collaborative Report on Assisted Reproductive Technology, 2002. *Human Reproduction* 2009, May 27, doi,10.1093/humrep/dep098.
42 M. Johnson, Reproduction in the Noughties: will the scientists have all the fun? *J Anat*, 2001; 198: 385-398.
43 A. Janvier, Jumping to premature conclusions. Virtual Mentor. *American Medical Association Journal of Ethics*, 2008; 10: 659-664.
44 S.C. Tough and others, Effects of in vitro fertilization on low birth weight, preterm delivery, and multiple births. *Journal of Pediatrics*, 2000; 136: 618-622.
45 R. Jackson and others, Perinatal outcomes in Singletons Following In Vitro Fertilization: A Meta-Analysis. Obstetrics and Gynecology, 2004;103:551-563.
46 A. Delpisheh and others, Pregnancy Late in Life: A Hospital-Based Study of Birth Outcomes. *Journal of Women's Health*, 2008; 17:1-6.
47 Farhi and Fisch, *Pediatric Endocrinology Reviews*, 2007).
48 S. Tough and other factors influencing childbearing decisions and knowledge of Perinatal Risk away. *Canadian men and women, Montreal* and *Build Health Journal, 2003; 11:189-198.*
49 M. Johnson, Reproduction in the Noughties 2001.
50 First ever class action lawsuit filed by sperm donor offspring in Canada http://www.arvayfinlay.com/news/news-oct28-2008.html.

Chapter Nine
Canadian Medical Codes of Ethics and the Issue of Gamete Provider Anonymity

Ian Mitchell and Juliet Guichon

1. Introduction

Do the oversight bodies that govern Canadian physicians regulate third party gamete use through their ethics codes of practice? Ought they to do so?

Medical ethics codes of practice in Canada are developed by organizations that represent physicians. In Canada, the Canadian Medical Association (CMA), is a national organization that is ultimately responsible to its physician members. Ethics codes are also promulgated by the Colleges of Physicians and Surgeons in each province which ultimately report not to physicians but to the public even though they have many physician members.

This chapter reviews these Canadian medical ethics codes. It argues that, even though the ethics codes do not require Canadian physicians to enable donor-conceived persons to know the identity of their progenitors, they should. Canadian medical ethics codes should be revised to require physicians to enable the donor-conceived to know the identity of their progenitors (prospectively) to be consistent with both CMA recommendations[1] and the important values on which the codes are based.

2. Ethical Regulation of Canadian Physicians

2.1 Bodies Governing Physicians in Canadian Provinces

Colleges of Physicians and Surgeons exist in every Canadian province to licence physicians and to govern their activities. (The Canadian Territories have other regulatory arrangements.[2]) Each College has the legislated responsibility to regulate the medical profession in its province. For example, in Alberta, the provincial government has given the College of Physicians and Surgeons of Alberta a broad and important mandate; the CPSA must *inter alia*: "provide direction to and regulate the practice of the regulated profession by its regulated members, and establish, maintain and enforce a code of ethics [...]."[3]

To fulfill this delegated authority and statutory duty, these provincial bodies issue policy statements regarding certain practical matters (such as, for example, transferring ownership of a medical practice and managing conflicts of interest). They also give advice about matters more directly related to the provision of medical care such as, for example, assessing and reporting unfit drivers.

To guide and direct physicians in matters involving ethics, the Colleges have either adopted a uniform code created by the Canadian Medical Association or created their own ethics code.

2.2 Ethics Codes Governing Physicians in Canadian Provinces

The purposes of such physician codes of ethics are many: to inspire members of the medical profession to achieve high levels of integrity; to provide the grounds upon which physicians are called to account if they fail to maintain such levels; to tell physicians about changes in expectations of them; to educate medical students about the values of their future profession; to inform members of the public about what ethical standards they can expect of physicians; and to justify, and to be the basis of, self-regulation of the profession. If a physician refuses to abide by the applicable code of ethics, he or she may face disciplinary proceedings before the relevant college of physicians and surgeons that has the power to remove a physician's license to practice medicine.[4]

Provincial colleges of physicians and surgeons have either adopted the Canadian Medical Association's *Code of Ethics*[5] in whole or with minor amendments, or have their own comprehensive ethics codes.

These codes all tend to set a high moral tone at the very outset. For example, the *Code of Ethics* of the CMA and the Manitoba Code begin by instructing physicians to "consider first the well-being of the patient."

These codes of ethics are living documents because they undergo frequent revision. Whereas they once addressed the immediate relationship between patient and physician, now they have adopted a broader scope and offer advice and direction about physicians' relationship to the public generally. For example, the CMA code contains an entire section entitled, "Responsibilities to Society" in which physicians are instructed, among other things, to[6] recognize the profession's responsibility to society in matters relating to public health, health education, environmental protection, legislation affecting the health or well-being of the community and the need for testimony at judicial proceedings.

2.3 How Canadian Ethics Codes Regulate Physician Conduct in Third Party Gamete Use

Despite the broad mandate of the Colleges of Physicians and Surgeons and the wide range of issues that their codes of ethics address, these codes do not specifically regulate physician conduct in third party gamete donation. They do not appear to contemplate the practice or to consider the interests of the resulting offspring.

To be sure, the ethics codes address some issues that are relevant in the context of third party gamete use. For example, the codes require that patient records be maintained, and that they be accurate and confidential.[7] Further, the codes reiterate the essential elements of consent. There are 10 paragraphs in the CMA code on "Communication, Decision-Making and Consent" including the initial statement that requires physicians to "provide your patients with the information they need to make informed decisions about their medical care, and answer their questions to the best of your ability."[8] That provision might be interpreted as requiring physicians to advise infertility patients that any children resulting from donor conception could express a strong desire to have full information about the gamete donor.

Nevertheless, it appears that the codes do not contemplate or regard the human being to be created by assisted human reproduction as a "patient" (or indeed a human) for the purposes of governing the physician's activities. The result is that if the "patient" in the medical practice of assisted reproduction is construed to mean only the adults involved (the woman who wishes to conceive, her partner and possibly also the gamete provider), then a physician is (generally speaking[9]) enjoined from disclosing the medical record without their consent. For example, the CMA Code specifically states, "Protect the personal health information of your patients"[10] and "Disclose your patients' personal health information to third parties only with their consent."[11] Indeed, the Ontario code seems specifically to exclude consideration of the donor-conceived in its statement that "Physicians should never forget that their primary responsibility is to the patient standing before them, either individually or collectively."[12] Leaving aside the confusing use of the word "collectively", it is clear that at the time they are being conceived, the donor-conceived are obviously not standing before the physician.

Yet the current Code of Ethics refers to "Physician's Responsibility to Society". This seems to lead to an implicit tension between the physician's responsibility to an individual patient and the physician's responsibility to the wider community. One interpretation of this ethical requirement, in the context of reproductive technology, is that a physician providing assisted reproductive technology can be expected to have some level of responsibility not just to the woman paying for gamete or embryo donation but also to egg and sperm providers and, most particularly, to the resulting offspring. While those who developed the current CMA Code of Ethics may not have had this specific situation in mind, a code of ethics should be capable of reinterpretation in the context of new facts.

Regarding the children of assisted human reproduction, there is a great deal of new information about their needs and desires to understand their genetic origins.

3. Should Canadian Medical Colleges have Medical Ethics Codes that Govern Third Party Gamete Use?

Even though Canadian medical codes of ethics governing physicians do not currently require physicians to contemplate the interests of the offspring, we contend that these codes ought to do so for four reasons: 1. The Canadian Medical Association has recommended that accurate records of gamete donation be created and retained, and that the interests of the donor-conceived in viewing these records be considered; 2. Medical ethics codes are revised according to changing understandings of moral obligation and such changes justify revision now; 3. The principles of bioethics require consideration of the interests of the donor-conceived; and 4. The fundamental values upon which such medical ethics codes are based support changes to the codes to require that physicians' actions be directed to ensuring the best interests of the children whom they help to create.

3.1 The Canadian Medical Association Has Itself Recommended that the Donor-Conceived be Given Access to their Records

The fact that the Canadian Medical codes do not specifically address the interests of those whom physicians aim to conceive with donor gametes, is curious in light of the detailed CMA report entitled, "New Human Reproductive Technologies". The CMA created the 298-page document in response to the Government of Canada appointment of a commission of inquiry to study and make recommendations regarding the regulation of new reproductive technologies.[13] This document therefore represents the CMA's official position on new reproductive technologies at that time.

The CMA Report commences by stating that assisted human reproduction can be discussed variously: from the perspectives of the woman, the child, the man, and society. With respect to the child, the CMA Report states:[14]

> It should never be forgotten that the primary reason for fertility associated efforts and for the development of techniques of reproductive technology is the birth of a child. The Association also wishes to reiterate that a child is a person. The Association believes that a child is entitled to the same respect and to the same treatment as all other people. It, therefore, wishes to go on record

as maintaining that if developments in the domain of reproductive technology cannot sustain such a perspective, if these developments reduce the child to the status of an object, or if they require that those who are involved adopt an instrumentalistic outlook toward children, the Association opposes such developments fundamentally and unalterably.

As a consequence of these strong words regarding the interests of the child, the CMA Report continues: [15]

> These considerations prompt the Association to suggest that this Commission pay particular regard in its deliberations to such matters as: ... record keeping to allow appropriate tracing of children and their genetic parents[.]

The CMA Report acknowledged that records have a special place in assisted human reproduction and stated that there is a need for "registries for gamete donors and for the children that are born as a result of the various techniques – especially techniques involving gamete donation." The CMA Report stated also that records were necessary to permit epidemiological studies and to enable psycho-social effects to be identified and traced and monitored. The Report further recommended that records should be held in a manner consistent with the need for confidentiality and informed consent and stipulations should be made regarding record quality, retention and access.[16]

The CMA Report also engaged in a lengthy analysis of whether CMA members who participate in reproductive technology might be at risk of legal action for failure to disclose a complete and accurate medical record of the donor and the donation to the person conceived thereby. The CMA Report expressed doubt that the interests of the child to be conceived in having access to the prenatal record of gamete donation could legally be ignored by infertility physicians.[17] If the court were to hold that the physician owes the donor-conceived person a duty to create and disclose a record of that person's progenitor, then failure to do so would be a breach of the duty. The donor-conceived person would then need to establish that the breach of the duty created harm which the donor-conceived person suffered. The CMA Report describes the possible extent of such harm.[18]

> In the case of the inability to ascertain genetic heritage resulting in potential harm, such harm might be a lack of inheritance rights, an imperfect status, insecurity with respect to prospective marriage due to inability to ascertain prohibited degrees of consanguinity, inability to give accurate medical history, and loss of a pool of potentially compatible donors.

The Canadian Medical Association has, therefore, clearly stated that the interests of the person to be conceived by donor-conception are of high importance and that physician members of the CMA ought to contemplate those interests. Given these CMA recommendations which require physicians to consider seriously the interest of the donor-conceived, it is important that the CMA Code of Ethics be revised to reflect what the CMA itself recommends.

3.2 Shift in Values Suggests that CMA Code Revisions are in Order

Since 1868, when the CMA first approved a Code of Ethics, the locus of decision-making in medicine has shifted from the physician to the patient. The current CMA Code of Ethics should reflect this change both by amending the Code to address the interests of those affected by the actions of physicians and by including them in the process of revising the Code. Thus we believe that the Code of Ethics should address the interests of those people whom physicians aim to create. We do not believe that this recommendation will make the application of the Code of Ethics unworkably broad. Indeed the recommendation is in keeping with the detailed submission of the CMA itself on the topic of reproductive technology.[2]

When the first CMA Code of Ethics was drafted in 1868, it demonstrated continuity with ancient times by referring to the Oath of Hippocrates; it articulated the then prevailing view that physicians were more knowledgeable than their patients who, therefore, should obey their doctors.

In an overview of the CMA Codes of Ethics from 1868 to 1996,[19] Brownell and Brownell state that the 1868 Code had three topics: (1) "The duties of physician to the patients and the obligation of patients to their physicians"; (2) "The duties of physicians to each other and to the profession"; (3) "The duties of the profession to the public, and the obligation to the public to the profession." The 1868 Code had some features that would surprise physicians of today, such as the duty to avoid "overly gloomy prognostications concerning the outcome of illnesses." The requirement to continue "to provide care even when the patient was incurable" suggests that physicians of the time were not always responsible or diligent in caring for patients. Yet the patients had a duty of obedience: the 1868 code stated that patients "need to follow physicians' prescriptions promptly and implicitly."

But the CMA Code of Ethics was not fixed in stone. By 1922, the section detailing patients' obligations to their physicians was eliminated. Over the next nearly 50 years there were a number of revisions to the Code of Ethics. The 1970 version established a new era by recognizing the patient's right to reject any recommended medical care. The 1986 and 1990 versions made it clear that physicians were expected to provide information to patients "to enable them to decide whether to accept physicians' recommendations." The 1996 Code continued the trend supporting patient's authority over prescribed treatment, and added recommendations to improve communication between physicians and patients and to ensure that physicians ascertained their patient's wishes about the initiation, continuation, or cessation of life-sustaining treatment.

In other words, the changes over time in the CMA Code of Ethics have reflected a fundamental shift in its philosophical underpinnings from the paternalistic "doctor knows best" to the position articulated by the Supreme Court of Canada in 1993 that people have "the right to decide what is to be done to one's own body."[20]

It seems surprising, therefore, that Canadian medical codes of ethics are still being developed by the medical profession itself without recourse to public opinion regarding how people would like physicians to treat them. The CMA Code of Ethics is drafted by the CMA Committee of Ethics. This committee reports to the General Council of the Canadian Medical Association, which has final authority regarding the document. Based on descriptions of the CMA Code predating the 1996 and 2004 revisions,[21] it seems unlikely that there was meaningful public participation.[22] John R. Williams, former Director, Department of Ethics and Legal Affairs of the CMA, stated that the process of creating the 1996 Code of Ethics included the following steps:[23]

> Review of other medical codes of ethics and related literature; determination of the type of code most appropriate for Canadian physicians in the late 20th Century; identification of the weaknesses of the then current version of the Code; preparation of a draft revised code.

Williams states that there was "extensive consultation" but does not specifically mention whether there was *public* consultation, suggesting that the general public is not involved in the process of creating a CMA Code of Ethics. Williams writes that the 1996 version was circulated in draft form to "Board of directors and to CMA councils, committees, provincial and territorial divisions and affiliated societies as well as the numerous other individuals and groups."[24] Again, public consultation is most noted by its absence. Although the physicians who develop codes of ethics are well aware of current trends of ethics and take them into account, the CMA Code of Ethics appears to have been developed by medical professionals and their staff alone.

If the CMA Code of Ethics is to be revised to address the interests of the people whom physicians deliberately participate in creating, then the public, including the donor-conceived, must be allowed to contribute to the development of the new CMA Code of Ethics.

3.3 The Canadian Medical Ethics Code's Implicit and Explicit Values Support Colleges in Requiring Physicians to Consider and Act upon Others' Interests

The fundamental values upon which medical ethics codes are based would support amendments to require that physicians consider and act upon the best interests of the children whom they help to create.

The values implicitly underpinning the CMA, Manitoba and Quebec codes are made explicit in the Ontario code, which articulates these: compassion, service, altruism and trustworthiness. The Ontario code explains that physicians as a group have entered into a social contract with the public whereby physicians are permitted to regulate themselves provided that they maintain their commitment to competence, integrity, altruism and the promotion of the public good within their domain.

Such high values arguably support a college's decision to direct physicians involved in third party reproduction to look beyond the patient before them to the person to be created. Four such values appear particularly important in guiding physician conduct regarding the interests of offspring. These are the values of compassion, trustworthiness, integrity and the promotion of the public good.

3.3.1 Compassion

Canadian ethics codes require physicians to respond with compassion to patients. This response is particularly appropriate with respect to infertility patients who are vulnerable. The pain of childlessness and the longing to overcome it are well-documented to be immense.[25] Given that the services of a Canadian physician providing *in vitro* fertilization tend to be paid out of pocket by the patient,[26] the patient might be regarded in some sense as a consumer or client and, therefore, neither vulnerable nor entitled to compassion. Yet while such patients might give "instructions" on how many cycles of treatment they would like to undergo, they are very dependent on their relationship with the reproductive physician who is in a position of knowledge and who must exercise that knowledge in a manner that minimizes harm. Infertility patients are often fragile and have an asymmetric relationship with the physician in terms of power. They are not customers to be negotiated with but patients to be helped. Like other patients, infertility patients are entitled to expect compassionate care from reproductive physicians.

Yet such compassion ought to extend also to the gamete provider and to the child to be created. Even if initially reluctant to be known, some gamete providers alter their views and do wish to know the outcome of their gamete sales or donations.[27] One author stated,[28]

> The rights of the donor is often overlooked and is something that I am also concerned about being a father myself. People's attitudes may change with time and they may no longer wish to remain anonymous. They may be open to disclosure of more information or even contact but the current system does not facilitate this. The donor should be able to know that the child is healthy and well cared for.

And even the American Society for Reproductive Medicine has acknowledged that gamete providers, "may also have an interest in having or not having contact with offspring."[29] Some gamete providers would like to meet the person whom their gametes helped create.[30]

Similarly, and as has been evident throughout this work, among the donor-conceived are those who strongly wish to know the identity of their progenitors. As with donors, those offspring who initially express no interest in knowing the identity of their progenitors can change their minds. According to one author:[31]

> I personally know a 30-year-old donor-conceived man who has known his status since early childhood. Initially he accepted it, until the birth of his own child when suddenly, as a father, he realized the importance of the biological link, and what the loss of his paternal kin had meant for him (and his daughter).

The value of compassion would support physicians taking steps to create systems to permit them to honour the wishes of the donor-conceived to learn the identity of their progenitors. The ethical duty for physicians to demonstrate compassion requires physicians to consider the interests of the donor-conceived even before they are conceived because that person will be affected by the physician's actions to the greatest extent and for the longest time. In other words, physicians should not use sperm contributed anonymously or by a provider who does not wish to be identified to his or her genetic children.

3.3.2 Trustworthiness

This value initially appears to put the physician in a difficult position. Physicians have claimed that donors should not be forced to release their identity[32] and that they are ethically bound to protect the anonymity of providers who were promised that their identities would never be disclosed.[33]

But even if the argument from promise keeping has some purchase with respect to the past, it cannot justify promising anonymity in the future given that some offspring are cogently criticizing anonymity on the basis that it does them serious harm.[34] Some physicians have responded that they must be free to promise anonymity in the future because they cannot otherwise obtain gametes for future adult patients. As Dr. Joseph Feldschuh of Idant Laboratories, New York City sperm bank, said "Most donors really don't want any kind of relationship with their offspring. Eliminate anonymity and you eliminate a great many donors."[35] This argument has been addressed in this volume by Eric Blyth and Lucy Frith who conclude that if supply initially declines because anonymity is banned, then there are ways to increase supply that are consistent with a ban on anonymity.

Even if we were to concede the accuracy of some physicians' concerns about supply, lack of supply is not, in itself, justification for what many offspring say is a harmful practice. In other words, it is appropriate to ask, "Is promising anonymity to gamete providers a good way to bring children into the world?" and then to conclude that it is not. Given what many offspring say about the harm anonymity causes them and that physicians are required by their governing colleges to be trustworthy, physicians must have an answer for the offspring when they ask the physician why they cannot see the medical record. It is not enough for a physician to respond, "I'm contractually bound not to show it to you." Offspring might retort, "If you are trustworthy, then why did you sign such an unethical undertaking?"

In other contexts, medical ethics codes do not permit physicians to bind themselves contractually to act unethically.[36] Specifically when involved in clinical research, physicians are exhorted by the CMA to avoid 'gag clauses' in contracts with pharmaceutical companies that sponsor the research.[37] These are clauses that would, for example, prevent researchers from disclosing matters that might adversely affect the marketability of the study drug without approval of the pharmaceutical sponsor. The body that oversees the three Canadian funding agencies (Social Sciences and Humanities Research Council, National Science and Engineering Research Council and the Canadian Institutes of Health Research) also recommends in its 2010 draft Tri-Council Policy Statement that physicians and other researchers avoid committing themselves to silence when to do so would harm others.[38]

3.3.3. Competence

The value of competence has been addressed, in part, in the discussion above of the value of compassion. Even when patients are paying physicians for service, the physician must act competently and professionally in the interests of the patient and of those whom his or her actions will affect. Just as they should refrain from impairing the outcome of the pregnancy and risking the pregnant woman's life and health by implanting too many blastocysts, so, too, should physicians refuse to create a situation in which the fetus's full health record cannot be obtained by a paediatrician or geneticist. Physicians must make accurate records of the circumstances and parties involved in conception and should retain those records in perpetuity.

3.3.4 Integrity

The value of integrity requires physicians to come to terms with what many offspring are telling them about the effects of anonymity on their lives, and to change their practices.

Such concerns are relevant to whether physicians ought to keep accurate records of the donation and to disclose those records to the donor-conceived. The wishes of a particular donor-conceived person obviously cannot be ascertained at the time that person is being conceived. But once the person has come into being and can maturely express his or her desire for information about the donor, then that person's wishes should be respected.

3.3.5 The Promotion of the Public Good Within Their Domains

This value of promoting the public good creates two important obligations for physicians in the field of reproductive technology. The first is to refrain from creating a situation in which people do not know those to whom they are genetically related. Colleges of physicians and surgeons might argue that, at the time of the attempted conception, there is no other person. But such a response appears to be an evasion of responsibility. The very point of using techniques of assisted human reproduction is intentionally to bring a child to life. Given that the reproductive physician's goal is to create a healthy child, it is odd deliberately to prevent the child from knowing one-half of its genetic heritage. (In the case of embryo donation, a person might know none of his or her genetic heritage.)

The harm that may result from this deliberately created situation has been articulated in the Statement of Claim[39] submitted to the British Columbia Supreme Court on behalf of Olivia Pratten:

1. The gamete donor suffers a genetically transmitted condition which, if communicated to his or her genetic offspring might permit them to take preventative steps to avoid suffering from the condition themselves. One such example is colon cancer, which with early screening can be prevented.

2. The genetic disorder suffered by a donor-conceived person cannot be traced back to the donor so that that person can receive diagnosis and treatment if required, and/or to prevent the further distribution and use of unhealthy gametes
3. A donor-conceived person might be genetically related to a sexual partner or proposed sexual partner without knowing, such that the health and dignity of their families and children could be at risk
4. A donor-conceived person may suffer from psychological distress and hardship from being irreparably cut off from crucial components of their identity, including the social, racial, cultural, religious, and/or linguistic history of their biological parents.

The value requiring physicians to promote the public good within their domain, also requires medical codes to stipulate that physicians engaged in reproductive technology must conduct research on the outcomes of what is, in essence, a social experiment. Generally speaking, the current Canadian medical ethics codes are deficient in failing to consider the interests of parties to assisted reproduction other than the patient herself. Assisted human reproduction focuses on immediate outcomes. But the revolution in human reproduction has not been accompanied by changes in medical ethics codes to require those engaged in innovative practice to develop data to validate their practice. There is no specified ethical duty to engage in research on these novel techniques to assess the outcomes especially for female gamete providers, for male gamete providers and for the children thereby created. The outcomes researched should include psychosocial effects of gamete use on the donor-conceived, the gamete providers, and the gamete providers' parents.

4. Recommendations

The Canadian codes of medical ethics have undergone many revisions since they were first published in 1868. It is time for such codes to undergo revision again for four important reasons: (1) The Canadian Medical Association has recommended that accurate records of gamete donation be maintained and that the interests of the donor-conceived in viewing them be considered; (2) The shift in values from physician paternalism requires that the interests of non-patients be considered and that their views be represented in the development of ethics codes; and (3) The fundamental values upon which Canadian medical ethics codes are based support changes to the codes to require that physicians' actions be directed to ensuring the best interests of the children whom they help to create.

Consequently, Canadian medical ethics codes should state that physicians have extensive duties to all who participate in assisted human reproduction that is, to the woman in whose uterus the conceptus will develop, her partner, to any donors who have provided sperm or eggs or fertilized embryos, and to their parents who can regard the donor-conceived as their grandchildren. In particular, physicians engaged in reproductive medicine have a strong duty to the children whom they aim to create. Such revisions to medical ethics codes will require physicians to engage in a different approach at all stages in the process, to maintain detailed records, and to make them available to the donor-conceived when they reach the age of majority.

In addition, the Canadian codes of medical ethics should contain sections on the positive duties of physicians to carry out research particularly when they are engaged in a novel practice. If Canadian physicians had been under such an ethical obligation, then we would now have much more useful information for the donor-conceived than what presently exists.

Such amendments to Canadian codes of medical ethics would likely best be accompanied by amendments to provincial and territorial legislation to make donors identifiable and to state that gamete donors are not financially responsible for the rearing of the donor-conceived.

Bibliography

Beauchamp and Childress. *Principles of Biomedical Ethics.* Sixth Edition, Oxford: Oxford University Press, 2009.

http://www.arvayfinlay.com/news/Writ of Summons and Statement of Claim.pdf

Canadian Medical Association. *New Human Reproductive Technologies: Perspective of the Canadian Medical Association.* Ottawa: Canadian Medical Association, 1991; 146.

Collier, Roger. "Disclosing the identity of sperm donors." *Canadian Medical Association Journal,* 2010; 182 (3): 232.

Ethics Committee of the American Society for Reproductive Medicine, "Interests, obligations and rights of the donor in gamete donation." *Fertility and Sterility,* 2009; 91(1): 22.

Hebert, Philip C. *Doing Right: A Practical Guide to Ethics for Medical Trainees and Physicians.* Don Mills, Ontario: Oxford University Press, 2009.

Lasker, Judith N. and Susan Borg. *In Search of Parenthood: Coping with Infertility and Hi Tech Conception.* Boston: Beacon Press, 1987.

Lorbach, Caroline. *Experiences of Donor Conception: Parents, Offspring and Donors throughout the years.* London: Jessica Kinsley Publishers, 2003.

Office of Ethics, Professionalism and International Affairs, Canadian Medical Association, *Research Guidelines*, http://www.cma.ca/multimedia/CMA/Content_Images/Inside_cma/Ethics/Final_Toolkit_Research.pdf, 32.

Robertson, John A. *Children by Choice: Freedom and the New Reproductive Technology.* Princeton, New Jersey, 1994.

Schmidt, L. "Social and psychological consequences of infertility and assisted reproduction – what are research priorities?" *Human Fertility*, 2009; 12 (1): 14-20.

Solberg, B. "Getting beyond the welfare of the child in assisted reproduction." *Journal of Medical Ethics*, 2009; 35.

Notes

1. Canadian Medical Association, *New Human Reproductive Technologies: A Preliminary Perspective of the Canadian Medical Association* (Ottawa: Canadian Medical Association, 1991), 146.
2. Yukon Territory physicians are governed by the Yukon Medical Council (Medical Profession Act, R.S.Y. 2002, c. 149 ss. 8-30), which has adopted the CMA Code of Ethics. Northwest Territories physicians are registered and disciplined under the Medical Profession Act, R.S.N.W.T. 1988, c. M-9 which creates a Medical Registration Committee (s. 5) and subjects physicians to the disciplinary authority of a Board of Inquiry established under s. 21 of the same statute. In Nunavut, physicians are registered as such under the Medical Profession Act, R.S.N.W.T. (Nu.) 1988, c. M-9 s 8 which effectively establishes a Medical Registration Committee of the Department of Health and Social Services.
3. Health Professions Act, R.S.A. 2000, c. H-7, s 3(1). Current version in force since Dec 17, 2008.
4. See, for example, Ontario College of Physicians and Surgeons description of its duties: http://www.cpso.on.ca/aboutus.
5. Canadian Medical Association, Code of Ethics 2004, http://policybase.cma.ca/PolicyPDF/PD04-06.pdf.
6. CMA Code, section 42 (supra, note 6).
7. CMA Code, ss. 31, 35; Manitoba Code, ss. 24, 26; Ontario Code section entitled "Maintaining Confidentiality", Quebec Code, ss. 20-21.
8. *Ibid.*, ss. 21-30.
9. There are exceptions when disclosure is required by law or there is a threat of substantial harm to a third party. See discussion below.
10. CMA Code, s 31.
11. *Ibid.*, s 35.
12. Ontario Code in section entitled, "Principles of Practice".
13. Williams, "Canadian Medical Association's Ethics Activities", 141.
14. *Ibid.*
15. *Ibid.*
16. *Ibid.*
17. *Ibid.*, 194-201.
18. *Ibid.*, 198.
19. Brownell and Brownell. "The Canadian Medical Association Code of Ethics 1868 to 1996", 240-243.
20. Ciarlariello v. Schacter, [1993] 2 S.C.R. 119.
21. Sawyer and Williams. "After 4 years work, revised code of ethics goes to General Council for decision", 314-315.
22. Williams, "Canadian Medical Association's Ethics Activities", 138-151.
23. *Ibid.*, 139.

24 Sawyer and Williams. "After 4 years work, revised code of ethics goes to General Council for decision", 314-315.
25 Lasker and Borg, *In Search of Parenthood*. Schmidt, "Social and psychological consequences of infertility and assisted reproduction", 14-20.
26 Diane Allen, "Insurance/IVF funding, Updated March 27, 2010," Infertility Network Website, http://www.infertilitynetwork.org/insurance. But see, Lia Lévesque The Canadian Press, Quebec women to get free fertility treatments, Canadian Press, July 13, 2010.
27 Laura Witjens, "Egg Donation: Why I Gave Up My Right to Remain Anonymous", *BioNews*, June 8, 2009, http://www.bionews.org.uk/page_45436.asp.
28 Damian H. Adams, "My Very Brief Story", Donated Generation, http://donatedgeneration.blogspot.com/2006/07/my-very-brief-story.html.
29 Ethics Committee of the American Society for Reproductive Medicine, "Interests, obligations and rights of the donor in gamete donation", 22.
30 Caroline Lorbach, *Experiences of Donor Conception*, 77-78.
31 Lauren Burns 'donor'-conceived perspective, Donor-Conceived Perspectives: Voices from the Offspring http://donorconceived.blogspot.com.
32 Roger Collier, "Disclosing the identity of sperm donors".
33 Kelly McParland, "The ethics of sperm donation", editorial, *National Post*, November 03, 2008, http://network.nationalpost.com/np/blogs/fullcomment/archive/2008/11/03/national-post-editorial-board-the-ethics-of-sperm-donation.aspx#ixzz0jJjt0TJR.
34 Joanna Rose, "From a bundle of joy to a person of sorrow, Disenfranchised grief for the donor-conceived adult," http://eprints.qut.edu.au/737/1/rose_fromabundle.PDF.
35 Judith Graham, "Sperm donor offspring reach out into past", *Chicago Tribune*, June 19, 2005, www.donorsiblingregistry.com/ChicagoTribune.pdf.
36 Lewis et al, "Dancing with the porcupine".
37 Office of Ethics, Professionalism and International Affairs, Canadian Medical Association, Research Guidelines: A web-based decision-guide for physicians, 2008 http://www.cma.ca/multimedia/CMA/Content_Images/Inside_cma/Ethics/Final_Toolkit_Research.pdf.
38 Interagency Advisory Panel on Research Ethics, Tri-Council of Canada, Revised Draft 2nd Edition of the TCPS (December 2009), Chapter 7, http://www.pre.ethics.gc.ca/eng/policy-politique/initiatives/revised-revisee/chapter7-chapitre7/#toc07-1c.
39 Writ and Statement of Claim, Pratten v. A.G. British Columbia and College of Physicians and Surgeons of British Columbia, Filed in the B.C. Supreme Court, October 24, 2009, Court File 087449, http://www.arvayfinlay.com/news/Writ%20of%20Summons%20and%20Statement%20of%20Claim.pdf.

Chapter Ten

Identity Harm: Lessons from Adoption for Donor Conception

Joanna Rose

1. Introduction

There is a history in the development of adoption practice that is pertinent to donor conception and therefore worthy of comparison and analysis. Many donor-conceived people and adoptees suffer from harms created by the disruption of biological relatedness. Both social practices engage in denial and disregard of relational loss. The common experience of those who are raised by one or more genetically unrelated persons is informative, and provides a starting point for making comparisons. This chapter examines the consequent issues of openness, denial, loss, and personal and social integration in relation to family systems and therapeutic support networks. It aims to highlight the complexity and ethical issues created by donor conception practices.

2. Competing Understandings of Openness

One of the most commonly discussed harms to the offspring of reproductive technology is dishonesty regarding the nature of their conception. This issue is often raised in the context of a call for greater openness, which is a growing trend in the practice. Openness is encouraged by many professionals, and major donor conception support groups. The current practice of not recording the nature of conception on birth certificates has led to suggestions that there should be a statutory requirement to support openness though governments have not gone so far as to advocate that the donor's identity be recorded on the birth certificate.[1] Even though openness is welcome, telling the truth about donor conception and providing medical information about the donor, do not address other significant moral issues.

The adoption experience demonstrates that interpretations of 'openness' vary. Treseliotis, Feast and Kyle's[2] description of the historical and legislative developments of adoption in the UK, shows that openness has resulted in a variety of practical and legislative outcomes. For example, during the late 1970's, governments made claims in support of openness, and at the same time decided that adopted children with special needs would benefit from a 'clean break' policy of total severance between the child and their birth family. This chapter provides other examples of how adults advance a policy of 'openness' regarding the fact of adoption but without exploring its meaning for the child.

Research into donor-conceived families reveals similar ambiguity in the application of openness towards donor offspring. In a UK-based study, the majority of parents were disinclined to tell the children about their donor conceptions. Researchers studying a sample of 46 donor insemination ("DI") families, with children between 4 and 8 years of age, reported that[3]

> 39% [of families] were inclined to openness and 61% were not. Thirteen per cent had already told their child, 26% intended to in the future, 43% had decided against telling their child and 17% were still uncertain.

While openness in donor conception is the current and popular theory, it is possible that many parents fear that the child's genetic connection (usually with strangers) might represent more significance for the child than the DI parents are comfortable with. Nearly 30% of parents reported also a concern that openness might affect the relationship between the social father and child. Some feared the child might reject the social father in favour of the biological father.[4]

Consequently, the definition of 'openness' can be adult-centric and interpreted to mean being open about the method of conception, but not about the kinship meaning and connection this might hold for the offspring. Even if the practice of donor conception embraces openness, as happened in adoption, adults can find it more comfortable to stick to adult-centric openness. Such popular concepts of parental 'openness' do not address the complexity and loss created for children and adults by adoption and donor conception.

3. Adoption and donor conception: "Denial? It's not a problem"

The social history of adoption practice has been influenced by commercial, sentimental and professional control; these influences have varied among countries and states, and led to "chronic uncertainty about what appropriate adoption standards should be."[5] There is evidence within the history of the management and mismanagement of adoption of both abuse and denial; there is particular emphasis on the denial of the loss and resulting complexity often experienced by adoptees, which is more commonly recognized now as inherent to adoption. Current adoption policies and protocols have developed in response to past practices, which have included baby farms and the use of adoption to supplement household labour, even after the abolishment of slavery.[6] While adoption practice and experience will continue to evolve, this history and the standards that have been achieved so far should be used to shed light on donor conception practices.

Denial and simplistic viewing in adoption has resulted from early protocols that focused on and prioritised the desires and interests of those adopting.[7] Such prioritization is now less common and has been replaced by an understanding of the lifelong impacts of kinship, identity loss and complexity for all the members affected. This recognition for adoptees has been supported by studies. A United Kingdom study summarized the issue by stating "the experience of loss is endemic to being adopted."[8]

Yet in donor conception, there are numerous examples of parents making the mistake that adoption has already overcome. Many DI parents disregard the kinship and identity loss for the offspring. Low presents a DI father who acknowledges that a child who is donor-conceived may well feel different, "but whether they consider such difference as being acceptable, technologically and socially, will depend on how well adjusted the child is.[9] Likewise, a single mother by choice evaded the existence and absence of her child's genetic father by asserting to the child that his family was comprised of his mother, himself and their dog.[10] The mother's response thus refuses to recognise the pain and relational absence expressed by the child. Dunne describes the process that occurs from such domination over children as their grief becomes "not just expressible and hence comprehensible unhappiness, but rather an inarticulate ache or a vague sense of missing or lost meaning."[11] This can result in obstacles and difficulties for Offspring in making sense of their lives: "for we make sense – or fail to make sense – of our lives by the kind of stories we can or cannot – tell about it."[12]

Researchers from adoption continue to remark on the incongruence that exists between adoption and donor conception:[13]

> Lessons learnt from the needs and experiences of adopted people appear to have had minimal influence on the attitudes and practices of donor assisted conceptions and the legislation that allows it.

4. Adoption and Donor Conception: The Significance of Intentional Loss

In order to understand or predict the impact of kinship loss, it is critical to look at the reason why it has occurred. Laing and Oderberg explain:[14]

> There is a fundamental distinction in both legal and moral theory between what one does and what happens to one; between creating a problem and a

> problem's happening.... it is one thing to allow adoption in order to minimize harm; it is another altogether to create an institution that traffics in human life (whether money is exchanged or not).

Thus there is an important distinction to be drawn between adoption, which happens as a matter of chance or misfortune, and donor conception which requires us to condone the intentional creation of loss for another, particularly when created as part of the bargaining for another's gain. In donor conception, the loss created for the child, caused by a pre-arranged and intentional separation from a genetic (donor) parent and extended family, suits the other (commissioning) parent's interest in experiencing parenthood, free from the other's legal and social encumbrances.

Research and experience in adoption have demonstrated that because of the absence of the family of origin, adoptees can experience a heightened propensity for feeling loss and rejection.[15] Research has demonstrated that to process this loss, adoptees need to establish the reasons why this loss has occurred. To learn "why", is a principle reason adoptees cite for making contact with their estranged kin.[16] It appears to be pivotal for adoptees to know that their relinquishment was a painfully arrived at decision – a last resort. Between one-half and two-thirds of the adoptees in the 2005 Triseliotis study stated that learning of the dire reasons behind their relinquishment lessened their feelings of rejection. Anger was found to be more likely when the adopted person found unsatisfactory the explanation as to why adoption had occurred.[17]

Yet this insight from the experience of adoption has not been applied to donor conception. Such anger and indignation as a result of the intentional creation of kinship loss for the donor offspring has been dismissed by some commentators as neither legitimate nor likely. For example, Montuschi asserts, "as far as blame is concerned ... it is highly unlikely that their method of conception will feature."[18]

Adoption is currently described as being child-focused: as "a way of providing a family for children who are not able to remain in their family of origin."[19] Best practice in adoption is no longer driven by the desire to provide children for people who cannot have a child between themselves. Yet in reproductive technology, Reitz and Watson have noted that there is a propensity for role reversal in terms of children meeting the adults' interests.[20] As such, "an adult's need to be a parent may jeopardize the long-range best interests of the child whose role it is to meet that need."[21] Whereas adoption is described as "a second choice for all the triad members",[22] gamete donation could hardly be described as a clinical 'need' or as a 'second choice' for the donor. It would be disingenuous for recipient parents to state that they regret that the child was not raised amongst their donated kin (unless the parents had re-evaluated their actions). Just like adoptees who are confronted by unsatisfactory explanations, some donor offspring do regard their situation as manufactured and profoundly unsatisfactory. These donor offspring have grounds to be indignant about the State's complicity in creating this loss.

5. The Consequences of the Immaturity of the Practice of Donor Conception

In 2006, concern quietly mounted that "insight into the consequences of reproductive technology is still in its infancy."[23] That year, Brodzinsky and Schechter explained that the search for birthparents in adoption can be best understood as occurring as a result of a deep need, driven by feelings of disconnectedness and disadvantage. They described this need as:[24]

> An attempt to repair aspects of the self that have to do with the sense of disconnectedness from the human race and with the sense of disadvantage vis-a-vis people who are born rather than adopted.

The exploration of kinship and identity loss appears to be motivated by more than just curiosity, at least for some. In adoption, its pursuit has been described as integral to the requirements of healthy psychological and social integration. For donor offspring, a similar type of drive for psychological repair and an attempt to come to terms with a disadvantage to their identity and kinship has received less recognition and support.

Reitz and Watson have applied their experience in adoption to appreciate the complexity of kinship loss and replacement for donor offspring and highlight the probability that this loss will affect family systems and life cycles.[25] They warn of "genetic confusion, difficulty in identity formation (especially, perhaps sexual identity formation), and poor self-esteem" as a potential consequence for donor offspring. It is possible that the lack of delineation between the recipient's interests in creating a family, and the child's consequent loss of contact with their donor family has resulted in a conceptual immaturity and arrested development in donor conception. The attainment of such maturity in this reproductive practice appears to be blocked, precisely because there is also no getting round the fact that to create a donor-conceived family, the donor family must be separated and dispersed and the donor offspring must also be displaced from their biological (donor) kin.

6. Personal and Social integration

It is common for adoptive parents to find it difficult to talk about adoption in their family.[26] Their failure or ability to attribute significance to the birth family has been found either to hinder or aid the integration of the social and genetic identity of the adoptee. This impediment in social and genetic integration appears to be common also for donor offspring because research is now showing that most parents have difficulty informing the child of their donor conception,[27] let alone embracing the offspring's continuity and kinship with the donors and their extended families. For heterosexual couples, this difficulty can be entangled with the concern that exposing the parents' infertility would compound social stigma and embarrassment for them.[28] The majority of such parents, therefore, seek to avoid this discomfort, to maintain an image of familial integrity, pretending that the donor offspring is genetically related to both social parents.[29] Thus the Offspring's need to integrate his or her social and genetic identities is placed in conflict with the parents' desire to maintain this family integrity. There are additional barriers and resistances to support for Offspring who seek to integrate both the biological and social aspects of their kinship and identity. This difficulty is further exacerbated by medical and government officials who are withholding records or recording birth certificates with misleading information. This situation bodes ill for Offspring and their families, because integration and acceptance is now recognised as critical for the well-being and outcomes of adoptive families.[30]

The process of achieving social and genetic integration in adoption can involve adoptees wondering what it would have been like to have been raised by their genetic parents, and mourning their absence.[31] Such processing is recognized as a normal human response in adoption, but for the donor offspring this response is not even acknowledged or understood by mental health professionals at large.[32] There is also recognition that there are some general issues that may affect an adoptee's passage into adulthood. The extra emotional burdens of adoption loss, dual heritage, and identity issues can cause adoptees to lag developmentally. Even when functioning well and on schedule in dealing with their adult role competence, adoptees may experience more anxiety than is typical.[33] But the donor-conceived are not generally regarded as needing recognition of social and genetic integration similar to adoptees. Therefore, the donor-conceived are not perceived to have extra emotional burdens that have the potential to cause developmental lags.

Indeed, physicians tend not to tell parents of the donor-conceived that they have special obligations of disclosure and of aiding complex identity integration for the Offspring. Rather, parents are told that if they are "good enough" parents, then their children's needs will be met. Attachment theory holds that if a baby's basic needs for food, comfort, warmth and security are met in a consistent way, then the baby and growing child will develop a sense of trust that his or her future needs can be met. On the basis of this theory, advocates of donor conception have asserted that:[34]

> Parents in families created through donor conception are much more likely to provide good or what is often referred to as 'good enough' parenting for their children. It is, therefore, much less likely that a [donor conception] young person, particularly one who has been brought up in an open household where qualities of trust and respect have been nurtured, would blame parents for their method of conception or bringing them into the world at all.

Yet important needs of Offspring can be overlooked. As adoption workers attest,[35]

> Our experience with adoption suggests that often the people who are most driven, and who have the resources to pursue their drive, [to obtain a child] are the most successful in achieving their ends; it also suggests that these people are not necessarily the ones who are best equipped to fill the unique parenting role that adoption requires.

The donor offspring are surrounded with this cognitive omission because:[36]

> Almost without exception, research [on donor conception] has failed to draw on appropriate psychological theory and has failed to predict not only the behaviour, but also the expectations and underlying cognitions of those involved.

The challenges to the donor offspring's integration tend to be disregarded, even by professionals in the field. Golombok, an 'expert' in DI families, advises DI parents that "difficulties would not necessarily be expected for the child."[37] In fact, the practice's total disregard of the donor offspring's genetic parents is supported by Golombok as one of the attractions of this means of conception. She appears to extol conception without the 'involvement' of the unwanted party by advancing qualities such as 'good enough parenting', and "a combination of warmth and control."[38] These are undisputedly important but nonetheless, such aspects of parenting should not be advanced without regard for the complexities of genetic kinship displacement. Personal and social integration is likely to be a continuing struggle for donor offspring.

7. The Limbo of Loss: Lack of Closure and Unacknowledged Grief

The loss of genetic continuity for those facing infertility and seeking treatment has been described by Becker as creating experiences of "chaos" and "limbo".[39] Becker's research acknowledged that those affected "felt unable to proceed to the next phase of life. Their culturally propelled sense of motion though time has stopped. They felt trapped in the present."[40] Such research makes evident that the limbo of loss in relation to genetic discontinuity is familiar to the infertile parents and those supporting and treating them. They define "the pursuit of fertility, itself [as] a symbol of continuity."[41] Russell explains that a limbo of loss is also created for adoptees who are thwarted in their search for their unknown kin, because there is[42]

> No death, no ending. In adoption, a state of limbo exists that is similar to the dynamics of mourning someone who is missing in action. Not knowing where the person is or if they are alive blocks the grieving process.

The limbo of loss has also been experienced by some birth parents who find similar trouble in achieving resolution to their situations.[43] Such a limbo, created from being unable to know of, contact or integrate, their absent genetic children can also be expected for some gamete donors, for whom this lack of resolution will be exacerbated, because donors often will not ever know the precise number of children that they have.

Interestingly, research into why most people changed their mind about donating spare embryos after they had achieved an IVF pregnancy, shows a tendency for such parents to develop an increased awareness and fear of such limbo or lack of closure from resultant pregnancies. Parents developed a fear that if others used their embryos "they would always be wondering where the child is."[44] Indeed there is a striking frame shift in the way such parents view the consequences of their reproductive actions, suddenly developing a concern about the risk of such limbo, which was not tangible to them until they had developed the maturity to foresee it.

Adoption experience has demonstrated that when adoptees seek resolution to lost relationships, and such contact or acknowledgement is hindered, the limbo can become chronic. When grief is arrested at one phase and denied, "that severe protracted grief has been consistently shown in research to be associated with major poor health outcomes."[45] The pain of relational blockage, especially when its significance is denied by others, can lead to depression. The severe effect of depression has been explained in this way: "the death rate among the depressed is of a similar order to that from heart disease."[46]

While Rickarby draws attention to such harm in relation to adoption, these insights are also applicable to donor conception for both donors and Offspring. Adding to this difficulty is the likelihood of very considerable numbers of relatives being displaced. A donor offspring notes that:[47]

> For those of us produced by DI or any other method of reproduction where we have been purposefully cut off from our biological roots, it means living with a wounded heart that will never heal.

Indeed, of the kin who can be found, some will have died, others will not acknowledge the seeker, and some will have language barriers. Additionally, there is a high potential for contact between donor and genetic relatives to place strain on the dynamics of the recipient family, which will be affected by searching.

In adoption, it is known that loss may well be exacerbated by significant events such as a birthday or Father or Mother's Day. Donor offspring are also likely to have times that represent their loss leading to inflamed feelings, accompanied by intense craving for resolution of this limbo. At such times, Offspring will also be predisposed to reflect on this burden, its lack of recognition, its international nature and the complicity of many actors in its creation, further intensifying this raw and painful experience.

There is no research to show the long-term effects on donor offspring who are unsupported in their loss and unable to contact missing relatives. Rickarby observed that, among adoptees who have unresolved grief, "there are more obvious links between irresolvable grief via the cigarettes, alcohol, benzodiazepines... Eating disorders and dietary problems are common" as are "risk taking behaviours" associated with unresolved grief.[48] The possibility of adoptees turning to self-destructive behaviour creates concern that donor offspring with irresolvable grief might similarly be at risk. Likewise, it is possible that adult Offsprings' grief may adversely affect their ability to form relationships in the future, because relating "in an intimate and trusting manner is difficult indeed when there is any element of grief overlaying personal development."[49] Even though such knowledge is available from adoption, it is still the case that this part of the social experiment on Offspring has not been monitored or properly studied. In fact, the general focus of research into the welfare of the donor-conceived is on their medical and psychological status.[50] At a deeper level concern has been expressed that there are "no mechanisms in place ensuring donor children's needs are met."[51]

8. Family Systems

Even though the realignment of kinship in adoption is generally recognized as both linking and affecting the family systems of both the birth family and adoptive family[52] this is not the case in donor conception. In fact, recognizing that donor conception links and affects all parties is an important task that promoters of donor conception tend to evade by pretending that reproductive technology "challenges", "redefines" and "brings about new constructions to kinship."[53] Thus they wrongly presume to have a licence to dismiss and recreate the rules of human kinship and identity. For Taylor, the removal of anonymity is described as the key that "re-establishes" the connection between donor and offspring, effectively re-entangling all the family systems involved. She articulates the concern that this may "threaten the bonds between grandparent, sibling, aunts and uncles."[54] Yet the notion that this connection is not present and lived with, until laws "re-establish" it, is misguided. It is not the laws that create genetic links but the genetic facts themselves, with or without acknowledgement.

A similar dynamic of evading the linking of family systems has been described in adoption.[55] This occurs when adoptive parents insist that they are the only 'real parents', putting the adoptee under pressure to support such evasions, which is noted to be unhealthy for them. According to Rosenberg, the adoptees who continue to support such notions are unable to progress developmentally to the recognized task of "forming an identity that integrates biology and upbringing", nor are they capable of the conscious recognition of issues of "abandonment", "self-esteem" or "ambivalence/splitting regarding two sets of parents."[56] Indeed, the adoptees' self-understanding can become stunted by the parents' preoccupations.

Donor offspring who experience reunion with genetic kin can face comparable struggles.[57] The conflicting needs of the family systems within donor conception are evidently worthy of greater appreciation, beyond the simplicity provided either by secrecy or openness. Despite the pretence that donor conception is merely a medical intervention, there are countless family systems linked by shared blood and kinship. Reproductive technology that uses donor gametes makes complex kinship systems of previously unknown proportions when hundreds of families have used the same donor.

Suggestions that we may need to "develop ways of coping with high-volume genetic connection, potentially embracing the families of the donors and the 'donor siblings' that have no parallel in contemporary western culture"[58] have an optimistic tone. It is striking that the intentional creation of this situation is not presented as cause for alarm, or moratorium. Instead, the onus is primarily placed on offspring to develop 'ways of coping' with this momentous and extraordinary demand. The intentional creation of such a cacophony of kinship, by one generation for the next generation to find ways to 'cope with', is ethically questionable.

New studies have begun to address the ambiguity and sensitivities of donor conception families in which contact has been achieved with the gamete donor and his or her wider family. This "notion of the destabilisation of the analytical opposition between 'biological' and 'social' kinship" is considered by Hargreaves as a:[59]

> Unique contribution to the field by including interviews not only with parents but also with extended family members, thereby making an argument that experiences of parenting and forming a family though DI are inextricably embedded in wider kin relations.

Notably, such issues are only just starting to be researched. Those who attempt to establish meaningful relationships between separated kin can experience the added difficulty of further exacerbating the complexities and sensitivities encountered in the recipient family members. Hargreaves has suggested that the prioritisation that extended family members show towards the sensitivities of the infertile family member is also a complicating factor in the expression and recognition of the child's genetic reality.[60] With the knowledge that "insight into the consequences of donor conception is still in its infancy,"[61] it is evident that the strains and constraints placed on the family systems, and offspring in particular, bear the need for far greater reflection and concern.

9. Therapeutic Support Networks

Rickarby states that, "While there are a minority of secure adoptive families, the vast majority are highly insecure and have dealt with their insecurity by establishing family myths."[62] These insecurities can result in their undermining the adoptee, in an effort to secure their attachments: "there are many binding behaviors: fostering dependency, undermining confidence and the young person's sense of capability, and by developing 'gratitude' and guilt."[63] The types of difficulties experienced by families affected by adoption are not always evident, but time and experience have enabled mental health professionals to know what to look for. Unlike donor conception, adoption is now presented as "a factor that therapists would do well to explore routinely as they gather family history and formulate assessments."[64]

Research in the United Kingdom continues to extol the notion that the donor offspring and families are 'ok', with titles such as "the kids are ok",[65] and "ART children are doing fine,"[66] commonly presenting the parent-child relationships founded on denial of donor conception as "well-adjusted".[67] Researchers and headline writers make such statements even when a significant percentage of the children in the studied families have not even been told that they are donor offspring, or the nature of the research conducted upon them.

Currently, in donor conception, there are few support networks or agencies comparable in quality with those for post adoption support, which specialise in offering help for the various issues that may be persistent and problematic for the donor-conceived. Malave[68] notes with dismay that there is still not even a framework presently available within such a therapeutic community to deal with the complexities of donor conception. He has expressed concern that donor conception has introduced "change that is a dramatic, historical, psychological event which necessarily has some very specific consequences."[69]

10. Conclusion

The history of adoption records a trail of harm and complexity that has been recognized for the individuals and family systems and which has much in common with the practice and trajectory of donor conception. The historic pattern of initial denial and then acceptance of the relevance and significance of the losses and harms found in adoption highlights the disparity and immaturity found in the practice of donor conception. There is a collective failure to demonstrate or give evidence as to why a different criterion than that developed in adoption is being used to frame and understand the identity and kinship for the child of donor conception and the family systems involved.

Donor conception is a relatively new addition to the field of human reproduction and experience. Secrecy and anonymity have aided a naïve or wilfully blind 'wait and see' approach to the rupturing and replacement of kinship and identity in this context. The consequent kinship loss and identity issues arising from donor conception are arguably compounded by being both avoidable and systemically created. In light of the lessons learnt from adoption, our human responsibility is to do what is right, not what is easy. In prioritizing the best interests of the child, including those created from reproductive technology, donor conception, with its intentional loss, should neither be condoned as an ethical solution to childlessness nor institutionally supported.

Bibliography

Ashbrook, T., " Single Mothers by Choice." *On Point*, (2006), http://www.onpointradio.org/shows/2006/03/20060317_b_main.asp.

Becker, G. "Metaphors in Disrupted Lives: Infertility and Cultural Constructions of Continuity." *Medical Anthropology Quarterly*, 1994; 8 (4): 383-410.

BioNews. "The kids are OK", (9 July 2001), http://www.bionews.org.uk/new.lasso?storyid=950.

-- "ART children doing fine." (March 25, 2002). http://www.bionews.org.uk/new.lasso?storyid=1198.

-- "Study finds egg donation families well-adjusted." (18 April 2006) http://www.bionews.org.uk/new.lasso?storyid=2984.

Blyth, E. "Information on Genetic Origins in Donor-Assisted Conception: Is Knowing Who You Are a Human Rights Issue?" *Human Fertility*, 2002; 5(4):185–192.

Brodzinsky, D.M. and M.D. Schechter. *The Psychology of Adoption*. New York: Oxford University Press, 1990.

de Lacey, S. "Parent Identity and 'Virtual' Children: Why Patients Discard Rather Than Donate Unused Embryos", *Human Reproduction*, 2005; 20 (6): 1661-1669.

Dunne, J. "Beyond Sovereignty and Deconstruction: The Storied Self." In *Paul Ricoeur: The Hermeneutics of Action*, R. Kearney, ed., London: Sage Publications, 1996, 137-157.

Franz, S. and D. Allen. *Report to Health Canada on The Offspring Speak – An International Conference of Donor Offspring*. Toronto: Infertility Network, 2001.

Golombok, S. "New Families, Old Values: Considerations Regarding the Welfare of The Child", *Human Reproduction*, 1998; 13 (9): 2342–2347.

Gottlieb, C., O. Lalos and F. Lindblad. "Disclosure of Donor Insemination to the Child: The Impact of Swedish Legislation on Couples' Attitudes", *Human Reproduction*, 2000; 15(9): 2052-2056.

Hargreaves, K. "Constructing Families and Kinship Through Donor Insemination", *Sociology of Health and Illness*, 2006; 28 (3): 261-283.

Herman, E. "The Paradoxical Rationalization of Modern Adoption", *Journal of Social History*, 2002; 36 (2): 229-385.

Howe, D., J. Feast and D. Coster. *Adoption, Search and Reunion: The Long Term Experience of Adopted Adults*. London: Children's Society, 2000.

Laing, J., and D. Oderberg. "Artificial Reproduction, the 'Welfare Principle', and the Common Good", *Medical Law Review*, 2005; 13 (3): 328-356.

Low, P. Reflections of a Father. In *Sperm Wars: The Rights and Wrongs of Reproduction*, H. G. Jones and M. Kirkman (eds.), Sydney: ABC Books, 2005, 108-111.

Lycett, E., K. Daniels, R. Curson and S. Golombok. "School-Aged Children of Donor Insemination: A Study of Parents' Disclosure Patterns", *Human Reproduction*, 2005, 20 (3): 810-819.

Malave, A. The Shadow Within, *Mental Health Professional Group Newsletter*, 4 & 6, 2006.

Montuschi, O. *You're Not My Father Anyway*. Donor Conception Network, (2005), http://donor-conception-network.org/notmyfather.htm.

Montuschi, "Telling Donor-Conceived Childrenabout their Origins". *BioNews,* http://www.bionews.org.uk/commentary.lasso?storyid=2811.

Pfeffer, N. "Artificial Insemination, In-Vitro Fertilization and The Stigma of Infertility". *Reproductive Technologies: Gender, Motherhood and Medicine,* edited by M. Stanworth, 81-97. Oxford: Polity Press, 1987.

Reitz, M. and K. W. Watson. *Adoption and the Family System: Strategies for Treatment.* New York: The Guilford Press, 1992.

Rickarby, G. A. "Continuation of Dr. Rickarby's Inquiry Submission" *Origins Inc,* 1997, http://www. angelfire. com/or/originsnsw/rickaby2.html.

Rosenberg, E. *The Adoption Life Cycle: The Children and Their Families Through the Years.* New York: The Free Press, 1992.

Russell, M. *Adoption Wisdom: A Guide to the Issues and Feelings of Adoption.* Santa Monica, CA: Broken Branch Productions, 1996.

Taylor, B. "Whose Baby Is It? The Impact of Reproductive Technologies on Kinship". *Human Fertility,* 2005; 8(3): 189-195.

van den Akker, O. "A Review of Family Donor Constructs: Current Research and Future Directions", *Human Reproduction Update,* 2006; 12(2): 91-101.

Triseliotis, J.P., J. Feast and F. Kyle. *The Adoption Triangle Revisited: A Study of Adoption, Search and Reunion Experiences.* London: British Association for Adoption and Fostering, 2005.

World Medical Association. "World Medical Association Declaration of Helsinki: Ethical Principles for Medical Research Involving Human Subjects." 2004, http://www.wma.net/e/policy/b3.htm.

Notes

1 Montuschi, *Telling Donor-Conceived Children about their Origins.*
2 Treseliotis, Feast and Kyle, *The Adoption Triangle Revisited,* 18.
3 Lycett, Daniels, Curson and Golombok, *School-Aged Children of Donor Insemination,* 810.
4 *Ibid.*
5 Herman, *The Paradoxical Rationalization of Modern Adoption,* 341.
6 *Ibid.,* 342.
7 Reitz and Watson, *Adoption and the Family System,* 3.
8 Howe, Feast and Coster, *Adoption, Search and Reunion,* 197.
9 Low, *Reflections of a Father,* 110.
10 Feinsod interviewed by Ashbrook, *Single Mothers by Choice.*
11 Dunne, *Beyond Sovereignty and Deconstruction,* 145.
12 *Ibid.*
13 *Supra,* note 8 at 198.
14 Laing and Oderberg, *Artificial Reproduction, the 'Welfare Principle', and the Common Good,* 334.
15 *Supra,* note 2 at 158.
16 *Ibid.*
17 *Ibid.,* 176.
18 Montuschi, *You're Not My Father Anyway.*
19 See note 8 above, 199.

20 See note 7 above, 318.
21 *Ibid.*
22 Russell, *Adoption Wisdom*, 35.
23 van den Akker, *A Review of Family Donor Constructs Current Research and Future Directions*, 98.
24 Brodzinsky and Schechter, *The Psychology of Adoption*, 74.
25 *Supra*, note 7 at 320.
26 Russell, Adoption Wisdom: A Guide to the Issues and Feeling of Adoption, 102.
27 Gottlieb, Lalos and Lindblad, *Disclosure of Donor Insemination to the Child,2052*.
28 Pfeffer, *Artificial Insemination, In-Vitro Fertilization and the Stigma of Infertility*, 82.
29 Taylor, *Whose Baby is it?*, 192.
30 *Supra*, note 7 at 319.
31 *Supra*, note 26 at 46.
32 Malave, *The Shadow Within*, 6.
33 *Supra*, note 7 at 221.
34 *Supra*, note 18.
35 See *Supra*, note 7 at 318.
36 *Supra*, note 23.
37 Golombok, *New Families, Old Values*, 2343.
38 *Ibid.*
39 Becker, *Metaphors in Disrupted Lives*, 383.
40 *Ibid.*, 396.
41 *Ibid.*, 397.
42 *Supra*, note 26 at 46-47.
43 *Ibid.*, 129.
44 de Lacey, *Parent Identity and 'Virtual' Children*, 1666.
45 Rickarby, *Continuation of Dr. Rickarby's Inquiry Submission.*
46 *Ibid.*
47 Ariel sighted by Franz and Allen, *Report to Health Canada*, 14.
48 *Supra*, note 49.
49 *Ibid.*
50 *Supra*, note 23 at 94.
51 *Ibid.*
52 *Supra*, note 7 at 12.
53 *Supra*, note 29 at 189.
54 *Ibid.*, 194.
55 Rosenberg, *The Adoption Life Cycle*, 197.
56 *Ibid.*
57 *Supra*, note 7 at 242.
58 Blyth, *Information on Genetic Origins in Donor-Assisted Conception*, 191.
59 Hargreaves, *Constructing Families and Kinship Through Donor Insemination*, 262.
60 *Ibid.*
61 *Supra*, note 23 at 98.
62 *Supra*, note 53.
63 *Ibid.*
64 *Supra*, note 7, 12.
65 BioNews, *The kids are OK.*
66 *Ibid.*, *ART Children Doing Fine.*
67 *Ibid.*, *Study Finds Egg Donation Families Well-Adjusted.*
68 Malave, *The Shadow Within*, 6.
69 *Ibid.*

PART THREE

WHAT DO COMMUNITY HEALTH, SOCIAL SCIENCE AND MEDICAL RESEARCH SUGGEST IS KNOWN ABOUT THE HEALTH AND WELL-BEING INTEREST OF THE DONOR-CONCEIVED?

Research in community health, social science and medicine commissioned to address the question, "Is donor anonymity in the health and well-being interest of the donor-conceived" produced mixed results. Some researchers concluded that the state of the existing research does not permit us to know, while others said there is sufficient evidence of anonymity's harm to conclude that it should be banned.

Stacey Page and Ben Gibbard are agreed that the psychosocial outcome data is preliminary. A review of studies on psychosocial outcomes for the donor-conceived conducted by *Stacey Page* reveals that the influence of creation by donor insemination cannot be fully understood in contexts where disclosure of genetic origins is not prevalent. The research has been conducted on families where the children are largely uninformed of their genetic origins. This fact limits the scope and resulting validity of research undertaken in this population. Further, the generalizability of the information generated is limited by small sample sizes and repeated observation of the same groups. Finally, the research conducted to date has depended primarily upon the perspectives of parents who have endorsed this method of procreation and who have chosen not to inform their offspring of their genetic origins. Dr. Page concludes that only when donor-conceived persons are informed of their origins and can provide their own opinions can researchers gain a more complete understanding of the consequences of being donor-conceived.

Ben Gibbard, a pediatrician specializing in the development of children, reviewed the medical literature to attempt to learn whether it is in the best interests of donor-conceived people to know about their donor conception in terms of psychosocial outcomes. He reports that it is not possible to answer the question because the existing research is insufficient. Like Stacey Page, Gibbard finds that the current psychosocial outcome research is preliminary, focuses only on those aware of their donor conception status, and explores only their emotional reactions. Gibbard argues that, to understand the effect of disclosure status on how offspring develop, it is important to know whether offspring differ according to whether they know or do not know about their conception, and whether they benefit from disclosure depending upon the age at which they were told this information. Moreover, Gibbard states that research should consider all variables that impact psychosocial development when attempting to assess the outcomes of donor-conceived people. Gibbard proposes new research directions. He suggests that future quantitative and qualitative research should review the details of risk and adaptation with respect to individual, family, community and cultural variables that together create positive and negative psychosocial outcomes for donor-conceived people. He recommends that research in this field should explore family therapy and adoption literature regarding whether encouraging disclosure is indeed best from both a family dynamic and child outcome perspective. Gibbard concludes by encouraging us to consider that whether disclosure is desirable for a donor-conceived person probably depends on the individual and his or her context.

In contrast to Page and Gibbard, *Jean Benward*, a licensed clinical social worker who provides counseling to the donor-conceived and their families, argues that there is enough information to reach a conclusion. She argues that donor anonymity is harmful to the donor-conceived because the important task of identity development can be seriously impeded by parents' failure to disclose the circumstances of the conception, and by the donor-conceived person's inability to meet his or her progenitor. Identity formation is a universal and vital task of human development in which people attempt to answer the question, "Who am I?" We all ask how we are alike or different from others in appearance, traits, personality and talents. This task is aided by being able to see genetic resemblance in relatives, hearing family members engage in resemblance talk (for example, "You look just like your grandmother!"), and knowing where one fits in the generations that preceded and will succeed oneself. Benward argues that, for healthy identity development in the donor-conceived, early disclosure is almost certainly best. She claims that all parties associated with the use of third-party gametes ought to understand the importance of kinship and family connections, and those families that use third-party gametes need to respect the complex relationships that their children have. She recommends the adoption of four measures: (1) Recognition of the emotional losses created by lack of donor information; (2) Provision of social and emotional support for the donor-conceived; (3) Preservation of donor information; and (4) Enabling and encouraging access to the donor.

Medical Geneticist, *Julie Lauzon*, considered whether the health and well-being of the donor-conceived is advanced by donor anonymity from the perspective of genetics and inherited conditions and concludes that it is not. In her chapter, Dr. Lauzon explores how health-care providers use family medical history not only to diagnose and treat disease but also to offer disease screening and prevention strategies to patients and at-risk family members. She then provides examples to illustrate the importance to donor offspring of knowing the health history of gamete donors and their family members, and how the health information of donor offspring may benefit also the gamete donor.

Chapter Eleven

A Review of Studies that Have Considered Family Functioning and Psychosocial Outcomes for Donor-Conceived Offspring

Stacey A. Page

1. Introduction

The primary purpose of this chapter is to summarize the findings of published studies that evaluated psychosocial outcomes for children who were conceived by donor insemination (DI) and raised in heterosexual families. This summary reveals that the full effect of creation by donor insemination on the psychosocial consequences for people conceived by DI is not known. Given the prevalence of secrecy regarding donor origins, most DI offspring are unaware of their genetic origins. This fact limits the scope and resulting validity of research that has been undertaken in this population. This chapter also considers, but to a lesser extent, research on offspring of ovum donation and embryo donation. The chapter concludes that researchers can gain a more complete understanding of the consequences of being a donor-conceived individual only when these individuals are informed of their origins.

2. Early Observation of Family Functioning and Psychosocial Outcomes for the Donor-Conceived

The first report of the psychological implications of donor insemination (DI) for the resulting family was published in the early 1960s.[1] Gerstel, a psychoanalyst, described her impressions of five families who had undergone donor insemination and their experiences over a period of several years. She postulated that these husbands were unable to fulfill the father role due to depression of varying duration and intensity. She hypothesized the experience of depression for the fathers resulted from several factors including the awareness that the biological need to survive through reproduction was not possible, the presence of the offspring as reminders of infertility and from feelings of hatred for the donors.

Gerstel described the mothers' experience of dread that the secret of their children's conception would be exposed. She observed severe and prolonged post-partum depression in all the women. Moreover, Gerstel reported that the mothers experienced feelings of hostility and subsequent guilt towards their infertile husbands.

The author opined that the mothers contributed to the compromised father-child relationships by over-protecting and over-indulging the children, and by further excluding the husbands, exacerbating his detachment from the child.[2]

Gerstel asserted that each of the resulting children was aware of a big family secret that involved their father and questioned their paternity in various ways. She stated that the compromised individual well-being of each parent combined with conflicted marital relationships resulted in family dynamics that were pathologically affected. Negative outcomes for the children included separation anxiety and disturbances in psychosexual development.

This psychoanalytic perspective provided the first theory of the effect of gamete donation on family relationships and outcomes for donor-conceived people.

3. Research Context

Since this early report, other researchers have investigated the effect of assisted reproductive techniques (ARTs) on a variety of outcomes for the resulting family members. They have considered the contributions of the experiences of infertility, genetics, sexuality, cultural factors, nature and quality of parental relationships when examining children's subsequent development.[3] Although the practice of DI is of relatively long-standing,[4] it is only recently that questions have been raised by researchers regarding the consequences for the well-being of the donor offspring. Ovum donation (OD) and embryo donation (ED), more recently developed assisted reproductive techniques, raise similar issues.[5]

Donor-conceived children are typically raised in families in which they are genetically related to just one of their parents. The creation of such families raises questions about the psychological consequences for these donor-conceived children, compared to children conceived in other ways. The fact that the children tend not to know about their unusual origins[6] raises separate questions about the effects of this lack of knowledge on the outcomes for both the child and the family.

When donor offspring have not been told of their origins, psychosocial sequelae cannot be directly attributed to their knowledge of their genetic history. Some researchers have hypothesized that negative consequences in the child's development are more likely attributable to the extent to which the lack of genetic ties interferes with the parent-child relationships, or to which secrecy surrounding the circumstances of conception negatively affects family relationships and functioning.[7] This hypothesis is based on the body of literature that demonstrates that children's healthy socio-emotional development depends in large part on the quality of children's attachment relationships with their parents.[8]

Other well-known factors which may influence the psychosocial health and development of children include the quality of the parent's marital relationship and their parents' mental health. Specifically, marital satisfaction and low levels of parental mental illness are conducive to healthy psychological adjustment and family relationships.[9]

Research available regarding outcomes for donor-conceived children is limited. What is available generally consists of studies describing psychosocial outcomes for families and children, and in which the majority of children do not know the truth about their genetic origins.

4. Identification of Research Studies and Methods

4.1 Search Strategy

This chapter summarizes the findings of published cohort studies that evaluated psychosocial outcomes for children conceived by donor insemination and raised in heterosexual families. Attempts to locate all such studies were made by searching in Pubmed, CINAHL, PsychINFO and ERIC using the MESH terms "artificial insemination" in combination with "psychosocial factors" and limited to human subjects. The key words "sperm donation" and "gamete donation" in combination with "donor offspring" and "psychosocial outcomes" were also entered. The online database, "Google Scholar" was searched using all of these terms as well. Other references were identified from review articles by Brewaeys (1996 and 2001).[10] Although the search was focused upon children conceived by sperm donation, a few studies of children conceived by ovum donation were found and also included.

4.2 Subjects Studied

Researchers have conducted a number of studies evaluating developmental outcomes for donor-conceived children, mainly in Europe. They have identified participants usually through fertility clinics and programs. In most protocols, the children have been preadolescent, with only a few including children over the age of 12. Early research described outcomes in groups of donor offspring.[11] Later studies have been comparative, considering outcomes for children conceived by donor insemination relative to outcomes for children in four other groups: those conceived naturally, those conceived by *in-vitro* fertilization (IVF), those raised in adoptive families (AD), and those raised in heterosexual families versus lesbian families.[12] A few investigators have considered outcomes in children conceived by ovum donation (OD) and embryo donation (ED).[13] The majority of the studied children raised in heterosexual families had not been told of their genetic origins.[14]

4.3 Outcomes Evaluated

Development outcomes evaluated have included: intellectual/cognitive development,[15] psychomotor development/developmental milestones,[16] and socio/emotional/behavioural adjustment.[17]

Additionally, some studies have recognized that children's psychosocial adjustment depends in part upon their parents' psychiatric status or psychological well-being.[18]

Aspects of the family relationships such as satisfaction with the marital relationship and parent-child relationships, have also been considered.[19]

5. Summary of Cognitive Development, Parental Psychiatric Status and Marital Satisfaction

5.1 Developmental Milestones, Cognitive Development

Among donor-conceived children, studies have found average or above average psychomotor development and achievement of developmental milestones,[20] faster language development[21] and average or above average IQs, and cognitive and psychosocial development.[22] Possible explanations offered for the above average outcomes were that these parents are more closely involved with their children and that they may have had advantaged socioeconomic and educational circumstances. In one comparative study, children conceived by donor insemination perceived themselves to be more cognitively competent than children who shared a genetic link with their fathers. A suggested explanation for this reported outcome is the observation that because many donors have been medical students, enhanced cognition may have genetic origins.[23]

Many of these early studies' findings of psychomotor and cognitive outcomes are limited due to methodological issues. Most of these investigations used small samples and lacked comparison or control groups. Limited information has been provided on the methods and instruments used to collect the data.[24] Much of the data has been reported by the parents, raising the possibility of a social desirability response bias where research subjects may respond in a way that makes them likely to be viewed in a positive manner.[25] A second problem is that, because the children in these families were typically young, concerns relating to these origins may not yet have affected them. Finally, most children did not have any knowledge of the circumstances of their conception, making the assessment of DI on psychosocial outcomes impossible to evaluate from the perspective of the children.

5.2 Parents' Psychiatric Status

Psychiatric status has been assessed across the groups of parents whose families were created in a variety of ways using standard measures of anxiety and depression. Some studies have shown no differences across family types for both parents[26] or for mothers.[27]

Other studies have revealed differences, though no clear pattern appears evident. For example, lower levels of depression or anxiety have been reported in families that had previously experienced fertility issues.[28] Lower levels of anxiety have been reported among DI mothers,[29] among mothers who have used ARTs (e.g., DI and IVF) compared to mothers who have conceived naturally (NC),[30] and among ED fathers.[31] Lower levels of depression have been found among ART mothers compared to NC mothers.[32] A significant country by family type relationship has been reported with greater anxiety and depression found among DI mothers in eastern Europe compared to those in western Europe.[33]

5.3 Parents' Marital Satisfaction

Satisfaction with marital status has also been evaluated across combinations of family types using primarily self-reporting measures of the quality of the marital relationship.

Some studies found no difference in marital satisfaction across family types.[34] As with psychiatric status, some differences have also been found, although no clear pattern has emerged. A lower incidence of relational problems has been reported in families that had previously experienced fertility issues[35] and among adoptive mothers[36] compared to families created by ART (both DI and IVF). Greater marital satisfaction among mothers who were genetically unrelated to their children (i.e., OD and AD) compared to those who were genetically related to their children (i.e., DI, IVF) has been reported.[37] A significant relationship between family type and country of residence has been found; Eastern European fathers of IVF and DI conceived children reported greater marital problems compared to AD and NC fathers from western European countries.[38]

Both lower[39] and higher rates[40] of family dissolution and marital breakdown in DI families have been found. The majority of these findings have generally suggested there are no negative effects on marital relationships in these families, however marital satisfaction has been assessed following successful reproduction, when the stressor of childlessness has been removed. Moreover, these studies may analyze an unrepresentative sample because couples whose relationships have dissolved may be less likely to participate in studies of family functioning and outcomes. Finally, it is not clear how marital satisfaction was taken into account among study participants who were already separated or divorced.[41] Higher ratings of marital satisfaction would be anticipated among those groups where a higher proportion of couples had separated, because marital satisfaction could not have been assessed among those who had separated or divorced.

6. The Research Program of Susan Golombok and Colleagues: Parent-Child Relationships and Children's Outcomes

Susan Golombok and her colleagues have contributed steadily to the literature on psychosocial outcomes for families with donor-conceived children. Generally, trained interviewers and standardized assessments have been used. Families have been matched as closely as possible for the age and sex of the child, and the age and social class of the parents. In some studies, these families have been followed over time.[42] The families have differed in their experiences of reproduction and subsequent choices in realizing parenthood. These studies have compared combinations of families (using artificial reproductive technologies including donor insemination, *in-vitro* fertilization, ovum donation and embryo donation) to families who chose to adopt children and who have been able to conceive naturally.

It is important to note that the data across publications of the Golombok research group are not always independent; some study groups are the same, or contain a substantial proportion of the same subjects, varying only with the addition of some subjects to a particular group or the inclusion or exclusion of comparison group(s).[43] This makes the available literature appear more substantial than it actually is.

6.1 Series 1: Families Created by Donor Insemination, *In Vitro* Fertilization, Adoption, Natural Conception (1995-2008)

In the first series of studies in which Golombok participated,[44] the quality of parent child relationships and the socio-emotional development of children created by ART including both donor insemination (DI) and *in vitro* fertilization (IVF) were compared with two control groups: families who had adopted (AD) and families with a naturally conceived child (NC). The authors state these groups allowed the role of genetic ties in family functioning and child development to be examined.

In the first phase of the study, 45 DI families (response rate 62%), 41 IVF (response rate 95%) families, 55 AD families (response rate 76%) and 43 NC (response rate 62%) families participated. The children were between four and eight years of age.[45] None of the DI children had been told of their genetic origins.

The researchers used standardized questionnaires and interviews to collect information from the children, the parents and the children's teachers. The findings of this study showed that the quality of parenting in families who had used reproductive technologies to conceive was superior to that in families with a naturally conceived child. The DI and IVF families scored higher on measures of mother's warmth toward the child, mother's emotional involvement with the child, mother-child interaction and father-child interaction compared to the families having conceived children naturally. Families with adopted children fell in between these groups. The authors emphasized that the families with a naturally conceived child were representative of the general population and did not represent a dysfunctional group. That is, the results should be interpreted as showing the ART families were functioning extremely well, and not that the naturally conceived families were experiencing problems. No differences were found with respect to any of the measures of children's emotions, behaviour or relationships with parents.

The families were subsequently approached for study participation when the children were 11-12 years of age.[46] Of the original families 37/45 created by donor insemination, and 49/ 55 created by adoption agreed to participate. Only 2/37 children had been told of their origins. Families created by IVF were not included. A new comparison group of 91 children conceived naturally, or with limited assistance (e.g., hormonal stimulation) following a period of infertility to control for the struggle in creating a family and desire for parenthood was included. The investigators hypothesized that as the children approached adolescence, difficulties would arise for DI children to the extent that conception by DI interfered with the parent-child relationships. A number of differences were found among family types and they appeared distinct for mothers and fathers. The mother-child relationships within DI families were again characterized as more positive, yielding higher levels of expressed warmth by the mothers, compared to AD and NC mothers and a greater tendency among the children to view their mothers as dependable (compared to NC mothers) and as confidents (compared to AD mothers). The investigators proposed this may have been due to the imbalance of the genetic relationship in DI families, leading mothers to feel they had a "special" relationship with their child given the existing genetic bond. Alternatively, researchers suggested that women who chose DI may have been most motivated to become mothers and as a result, may have been more warmly involved with their children than those mothers who conceived naturally. The father-child relationships differed on the construct of control, with DI fathers less likely to become involved in serious disputes with their children (compared to NC fathers) and less likely to reason with the children when they did occur (compared to AD and NC fathers). This could be interpreted as an indicator of paternal detachment from the children; however no differences were found on measures of warmth or involvement in parenting. Alternatively, it could be there were simply fewer disputes in these families. Considering the children, no differences were found among family types with respect to children's psychiatric ratings, school adjustment or peer relationships.

The most recent phase in this study examined the quality of parent-child relationships close to the adolescents' 18th birthdays.[47] The number of subjects dropped again from those originally participating with 26/45 DI families, 26/41 IVF families, and 38/55 adoptive families taking part. From the second phase of the study, 63/91 families who had a child naturally after a period of infertility agreed to participate.

When these researchers examined parent-child relationships, they found that DI mothers generally showed higher levels of warmth in their relationships compared to the other groups and these findings were consistent with the two previous phases of the study. Again the authors stated this was a function of exceptionally high warmth shown in these families rather than lower than normal levels of warmth among the others. On measures of conflict, DI mothers showed a higher level of disciplinary aggression compared to IVF mothers, where "disciplinary aggression" referred to parental reaction to the child in a situation of conflict. In contrast to the previous phase of this study, no differences were found among fathers on measures of warmth or conflict for any of the family types. Higher proportions of marital breakdown (separation/divorce) were found among the DI and NC families relative to the others, however no differences in marital satisfaction were found among those couples who were still together. DI mothers reported lower levels of trait anxiety. The higher proportion of divorce and separation among DI families, and resulting higher prevalence of single motherhood, was offered by the authors as an explanation for the increased maternal warmth shown by DI mothers, though this outcome has also been attributed to the presence of the genetic bond.[48] Researchers used the higher rate of marital dissolution in conjunction with a lower participation rate among DI fathers in the study as an explanation for the shift in the father-child relationship observed in the previous study.[49]

In this study, no outcome measures were taken on the children because only 2 of the children had been told of their genetic origins. The majority was unaware of the truth about their conception and therefore could not give informed consent for study participation. The researchers provided limited information about the outcomes for the two children who knew the truth: the authors reported these children, while reportedly distressed at the time of disclosure in mid-childhood, were not distressed by this information at age 18.[50]

6.2 Series 2: Families Created by Donor Insemination, *In Vitro* Fertilization, Ovum Donation, Adoption (1995-2006)

The study groups in Phase 1[51] and Phase 2[52] of the foregoing studies were extended in two subsequent investigations by the addition of a group of children conceived by ovum donation.[53]

In the first of these studies that included OD, researchers compared families created by DI (N=45), IVF (N=41), AD (N=55) and OD (N=21, response rate 81%) to evaluate differences in outcomes according to the degree of genetic relatedness between the child and each of the parents (e.g., mother only, father only, both, neither), or as described by the investigators, social vs. biological parenting. All groups had experienced significant fertility issues and therefore the desire for a child and motivation for parenthood was believed to be constant. The children in this study were between three and a half, and eight years of age. Only one of the children conceived by gamete donation (DI and OD) had been told of his or her origins.

Researchers reported less trait anxiety and less stress associated with parenting among all fathers in families where the child was not genetically related to the mother. In families where the children were genetically related to the fathers, but not the mothers, mothers reported lower levels of parental distress and more coordination with the fathers over discipline. When children were genetically related to their fathers, and regardless of their relationship with the mothers, mothers expressed less warmth toward the child. The investigators noted that the lack of a genetic link between the child and the mother was associated with greater psychological well-being among the parents, but no differences in the quality of their parenting. The authors hypothesized that raising a child genetically unrelated to the mother is somehow experienced as a more significant venture than other assisted reproductive methods and as a result, these parents are more committed to their roles and find parenting more satisfying. This explanation directly contrasts to hypotheses offered in other studies where genetically related mothers were found to express more warmth, or were emotionally over-involved with their children. This increased warmth and over-involvement was attributed to the special nature of the mother-child genetic bond.[54]

Assessments of the children's development did not show any differences between family types on measures of social or emotional development, with the exception of DI children's self reports of greater cognitive competence than those genetically related to their fathers.

The researchers followed up this study group when the children reached 12 years of age.[55] Again, two of the study groups in this report were included in a previous publication.[56] This study differs from the original[57] by the inclusion of an OD family type and differs from the Phase 1 report[58] by the exclusion of the adopted families. At the time of this study, 35/45 DI, 34/41 IVF and 17/21 OD families agreed to participate, though in this study only mothers and children took part. As in the second phase of the study, very few DI (11%) and ED (35%) parents had already told, or planned to tell, their children about the circumstances of their conception.

Researchers reported no parenting differences between the IVF and OD families. A few differences were found between OD and DI mothers. OD mothers demonstrated less sensitive responding to the child's needs. The investigators suggested this may have been due to the lack of a genetic bond between OD mothers and their children interfering with their ability to respond to the child; the researchers qualified this explanation, however, by noting the mean difference represented a shift from "average" to "above average" on the measurement scale and reflected appropriate function on the part of the OD mothers. Another observation reported by the investigators was that DI mothers were more likely to be over-involved with their children compared to OD mothers. As previously noted, this was hypothesized to be related to the presence of a genetic bond in the DI relationship. Again, however, the researchers did not deem the increased rating to be sufficient to be problematic for the parent-child relationships.[59] Finally, DI mothers reported their partners shared more of the parenting load compared to those in OD families. The researchers proposed this result may have been due to the following: the lack of a genetic tie motivated the DI fathers to be more involved with parenting, or conversely, that DI mothers presented the DI fathers in a more positive light.

6.3 Series 3: Families Created by Donor Insemination, *In Vitro* Fertilization, Adoption, Natural Conception in Eastern and Western Europe (1995-2002)

Golombok's initial study of UK families[60] was subsequently extended by including families from other European countries including Italy, Spain and The Netherlands.[61] This study, in turn, was extended by including families from Bulgaria,[62] in addition to the UK samples, to examine both cultural variation towards assisted reproduction, and the quality of parent-child relationships and socio-emotional development of the children.

In the first European study, the investigators hypothesized that DI parents of four to eight year olds from the predominantly Protestant Northern countries (UK and the Netherlands) would be more likely to tell their children of their genetic origins and that children who had been told would be better psychologically adjusted than those not told the truth.[63] Across countries, there were 111 DI families (response rate 47%), 116 IVF families (response rate 76%), 115 AD families (response rate 72%) and 120 NC families (response rate 65%), making this one of the largest comparative studies to date.

Considering the outcomes for quality of parenting, mothers with children conceived by assisted reproductive technologies differed from mothers of naturally conceived children, but not mothers of adopted children on a couple of outcomes. The type of ART (i.e., DI or IVF) did not matter. Specifically, mothers of ART children (to whom they were genetically related) were shown to express significantly more warmth, more emotional involvement, more interaction with their children and to experience less stress with parenting. Similarly, fathers of ART children were shown to have greater interaction with their children compared to fathers of NC children. Fathers of adopted children were found to contribute more to discipline than the ART fathers did. These patterns of group differences were consistent across countries. For fathers, a few differences were noted by country. DI fathers in Spain reported less parenting stress, AD fathers in Italy reported more parenting stress and fathers from the Netherlands were reported to contribute more to parenting.[64]

Researchers reported that the ratings of children's emotions, behaviour and relationships were similar across family types and countries with few exceptions. DI children in The Netherlands showed more evidence of emotional and behavioural problems than DI children in other countries as rated by both mothers and teachers. The authors suggested that this may be attributable to factors associated with a lower social class among this particular group (i.e., children conceived by DI).[65]

Regarding disclosure, none of the families of DI children had told their child about his/her method of conception and the investigators concluded that attitudes towards ART do not differ between these countries.[66] Thus failing to disclose may be interpreted as an indication that attitudes towards DI across countries are not very accepting.

Subsequently, this 1996 study[67] was extended to include a sample from Bulgaria, an Eastern European study to assess the influence of another cultural environment.[68] The authors described the context in Bulgaria as less accepting of childlessness, leading to more pressure to accept reproductive technologies. At the same time, it was suggested that donor insemination was less socially acceptable and a culture of secrecy surrounded ART. The authors hypothesized that greater difficulties and more negative outcomes would be experienced by Bulgarian families who had used ART generally, and DI specifically. This study contributed 19 DI families (response rate 53%), 20 IVF families (response rate 74%), 20 AD families (response rate 65%) and 20 NC families (response rate 77%) to the foregoing study samples. The children were between four and eight years of age. None of the DI families had told the children of their genetic origins.

Analyses were carried out comparing outcomes between groups (IVF, DI, AD, and NC) and regions (Eastern and Western Europe). The investigators reported a number of family groups by country relationships, possibly illustrative of the impact of social context on outcomes. In Eastern European families with a child conceived by DI, both mothers and fathers reported increased levels of parenting stress compared to their Western European counterparts. IVF fathers in Eastern Europe also reported higher levels of parenting stress. Eastern European fathers showed greater involvement in care giving and contributed less to discipline than Western European fathers. DI fathers in Eastern Europe showed less involvement with discipline and the authors speculated this was due to the fathers' feelings this may not be their "real" child. More positive relationships were found between Eastern European children and their mothers compared to those in the Western countries and children in Eastern Europe scored higher on measures of peer acceptance, particularly those naturally conceived. Eastern European children conceived by DI and IVF showed higher levels of behavioural and emotional problems compared with those in the Western countries and this may be associated with the higher levels of parenting stress, greater marital difficulties and higher anxiety experienced among Eastern European parents. Cook concluded that the problems encountered by parents were exacerbated when the children had been conceived by ARTs and that social context (i.e., being Eastern European) influenced outcomes as well.[69]

A third European study which was published in 1997[70] focused on data gathered from the Netherlands in the original European study published in

1996.[71] The researchers increased the Dutch DI sample from 29 to 38 families (response rate 53%) and modified the control groups to include only IVF (N=30; response rate 67%) and NC families (N=30; response rate 60%) from the Netherlands. The number of NC families participating in the original study was 26: it is assumed that four new NC families were recruited for this investigation.[72] Outcomes investigated in this study were the emotional/behavioural development of the DI children and whether or not secrecy was associated with differences in adjustment. The children were between four and eight years of age. One DI family had told the child of its origins.

More emotional/behavioural problems were identified among the children conceived by donor insemination than among those conceived naturally; moreover, their total problem scores were found to be higher than that of the Dutch population sample. The effect of secrecy on functioning was compared by examining the differences in outcomes between those parents who had disclosed or intended to disclose their children's genetic origins and those opting for secrecy. No evidence was found to support an association between secrecy and emotional behavioural adjustment of the child. Unfortunately, researchers did not assess other factors (e.g., family functioning, parent-child relationships) and therefore their association could not be measured. The authors of this study attributed the finding of elevated problem scores to methodological limitations, most likely random sampling error because the response rate of the DI families was only 53%. The findings of more behavioural/emotional adjustment problems in the DI group were consistent with the earlier studies, which is not surprising given that the majority of the sample was the same.[73] In the previous studies, these authors postulated the problems were due to social class and sociocultural factors.[74]

Findings of behavioural problems have been reported previously by other researchers. An early Australian study followed up with 50 couples who had conceived children using donor semen.[75] Although it was concluded that there weren't any major paediatric or emotional problems, 14 parents indicated their children (1-3 years old) were hyperactive with six requiring sedation. Five wives reported anxiety about their husbands' reactions to the children with two describing the husbands as being overprotective and one stating she did not believe the husband had accepted the child. In addition, two men reported difficulties, with one describing problems enforcing discipline and one feeling the child was a constant reminder of his infertility. The generalizability of these results is limited by the small sample size, lack of control group and limited information on the methods used.

The last study, published in 2002, in the European series by Golombok and colleagues followed up the families from the original study[76] as the children approached adolescence (11-12 years of age).[77] From the original sample, researchers compared 94/111 DI families, 102/116 IVF families, 102/115 AD families and 102/120 NC. Eight of the DI families had told the children about their method of conception. No differences were found between IVF and DI families on any measures relating to mother-child warmth, father-child warmth, mother-child control or father-child control. There were also no differences between these family types relating to children's socio-emotional functioning. A few differences were found when these ART families (i.e., IVF and DI families) were compared to AD and NC families. Although ART mothers were not different with respect to expressed warmth, sensitivity or affection towards their children compared to adoptive or natural mothers, a higher proportion of ART mothers were classified as enmeshed, suggesting that ART mothers were more likely to be over-concerned or over-protective of their children. In turn, the children of enmeshed mothers reported less criticism from their mothers and also less time spent with peers. ART fathers demonstrated higher scores on expressed warmth than both natural conception and adoptive fathers, and greater enjoyment of fatherhood than natural conception fathers. Similar to findings for the mothers, a higher proportion of ART fathers were classified as enmeshed, and children of ART fathers perceived less criticism and more lenient discipline by their fathers.[78]

This study also compared variables relating to the quality of parent-child relationships and the children's socio-emotional functioning between those who had disclosed DI status and those who had not. No differences were found for any of the warmth or children's outcome variables. Children who had been told of their DI status reported less frequent and less severe disputes with their mothers, and perceived their mothers to be less strict than those who had not been told, suggesting that disclosure may have a beneficial effect on the parent-child relationship. The authors caution these comparisons were exploratory and based on a very small number of observations.

Enmeshment has been reported by others. Manuel and colleagues (1990) compared outcomes for 94 children conceived by DI to children conceived after fertility treatment not involving a donor, and to NC children at three months, eighteen months and three years of age.[79] The investigators described an "anxious overinvestment" in parents who had undergone fertility treatment (DI and IVF) compared to parents of NC children; however no differences were found between the donor-conceived children and the children born after fertility treatments. Compared to NC children, the children created through reproductive technologies reportedly exhibited signs of increased emotional vulnerability evidenced by disturbed sleeping and eating patterns, more visits to the MD's office and increased aggressive behaviour. The authors suggested factors relating to long struggles with fertility, and a prolonged life period without children, rather than the lack of a genetic link, may have produced these sequelae. McWhinnie has similarly reported parental self-perceptions of protection or over protection in her study of 54 DI and IVF families.[80]

6.4 Series 4: Families Created by Donor Insemination, Ovum Donation, and Natural Conception: New Cohorts (2004-2006)

A final series of longitudinal cohort studies was initiated by Golombok et al in 2004.[81] This research group undertook these studies to examine family outcomes in a cohort of children conceived by gamete donation in an era that the investigators hypothesized was less inclined towards secrecy. This fourth series of studies commenced 15 years after the first series of studies. It considered the effect of a perceived climate of societal encouragement of openness and disclosure. As in previous investigations, the researchers used standardized interview and questionnaire measures to examine the psychological well-being of the parents, the quality of the parent-child relationships and in this case, infant temperament.

The first study compared 50 families (response rate 50%) with a child conceived by DI and 51 families (response rate 75%) with a child conceived by OD with 80 families (response rate 73%) who had a naturally conceived infant (9-12 months of age).[82] All of the DI children and 36 of the OD children were conceived using anonymous donors.

The differences identified among the groups suggested more positive parent-child relationships for the gamete donation parents compared to the natural conception parents. Mothers of donor gamete conceived infants showed higher levels of expressed warmth, greater emotional over-involvement and greater enjoyment of parenthood. Among fathers, greater emotional involvement was shown by gamete donation fathers. With the exception of fathers of infants conceived by ovum donation showing higher levels of involvement than the donor insemination fathers, no differences between the ovum donation and donor insemination families were found for parent-child relationships. No differences were observed among the three groups for infant temperament.

Regarding the intention to tell their offspring of their origins, 46% of DI families and 56% of ovum donation families indicated that they planned to disclose, while 30% and 22% respectively had decided not to. The most common reasons given for deciding to tell their children were that the child had a right to know and to avoid disclosure by someone else. Reasons given for non-disclosure were to protect the child and to protect the non-biological parent.

The researchers conducted a second phase of this study when the children reached two years of age.[83] Again, the focus was on the quality of parent-child relationships and the psychological development of the child. The investigator hypothesized that parents who had used gamete donation to create families would show less positive emotions and more negative emotions in their relationships with their children than parents of naturally conceived children because of the absence of a genetic link. Moreover, they hypothesized that these emotional patterns would be exacerbated in those families where the parents did not intend to tell the child about the donor conception. Ninety-two percent of the original DI group (46/50), 94% of the original OD group (48/51) and 85% of the NC group (68/80) participated. Contrary to the stated hypothesis, comparisons between the gamete donation mothers and the natural conception mothers showed significantly more joy or pleasure among the gamete donation mothers, along with a greater perception of their child's vulnerability. Within the gamete donation families, the ovum donation mothers showed higher levels of joy or pleasure while the donor insemination mothers showed higher levels of over-protectiveness towards the child. The investigators suggested the former relationship may be attributable to a compensatory reaction experienced by the women who had previously believed they were infertile and unlikely to become mothers. In the latter comparison, the investigators suggested the feelings of (over) protection may be attributable to the genetic bond shared by the DI mother alone as they have suggested in previous investigations.[84]

Researchers observed no differences between the gamete donation fathers and the natural conception fathers with respect to the quality of their parent-child relationships, nor were any differences found between the DI fathers and the OD fathers. The authors suggested this was possibly due to the father's sense of identity being less influenced by their role as a parent.[85] It may be however that the father's sense of parental identity is less influenced by their genetic contribution regarding the quality of the parent-child relationship.

The influence of intention to disclose origins on the quality of the parent-child relationships was not significant across groups. Nor were any differences observed in the psychological development or cognitive functioning among the groups of children.

The third phase of this longitudinal study took place when the children were three years of age. From the original sample, 82% (41/50) of the DI families, 80% (41/51) of the OD families and 84% (67/80) of the NC families continued their participation. In this study, 34 families who had used a surrogate gestational mother were included. In the majority of these latter families, the surrogate mother was also the genetic mother (59%), while in the remaining proportion, the commissioning mother was the genetic mother. Standardized interviews and questionnaire measures of the psychological well-being of the parents, the mother-child relationships alone and the psychological well-being of the child were conducted. The investigators were interested in assessing whether differences in parenting existed among the families where the mothers lacked a genetic and/or gestational link with the child and families where the fathers lacked the genetic link.

Consistent with the findings when the children were 1 and 2 years of age, the findings showed the absence of a genetic link between the mother and the child did not negatively affect the parent-child relationships. Again, as before, the differences found in parent-child relationships reflected higher levels of warmth and interaction between mothers and their children in the assisted reproduction families than in the naturally conceived comparison group.

When researchers compared the maternal and paternal genetic links, they found that the surrogacy and ovum donation mothers (no genetic link and/or no gestational link) had a higher level of interaction with their children than the mothers of children conceived by DI. The authors explained this higher interaction might be due to the former group of mothers being especially committed to parenting and possibly trying to compensate for the absence of a genetic/gestational link. This finding contrasts with that reported by Murray, and described previously,[86] where OD mothers were observed to respond less sensitively to their children compared to DI mothers, and where the DI mothers were reportedly more involved with their children compared to OD mothers. In the Murray study, these parameters were hypothesized to be directly related to the genetic relationship.

Considering the psychological well-being of the children, no differences were found between family types and all were functioning within the normal range.

Regarding disclosure, 46% of the DI parents and 22% of the OD parents had decided against telling their children of their genetic origins. This reflects an increase in the proportion of DI families who had decided against disclosure compared in the original study, though this increase may reflect a change in sample size, rather than a change in opinion of the subjects.

6.5 Embryo Donation Study (2007)

Studies reviewed to this point have considered families who have used artificial techniques to have children. A 2007 study considered the case where the gametes came from two rather than just one person. Unlike gamete donation where at least one parent has had a genetic relationship to the resulting child, in embryo donation (ED), neither parent has a genetic relationship. ED differs from adoption, however, in that the parents to be have a gestational relationship with the child. The 2007 study was conducted by MaCallum, Golombok and Brinsden who undertook a preliminary investigation of families created by embryo donation.[87] In this study, the researchers compared 21 ED families to 28 AD families and 30 IVF families when the children were two to five years of age. The purpose was to explore for differences in marital satisfaction, psychological state, parent-child relationships and the children's psychological development possibly attributable to genetic and gestational characteristics. Of the 21 ED families, only two (9%) had told their children about their method of conception, while nine (43%) had definitely decided against telling their child and five (24%) were undecided.

ED mothers and fathers showed higher levels of emotional over-involvement compared to the AD mothers and fathers but not to the IVF group, leading the authors to suggest this difference in involvement may have been due to the experience of reproductive technology procedures and to the bonds formed with the child during pregnancy. As in a previous study[88] the investigators noted that the level of over-involvement represented a moderate rather than pathological level. They suggested that having had such difficulty conceiving, this involvement simply reflected the ED parents wanting to spend as much time as possible with their child.

ED mothers and fathers were also more likely to respond defensively when asked questions about their child and family life than were adoptive parents. ED mothers, but not fathers were found to respond more defensively than IVF mothers.

When the researchers examined the children's socio-emotional adjustment, they found that the children in the adoptive families showed significantly higher levels of conduct-related problems than children in the other two groups.

7. Summary

7.1 Studies to Date Suggest that the Donor-Conceived Are Doing Well

The pervasive negative outcomes for families created by donor insemination described by Gerstel in the 1960s do not appear to have been observed in later investigations.[89] Most of the early studies of these families, though limited by methodological weaknesses, do not systematically reveal evidence of compromised family relationships or impaired psychosocial and emotional outcomes for the children.

Later studies, conducted by Golombok and her colleagues, have addressed some of these earlier methodological limitations by using comparison groups and standardized assessments.

Considering outcomes for parent-child relationships and the children's psychosocial outcomes, this research group has repeatedly concluded that the lack of a genetic relationship between a parent (typically the father) and the child does not appear to adversely affect the quality of parenting or the child's psychological development. These authors have presented results illustrating more positive parent-child relationships in combination with greater parental involvement among families created using donor insemination than families created in other ways. They have suggested that a genetic bond is not as important for family functioning and positive child outcomes as is a strong desire for parenthood. In other words, a strong desire for parenthood may outweigh any negative effects arising from the lack of genetic link. Infertile couples who choose to have a child who is genetically unrelated to one of the parents may be more committed to parenthood and consequently find parenthood a more satisfying experience than those who become mothers and fathers by other means.

7.2 Limitations of These Findings

7.2.1 Secrecy and Failure to Disclose

The central caution to the interpretation of these findings, acknowledged by the authors, is that these studies have taken place in a context of secrecy; most children were young, and had not been told of their genetic origins. The outcome measures relating to the children's psychosocial development have been limited to proxy indicators of outcomes in the sense that the construct of identity, and acceptance of genetic history, have not been directly assessed because the children were not aware of how they came to be. Likewise, researchers could not assess with any accuracy the effect of such origins on parent-child relationships. The authors have suggested that the secrecy regarding conception does not seem to affect negatively family relationships or the children's functioning for the time being, and they have appropriately cautioned that these conclusions may not hold when the children become older, issues of identity become more salient or the children learn of their origins.

7.2.2 Sample Bias

Across studies, the sample sizes and response rates of the donor inseminations families are low, hovering around 50%, and tend to decrease over time within the longitudinal studies. The low number of participants is most likely attributable to the enduring secrecy surrounding DI and fear that the children's genetic history might be revealed. Parents of children conceived by DI are reticent to take part in research themselves and are perhaps even more reluctant to allow their children to participate, biasing the samples and limiting the generalizability of study results. Therefore, those parents who have agreed to participate in these studies may differ substantively from those who have declined.

7.2.3 Small Numbers of Subjects

Related to this sampling bias is the problem of small numbers of study subjects. These low numbers may have affected the power of the statistical tests used to evaluate outcomes because differences among groups may not have been detected. Also, the sample sizes within the studies may have been inadequate for the statistics used to be meaningful, given the ratio of subjects to outcome variables.[90] Although a few studies corrected for multiple testing[91] this was not usually undertaken; consequently, some differences reported to be significant might have been, in fact, spurious effects. In other words, the effects might be due to chance rather than actual differences.

7.2.4. Social Desirability Bias

As previously noted, the self-report methods used within the studies can engender social desirability bias; such self-report methods may, therefore, threaten the validity of the study conclusions. In general, assessments of parenting are prone to the effects of social desirability bias where parents are inclined to provide responses that garner social approval.[92] This bias or contamination may be exacerbated in populations of parents who have created a family by non-conventional means. Parents of non-genetically related children may be reluctant to report any negative feelings about family dynamics or parenting and may have attempted to present their relationships in the best possible light due to perceived negative attitudes associated with non-genetic parenting.

7.2.5 "Snapshot" Views Prevent Understandings of Possible Causation

Finally, the studies undertaken in this area have been descriptive. The intent has been to describe psychosocial outcomes in relation to a set of perceived "risk factors" (e.g., genetic history, parental psychiatric status, marital satisfaction). The validity of postulated associations is limited by the fact that they are described at one time point and do not take into account the sequence of events. It cannot be determined if problems in marital adjustment, psychiatric adjustment or family relationships were present prior to parenthood or developed afterwards. Consequently, it is impossible to infer causality with any certainty.[93]

8. Recommendations for Future Research

The full impact of creation by donor insemination on the psychosocial consequences for DI offspring in Canada is not known. Given the prevalence of secrecy regarding donor origins, most DI offspring are unaware of their genetic origins. This lack of knowledge limits the scope and resulting validity of research that can be undertaken in this population. A more complete understanding of the consequences of being a donor-conceived individual, can be obtained only when these individuals are informed of their origins.

Bibliography

Amuzu, B., R. Laxova and S.S. Shapiro. "Pregnancy outcome, health of children, and family adjustment after donor insemination." *Obstetrics and Gynecology* 75, no. 6 (1990): 899-905.

Applegarth, L., N.C. Goldberg, I. Cholst, N. McGoff, D. Fantini, N. Zellers, A. Black and Z. Rosenwaks. "Families created through ovum donation: a preliminary investigation of obstetrical outcome and psychosocial adjustment." *Journal of Assisted Reproduction and Genetics* 12, no. 9 (1995): 574-580.

Baran, A. and R. Pannor. *Lethal secrets.* 2 ed. New York: Amistad, 1993.

Bos, H.M.W., F. van Balen and D.C. van den Boom. "Child adjustment and parenting in planned lesbian-parent families." *American Journal of Orthopsychiatry* 77, no. 1 (2007): 38-48.

Bowlby, J. *A secure base: clinical applications of attachment theory.* London: Routledge, 1988.

Brewaeys, Anne. "Donor insemination, the impact on family and child development." *Journal of Psychosomatic Obstetrics and Gynaecology* 17, no. 1 (1996): 1-13.

-- "Review: parent-child relationships and child development in donor insemination families." *Human Reproduction* Update 7, no. 1 (2001): 38-46.

-- and S. Golombok, N. Naaktgeboren, J.K. de Bruyn and E.V. van Hall. "Donor insemination: Dutch parents' opinions about confidentiality and donor anonymity and the emotional adjustment of their children." *Human Reproduction* 12, no. 7. (1997): 1591-1597.

Chan, R.W., B. Raboy and C.J. Patterson. "Psychosocial adjustment among children conceived via donor insemination by lesbian and heterosexual mothers." *Child Development* 69, no. 2 (1998): 443-457.

Clamar, A. "Psychological implications of the anonymous pregnancy." In *Gender in Transition: a new frontier.* J. Offerman-Zuckerberg, ed. New York: Plenum, 1998.

Clayton, C.E. and G.T. Kovacs. "AID offspring: initial follow-up of 50 couples." *Medical Journal of Australia* 1 (1982): 338-339.

Cummings E.M. and P.T. Davies. "Effects of marital conflict on children: recent advances and emerging themes in process-oriented research." Journal of Child *Psychology and Psychiatry* 43, no. 1 (2002): 31-63.

-- and P.T. Davies. "Maternal depression and child development." *Journal of Child Psychology and Psychiatry* 35, no. 1 (1994): 73-112.

Daniels, K. "Donor gametes: anonymous or identified?" *Best Practice and Research Clinical Obstetrics and Gynaecology* 21, no. 1 (2007): 113-128.

Dean, N.L., and R.G. Edwards. "Oocyte donation – implications for fertility treatment in the nineties." [Editorial]. *Current Opinions in Obstetrics and Gynecology* 6, no. 2 (1994): 160-165.

Gerstel, G. "American psychoanalytic view of artificial donor insemination." *American Journal Psychotherapy* 17 (1963): 64-77.

Golombok, S., A. Brewaeys, M.T. Giavazzi, D. Guerra, F. Maccallum and J. Rust. "The European study of assisted reproduction families: the transition to adolescence." *Human Reproduction* 17, no. 3 (2002): 830-840.

-- and A. Brewaeys, R. Cook, M.T. Giavazzi, D. Guerra and A. Mantovani A. "The European study of assisted reproduction families: family functioning and child development." *Human Reproduction* 11, no. 10 (1996): 2324-2331.

-- and C. Murray, P. Brinsden and H. Abdalla. "Social versus biological parenting: family functioning and the socioemotional development of children conceived by egg or sperm donation." *Journal of Child Psychology and Psychiatry* 40, no. 4 (1999): 519-527.

-- and C. Murray, V. Jadva, E. Lycett, F. Maccallum and J. Rust. "Non-genetic and non-gestational parenthood: consequences for parent-child relationships and the psychological well-being of mothers, fathers and children at age 3." *Human Reproduction* 21, no. 7 (2006): 1918-1924.

-- and E. Lycett, F. MacCallum, V. Jadva, C. Murray, J. Rust, H. Abdalla, J. Jenkins and R. Margara. "Parenting infants conceived by gamete donation." *Journal of Family Psychology* 18, no. 3 (2004): 443-452.

-- and F. MacCallum, C. Murray, E. Lycett and V. Jadva. "Surrogacy families: parental functioning, parent-child relationships and children's psychological development at age 2." *Journal of Child Psychology and Psychiatry* 47, no. 2 (2006): 213-222.

-- and F. Maccallum, E. Goodman and M. Rutter. "Families with children conceived by donor insemination: a follow-up at age twelve." *Child Development* 73, no. 3 (2002): 952-968.

-- and R. Cook, A. Bish and C. Murray. "Families created by the new reproductive technologies: Quality of parenting and social and emotional development of the children." *Child Development* 66, no. 2 (1995): 285-298.

-- and R. Cook, A. Bish, and C. Murray. Quality of parenting in families created by the new reproductive technologies: a brief report of preliminary findings. *Journal of Psychosomatic Obstetrics and Gynecology* 1993; 14: 17-22.

-- and V. Jadva, E. Lycett, C. Murray and F. Maccallum. "Families created by gamete donation: follow-up at age 2." *Human Reproduction* 20, no. 1 (2005): 286-293.

Gregoire, A.T., and R.C. Mayer. "The impregnators." *Fertility and Sterility* 16, no. 1 (1965): 130-134.

Iizuka, R., Y. Sawada, N. Nishina and M. Ohi. "The physical and mental development of children born following artificial insemination." *International Journal of Fertility* 13, no. 1 (1968): 24-32.

Kovacs, G.T., D. Mushin, H. Kane and H.W.G. Baker. "A controlled study of the psychosocial development of children conceived following insemination with donor semen." *Human Reproduction* 8, no. 5 (1993): 788-790.

Leeton, J. and A. Backwell. "A preliminary psychosocial follow-up of parents and their children conceived by artificial insemination by donor (AID)." *Clinical Reproduction and Fertility* 1 (1982): 307-310.

Lycett, E., K. Daniels, R. Curson and S. Golombok. "Offspring created as a result of donor insemination: a study of family relationships, child adjustment, and disclosure." *Fertility and Sterility* 82, no. 1 (2004): 172-179.

Maccallum, F., S. Golombok and P. Brinsden. "Parenting and child development in families with a child conceived through embryo donation." *Journal of Family Psychology* 21, no. 2 (2007): 278-287.

Manuel, C., F. Facy, M. Choquet, H. Grandjean and J.C. Czyba. "Les risques psychologiques de la conception par insemination artificielle avec donneur (IAD) pour l'enfant." *Neuropsychiatrie de l'Enfance* 38, no. 12 (1990): 642-658.

McWhinnie, A. "Outcomes for families created by assisted conception programmes." *Journal of Assisted Reproduction and Genetics* 13, no. 4 (1996): 363-365.

Milsom, I. and P. Bergman. "A Study of Parental Attitudes after Donor Insemination (AID)." *Acta Obstetricia et Gynecologica Scandinavica* 61, no. 2 (1982): 125-128.

Murray, C., F. Maccallum and S. Golombok. "Egg donation parents and their children: follow-up at age 12 years." *Fertility and Sterility* 85, no. 3 (2006): 610-618.

-- and S. Golombok. "Going it alone: solo mothers and their infants conceived by donor insemination." *American Journal of Orthopsychiatry* 75, no. 2 (2006): 242-253.

Morsbach, S.K. and R.J. Prinz. "Understanding and improving the validity of self-report of parenting." *Clinical Child and Family Psychology Review* 9, no. 1 (2006):1-21.

Nachtigall, R.D., J.M. Tschann, S.S. Quiroga, L. Pitcher and G. Becker. "Stigma, disclosure and family functioning among parents of children conceived through donor insemination." *Fertility and Sterility* 68, no. 1 (1997): 83-89.

Owen, L. and S. Golombok. "Families created by assisted reproduction: Parent-child relationships in late adolescence." *Journal of Adolescence* (forthcoming).

Portney, Leslie Gross, and Mary P. Watkins. "Epidemiology." In *Foundations of Clinical Research: Applications to Practice.* Toronto: Prentice Hall Canada, Inc., 1993: 271-297.

-- "Statistical Inference." In *Foundations of Clinical Research.* Toronto: Prentice Hall Canada, Inc., 1993: 335-359.

Raoul-Duval, A., H. Letur-Konirsch and R. Frydman. "Anonymous oocyte donation: a psychological study of recipients, donors and children." *Human Reproduction* 7, no. 1 (1992): 51-54.

Richman, J.M., M.V. Chapman and G.L. Bowen. "Recognizing the impact of marital discord and parental depression on children: a family-centered approach." *Pediatric Clinics of North America* 42, no. 1 (1995): 167-180.

Soderstrom-Anttila, V., N. Sajaniemi, A. Tiitinen and O. Hovatta. "Health and development of children born after oocyte donation compared with that of those born after in-vitro fertilization, and parents' attitudes regarding secrecy." *Human Reproduction* 13, no. 7 (1998): 2009-2015.

Notes

1 Gertsel, "A psychoanalytic view of artificial donor insemination," 64-77.
2 *Ibid.*
3 Brewaeys, "Donor insemination," 1-13; Bos, van Balen and van den Boom, "Child adjustment and parenting in planned lesbian-parent families," 38-48; Cook and others, "European study of assisted reproduction families," 203-212; Golombok and others, "European study of assisted reproduction," 2324-31; McWhinnie, "Outcomes for families created by assisted conception programmes," 363-5.
4 Gregoire and Mayer, "The impregnators," 130-4.
5 Dean and Edwards, "Oocyte donation," 160-5; Murray, Maccallum, Golombok, "Egg donation parents and their children," 610-8.
6 Daniels, "Donor gametes," 113-28.
7 Baran and Pannor, *Lethal Secrets*; Clamar, "Psychological implications of the anonymous pregnancy" in *Gender in Transition.*
8 Bowlby, *A secure base.*
9 Cummings and Davies, "Maternal depression and child development," 73-112; Richman, Chapman and Bowen, "Recognizing the impact of marital discord and parental depression on children," 167-180; Cummings and Davies, "Effects of marital conflict on children," 31-63.
10 Brewaeys, see note 3 above; 17.
11 Amuzu, Laxova and Shapiro, "Pregnancy outcome," 899-905; Applegarth and others, "Families created through ovum donation," 574-580; Clayton and Kovacs, "AID offspring," 338-9.
12 Brewaeys and others, "Donor insemination," 1591-7; Chan, Raboy and Patterson, "Psychosocial adjustment among children conceived via donor insemination by lesbian and heterosexual mothers, 443-57; Golombok and others, "European study of assisted reproduction families," 830-40.
13 Golombok and others, "Parenting infants conceived by gamete donation," 443-52; Golombok and others, "Non-genetic and non-gestational parenthood," 1918-24; Maccallum, Golombok and Brinsden, "Parenting and child development in families with a child conceived through embryo donation," 278-87; Raoul-Duval, Letur-Konirsch and Frydman, "Anonymous oocyte donation," 51-4.

14 Cook and others, see note 3 above; McWhinnie, see note 3 above; Golombok and others, "Surrogacy families," 213-22.
15 Amuzu, Laxova and Shapiro, see note 11 above; Golombok and others, "Families created by gamete donation," 286-93; Iizuka and others, "The physical and mental development of children born following artificial insemination," 24-32; Leeton and Backwell, "A preliminary psychosocial follow-up of parents and their children conceived by artificial insemination by donor (AID)," 307-10.
16 McWhinnie, see note 3 above; Applegarth and others, see note 11 above; Clayton and Kovacs, see note 11 above; Raoul-Duval, Letur-Konirsch and Frydman, see note 13 above; Leeton and Backwell, see note 15 above; Milsom and Bergman, "A Study of Parental Attitudes after Donor Imsemination (AID), 125-8; Manuel and others, "Les risques psychologiques de la conception par insemination artificielle avec donneur (IAD) pour l'enfant," 642-58; Soderstrom-Antilla and others, "Health and development of children," 2009-15.
17 Cook and others, see note 3 above; Golombok and others, "European study of assisted reproduction," 2324-31; Murray, Maccallum and Golombok, see note 5 above; Clayton and Kovacs, see note 11 above; Brewaeys and others, see note 12 above; Golombok and others, see note 12 above; Golombok and others, see note 13 above; Maccallum, Golombok and Brinsden, see note 13 above; Golombok and others, see note 14 above; Golombok and others, see note 15 above; Leeton and Backwell, see note 15 above; Manuel and others, see note 16 above; Soderstrom-Antilla, see note 16 above; Kovacs and others, "A controlled study of the psycho-social development of children conceived following insemination with donor semen," 788-790; Golombok and others, "Families created by the new reproductive technologies," 285-98; Golombok and others, "Social versus biological parenting," 519-27; Golombok and others, "Families with children conceived by donor insemination," 952-68; Lycett and others, "Offspring created as a result of donor insemination," 172-179.
18 Murray, Maccallum and Golombok, see note 5 above; Golombok and others, see note 12 above; Golombok and others, see note 13 above; Golombok and others, see note 13 above; Maccallum, Golombok and Brinsden, see note 13 above; Golombok and others, see note 15 above; Golombok and others, see note 17 above.
19 Cook and others, see note 3 above; Golombok and others, see note 17 above; McWhinnie, see note 3 above; Murray, Maccallum and Golombok, see note 5 above; Applegarth and others, see note 11 above; Golombok and others, see note 12 above; Golombok and others, see note 13 above; Macallum, Golombok and Brinsden, see note 13 above; Raoul-Duval, Letur-Konirsch and Frydman, see note 13 above; Golombok and others, see note 14 above; Golombok and others, see note 15 above; Leeton and Backwell, see note 15 above; Milsom and Bergman, see note 16 above; Manuel and others, see note 16 above; Soderstrom-Antilla, see note 16 above; Golombok and others, see note 17 above; Lycett and others, see note 17 above; Nachtigall and others, "Stigma, disclosure and functioning and family functioning," 83-9; Golombok and others, "Quality of parenting in families created by the new reproductive technologies," 17-22.
20 McWhinnie, see note 3 above; Amuzu, Laxova and Shapiro, see note 11 above; Applegarth and others, see note 11 above; Clayton and Kovacs, see note 11 above; Raoul-Duval, Letur-Konirsch and Frydman, see note 13 above; Leeton and Backwell, see note 15 above; Milsom and Bergman, see note 16 above; Manuel and others, see note 16 above; Soderstrom-Antilla, see note 16 above.
21 Manuel and others, see note 16 above.
22 Golombok and others, see note 15 above; Iizuka and others, see note 16 above; Leeton and Backwell, see note 15 above; Kovacs and others, see note 17 above.
23 Golombok and others, "Social versus biological parenting," 519-27.
24 Clayton and Kovacs, see note 11 above; Raoul-Duval, Letur-Konirsch and Frydman, see note 13 above; Leeton and Backwell, see note 15 above.
25 Clayton and Kovacs, see note 11 above; Raoul-Duval, Letur-Konirsch and Frydman, see note 13 above; Leeton and Backwell, see note 15 above; Milsom and Bergman, see note 16 above.
26 Golombok and others, see note 12 above; Golombok and others, see note 13 above; Golombok and others, see note 14 above; Golombok and others, see note 15 above.
27 Murray, Maccallum and Golombok, see note 5 above; Macallum, Golombok and Brinsden, see note 13 above; Golombok and others, see note 23 above.

A Review of Studies

28 Golombok and others, see note 17 above; Golombok and others, "Families created by the new reproductive technologies," 285-98.
29 Owen and Golombok, "Families created by assisted reproduction."
30 Golombok and others, see note 17 above.
31 Golombok and others, see note 23 above.
32 Golombok and others, see note 17 above.
33 Cook and others, see note 3 above.
34 Murray, Maccallum and Golombok, see note 5 above; Golombok and others, see note 12 above; Golombok and others, see note 13 above; Macallum, Golombok and Brinsden, see note 13 above; Golombok and others, see note 15 above; Golombok and others, see note 17 above; Owen and Golombok, "Families created by assisted reproduction," forthcoming.
35 Golombok and others, see note 17 above; Golombok and others, see note 28 above.
36 Golombok and others, see note 17 above.
37 Golombok and others, see note 23 above.
38 Cook and others, see note 3 above.
39 Amuzu, Laxova and Shapiro, see note 11 above.
40 Golombok and others, see note 17 above; Owen and Golombok, see note 34 above.
41 Golombok and others, see note 17 above; Owen and Golombok, see note 34 above.
42 Golombok and others, see note 17 above; Murray, Maccallum and Golombok, see note 5 above; Golombok and others, see note 12 above; Golombok and others, see note 13 above; 25, Golombok and others, see note 15 above; Golombok and others, see note 28 above; Golombok and others, see note 23 above; Golombok and others, see note 17 above; Owen and Golombok, see note 34 above.
43 Cook and others, see note 3 above; Golombok and others, see note 17 above; 9, 21, Golombok and others, see note 28 above; Golombok and others, see note 23 above; Golombok and others, see note 17 above; Owen and Golombok, see note 34 above.
44 Golombok and others, see note 28 above; Golombok and others, see note 17 above; Owen and Golombok, see note 34 above.
45 Golombok and others, see note 28 above.
46 Golombok and others, see note 17 above.
47 Owen and Golombok, see note 34 above.
48 Golombok and others, see note 17 above.
49 Owen and Golombok, see note 34 above.
50 *Ibid*.
51 Golombok and others, see note 28 above.
52 Golombok and others, see note 17 above.
53 Murray, Maccallum and Golombok, see note 5 above; Golombok and others, see note 23 above.
54 Murray, Maccallum and Golombok, see note 5 above; Golombok and others, see note 17 above.
55 Murray, Maccallum and Golombok, see note 5 above.
56 Golombok and others, see note 17 above.
57 *Ibid*.
58 Golombok and others, see note 28 above.
59 Murray, Maccallum and Golombok, see note 5 above.
60 Golombok and others, see note 28 above.
61 Golombok and others, see note 17 above.
62 Cook and others, see note 3 above.
63 Golombok and others, see note 17 above.
64 *Ibid*.
65 *Ibid*.
66 *Ibid*.
67 *Ibid*.
68 Cook and others, see note 3 above.
69 *Ibid*.
70 Brewaeys and others, see note 12 above.
71 Golombok and others, see note 17 above.
72 Brewaeys and others, see note 12 above.

73 *Ibid.*
74 Cook and others, see note 3 above; Golombok and others, see note 17 above.
75 Clayton and Kovacs, see note 11 above.
76 Golombok and others, see note 17 above.
77 Golombok and others, see note 12 above.
78 *Ibid.*
79 Manuel and others, see note 16 above.
80 McWhinnie, see note 3 above.
81 Golombok and others, see note 13 above; 25, Golombok and others, see note 15 above.
82 Golombok and others, see note 13 above.
83 Golombok and others, see note 15 above.
84 Golombok and others, see note 17 above.
85 Golombok and others, see note 15 above.
86 Murray and Golombok, "Going it alone," 242-53.
87 Macallum, Golombok and Brinsden, see note 13 above.
88 Golombok and others, see note 28 above.
89 Gertsel, see note 1 above.
90 Portney and Watkins, "Statistical Inference" in *Foundations of Clinical Research*, 335-59.
91 Brewaeys, see note 13 above; Macallum, Golombok and Brinsden, see note 13 above.
92 Morsbach and Prinz, "Understanding and improving the validity of self-reporting of parenting," 1-21.
93 Portney and Watkins, "Epidemiology" in *Foundations of Clinical Research: Applications to Practice*, 271-97.

Chapter Twelve

The Effect of Disclosure or Non-Disclosure on the Psychosocial Development of Donor-Conceived People: A Review and Synthesis of the Literature

W. Ben Gibbard

1. Introduction

This chapter reviews the consequences of disclosure or non-disclosure of donor conception on the psychosocial development of children and adolescents conceived by gamete donation. Having reviewed the available medical literature, the chapter concludes that there are serious limitations to what we know about the effects of disclosure on the psychosocial wellbeing of donor-conceived young people. Consequently, the chapter offers suggestions for future research possibilities and methodology to advance our understanding in this area. It advocates that future research should draw upon existing concepts and knowledge in the literature of adoption, family therapy, and developmental psychopathology.

1.1 Extent of Canadian Data

At the outset, it is important to recognize that not all donor-conceived people are told about their origins. This fact creates significant impediments to research especially in North America. Even though new research is emerging that describes the psychosocial outcomes of donor-conceived people, this research has developed, in part, because some jurisdictions in Europe and Australia have banned donor anonymity. But there is little information in the literature about North American offspring outcomes related to disclosure, because donor anonymity is legally permitted or is common practice in Canada and the United States. Historically, most parents do not disclose to their offspring that they were conceived using donor gametes, and most fertility clinics have encouraged non-disclosure. As a result, there is much we do not know about the psychosocial outcomes for children and adolescents related to disclosure, non-disclosure or accidental disclosure.

Only two Canadian surveys were located. The first surveyed the opinions of Canadian pediatricians regarding disclosure of donor conception to offspring.[1] This study found that most pediatricians (57 percent) were in favour of telling donor-conceived children about their mode of conception, and 43 percent believed that donor-conceived individuals had a right to know about their biological origins. The second Canadian study surveyed parents who had used donor conception and found that only 30 percent of parents disclosed to their children that they had been conceived using donor gametes.[2]

2. Matters Related to Disclosure of Donor Conception

2.1 Rates of Disclosure

Research to date in the English language and without geographic limitation indicates that few parents disclose the details of conception to their donor-conceived children.[3] Consecutive follow-up of a cohort of European children conceived by donor insemination found that none of the parents had told their 4- to 8-year-old children about their donor-conception origins,[4] but that this increased marginally to 8.6 percent in the same sample when the children were aged 12 years.[5] Even in Sweden, where legislation has existed since 1985 establishing the right of donor-conceived individuals to receive information about their donor, research suggests a similar disclosure pattern to offspring. Only 11 percent of those children were told about their conception; the mean child age at disclosure was 5.5 years.[6] The parents in this study who had informed their child of their donor conception origins tended to be satisfied with their decision to do so, and no direct immediate negative effects were noted for the children.[7] Similar disclosure rates (9 percent) have also recently been reported in a sample of children aged 2 to 5 years conceived by embryo donation.[8] Another study found that children were less likely to be told of their donor conception origins as they became older.[9] Unfortunately, no prospective research is available regarding whether disclosure rates continue to change as children grow into adolescence, or what the rate might be for disclosure to adult donor-conceived individuals.

Many parents surveyed reported an intention to disclose to their children their donor conception status, but this intention is not expressed by all, and those who claim an intention to disclose often do not. The Swedish study referenced above found that 58 percent of couples who had conceived using donor gametes indicated that they intended to tell their child at a later date, 15 percent were not sure whether to disclose, and 27 percent intended not to inform the child.[10] Another sample from the United Kingdom found that while 46 percent of parents of 1 year old children conceived using donor gametes intended to disclose this information to their children,[11] only 5 percent of these families had done so when the child was 3 years of age,[12] and only 29 percent had done so by the time the child was aged 7.[13]

However, parents often tell a third party about their child's donor conception even if they do not tell the resulting child. In the previously described Swedish study, 59 percent of parents had disclosed this information to someone else – generally a close family member.[14] Moreover, among those parents who had not told their child about their donor conception origins, 53 percent had told someone else. Of those parents who had told their child, 100 percent had told a third party.[15]

2.2 Rationale for Disclosure or Non-disclosure

There are a variety of arguments offered by theorists and advocates regarding whether or not to tell children about their donor conception. Arguments in favour of disclosure include: non-disclosure or secrecy might undermine trust among the parents and child;[16] a child has an inherent right to know his or her biological origins;[17] and adolescents may face challenges with respect to identity formation if they do not have knowledge about their donor.[18] Arguments against disclosure include: non-disclosure protects both the couple and the child from negative societal reactions;[19] the relationship between father and child and the psychological health of the child might be jeopardized should the child know his or her donor conception status;[20] and the parental right to privacy and to make decisions affecting the welfare of the child are as important as children's right to know about their conception.[21]

Parents themselves report various reasons for disclosure or non-disclosure. Parents' reasons for telling children about their donor conception include: the desire to be honest and open with their children; a concern that accidental disclosure by someone other than the parent might occur; respect for a child's right to know his or her origins; a belief that genetic information may be valuable to their children; and a wish to decrease family tension.[22]

Parents who chose not to disclose state as their reasons: a desire to protect children from the distress of learning that their father was not genetically related; the inability to give information to the child about his or her donor; the opinion that the nature of conception is a personal matter between parents and irrelevant to the child; and concerns about the effect disclosure may have on family relationships – in particular, a desire to protect the father from potential rejection by the child or from social stigma associated with male infertility.[23] Some parents reported that they were unsure about how to tell their child about their donor conception and that this uncertainty amounted to a reason in favour of non-disclosure.[24]

A survey by Nachtigall and colleagues found that parents who disclose consider the issue in terms of honesty, and believe that disclosure safeguards family emotional stability from threats of non-disclosure or accidental disclosure.[25] They also found that non-disclosing parents often view confidentiality as the most important issue, and seek to protect the family from the external threat of social stigma.[26]

The reasons described in the literature regarding parental motive for disclosure or non-disclosure provide an important backdrop for the development of effective social policy regarding banning donor anonymity and encouraging disclosure to donor-conceived people. Further research is necessary concerning parental motives and concerns related to disclosure, because understanding and addressing these issues may increase disclosure rates and improve the quality of the disclosure experience for both offspring and their parents.

2.3 Effect of Family Type on Disclosure

Some research has found that the decision to disclose varies among family types. Most research regarding the psychosocial outcomes of donor-conceived children and their families has been conducted with heterosexual parents. However, many studies do not indicate the parent type, and only a minority of studies report outcomes for homosexual or single mother families. Lesbian parents or single female parents are reported to be more likely to disclose to their children the truth about their donor conception, probably because of the obvious absence of a father in these families.[27] One recent survey of adolescents and adults who knew about their donor conception origins found that 9 percent of children parented by heterosexual couples were told at a young age (less than 3 years), and 33 percent indicated that they were told about their donor conception origins when they were 18 years of age or older.[28] By contrast, 56 percent of individuals in this survey who were told about their donor conception status were parented by homosexual couples.[29]

3. Effect of Disclosure on Psychosocial Outcomes of Donor-Conceived People

To determine whether, and how, to tell donor-conceived people about their conception, it would be helpful to know the psychosocial effects of disclosure on offspring. Unfortunately, we do not know much about the views and experiences of donor-conceived people who have been told their donor conception status because very few studies have been conducted on this issue. Moreover, there is little research that compares families who disclose with those who do not when attempting to assess the effect that disclosure has on offspring psychosocial wellbeing. Consequently, we have little empirical evidence to support the assertion that disclosure is beneficial or that non-disclosure is harmful for the psychosocial development of donor-conceived people.

Although studies to date have recorded the emotional reaction of offspring to the knowledge of their donor conception status, little detailed research has been undertaken to explore differences in psychosocial functioning in offspring who know about their donor conception status compared to those who do not. Similarly, no research has explored these core outcome variables in relation to age at disclosure. If such research were undertaken, the resulting information would be useful to guide parents who have used donor conception in determining: whether there is an optimal age for disclosure and, if so, what that might be; if disclosure is delayed but desired by parents who have used donor conception, what to expect with disclosure by age; and how to mitigate the effects of disclosure on the psychosocial development of their children. The relationship between disclosure status and child emotional and behavioral outcomes is reviewed elsewhere in this book by Page, but literature to date suggests that there is minimal negative effect on offspring related to non-disclosure.[30]

Some adults have reported negative feelings about being donor-conceived, including anger about being lied to, and frustration at not having access to medical or genetic information.[31] A recent study surveyed 29 adolescents who were conceived using open identity donors; all participants had been informed of their donor conception status prior to the age of 10 years. All those surveyed reported being comfortable with the way they were conceived, and the majority indicated that knowing about their donor conception had a positive effect on their relationship with their parents.[32]

Another recent study surveyed a group of adolescents and adults who knew about their donor conception origins regarding their feelings about being donor-conceived.[33] This group was recruited from a worldwide on-line registry of donor- conceived people, and may not be representative due to sampling bias. In this group of 165 individuals conceived by sperm donation, 30 percent learned of their donor conception origins when they were aged 3 years or earlier, and 19 percent learned when they were older than 18 years (the mean age of disclosure was 14 years). The majority of individuals reported being told intentionally, with a small minority finding out accidentally. The most common response at the time of disclosure by study participants was curiosity (72 percent), but this varied by the individual's age at the time of disclosure. If the individual was an adult at the time of disclosure, common responses included anger, confusion, numbness, shock, being upset, and relief. Respondents were also asked about their present emotional response to being conceived by donor conception, and again the most common response was that of curiosity (69 percent). Similarly, if the individual was an adult at the time of disclosure, the individual's present emotional reactions were dominated by feelings of anger, shock, and relief. Information regarding participants' feelings towards their parents was varied; some individuals who were told about their donor conception later in life reported more positive feelings, and others reported negative feelings. Children raised by heterosexual parents were more likely to feel angry at being lied to by their mothers than by their fathers. The most common feeling towards social fathers was sympathy.

Golombok and colleagues theoretically explored the issue of secrecy of donor conception in the context of a study examining outcomes related to family functioning, and child-related developmental and mental health outcomes.[34] Because almost no parents in their sample had disclosed (2 of 37 subjects studied), the researchers could not make inferences regarding negative adolescent, parent, or family functioning outcomes as a consequence of non-disclosure. Some parents in this study reported that they regretted not disclosing donor conception information to their children, and somewhat paradoxically felt more reluctant to do so over time. The authors concluded that research is required that compares children who have been told about their donor conception with those who have not, so that researchers can establish the psychological effects of openness about donor conception.

Initial research suggests that age of disclosure may be an important determinant of an offspring's response to their donor conception origin, because those told during adulthood have reported more negative experiences than those told in childhood or adolescence.[35] Some researchers have advocated for early disclosure on the basis that it would permit the information to be incorporated into a child's identity.[36] One survey completed by parents of young donor-conceived children (mean age 5 years) indicated positive child responses to being told of their origins.[37] A recent study using a convenience sample of adults aged 21 to 34 years found that 56 percent had learned of their donor conception at the age of 16 years or older.[38] This study did not find an association between child age at the time of disclosure and family functioning.[39]

There is little research examining the actual effects of accidental disclosure on the psychosocial outcomes of donor-conceived people. However, it has been postulated that accidental disclosure may damage trust among parents and children, and it has been suggested that this may be more harmful than planned disclosure.[40] Because the possibility of accidental disclosure increases as a child ages, both late disclosure and non-disclosure could potentially cause negative psychosocial outcomes for donor-conceived individuals and their families by creating the conditions for accidental disclosure.

4. Critique of Previous Research

Not only is research examining the psychosocial outcomes of donor-conceived people preliminary, the studies undertaken to date have a number of limitations. Because it is difficult to generalize the conclusions of research reviewed here to populations of all donor-conceived people for the purposes of developing social and legal policy, this section highlights some of the methodological limitations of these studies and suggests future research directions.

Almost uniformly, studies about donor conception indicate generally normal family and offspring outcomes. However, these studies are based on samples where non-disclosure is predominant. There are no true population-based longitudinal studies comparing groups of children who know their donor conception status to those who do not, in terms of psychosocial outcomes and antecedent risk and resiliency factors. There is also little information about psychosocial outcomes based on age of the child at time of disclosure, especially in adolescent and adult populations of donor-conceived people. In particular, there are no Canadian studies in this area. As a result, there is little psychosocial evidence to apply to the development of social or legal policy regarding whether to ban donor anonymity and whether to facilitate the ability of offspring to learn about their origins.

Most outcome research concerning donor-conceived people consists of descriptive cross sectional surveys or longitudinal cohorts. These studies have collected risk factor and outcome data based on predetermined variables, but it is possible that important individual and family functioning variables were not included. In addition, many of the studies reviewed used unknown measures of psychosocial outcome, or were limited by the use of self-report questionnaires which are prone to bias.[41] In addition, because the research methods are descriptive in nature, it is not possible to determine if there is a causal link between risk factors such as donor conception disclosure and psychosocial outcomes for donor-conceived people.

Quantitative studies to date are also flawed by a number of sources of bias which limit their generalizability. In particular, all studies reviewed report small sample sizes and low response rates. Other sources of bias in research to date include selection bias, non-response bias, and recall bias. Selection bias refers to systematic differences in characteristics between those selected for a study and those who are not. Non-response bias is the systematic error that may occur due to differences between those who responded to the surveys and those who did not. Those who agree to participate in a study may be systematically different from those who do not participate because of causally important variables that are not taken into account. For example, those with negative experiences following disclosure of donor conception may be more likely to take part in a survey and impart their experiences than those with more positive experiences. Recall bias entails the systematic error due to differences in the accuracy or completeness of a research subject's recollection of past experiences. For instance, subjects asked about their emotional reactions to donor conception disclosure might be biased in their reporting if disclosure occurred at a point early in their childhood when their memory of events may be unclear or affected by other events subsequent to disclosure. Consequently, because of significant issues of bias, these preliminary studies cannot be generalized to all donor-conceived people regardless of disclosure status.

Qualitative research examining the experiences of donor-conceived people is often limited by the lack of rigour in methodology; for example, many studies are purely descriptive. Qualitative research in the field is also limited by selection bias. Moreover, many authors cited in the literature are, themselves offspring of donor conception. While these anecdotal descriptions or case studies provide important perspectives on the personal experiences of individuals, there are significant challenges in moving from such perspectives toward the development of social policy. Future research might engage in more rigorous qualitative methodology with groups of individuals who have different outcomes and antecedent risk and resiliency factors. Moreover, future in-depth qualitative research should focus on providing a description of family dynamics and child psychosocial development in donor-conceived people over time.[42]

5. Proposals for Future Research

This review of research to date does not show that donor-conceived people either experience or demonstrate significant adverse psychosocial outcomes related to knowledge of their donor conception status. But for the reasons just outlined, the existing research cannot be regarded as the final word on the subject. Existing psychosocial outcome research is preliminary, focuses only on those aware of their donor conception status, and explores only their emotional reactions. To better understand the effect of disclosure status on offspring psychosocial outcomes, future research must determine whether offspring differ in relation to disclosure status and subsequent core psychosocial outcomes, and also whether these outcomes differ in the disclosed group by age at disclosure.

Moreover, it is naïve to believe that a single factor such as donor conception can, in itself, explain the psychosocial status of donor-conceived individuals. Such a notion does not find support in developmental psychopathology theory, which is a leading approach to understanding how individuals develop over time to adulthood. Developmental psychopathology asserts that there are no linear outcomes by which a single exposure is entirely responsible for an expected outcome, and no single candidate factor acts alone.[43] On the contrary, development arises from a dynamic interplay between physiological, genetic, social, cognitive, emotional, and cultural influences across time. Consequently, developmental psychopathology principles caution against focusing on one factor or variable (for example, donor conception disclosure status) to explain human behavior or psychological outcomes.[44] Multifactoral models of psychosocial outcome should be used to inform future research in this area. Therefore, future quantitative and qualitative research should review the details of risk and adaptation with respect to individual, family, community and cultural variables that together create positive and negative psychosocial outcomes for donor-conceived people.

In addition, family therapy literature in particular requires more exploration regarding whether banning donor anonymity and encouraging disclosure are indeed best from both a family dynamic and child outcome perspective. It will be important to understand parent perspectives on disclosure, especially narratives of loss, discontinuity and difference, and how these might shape their interactions with and parenting of donor-conceived children.[45] Adoption literature reports that many factors influence the degree to which parents desire or are able to be open about their family history with their children, and that parents are in the best position themselves to decide whether disclosure is the optimal course of action for their particular family circumstances.[46] If policy or law makers contemplate a ban on donor anonymity and to facilitate disclosure of information to offspring about their donor conception origins, then it would be important to learn from established perspectives in the adoption literature regarding parental desires and control over disclosure. Recent studies exploring the disclosure decisions of parents using explicit qualitative methodology reveal that these decisions are complex and reflect a wide range of influences and contexts.[47] The recent social policy trend toward openness about donor conception contrasts with the majority of parents who have used donor conception who view that non-disclosure is best. All parties involved might be assisted by considering the notion that disclosure is dependent on individual and contextual variables, and may not be universally advantageous to donor-conceived people.[48]

Future research should also attempt to resolve the dilemma apparent in the literature regarding whether parental attitudes or openness toward disclosure change over time.[49] This question has arisen because some research reports little change in parental decisions regarding disclosure as their children mature,[50] while other research suggests that disclosure decreases as offspring grow older.[51]

6. Conclusion

Sound Canadian policy and law regarding the practice of donor conception would be aided by the development of a Canadian and international research agenda related to the psychosocial development of donor-conceived people. In developing such an agenda, investigators must grapple with the fact that most people who are donor-conceived are not told about their origins. This fact presents considerable challenges to research aimed at understanding the effect of disclosure versus non-disclosure on offspring psychosocial development. If social and legal policy develop in Canada to establish mandatory disclosure, then careful prospective research will be necessary that explores individual, parent, and family-related variables that contribute to best outcomes. Ideally, a research agenda should be informed by all parties involved: the donor-conceived, parents (both social and genetically related), siblings, clinicians, and other community stakeholders.

If policy and law makers decide that encouraging disclosure to all donor-conceived people is appropriate and desirable, then future research will be needed to guide parents in how and when to disclose this information to their children. Despite the fact that many European countries and Australian states now ban donor anonymity, the majority of parents surveyed in those jurisdictions still have not disclosed the fact of donor conception to their children, and many have voiced a preference never to disclose this information to their children. Understanding individual parent, child, and family-based factors that affect disclosure will, therefore, be paramount to the success of legislation that would encourage parents to disclose. Such information would also inform debate about whether the State should make it possible for adult offspring to learn the truth, irrespective of their parents' wishes in this regard. Moreover, providing parents and families with longitudinal support, guidance and counseling regarding the issues that frame disclosure in their particular family circumstances will be equally important.[52] Such work will require the thoughtful and collaborative integration of the perspectives regarding disclosure of not only donor-conceived individuals, but also of parents, fertility clinicians and, most notably, experts in family therapy.

Developing a comprehensive Canadian and international research agenda related to the factors and processes that frame disclosure and best psychosocial outcomes for donor-conceived people is crucial to inform Canadian social and legal policy. This information could be used to determine whether banning anonymity and encouraging disclosure are desirable and, if so, how these changes could best be implemented. Future research should draw upon existing knowledge in the fields of adoption and family therapy, and be informed by the conceptual framework of developmental psychopathology.

Bibliography

Berger, D.M., A. Eisen, J. Shuber J and K.F. Doody. "Psychological Patterns In Donor Insemination Couples." *Canadian Journal of Psychiatry* 31 (1986): 818-23.

Braverman, A.M., A.S. Boxer, S.L. Corson, C. Coutifaris and A, Hendrix. "Characteristics and Attitudes of Parents of Children Born with the Use of Assisted Reproductive Technology." *Fertility and Sterility* 70 (1998): 860-65.

Brewaeys, A. "Donor Insemination, the Effect on Family and Child Development." *Journal of Psychosomatic Obstetrics and Gynecology* 17 (1996): 1-13.

-- "Review: Parent-Child Relationships and Child Development in Donor Insemination Families." *Human Reproduction* Update 7 (2001): 38-46.

-- S. Golombok, N. Naaktgeboren, J.K. de Bruyn and E.V. van Hall. "Donor Insemination: Dutch Parents' Opinions about Confidentiality and Donor Anonymity and the Emotional Adjustment of Their Children." *Human Reproduction* 12 (1997): 1591-97.

Casey, P., J. Readings, L. Blake, V. Jadva and S. Golombok. "Child Development and Parent-Child Relationships in Surrogacy, Egg Donation and Donor Insemination Families at Age 7." Paper, presented at the 24th Annual Meeting of the European Society of Human Reproduction and Embryology (ESHRE), Barcelona, Spain, July 2008.

Colpin, H. and S. Soenen. "Parenting and Psychosocial Development of IVF Children: A Follow-Up Study." *Human Reproduction* 17 (2002): 1116-23.

Cook, R., S. Golombok, A. Bish and C. Murray. "Disclosure of Donor Insemination: Parental Attitudes." *American Journal of Orthopsychiatry* 65 (1995): 549-59.

Daniels, K.R. and K. Taylor. "Secrecy and Openness in Donor Insemination." *Politics and the Life Sciences* 12 (1993): 155-170.

Durna, E.M., J. Bebe, S.J. Steigrad, L. Leader and D.G. Garrett. "Donor Insemination: Attitudes of Parents towards Disclosure." *Medical Journal of Australia* 167 (1997): 256-59.

Golombok, Susan. "Parenting and Secrecy Issues Related to Children of Assisted Reproduction." *Journal of Assisted Reproduction and Genetics* 14 (1997): 375-78.

-- A. Brewaeys, R. Cook, M.T. Giavazzi, D. Guerra, A. Mantovani, E. van Hall, P.G. Crosignani and S. Dexeus. "The European Study of Assisted Reproduction Families: Family Functioning and Child Development." *Human Reproduction* 11 (1996): 2324-31.

-- A. Brewaeys, M.T. Giavazzi, D. Guerra, F. MacCallum, J. Rust. "The European Study of Assisted Reproduction Families: The Transition to Adolescence." *Human Reproduction* 17 (2002):830-40.
-- E. Lycett, F. MacCallum, V. Jadva, C. Murray, J. Rust, H. Abdalla, J. Jenkins and R. Margara. "Parenting Children Conceived by Gamete Donation." *Journal of Family Psychology* 18 (2004): 443-52.
-- F. MacCallum, E. Goodman and M. Rutter. "Families with Children Conceived By Donor Insemination: A Follow-Up at Age Twelve." *Child Development* 73 (2002): 952-68.
-- S.C. Murray, V. Jadva, E. Lycett, F. MacCallum and J. Rust. "Non-Genetic and Non-Gestational Parenthood: Consequences for Parent-Child Relationships and the Psychological Well-Being of Mothers, Fathers and Children at Age 3." *Human Reproduction* 29 (2006): 1918-24.
Gottlieb, Claes, Othon Lalos and Frank Lindblad. "Disclosure of Donor Insemination to the Child: The Effect of Swedish Legislation on Couples' Attitudes." *Human Reproduction* 15 (2000): 2052-56.
Hershberger, P., S.C. Klock and R.B. Barnes. "Disclosure Decisions among Pregnant Women Who Received Donor Oocytes: A Phenomenological Study." *Fertility and Sterility* 87 (2007): 288-96.
Hunter, M., N. Salter-Ling and L. Glover. "Donor Insemination: Telling Children about Their Origins." *Child Psychology and Psychiatry Review* 5 (2000): 157-63.
Jadva, Vasanti, Tabitha Freeman, Wendy Kramer and Susan Golombok. "The Experiences of Adolescents and Adults Conceived by Sperm Donation: Comparisons by Age of Disclosure and Family Type." *Human Reproduction* 24 (2009): 1909-19.
Kirkman, M. "Parents' Contributions to the Narrative Identity of Offspring of Donor-Assisted Conception." *Social Science and Medicine* 57 (2003): 2229-42.
Klock, S. "The Controversy Surrounding Privacy or Disclosure among Donor Gamete Recipients." *Journal of Assisted Reproduction and Genetics* 14 (1997): 378-80.
Lalos, A., C. Gottlieb and O. Lalos. "Legislated Right for Donor-Insemination Children to Know Their Genetic Origin: A Study of Parental Thinking." *Human Reproduction* 22 (2007): 1759-68.
Lindblad, F., C. Gottlieb and O. Lalos. "To Tell or Not To Tell – What Parents Think about Telling Their Children that They Were Born Following Donor Insemination." *Journal of Psychosomatic Obstetrics and Gynecology* 21 (2000): 193-203.
Lycett, E., K. Daniels, R. Curson and S. Golombok. "School-Aged Children of Donor Insemination: A Study of Parents' Disclosing Patterns." *Human Reproduction* 20 (2005): 810-9.
MacCallum, Fiona and Susan Golombok. "Embryo Donation Families: Mothers' Decisions Regarding Disclosure of Donor Conception." *Human Reproduction* 22 (2007): 2888-95.
McWhinnie, A. "Families from Assisted Conception: Ethical and Psychological Issues." *Human Fertility* 3 (2000): 13-19.
-- "A Study of Parenting of IVF and DI Children." *Medical Law Review* 14 (1995): 501-508.

Murray, C. and S. Golombok. "Going it Alone: Solo Mothers and Their Infants Conceived by Donor Insemination." *American Journal of Orthopsychiatry* 75 (2005): 242-53.

Nachtigall, R.D., G. Becker, S.S. Quiroga and J.M. Tschann. "The Disclosure Decision: Concerns and Issues of Parents of Children Conceived Through Donor Insemination." *American Journal of Obstetrics and Gynecology* 178 (1998):1165-1170.

-- J.M. Tschann, S.S. Quiroga L. Pitcher and G. Becker. "Stigma, Disclosure, and Family Functioning among Parents of Children Conceived Through Donor Insemination." *Fertility and Sterility* 68 (1997): 83-89.

Owen, L. and S. Golombok. "Families Created by Assisted Reproduction: Parent-Child Relationships in Late Adolescence." *Journal of Adolescence* 32 (2009): 835-48.

Patrizio, Pasquale, Anna C. Mastroianni and Luigi Mastroianni. "Gamete Donation and Anonymity: Disclosure to Children Conceived with Donor Gametes Should be Optional." *Human Reproduction* 16 (2001): 2036-39.

Paul, M.S. and R. Berger. "Topic Avoidance and Family Functioning in Families Conceived with Donor Insemination." *Human Reproduction* 22 (2007): 2566-71.

Pearce, J.W. and T.D. Pezzot-Pearce. *Psychotherapy of Abused and Neglected Children.* 2nd ed. New York: The Guilford Press, 2007.

Rumball, Anna and Vivienne Adair. "Telling the Story: Parents' Scripts for Donor Offspring." *Human Reproduction* 14 (1999): 1392-99.

Sanschagrin, M.L., E.B. Humber, C.C. Speirs and S. Duder. "A Survey of Quebec Pediatricians' Attitudes toward Donor Insemination." *Clinical Pediatrics* 32 (1993): 226-30.

Scheib, J.E., M. Riordan and S. Rubins. "Adolescents with Open-Identity Sperm Donors: Reports from 12-17 Year Olds." *Human Reproduction* 20 (2005): 239-52

Shapiro, V.B., J.R. Shapiro and I.H. Paret. *Complex Adoption and Assisted Reproductive Technology: A Developmental Approach to Clinical Practice.* New York: The Guilford Press, 2001.

Shehab, D., J. Duff, L.A. Pasch, K. MacDougall, J.E. Scheib and R.D. Nachtigall. "How Parents Whose Children have been Conceived with Donor Gametes Make Their Disclosure Decision: Contexts, Influences, and Couple Dynamics." *Fertility and Sterility* 89 (2008): 179-87.

Shenfield, F. and S.J. Steele. "What are the Effects of Anonymity and Secrecy on the Welfare of the Child in Gamete Donation?" *Human Reproduction* 12 (1997): 392-95.

Snowden, R., G.D. Mitchell GD and E.M. Snowden. "AID and Secrecy." In *Artificial Reproduction: a Social Investigation.* London: George Allen and Unwin, 1983.

Sroufe, L.A., B. Egeland, E.A. Carlson EA and W.A. Collins. *The Development of the Person: The Minnesota Study of Risk and Adaptation from Birth to Adulthood.* New York: The Guilford Press, 2005.

Suess, G.J. and J. Sroufe. "Clinical Implications of the Development of the Person." *Attachment and Human Development* 7 (2005): 381-92.

Turner, A.J. and A. Coyle. "What Does it Mean to be a Donor Offspring? The Identity Experiences of Adults Conceived by Donor Insemination and the Implications for Counseling and Therapy." *Human Reproduction* 15 (2000): 2041-51.

Van den Akker, Olga. "A Review Of Family Donor Constructs: Current Research And Future Directions." *Human Reproduction* update 12 (2006): 91-101.

Vaughn, B.E. "Discovering Pattern in Developing Lives: Reflections on the Minnesota Study of Risk and Adaptation from Birth to Adulthood." *Attachment and Human Development* 7 (2005): 369-80.

Wendland, C.L., F. Byrn and C. Hill. "Donor Insemination: A Comparison of Lesbian Couples, Heterosexual Couples and Single Women." *Fertility and Sterility* 65 (1996): 764-70.

Notes

1 Sanschagrin and others, "A Survey of Quebec Pediatricians' Attitudes," 226-30.
2 Berger and others, "Psychological Patterns in Donor Insemination Couples," 818-23.
3 Berger and others, see note 2 above; Brewaeys, "Donor Insemination," 1-13; Braverman and others, "Characteristics and Attitudes of Parents," 860-865; Gottlieb, Lalos and Lindblad, "Disclosure of Donor Insemination to the Child," 2052-56; Brewaeys, "Review," 38-46; Colpin and Soenen, "Parenting and Psychosocial Development of IVF Children," 1116-1123; Lycett and others, "School-Aged Children of Donor Insemination," 810-9; Jadva and others, "Experiences of Adolescents and Adults Conceived by Sperm Donation," 1909-19; Owen and Golombok, "Families Created by Assisted Reproduction," 835-48.
4 Golombok and others, "European Study of Assisted Reproduction Families," 2324-31.
5 *Ibid.*, 830-840.
6 Gottlieb, Lalos and Lindblad, see note 3 above.
7 Ibid.
8 MacCallum and Golombok, "Embryo Donation Families," 2888-95.
9 Durna and others, "Donor Insemination," 256-59.
10 Gottlieb, Lalos and Lindblad, see note 3 above.
11 Golombok and others, "Parenting Children Conceived by Gamete Donation," 443-52.
12 Golombok and others, "Non-Genetic and Non-Gestational Parenthood," 1918-24.
13 Casey and others, "Child Development and Parent-Child Relationships in Surrogacy, Egg Donation and Donor Insemination Families at Age 7," (paper, presented at 24th Annual Meeting of the European Society of Human Reproduction and Embryology, Barcelona, Spain, July, 2008).
14 Gottlieb, Lalos and Lindblad, see note 3 above.
15 *Ibid.*
16 *Ibid.*
17 Daniels and Taylor, "Secrecy and Openness in Donor Insemination," 155-170; Snowden, Mitchell and Snowden, "AID and secrecy" in *Artificial Reproduction: A Social Investigation.*
18 Snowden, Mitchell and Snowden, see note 17 above.
19 Nachtigall and others, "Stigma, Disclosure and Family Functioning," 83-89.
20 Cook and others, "Disclosure of Donor Insemination," 549-59; Shenfield and Steele, "What are the Effects of Anonymity and Secrecy?" 392-95.
21 Shenfield and Steele, see note 20 above; Patrizio, Mastroianni and Mastroianni, "Gamete Donation and Anonymity," 2036-39.
22 Lycett and others, see note 3 above; Golombok and others, see note 11 above; Golombok and others, see note 12 above; Rumball and Adair, "Telling the Story," 1392-99; Hunter, Salter-Ling and Glover, "Donor Insemination," 157-53; Lindblad, Gottlieb and Lalos, "To Tell or Not to Tell," 193-203; Lalos, Gottlieb and Lalos, "Legislated Right for Donor-Insemination Children to Know Their Genetic Origin," 1759-68.
23 Lycett and others, see note 3 above; Golombok and others, see note 11 above; Golombok and others, see note 12 above; Cook and others, see note 20 above; Lindblad, Gottlieb and Lalos, see note 22 above; Lalos, Gottlieb and Lalos, see note 22 above; McWhinnie, "Families from

Assisted Conception," 13-19; McWhinnie, "A Study of Parenting of IVF and DI Children," 501-508; Kirkman, "Parents' Contributions to Narrative Identity," 2229-42.
24 Cook and others, see note 20 above; Lindblad, Gottlieb and Lalos, see note 22 above; Wendland, Byrn and Hill, "Donor Insemination," 764-70.
25 Wendland, Byrn and Hill, see note 24 above.
26 *Ibid.*
27 Brewaeys and others, "Donor Insemination," 1591-97; Wendland, Byrn and Hill, see note 24 above.
28 Jadva and others, see note 3 above.
29 *Ibid.*
30 Brewaeys, "Review," 38-46; Colpin and Soenen, see note 3 above; Nachtigall and others, see note 19 above; Murray and Golombok, "Going it Alone," 242-53.
31 Kirkman, see note 23 above; Turner and Coyle, "What Does It Mean to Be a Donor Offspring?" 2041-51.
32 Scheib, Riordan and Rubins, "Adolescents with Open-Identity Sperm Donors," 239-52.
33 Jadva and others, see note 3 above.
34 Golombok and others, "Families with Children Conceived by Donor Insemination," 952-68.
35 Jadva and others, see note 3 above; Kirkman, see note 31 above.
36 Rumball and Adair, see note 22 above; Kirkman, see note 23 above.
37 Braverman and others, see note 3 above.
38 Paul and Berger, "Topic Avoidance and Family Functioning," 2566-71.
39 *Ibid.*
40 McWhinnie, see note 23 above.
41 Brewaeys, "Review," 38-46.
42 Shapiro, Shapiro and Paret, *Complex Adoption and Assisted Reproductive Technology*.
43 Vaughn, "Discovering Pattern in Developing Lives," 369-80, Suess and Sroufe, "Clinical Implications of the Development of the Person," 381-92; Sroufe and others, *The Development of the Person*.
44 Pearce and Pezzot-Pearce, *Psychotherapy of Abused Children*.
45 Shapiro, Shapiro and Paret, see note 42 above.
46 *Ibid.*
47 Berger and others, see note 2 above; Shehab and others, "How Parents Whose Children have been Conceived with Donor Gametes Make Their Disclosure Decision," 179-97; Hershberger, Klock And Barnes, "Disclosure Decisions among Pregnant Women who Received Donor Oocytes," 288-96; Van Der Akker, "A Review of Family Donor Constructs," 91-101.
48 Golombok, "Parenting and Secrecy Issues," 375-78.
49 Klock, "The Controversy Surrounding Privacy or Disclosure," 378-80.
50 Brewaeys, "Review," 38-46.
51 Durna and others, see note 9 above.
52 Berger and others, see note 2 above; Klock, see note 49 above.

Chapter Thirteen
Identity Development In The Donor-Conceived

Jean Benward

1. Introduction

This chapter discusses the concept of identity formation in psychological development. It argues that lack of knowledge of, and lack of access to, one's progenitors presents serious obstacles to identity formation in the donor-conceived. The chapter concludes with recommendations.

2. Identity Formation

2.1 Definition

Identity formation is a universal psychological task in development that starts in early childhood and continues throughout adulthood.[1] At its simplest, identity-creation answers the question, "Who am I?" Identity is the combination of personal and social attributes by which we define ourselves. It provides a sense of self, purpose, and place in the larger community. In creating identity, one asks questions about how one is alike or different from others, about belonging, about rootedness and about one's place in a larger genealogical lineage. Successful or workable identity formation provides an individual with a sense of well being, belonging and self-mastery.

2.2 Origins of Identity Formation Theory

The theoretical basis for understanding identity formation was pioneered by Eric H. Erikson, developmental psychologist and psychoanalyst. Erikson asserted that identity consists of three essential parts: (1) biological – knowledge of one's origins; (2) psychological – the internal sense of self; and (3) cultural – the adoption of beliefs and values from the larger community. Erikson described identity formation as "a process located in the core of the individual and yet also in the core of his communal culture."[2] For Erikson, identity is an understanding of one's self and of one's place not only within a system of social relations but also in genealogical relationships.

2.2.1 Mirroring

In emphasizing the relational component of identity, psychologists have often used the metaphor of the "mirror."[3] Without a mirror, one cannot see or recognize oneself. Psychologist Heinz Kohut, for example, contended that our sense of self depends on what others, our family and community, reflect back: what they know, say and feel about us.[4] To paraphrase Erikson, I see myself the ways others perceive me.[5] For the donor-conceived, an essential piece of the mirror needed for identity formation is missing:[6] the information that exists in genetic heritage and resemblance and in genetic continuity and family history.

2.2.1.1 Genetic Heritage and Resemblance

One's genetic heritage is evident in one's appearance, temperament, interests, abilities and other traits. In this sense, biologically based experiences of the self are core parts of one's identity.

People deprived of knowledge of their progenitors – whether because of adoption or donor conception – have lost this important component of self-knowledge.[7] Identity is a story, a narrative of our personal history and what it means. David Gollancz describes his donor conception as a "half hidden story in the genes, that story which we cannot read but whose narrative will inescapably unfold in our own lifetimes and be passed to our own children."[8] The absence of a mirror and the opportunity to see oneself in one's biological ties hinders identity formation for the donor-conceived.

2.2.1.2 Resemblance Talk

The psychological importance of genetic resemblance is evident and amplified in what anthropologist Gaylene Becker calls "resemblance talk."[9] Adults look at children for their resemblance to other family members in appearance, attitudes and behavior, and they talk to children and others in the community about such resemblances. Family resemblance talk communicates many things our family "knows" about us, and how we are like both our current relatives and our ancestors.[10]

2.2.1.3 Genetic Continuity and Family History

Family resemblance talk reveals the importance our culture places on knowing our place in the generations of ancestors preceding us. Gametes from the donor contribute half of a person's genetic identity, and they represent links from one generation to the next.

Because people conceived with donor gametes typically have no or little information about their genetic origins,[11] they have lost the sense of resemblance to half of their immediate family, extended family and ancestors. The loss of opportunity to see their resemblance to genetic relatives deprives them of a major element in identity formation.

2.2.1.4 Pain caused by loss of family resemblance

The denial of this important opportunity to see oneself reflected in family can create emotional pain for the donor-conceived. Erikson claimed that identity formation proceeds smoothly "except where inner conditions and outer circumstance combine to aggravate a painful [...] identity-consciousness."[12] The reports of donor-conceived adults, who have no access to their genetic origins, echo Erikson's description of the painful identity consciousness. Unable to meet the donor or to obtain information about the donor, they describe a sense of genetic discontinuity, sadness, and frustration. They wish for more information about the donor and the donor's identity.[13] The lack of donor information and the inability to see oneself reflected in biological ties creates an ongoing sense of grief and isolation.[14] The absence of genetic origins information can create an ongoing obstacle to answer the question, "Who am I?" and "Where do I belong?"

One donor-conceived person describes the implications of a genetic mirror's absence in this way:

> When children are told they have father's eyes, mother's laugh, grandma's strength, they build a strong internal impression of themselves. When you are raised in family with different genetic origins, nobody tells you that you have dad's eyes. The face in the mirror does not belong to anyone.[15]

The loss of genetic information disrupts the creation of an identity and leaves pieces of the donor-conceived person's identity missing.

In their rearing families, the donor-conceived can find it difficult to ignore the resemblance talk around them: "Who do you look like?", "From whom did you get that trait?" The absence of resemblance talk creates a loss of self:

> I remember examining my hands and face in the mirror seeking physical evidence of this ... biological father's presence, and being fascinated ... that half of me was unknown. I also felt sadness and frustration....[16]

3. Effect of absent information on identity formation and secrecy

The struggle to cope with the loss of genetic connection and to create a coherent identity story repeats over the life cycle. The loss of genetic connection of the donor-conceived is passed on to yet a third generation and is one that they must share with their children. A donor-conceived woman explained,

> Sometimes when I look at [my children] I see mannerisms and physical details such as the shape of their eyes, and they look strange to me. I realize then that these are characteristics inherited from a grandfather they will never know.[17]

Given the importance of the genetic mirror in identity formation, people who are denied knowledge of their donor not only struggle to create their own identity narrative, the loss of genetic information disrupts the sense of genetic continuity in the generations that follow them.

In addition to experiencing the loss of three aspects of identity (genetic resemblance, resemblance talk, and genetic continuity), donor-conceived people experience also the secrecy and shame that has surrounded their conception and that can intensify the "painful identity consciousness." The pain of secrecy is a frequent theme among many persons conceived by donor insemination. Even if parents tell their donor-conceived adults the truth, the shame and the long years of silence can make it difficult to communicate in the family about the donor conception. One donor-conceived woman reports, "My family is open … but only now. For 12 years they carried a secret which ate away at their hearts and mind."[18]

The secrecy creates obstacles to the exploration of self and the meaning of one's donor conception. The absence of information about the donor, or the possibility of meeting the donor, coupled with the stigma of donor conception and their parents' fears about the donor result in multiple levels of loss, missing pieces of identity and self.[19]

Donor-conceived people realize that resemblance talk both reflects the expectation of a genetic connection between parent and child, and it reinforces the legitimacy of the child as part of the family. The donor-conceived who were not told of their donor conception report a sense of not belonging fully in their family. They notice not just what their parents say but also what they do not say, and, from this silence, they sense something is different about their status in their family. Using psychoanalyst Christopher Bollas' concept of the "unthought known" – that which we know or have a sense for but cannot think about – psychologist Diane Ehrensaft posits that the donor-conceived subliminally know about their donor conception.[20] Ehrensaft describes the case of 15-year-old David who "reported that 'I feel like Dad and I are from different planets'. Later when told about his donor conception, he says, 'I was wondering if I sort of knew this without knowing it.'"[21] An adult donor-conceived person also found the revelation of the truth to be a confirmation of what she had known all along:

> At age 41, I received a letter from my mother informing me that I had been conceived by donor insemination. ... In the instant I read the truth, I felt enormous relief. ... I was vindicated in my long held assumption that I was not the person I had been led to believe I was.[22]

Furthermore, the family's secrecy about donor conception can lead to traumatic disclosure and intensified loss. Adults who are told of their donor-conceived status after years of secrecy and denial, commonly report feelings that include grief, anger, a sense of not belonging, and a sense of an incomplete identity.[23]

Faced with a sudden and unexpected disclosure of her donor conception, a woman explains, "[I was] experiencing the death of a version of myself and, in particular, the death of myself in relation to my father: the death of that relationship."[24]

4. Absence of Information is An Identity Loss

People who are denied knowledge of their donor not only struggle to create their identity but struggle to cope with bereavement stemming from the loss of a meaningful link in their genetic origins. The historical lack of recognition of the loss and lack of social support of the donor-conceived's loss of genetic identity have contributed to unrecognized and ongoing mourning.

4.1 Unrecognized Nature of the Loss

The loss of knowledge of one's progenitor is a loss that is exacerbated by the way in which society fails to recognize the significant nature of the loss. Until recently, the donor-conceived have had few opportunities for sharing their loss and thus having the loss validated. This results in an invisible grief or what grief specialist Kenneth Doka called a hidden sorrow, "a disenfranchised grief",[25] losses that are negated by society and viewed as non-losses.

Those whose psychological relationships are not recognized experience disenfranchised grief. In examining the impact of disenfranchised grief on the donor-conceived, social scientist Joanna Rose quotes from Evelyn Burns Robinson's work on grief and adoption, "The mourners whose grief is disenfranchised are [...] cut off from ... social supports and ... have few opportunities to express and resolve their feelings."[26] If their families, infertility treatment providers and the larger social institutions that control access to donor information do not recognize a donor-conceived person's loss, then the donor-conceived can live in a state of chronic sorrow.

Donor-conceived persons have described their personal encounters with disenfranchised grief and the refusal of others to recognize their feelings. For example, one woman said, "My mother told us about the sperm donor and said she thought that would be the end of it. *She expected us to not have any feelings about it.* [emphasis added]"[27] Another explains: "Dad doesn't want to speak about it. Mum sometimes will, other times not. *She just wants me to forget it* [emphasis added]."[28]

4.1.1 Unrecognized Grief can Lead to Pain and Isolation

Donor-conceived people report difficulty in finding a place to talk about their experiences, even with other donor-conceived persons.[29] "No one has questioned us, nor provided support for us. We cannot even talk about it with other children of donor insemination."[30] One person noted that shame can inhibit donor-conceived people from talking to others. Some express frustration that they are not supposed to speak about their feelings with family members:

> For 16 years, I have known. My mum told me, my dad was embarrassed, and no one other than my parents knew. The topic was taboo and I was not to tell friends or family. To this day, I still have not been able to discuss it at all with my dad, nor with my sister (also conceived by donor insemination).[31]

The unrecognized loss is compounded by powerlessness "because others control the information about an essential aspect of self."[32] Psychologist Amanda Turner describes the problem that secrecy in donor conception presents to the donor-conceived, "When self disclosure becomes difficult, it can limit the choice of interpersonal coping strategies. Isolation cuts down the possibility of forming social support networks."[33]

4.1.2. Meeting Other Donor-Conceived People and Sharing Common Loss Can Contribute to Healing

Sociologist, Erving Goffman, in discussing responses to stigma, describes how people join with others of the same status to give voice to their experience.[34] In their journey to construct or reconstruct an identity, the donor-conceived find themselves longing to share their donor-conception story with others, to develop supportive relationships and to make meaning of their experience. One donor-conceived person explained, "I was amazed … at the openness and strong feelings that were being shared via email, by so many donor offspring worldwide."[35] Powerless to obtain information about their genetic origins, and facing both denial of their experience and ongoing loss, the donor-conceived individual must create and tell his or her own story to restore his sense of wholeness. One adult man describes a stage in his life when he started to speak for himself:

> [I]t turned out to be an enormously healing step. First, I was saying I own this. Second, I was 45 and it was one of the first times I really felt like a person.[36]

Another woman reports,

> "I hope that through my experiences others will realise that they are not alone and [that there are people] who are in a position to help us gain an insight into our isolation."[37]

To quote psychoanalyst, Dori Laub, "No one finds peace in silence."[38]

As described and discussed elsewhere in this volume by Harris and Shanner,[39] the community of donor-conceived has connected in various groups on the internet,[40] in forums sponsored by institutions[41] and in donor conception support networks. The sites reflect the need for validation and a voice, as they permit the donor-conceived to share their losses, quandaries, and begin to understand their identity. One donor-conceived person reported:

> My quest began a little over a year ago, and what a surprising, intense experience it has been. The Internet has been an invaluable tool. It has allowed me to communicate with others … who live across the globe. I have been amazed at how incredibly open people have been in sharing such personal, detailed stories of their own.[42]

5. Identity Formation and Searching for Genetic Relatives

In attempting to deal with the loss of genetic identity, donor-conceived persons seek more than information about the donor. They search for a better sense of themselves by knowing the persons to whom they are genetically related, both the donor and half-siblings.

5.1 Searching For the Donor

As was true previously for adoption, a growing number of donor-conceived people have begun to search for their donor. The task can be overwhelming, exhausting and frustrating. One woman reported that:

> Despite several hundred hours invested in my search, letters to 450 male graduates from my biological father's medical school, responses from 100 men from the yearbooks, and numerous negative DNA tests, for now I will continue to communicate to my biological father only … in my dreams."[43]

In addition to bearing the frustration of not finding one's progenitor, donor-conceived people can find the responses of infertility treatment providers to be deceptive and uncaring:

> I wrote several letters to my mother's physician. He replied he was searching for my information. … When I asked again, he said, "it seems that I misplaced it."[44]

The donor-conceived can experience the search for their progenitor as hopeless. "Some days I feel impassioned to find the answers, other days I feel beaten and think why bother. What's the use?"[45]

5.2. Searching for Genetic Siblings

The wish for genetic understanding of "self" is evident also in the desire of the donor-conceived to meet genetic siblings. For many, the search for genetic siblings is as important as meeting their donors.[46]

> Perhaps if I could find my half siblings, then this urge to see my other traits accounted for would be somewhat alleviated.[47]

Meeting a genetic relative can be a healing and meaningful experience. One donor-conceived person described it thus:

> You get to see a bit of yourself in the mirror. You get to see a bit of familiarity. And I think that's really important.[48]

Another commented on the nature of the relationship that can develop:

> Maybe it's because I know he's my half brother, and the knowledge gives me permission to trust him at a certain level. Or maybe there is some bond between us that I instinctively know. Certainly there is something about mirrors and seeing yourself in others.[49]

5.3 Rethinking the Family and Genetic Relationships Would Help the Donor-Conceived in Their Identity Formation

The relatively narrow view of family currently in the ascendance in North America is at the heart of one of the challenges the donor-conceived face in identity formation. A broader paradigm of extended kinship would allow donor-conceived individuals to create an identity that acknowledges different kinds of attachments – genetic and non-genetic.

The relative narrowness of our cultural understandings of family can be seen in relation to the diversity described by cultural anthropologists. Cultures vary widely in types of family constellations, in relationships among kin and in the different terms for kin. Based on research in South-East Asian communities, anthropologist Carsten reports that children are able to accept knowledge about their birth parentage while experiencing a parentage within a kinship system that does not include biological ties.[50] Children can grow in diverse family structures with attachments to both genetic and non-genetic kin. It seems reasonable and supportive to the donor-conceived to accept that their kinship system, a basis for identity, would include both their genetic relatives including their donor and donor siblings, and their non-genetic relatives such as their parents.[51]

6. Recommendations Regarding Disclosure and Identity Development

Disclosure[52] of donor conception has the potential to be either constructive or destructive. The donor-conceived response to learning about their origins will vary depending on the age of the donor-conceived person, how much information is available about the donor, and how supportive and understanding are their family and social networks.[53]

6.1 Non Disclosure in Childhood Can Lead to Traumatic Disclosure in Adulthood

The circumstances of disclosure appear to be critical factors in how the donor-conceived construct their identity. Particularly relevant are factors such as parental unwillingness to disclose, the age at which the donor-conceived person learned the circumstances of his or her conception, and the circumstances of disclosure. Most donor-conceived persons who are adults today were not reared with knowledge of their donor-conception. Many learned the truth only as adults and often in a traumatic way.[54] Such unexpected or sudden disclosure is disruptive and can lead to the destruction of the identity that the donor-conceived adult has already developed.[55]

> When my father told me the truth back in 1965, I felt as though someone was standing in front of me, tearing up my autobiography page by page. Of course, all the things in my story had happened – but the "me" to whom they had happened was not the me who had been telling himself the story."[56]

6.2 Recommendations for Early Disclosure with Attention to the Child's Perspective

Current research tends to reinforce the argument for early disclosure as a support for identity development.[57] Telling from a young age enables children to incorporate their donor conception into their sense of identity, rather than requiring a traumatic adjustment of their established sense of self.[58] Early disclosure has been associated with better outcomes: a more positive response, greater acceptance and comfort with their donor conception, and satisfaction that their parents had been honest.[59] Adolescents reared with knowledge of their donor conception report greater comfort with their donor conception than those who discovered at 18 or over.[60]

Early disclosure nonetheless reveals the difficulty that both professionals and parents have recognizing the donor as a biological fact or acknowledging that some connections exists between the parents, their children and the donor.[61] Some children's books do not reference the donor at all, instead referring to seeds and cells.[62]

These early stories also contain the potential for later division between the parents and their children in the meaning each attaches to the genetic connection with the donor.[63] Some of these early stories about seeds and cells or the 'gene lady' discount the possibility that the donor-conceived person may have more substantial feelings about the donor, who is not seeds but a person.[64] As Kirkman argues, "The relative contribution of genes and relationships to meaning varies not only among participants as a whole but for individual people according to time and circumstances."[65]

7. Disclosure and Identity Formation in Childhood

How might young donor-conceived people integrate this information into their sense of self in a positive and non-traumatic way? Drawing upon the reports of parents, the donor-conceived and the psychological literature, I propose the following path.

7.1 Early Childhood (ages 2-5)

If allowed to process the story according to their own development needs, young children will create a narrative where both the donor and the parent are part of their story. Early in their young lives, these children work on figuring out where to "put" the donor and how to integrate him or her into their story.

Young children make social maps of their world and can imagine the donor as part of their world. For example, three and one half year-old Max asked his mother as they sat down to lunch, "So, the donor's not coming, right?"[66] Another mother's story describes how her 5-year-old son drew a picture of his family and included the donor:

> Adam (5) was ... making a Mother's Day Card. He had drawn people on the front, inside and on the back of the card. Inside he drew a picture of himself, his mother, his father and two sisters. His mother asks who the man on the front is: "He's the guy who gave you sperm."[67]

An example given by one mother illustrates how the child's identification with and love for her mother is interwoven with her conception story:

> I have been telling my three-year-old daughter as a bedtime story ... we were reading and she began to tell me that when she grew up, she would find a nice lady to give her some eggs, and that they would be mixed with daddy's sperm, and then would be put in her belly to grow into a baby. She said that she wanted to have babies the same way that I had her.[68]

7.2 Early School Years (ages 6-12)

During the early school years, children continue to work on the donor construct and express a wider range of feelings and questions. Their concerns and comments can express a high degree of sophistication, emotional sensitivity and problem solving. They can grasp that there was a time when they did not exist, and they can see themselves in relation to others.[69]

One boy wanted to know, "How does the sperm get out?"[70] School-aged children can also show empathy toward their parents. For example, six-year-old Jack came up with an altruistic solution to his dad's infertility, "I've got a good idea, Daddy. If you have not got any sperm, you can have some of mine."[71] An eight-year-old boy asked, "Did that make daddy sad?"[72]

Children can understand that conception requires sperm and eggs but be uncertain as to how it all works. As children grow, their concept of the donor broadens, as does their understanding of their connection to the donor. Consider these words of a nine-year-old girl named Lisa:

> I was born in my mom's uterus, but I was born from another lady's egg. My mom's hair is brown, my dad's hair is black and … mine is blond. The … reason is that the lady that made the egg that I was born from … her hair was blond, like mine. So, I have my dad's "chubby" cheeks, my mom's curly hair and the lady's blond hair.[73]

From children's stories, we can see that the donor starts to exist as both an inner figure and a physical reality. During this period of development, children express their thoughts and feelings about the donor: "We should buy that man a present",[74] "I call him a friend. … He helped us. … That's what friends do."[75] Meagan wanted to know why the donor 'gave away his sperm.' "She said it was important [to know] because she would be able to tell her children and they could pass on that knowledge to their children."[76]

Elementary school age children have a growing sense that genetics and physical similarity are part of the meaning of donor conception. They begin to explore how genetics plays a part in their personal story, for example, in these ways:

> I think I am so bright because of the man who gave us sperm.
> 4 → 8-year-old boy[77]
> Why don't I look like you? Hannah looks like her mother.
> 5 → 10-year-old girl[78]

Children can express an interest in having more information about the donor at this stage. They can ask what the donor looks like and wonder if they can meet him or her as they explore what the donor's genetic contribution means for them.[79] They continue to create a sense of both who this person is and who they are in relation to this person. For example, children in this age group have asked:

> Do you have a picture of the donor?
> 6 → 10-year-old girl[80]
> Will I ever find out who is the donor?
> 7 → 11-year-old boy[81]
> Are you allowed to meet the donor?
> 8 → 9-year-old girl[82]
> What is her name?
> - 10-year-old girl.[83]

7.3 Junior High School Years (ages 11-15)

As young people move into late childhood and early adolescence, the genetic connection assumes new significance. Donor-conceived children wish to make sense of their attachments and to know who is related to whom. They can strive to understand what it means to have two connections: from the family they are born into and from genetics. They understand that in the larger culture, families are usually defined by genetic relationships. The children, as the adults, have no simple way to talk about genetics and relationships that does not assume parenthood is based on genetics. Using the given cultural framework, the young donor-conceived can attempt to clarify the genetic connection to the donor in juxtaposition with their connection to their parent. As Ehrensaft points out, children's musings reflect the child's self-exploration and not, as some fear, rejection of the parents.[84] Examples of such musings are:

> I am half adopted.
> $9 \rightarrow$ 10-year-old girl[85]
> Mom, technically speaking, you aren't my mother.
> $10 \rightarrow$ 12-year-old girl[86]
> Oh yes, it's almost like she is our-ex mother.
> $11 \rightarrow$ 10-year-old boy[87]

At this stage of late childhood and early adolescence, parents can help or impede the integration of these connections into a coherent sense of self. Consider Diane Ehrensaft's story of one mother and her egg donor-conceived daughter:

Alexandra, now 11, says "Mom I know you are my mom, but do you ever feel that I am not quite as much yours as I am Daddy's? Are you ever jealous that [the donor] is my 'real mother'?" This mother was able to listen to her daughter's questions, and answer truthfully and openly. The result was shared hugs and tears.[88]

Compare Alexandra's experience to that of an adult woman, Shirley: "Anything I try to discuss with Dad, he just does not want to talk about. He gets really angry."[89]

7.4 Late Adolescence

Adolescence brings identity development to the forefront. Like the adopted adolescent, the adolescent donor-conceived is in an unusual position when asking, "Who am I?" Both groups of adolescents are asking a two-part question:

not only who they are but also who they are in relation to their genetic origins. Those who achieve a workable identity at this age are likely to be those who learned the truth at an earlier age,[90] whose families have facilitated conversations about donor conception[91] and who have access to information about their donor.[92]

Adoption researcher, David M. Brodzinsky, stresses the importance of providing an "information rich" environment so that the adolescent's sense of adoptive identity is based on fact rather than fantasy or assumption.[93] While this is now considered best practice in adoption, parents in donor conception continue to be provided with inadequate amounts of information about their children's donors. The lack of information leaves their children at risk for "identity diffusion", feeling out of place or unable to pursue further identity building.

Searching for genetic relatives is now recognized as a healthy part of adoptive identity development. Social policies and social institutions have changed to support adoptees' wish for information and to meet their birth parents.[94] Yet the situation is far different for adolescent donor-conceived people, most of whom face the important task of constructing an identity with only limited and incomplete information.

7.5 Early Disclosure Does Not Prevent Loss or Remedy the Lack of Information Created by Donor Anonymity

In a qualitative research study of the donor-conceived, parents and donors, Kirkman concludes that despite the benefits of early disclosure, there is no guarantee that early disclosure will mitigate the grief that some people feel about permanent and irretrievable loss of genetic identity.[95] As one donor-conceived person said:

> As I grew older, however, the idea of anonymous and non-identity release donations became ... significantly more distressing, and the reality behind being a donor-conceived offspring began to hit.[96]

Among some donor-conceived teens, healthy identity formation requires not only early disclosure, but also the possibility of meeting the donor. A study of donor-conceived adolescents who had open-identity donors, reported that the large majority of the donor-conceived were comfortable with their conception. They had learned the truth about their conception before the age of 10. One commented, "I am curious as to what he is like and how he has changed from the papers that tell me of his life."[97] Others reported wanting to know what the donor was like and being curious about whether they shared their looks. Most of the teenagers reported that they would contact the donor because this would help them learn more about themselves.[98]

One such young adult had this experience:

> From age 10, says Christina, "I kept asking, 'When can I meet him?'"[99] When Christina turned 18, [the Sperm Bank gave her] her donor's name. She had questions about herself such as, "Why is she taller than most of her mother's family?", "Why is her sense of humor so different from her mother's?" Christina's first question to her donor was, "Do you have big feet?" When he said, "Yes," she shouted, "I knew it! That's where mine come from." Christina says she's been rewarded by a better understanding of that part of her she can learn about only from her donor. She describes their first meeting "We have a lot of the same features, a lot of the same personality traits. We have a lot of the same everything. It's uncanny." Her mother agrees.[100]

The history of secrecy, the frequency of late disclosure, and the absent information about their donor, mean that the struggle of most adult donor-conceived people alive today will be ongoing, perhaps for decades, as they deconstruct who they thought they were and reconstruct a new identity in the light of their donor-conceived status. Identity development in the donor-conceived is a process affected by developmental factors and context; it is life-long in scope.

8. Adoption Research and Donor-Conception

A unique study in adoption research looked at how adult adoptees described the ongoing task of identity formation in adulthood. The researchers noted distinct patterns, not necessarily linear, as the adoptees reported their efforts to find meaning in, or to reconstruct, their adoption experience. The researchers grouped these patterns into five phases: no awareness, emerging awareness, drowning in awareness, reemerging from awareness, finding peace.[101] Dunbar and Grotevant, in their research, identified similar patterns in the identity development of adolescent adoptees.[102]

8.1 Constructing the Meaning of Donor Conception and its Place in Their Identity is an Ongoing Process.

As with adult adoptees, the narratives of the adult donor-conceived suggest that they reconstruct the meaning of their donor-conceived status and its place in their identity, in an ongoing process.

> For some time, I didn't do much about this information. ... As I enter the middle of my life, I am now 36, I wonder about what it means for me. ... I have made some attempts to find out who the donor was.[103]

After having time to process the original information, awareness of identity issues may emerge in painful ways.

> I remember crying a lot because I had no one to talk to. I only told one of my friends. ... She was as shocked or more than me. ...[104]

A man, who discovered his conception 13 years previously, has not found either his donor or any genetic siblings. Now at mid life, he finds himself reaching for some sense of peace, "The only lingering emotion I have from ... disclosure ... is regret. I am no longer angry, confused, embarrassed, or relieved."[105]

In the end, the process of understanding the meaning of donor conception is probably a life-long process. As one donor-conceived man said:

> One summer evening ... when I was 12, my father ... explained that: I ... had been conceived using the sperm of an anonymous donor. That was the start of a long journey. I am 54 now; I have had the extraordinary experience of finding a number of half-siblings, ranging in age from their early 80s to their early 40s and living in the UK, US and Canada, all children of the same man; and I have had the privilege of meeting and sharing the stories of many, many people whose lives have been touched and shaped by ... donor conception.[106]

He concludes, decades after learning of his donor conception, "I am still making sense of what I was told that evening."[107]

8.2 The Donor-Conceived and the Role of Non-Genetic Parents in Identity.

Several dilemmas confront the donor-conceived on their path to identity formation. These include facing the loss of genetic connection, finding emotional support, overcoming the shame and secrecy associated with their conception, and deciding whether to learn more about their donor and genetic siblings. An additional task centers on understanding themselves in relation to their non-genetic parents. Individuals experience a continuity of self, a core ingredient in identity, in relationships to kin, which include both people who are biologically related and those who are not.

As they sort out their experiences of kinship and relatedness, donor-conceived people often deconstruct and re-construct the meaning of their relationships with their rearing parents. When they first learned about their origins, some donor-conceived people, primarily those learning at an older age, report feeling sadness, frustration and anger.

Kirkman reports the story of a donor-conceived person named, "Kelly":

> It was so painful to find out my dad had lied to me our whole life together about our true relationship and that he felt it was none of my business. I had to redevelop my sense of identity, because I wasn't the person I thought I was.[108]

Although donor-conceived people can experience alienation, pain, and anger, they can also reconcile themselves with the person who reared them:

> During the final five years of his life we became close at last. We spent many intimate hours alone together ... I began to feel like his true son. Our relationship [also] improved once I became a father myself.[109]

Another obstacle that donor-conceived people confront in forming an identity is the fact that they can find that their experience of kinship and relatedness is at odds with the dominant culture which expects that "blood" relationships are the "real ones". Rather than seeing all the donor-conceived's relationships – genetic and non-genetic – as kinship relations, the larger culture continues to interpret one form of relatedness as superior to another and to expect the donor-conceived to see one parent as the "real parent".

In the understanding of self and family, donor-conceived people attach significance to bonds formed by genetics and by relationships. They describe emotional and psychological connections to donor and parent. They want and need to have both bonds, without rejecting one in favour of the other.

One donor-conceived adult reports:

> Throughout life when people ask, "Who's your real father?", I ... stop ... and say, "My real father is the man who raised me." That's real to me ... There's a sperm donor and a ... father and these roles both exist.[110]

Other donor-conceived people report:

> In spite of her profound regret that she does not know the identity of her donor, she wanted to convey, "How much I feel [that I am] my father's daughter

because of all the things I see in myself that he gave me, through environment, though not through genetics'".[111]

So I have come full circle, I suppose: once again, I believe that family is about so much more than blood.[112]

Identity formation is a life-long developmental process that is affected by changing perspectives and is shaped by context. Early disclosure appears best for the young donor-conceived and supports identity integration at normal stages of childhood development. The child's understanding of the donor will vary with the stage of development, changing over time. Likewise, children will evaluate and reconstruct their relationships with their parents. Even with early disclosure, however, lack of donor information may be a serious impediment to identity resolution.

Factors that facilitate the creation of a workable identity include family comfort with open discussion rather than avoidance of the subject, sensitivity of family members and of significant others to the psychological importance of the donor, the provision of social support, the availability of substantial information about the donor; and information from the donor directly.

9. Conclusion

Donor conception raises important questions about its effect on the identity development of the donor-conceived. The multiple historical and institutional forces that have surrounded donor conception have led to secrecy, donor anonymity, lack of preservation of the information about donors, and lack of access to donors by their offspring. In recent years, the donor-conceived have questioned the closed system of gamete donation and the imbalance in power relations between providers and donor-conceived families. As the larger culture has become more open about donor conception, the narratives and personal accounts of the donor-conceived have served to focus attention on their identity needs. Gamete donation is now understood to have ongoing psychological meaning in the lives of the donor-conceived[113] with long-term impacts.[114]

A number of measures could ease the difficulty of identity formation for the donor-conceived: (1) Recognition of the emotional losses created by lack of donor information; (2) Provision of social and emotional support for the donor-conceived; (3) Preservation of donor information; and (4) Enabling access to the donor. The achievement of these goals will necessarily require decreased institutional paternalism and increased autonomy for the donor-conceived.

Because past decisions by infertility treatment providers and parents cannot be unmade, most donor-conceived people and their families must live without essential knowledge about the donor. However, for future generations, things can change. Providing identifiable donors, and preserving extensive donor information strongly supports identity development in the donor-conceived. Providing the donor-conceived access to their donors would recognize the biological kinship connections of the donor-conceived and would not negate the meaning of their relationships with their non-genetic parents. Providing access to donors would also recognize that identity develops through multiple sources for the donor-conceived.

Although the debate about whether to remove donor anonymity will continue, it is also clear that an increasing number of donor-conceived people are finding and meeting genetic relatives, usually with little help from the institutions and treatment providers that make donor conception possible.[115] The question now is how and when policy and lawmakers, and reproductive health professionals will recognize and support the need of the donor-conceived for information about, and contact with, their donors and genetic siblings. It is up to them to explain why they have created a system that creates such obstacles to identity development for the donor-conceived. As one donor-conceived person argues, the burden of justifying the current system rests on those who would maintain it,

> I have often wondered why the people fighting for a system based on honesty, openness, and trust are the ones having to explain themselves. Why aren't those who want to continue the present system of secrets, lies, and deception called upon to justify themselves?[116]

Bibliography

Aldgate, J. et al., editors "The Developing World of the Child", Jessica Kingsley, 2006.
Allen, D. "The future of donor conception: where do we go from here?" In *The Infertility Network. Conference proceedings*, Toronto, Canada, 2006.
Allen, P. "I find myself wondering." In *Let the Offspring Speak: Discussions on donor conception*. Sydney: The Donor Conception Group of Australia, 1997.
Becker, G., A. Butler and R.D. Nachtigall. "Resemblance talk: A challenge for parents whose children were offspring with donor gametes in the US." *Social Science and Medicine* 61 (2005): 1300-9.
"Becky's Story," Donor Conception Network, 2006, www.dcnetwork.org/beckysjourney finding sibs.htm.

Bennett, S. "The emotional and biological consequences of DI." In *Let the Offspring Speak: Discussions on Donor Conception.* Sydney: The Donor Conception Group of Australia, 1997.

Bernstein, A. *Flight of the Stork.* Indianapolis: Perspectives Press, 1994.

Botsford, J.S. "A personal story of Blood and Belonging," Donor Conception Network, 2000, http://www.donor-conception-network.org/offspring2.htm.http://www.donor-conception-network.org/offspring2.htm.http://www.donor-conception-network.org/offspring2.htm.

Brodzinsky, D. "Family structural openness and communication openness as predictors in the adjustment of adopted children." *Adoption Quarterly* 9, no. 4 (2006): 1-18.

Cahn, N. "Necessary subjects: the need for a mandatory national donor gamete registry." *DePaul Journal of Health Care Law* 12, no. 1 (2009): 203-223.

Canada. Standing Senate Committee on Human Rights. *Proceedings of the Standing Senate Committee on Human Rights* (2006), Issue 10 – Evidence (B. Stevens), http://www.parl.gc.ca/39/1/parlbus/commbus/senate/Com-e/huma-e/10ev-e.htm?Language=E&Parl=39&Ses=1&comm_id=77.

Carsten, J. "Kinship and the identity of the child: a perspective from anthropology." In *Truth and the Child 10 years on: information exchange in donor assisted conception,* E. Blyth, M. Crawshaw and J. Speirs, eds. Birmingham: British Association of Social Workers, 1998.

http://www.people.com/people/archive/article/0,20140544,00.html.

http://www.washingtonpost.com/wp-dyn/content/article/2006/12/15/AR2006121501820.htmlhttp://www.people.com/people/archive/article/0,20140544,00.htmlCordray, W. "The need for self identity." In *Let the Offspring Speak: Discussions on Donor Conception.* Sydney: The Donor Conception Group of Australia, 1997.

Daniels, K. *Building a Family: with the Assistance of Donor Insemination.* Palmerston North: Dunmore Press, 2004.

-- and L. Meadows. "Sharing information with adults conceived as a result of donor insemination." *Human Fertility* 9 (2006): 93-99.

-- and P Thorn Toward a family-building approach to donor insemination. *J Obstet Gynaecol Can.* 24(2):125-6.

http://www.ncbi.nlm.nih.gov/sites/entrez?Db=pubmed&Cmd=Search&Term=http://www.ncbi.nlm.nih.gov/sites/entrez?Db=pubmed&Cmd=Search&Term=Doka, K.J., ed. *Disenfranchised grief: Recognizing hidden sorrow.* Lanham: Lexington Books/D. C. Heath and Co., 1989.

Dovido, J, B. Major and J. Crocker. "Stigma: introduction and overview." In *The Social Psychology of Stigma,* T.F. Heatherton and R. Kleck, eds. The Guilford Press. New York.

Dunbar, N., and H. Grotevant. Adoption Narratives: The Construction of Adoptive Identity During Adolescence. In *Family Stories and the Life course,* M. Pratt and B. Fiese, eds. Mahwah: Lawrence Erlbaum Publishers.

Ehrensaft, D. *Mommies, Daddies, Donors and Surrogates.* New York: The Guildford Press, 2005.

-- "When Baby Makes Three or Four or More." *Psychoanalytic Study of the Child* 63 (2008): 3-23.

Erikson, E.H. *Identity and the Life Cycle.* New York: W.W. Norton & Company, Inc, 1980.

-- *Identity Youth and Crisis.* New York: W. W. Norton & Company, Inc, 1968.

Franz, S. and D. Allen. "Report to Health Canada." In *The Offspring Speak: An International Conference of Donor Offspring.* Toronto: The Infertility Network. Toronto, 2001.

Freeman, T., V. Jadva, W. Kramer, and S. Golombok. "Gamete donation: parents' experiences of searching for their child's donor siblings and donor." *Human Reproduction* 24 (2009): 505–516.

Friedeman, J. *Building Your Family Through Egg Donation.* Jolance Press, 2007.

Frith, L. "Gamete donation and anonymity: the ethical and legal debate." *Human Reproduction* 16 (2001): 818-824.

Gollancz, D "Give me my own history," *The Guardian News,* 22 May 2002. http://www.guardian.co.uk/http://www.buzzle.com/http://www.guardian.co.uk/

Grotevant, H., N. Dunbar, J. Kohler and A. Esau. "Adoptive identity: How contexts within and beyond the family shape developmental pathways." *Family Relations* 49 (2000): 379-387.

Hamilton, R. "Open Parents, Closed System." In *Voices of Donor Conception, Behind Closed Doors: Moving Beyond Secrecy and Shame,* M. Morrissette, ed., Minnesota: Be-Mondo Publishing. http://www.nytimes.com/2005/11/20/national/20siblings.htmlhttp://articles. latimes.com/2003/jul/04/entertainment/et-harris4Harris, Rhonda E., and Laura Shanner. "Seeking Answers in the Ether: Longing to Know One's Origins is Evident from Donor Conception Websites."

Hewitt, G. "Missing links: identity issues of donor-conceived people." *Journal of Fertility Counselling,* 9 (2002): 14-20.

"How it feels to be a child of donor insemination." *British Medical Journal* 324 (2002): 767.

Jadva, V., T. Freeman, W. Kramer, S. Golombok. "The experiences of adolescents and adults conceived by sperm donation: comparisons by age of disclosure and family type." *Human Reproduction* 1, no.1 (2009): 1–11.

Kirkman, M. "Parents' contributions to the narrative identity of offspring of donor-assisted conception." *Social Science & Medicine* 57 (2003): 2229-2242.

-- "Genetic Connection and Relationships in Narratives of Donor Assisted Conception." *Australian Journal of Emerging Technologies and Society* 2 (2004): 1-20.

-- *Telling About Donor Assisted Conception.* Victoria, Australia: Infertility Treatment Authority, Department of Human Services, 2006.

Kroger, J. *Identity Development: adolescence through adulthood.* Sage Publications, 2006.

Laub, D. "Truth and Testimony: the Process and the Struggle." *American Imago* 48 (1991):75-91.

Lauren. "Issues for Donor Inseminated Offspring." In *Truth and the Child 10 years on: information exchange in donor assisted conception,* E. Blyth, M. Crawshaw and J. Speirs, eds., Birmingham: British Association of Social Workers, 1998.

Lorbach, C. *Experiences of Donor Conception: Parents, Offspring and Donors Through the Years.* London: Jessica Kingsley Publishers, 2003.

-- and P. Lorbach. "Naivety." *Let the Offspring Speak: Discussions on Donor Conception.* Sydney: The Donor Conception Group of Australia, 1997.

Lycett, E., K. Daniels, R. Curson and S. Golombok. "Offspring created as a result of donor insemination: a study of family relationships, child adjustment, and disclosure." *Fertility and Sterility* 82 (2004):172-179.

-- "School-aged children of donor insemination: a study of parents' disclosure patterns." *Human Reproduction* 20 (2005): 810-819.

MacDougall, K., G. Becker, J.E. Scheib and R.D. Nachtigall R.D. "Strategies for disclosure: how parents approach telling their children that they were conceived with donor gametes." *Fertility and Sterility* 87 (2007): 524-533.

Mahlstedt, P., K. LaBounty and W.T. Kennedy. "The views of adult offspring of sperm donation: essential feedback for the development of ethical guidelines within the practice of assisted reproductive technology in the United States." *Fertility and Sterility* 93 (2010): 2236-46.

Mick, Hayley "Contact with donor siblings a good experience for most families," *The Globe and Mail,* February 26, 2009. http://www.theglobeandmail.com/servlet/story/RTGAM.20090226.wldonor26/BNStory/lifeFamily/home http://www.thenewatlantis.com/blog/conceptions/questions-for-damian-adams-donor-conceived-adult-2 http://www.thecanadianencyclopedia.com/index.cfm?PgNm=TCE&Params=M1ARTM0012412 http://www.thecanadianencyclopedia.com/index.cfm?PgNm=TCE&Params=M1ARTM0012412.

Nicky. "To whom it may concern." *Let the Offspring Speak: Discussions on Donor Conception.* Sydney: The Donor Conception Group of Australia, 1997.

Penny, J., L.D. Borders and F. Portnoy. "Reconstruction of Adoption Issues: Delineation of Five Phases among Adult Adoptees." *Journal of Counseling and Development* 85 (2007).

Pratten, S. "Building families through donor conception: An international forum on the personal, professional & public policy issues." *Journal of Infertility Counseling* 9, no. 2 (2002).

Rose, J. "From a 'bundle of joy' to a person with sorrow: Disenfranchised grief for the donor-conceived adult." Lecture for the Queensland University of Technology Applied Ethics Seminar Series, Queensland, Australia, 2001. http://www.parliament.nsw.gov.au/Prod/parlment/committee.nsf/0/9f164d5dd1a5d158ca2574f9007c3c15/$FILE/081106 Tabled document - Tim Cannon.pdf.

Rumball, A., and V. Adair. "Telling the story: parents' scripts for donor offspring." *Human Reproduction* 14 (1999): 1392-1399.

Scheib, J., J. Benward and A. Ruby A. "Who requests their sperm donor's identity? Analysis of donor-conceived adults requests at an open-identity program." *Fertility & Sterility* 90 (2008): S8-9.

-- and R.A. Cushing. "Open-identity donor insemination in the United States: Is it on the rise?" *Fertility & Sterility* 88 (2007): 231-232.

-- M. Riordan and S. Rubin. "Adolescents with open-identity sperm donors: reports from 12-17 year olds." *Human Reproduction* 20 (2005): 239-252.
-- M. Riordan and S. Rubin. "Choosing identity-release sperm donors: the parents' perspective 13-18 years later." *Human Reproduction* 18 (2003): 1115-1127.
-- and A. Ruby. "Impact of sperm donor information on parents and children." *Sexuality, Reproduction & Menopause* 4 (2006): 17-19.
Siegel, A.M. Heinz Kohut and the Psychology of the Self. New York: Routledge, 1996.
Speirs, J. "Children's rights or Adult rights?" In *Truth and the Child 10 years on: information exchange in donor assisted conception*, E. Blyth, M. Crawshaw and J. Speirs, eds. Birmingham: British Association of Social Workers, 1998.
Spencer, L. "Your father may not be your real father." *Let the Offspring Speak: Discussions on donor conception*. Sydney: The Donor Conception Group of Australia, 1997.
Squire, AS, "A generation of sperm donor children are discovering that the father they know and love is NOT their father at all," *The Daily Mail*, 19 March 2009.
Turner, A.J. and A. Coyle. "What does it mean to be a donor offspring? The identity experience of adults conceived by donor insemination and the implications for counseling and therapy." *Human Reproduction* 15 (2000): 2041-2051.
Vanfraussen, K., I. Ponjaert-Kristoffersen and A. Brewaeys. "An Attempt to reconstruct children's donor concept: a comparison between children's and lesbian parents' attitudes toward donor anonymity." *Human Reproduction* 16, no.9 (2001): 2019-2025.
-- "Why do children want to know more about the donor? The experience of youngsters raised in lesbian families." *Journal of Psychosomatic Obstetrics and Gynaecology* 24 (2003): 31-38.
Velleman, D. "Family History," *Philosophical Papers* 34 (2005): 357-78. http://papers.ssrn.com/sol3/papers.cfm?abstract_id=1006993.
Whipp, C. "The Legacy of Deceit." In *Truth and the Child 10 years on: information exchange in donor assisted conception*, E. Blyth, M. Crawshaw and J. Speirs, eds. Birmingham: British Association of Social Workers, 1998. http://www.donor-conception-network.org/zannah.htm.

Notes

1 Kroger, *Identity Development*, 3.
2 Erikson, *Identity, Youth and Crisis*, 22.
3 Ehrensaft, "When Baby Makes Three or Four or More," 3.
4 Siegel, Heinz Kohut.
5 Erikson. Identity Youth and Crisis, 23. "The individual judges himself in the light of what he perceives to be the way in which others judge him".
6 Ehrensaft, see note 3, above.
7 Owusu-Bempah, J "Socio-Genealogical connectedness, Knowledge and Identity," 119 in The Developing World of the Child.
8 Gollancz, "Give me my own history," *The Guardian News*, 22 May 2002.
9 Becker, Butler and Nachtigall, "Resemblance talk," 1300.
10 Velleman, "Family History," 357-78.

11 Jadva and others, "The experience of adolescents and adults conceived by sperm donations," 17-19.
12 Erikson, Identity, Youth and Crisis, 23.
13 Franz and Allen, *The Offspring Speak*; Daniels and Meadows, "Sharing information with adults conceived as a result of donor insemination, 93-99. Turner and Coyle, "What does it mean to be a donor offspring," 2041-51; Mahlstedt, LaBounty and Kennedy, "The views of adult offspring of sperm donation," 2009.
14 Turner and Coyle, see note 13 above; Allen, "The future of donor conception," in The Infertility Network: Conference proceedings; Kirkman, "Parents' contributions to the narrative identity of offspring of donor-assisted conception," 2229-42.
15 Bennett, "The emotional and biological consequences of DI," in *Let The Offspring Speak*, 138.
16 Botsford, "A personal story of Blood and Belonging," Donor Conception Network, 2000, http://www.donor-conception-network.org/offspring2.htm.
17 Squire, "A generation of sperm donor children are discovering that the father they know and love is NOT their father at all," *The Daily Mail*, 19 March 2009.
18 Lauren, "Issues for Donor Inseminated Offspring," in *Truth and the Child 10 years on*," 65.
19 Scheib, Riordan and Rubin, "Adolescents with open-identity sperm donors," 239-52; Vanfraussen, Ponjaert-Kristoffersen and Brewaeys, "An attempt to reconstruct children's donor concept," 2019-25; Frith, "Gamete Donation, Identity, and the Offspring's Right to Know," 818-24; Jadva and others, "The experiences of adolescents and adults conceived by sperm donation", 1-11.
20 Ehrensaft, *Mommies, Daddies and Surrogates*, 153. Eherensaft introduces the clinical work of Marsha Levy Warren, author of A Clinical Look at Knowing and Telling: Secrets, Lies and Disillusionments in Complex Adoption and Assisted Reproductive Technology.
21 *Ibid.*
22 Whipp, "The Legacy of Deceit," in *Truth and the Child 10 Years on*, 61.
23 Lauren, see note 18 above; Turner and Coyle, see note 13 above; Hewitt, "Missing links," 14-20; Daniels, *Building a family*; Jadva and others, see note 13 above.
24 "Becky's Story," Donor Conception Network, 2006, www.dcnetwork.org/beckys journey finding sibs.htm.
25 Doka, ed., *Disenfranchised Grief*, 3-11. The concept of disenfranchised grief was first applied to the experience of the donor-conceived in a paper written by J. Rose in 2001.
26 Joanna Rose, "From a 'bundle of joy' to a person with sorrow," (lecture, Queensland University of Technology, Queensland, Australia, 2001).
27 Spencer, "Your father may not be your real father," in *Let the Offspring Speak*.
28 Kirkman, see note 14 above.
29 LaBounty, 2008.
30 Anonymous."How it feels to be a child of donor insemination," 767.
31 Kirkman, *see note 14 above*.
32 Speirs, "Children's rights or Adult rights?" in *Truth and the Child 10 Years on*, 15.
33 Turner and Coyle, see note 12 above.
34 Dovido, J, B. Major and J. Crocker. "Stigma: introduction and overview." In *The Social Psychology of Stigma*, T.F. Heatherton and R. Kleck, eds. The Guilford Press. New York.
35 Turner and Coyle, see note 13 above.
36 Rose, see note 24 above.
37 Anonymous, see note 30 above.
38 Laub, "Truth and Testimony," 75-91. Doris Laub is a psychoanalyst who has written extensively about trauma and healing.
39 Harris and Shanner, "Seeking Answers in the Ether: Longing to Know On'es Origins is evident from Donor Conception Websites".
40 For example, the Donor Sibling Registry, a non-profit organization, operates a voluntary mutual-consent, internet-based registry for matching offspring with donors and genetic siblings. More than 22,000 donors, parents, and children have signed up since the registry began in 2000, and more than 6,000 half-siblings and/or donors have been connected through it, indicating a significant desire for contact for families already formed through gamete donation. See also www.donorsiblingregistry.com, www.donoroffspring.com, its offshoot www.

donoroffspringmatches.com, donoroffspringhealth.com; AmFORDonorOffspringRegistry; www.birthparentfinder.com/donor.html. www.donorsiblinggroups.com and www.cabrimed.org/donorconceivedservices.jsp; Australian donor conception registry on Yahoogroups.com; SMC Sibling registry; California Cryobank Sibling Registry; TSBC Family Match; UKDonorLInk.

41 For example the "Let the Offspring Speak" conference organized by the Donor Conception Support Group of Australia. Or The Offspring Speak: An International Conference of Donor Offspring, organized by Health Canada.
42 Botsford, see note 16 above.
43 LaBounty, see note 13 above.
44 Lauren, see note 18 above.
45 Nicky, To whom it may concern," in *Let the Offspring Speak*, 30.
46 Mahlstedt, LaBounty and Kennedy, see note 13 above.
47 Hamilton, "Open Parents, Closed System," in *Voices of Donor Conception: Behind Closed Doors*.
48 Hayley Mick, "Contact with donor siblings a good experience for most families," *The Globe and Mail*, February 26, 2009.
49 Susan McClelland, "Controversy over sperm donor anonymity," *Maclean's*, May 20, 2002.
50 Carsten, "Kinship and the identity of the child," in *Truth and the Child 10 Years on*, 1-4.
51 Ibid.
52 As others have noted, the term disclosure is not ideal. (See Daniels and Thorn, 2001, Kirkman, 2003). Nonetheless, since this term is commonly recognized I have used it.
53 Jadva and others, see note 11 above.
54 Mahlstedt, LaBounty and Kennedy, see note 13 above; Hewitt, see note 23 above Missing links: identity issues of donor-conceived people 2002.
55 Turner and Coyle, see note 13 above; Hewitt see note 23 above.
56 Gollancz, see note 18 above.
57 Kirkman, see note 14 above; Rumball and Adair, "Telling the story," 1392-1399; Scheib, Riordan and Rubin, see note 23 above.
58 Rumball and Adair, see note 57 above.
59 Hamilton, 2006, 48.
60 Scheib, Riordan and Rubin, see note 23 above; Mahlstedt, LaBounty and Kennedy, see note 13 above.
61 MacDougall and others, Strategies for disclosure, 524 – 33.
62 Vanfraussen, Ponjaert-Kristoffersen and Brewaeys, see note 23 above, 2024.
63 VanFrausssen, Ponjaert-Kristoffersen and Brewaeys, see note 23 above; VanFraussen, Ponjaert-Kristoffersen and Brewaeys, "Why do children want to know more about the donor?" 31-38.
64 Ibid.
65 Kirkman, "Genetic Connection and Relationships," 5.
66 Anonymous parent, Donor Sibling Registry, http://www.donorsiblingregistry.com.
67 Daniels, *Building a Family*, 173.
68 Anonymous mother of an egg donor-conceived daughter, personal communication.
69 See Bernstein, 1994.
70 Daniels, *Building a Family*, 146.
71 Ibid. 138.
72 Anonymous interview with parents of child conceived by donor insemination, personal communication.
73 Anonymous mother of girl conceived via egg donation, personal communication.
74 Daniels, *Building a Family*, 218.
75 Ibid. 175.
76 Daniels, *Building a Family*, 175.
77 Lorbach 2003, 128.
78 Anonymous mother of a 10-year-old girl conceived by egg donation, personal communication.
79 VanFraussen, Ponjaert-Kristoffersen and Brewaeys, see note 19 above.2001 2021.
80 Anonymous interview with mother of a 10-year-old girl conceived with egg donation, personal communication.

81 Lorbach, 2003, 131.
82 *Ibid.*, 131.
83 *Ibid.*
84 Ehrensaft, 2008, 20.
85 Anonymous interview with 11-year-old girl, personal communication.
86 Anonymous interview with 12-year-old girl, personal communication.
87 *Ibid.*, 131.
88 Ehrensaft, see note 3.
89 Lorbach, 2003, 157.
90 Scheib, Riordan and Rubin, see note 23 above; Jadva, see note 11 above.
91 Mahlstedt, LaBounty and Kennedy, see note 13 above.
92 Hewitt, see note 23 above; Scheib, Riordan and Rubin, see note 23 above.
93 Brodzinsky, "Family structural openness," 1-18.
94 Cahn, "Necessary subjects," 203-23.
95 Kirkman, Genetic Connection and Relationships in Narratives of Donor Assisted Conception. 2239.
96 LaBounty, see note 28 above.
97 Scheib, Riordan and Rubin, see note 19 above.
98 *Ibid.*
99 Christina Cheakalos, "Discovering Dad," *People*, July 14, 2003.
100 Scott Duke Harris, "Runs in the family," *Los Angeles Times*, July 4, 2003.
101 Penny, Borders and Portnoy, "Reconstruction of Adoption Issues."
102 Dunbar and Grotevant, "Adoption Narratives," in *Family Stories and the Life course,* 135-163.
103 Allen, "I find myself wondering," in *Let the Offspring Speak*, 45.
104 Kirkman, *Telling About Donor Assisted Conception*, 22.
105 Cordray, "The need for self identity," in *Let the Offspring Speak*, 35.
106 David Gollancz, "Time to stop lying," *The Guardian*, August 2, 2007.
107 Gollancz, see note 8 above.
108 *Ibid.*
109 Cordray, "The need for self identity", 1997.
110 McClelland, see note 48 above.
111 Kirkman, 2004, 16.
112 "Becky's Story," see note 24 above.
113 Scheib and Cushing, *2007, 232*.
114 Daniels, "Toward a family-building approach to donor insemination," 125-6.
115 See www.donorsiblingregistry.com, www.donoroffspring.com, its offshoot www.donoroffspringmatches.com, donoroffspringhealth.com; AmFORDonorOffspringRegistry; www.birthparentfinder.com/donor.html. www.donorsibinggroups.com/ and www.cabrimed.org/donorconceivedservices.jsp; Australian donor conception registry on Yahoogroups.com; UKDonorLink. See www.cryokidconfessions.blogspot.com; The International Network of Donor Conception Networks; www.voicesofdonorconception.com. These groups report increasing memberships of offspring, donors and parents.
116 Pratten, "Buiding families through donor conception."

Chapter Fourteen

The Health Benefits to Children Having their Genetic Information
The Importance of Constructing Family Trees

Julie L. Lauzon

1. Introduction

The innate desire of people with fertility challenges to have a family of their own has fuelled the development of assisted reproductive technologies such as in vitro fertilisation, intra-cytoplasmic sperm injection and pre-implantation genetic diagnosis. The majority of people who undergo these procedures have been diagnosed with infertility of known or unknown cause. Some may seek these treatments because they are at risk of having a child with a specific genetic condition. Gamete donation is often used in the context of infertility treatment. Its use has expanded to enable single parents and same sex couples to have children.

Most children born through gamete donation (referred to as "donor offspring") do not know that they have been conceived by these means.[1,2] Those who are aware of the circumstances of their conception tend not to have access to their family medical history if the gametes were donated anonymously. Consequently, the use of anonymous donor gametes has created children who do not know at least one of their biological parents and who are therefore separated from half of their genetic heritage.

The purpose of this chapter is to assess whether the lack of knowledge of one's biological parents creates a situation that could compromise one's health and well being from the perspective of genetics. The chapter first reviews some of the basic concepts regarding how our genetic information plays a role in disease and then explores how family medical history is important in assessing risks for disease. It then addresses specific concerns regarding the determination of genetic disease risks in the context of gamete donation. The chapter concludes that the inability of people to know their genetic or family history is a health disadvantage, which can be a significant and even life-threatening health disadvantage in particular cases.

2. Genetics Primer

Genetic information is both personal and familial. Our genetic information is packaged in structures called chromosomes that are found in each of our body's cells. Our genes are encoded in a molecule called DNA (deoxyribonucleic acid) and are found on these chromosomes. Genes serve as a "blue print" that guides our growth and development.[3]

Specific changes in our genetic information, often called "mutations", can cause disease. However, gene-gene interactions and gene-environment interactions are also very important in determining how susceptible we each are to disease.[4]

3. Genetics in Medicine

Our knowledge of genetics and inherited conditions is rapidly increasing for at least two reasons. The Human Genome Project, which was completed in 2003, fostered progress in conditions that are due to changes in specific genes (single gene disorders), such as cystic fibrosis and certain blood disorders (e.g. thalassemias and hemophilia). The Human Genome Project also affirmed our knowledge that the genetic make-up of people plays a significant role in their health by influencing everything from their risk of congenital anomalies to their chance of developing a common disorder such as cardiovascular disease, asthma, and obesity.[5] The second reason for the rapid increase in knowledge of genetics is the development of newly emerging technologies such as array comparative genomic hybridization, genome-wide association studies, and next generation sequencing. With their help, we are now beginning to learn how genetics contributes to the disease development of common genetic disorders.

We aim to use the results obtained by new technologies to gain a better understanding of the individual characteristics of common disease conditions including specific disease risk or susceptibility, predictability of genetic testing, treatment or cure for genetic conditions and available preventative measures. The medical goal is to decrease both the seriousness of the disease and the likelihood of it causing death. Because of what genetic testing thus offers, it has become part of routine medical practice in many specialties.

This fast growth in knowledge of genetics is exciting and holds much promise for the future. The integration of genetic information into medical practice gives physicians the tools to identify individuals who are at risk of developing medical problems or to diagnose those already affected so that effective preventive treatment measures can be instituted and family members offered counselling.

3.1 Genes and Disease

Genes play a role in developing disease in a variety of ways. Most genetic conditions are inherited; in other words, genetic changes have been passed on through generations. Many of these conditions are due to changes in specific genes and are inherited in a variety of ways including autosomal dominant, autosomal recessive and X-linked inheritance. For some conditions the genetic change is a new change (called *de novo*) and occurred in the affected individual. This individual would not have a family member with the genetic condition but the individual's biological children may be at-risk of developing the disease.

Genetic changes can occur also in our somatic cells (i.e. non germ cells). These are not inherited and cannot be "passed on" to offspring. Genetic changes in our somatic cells can lead to the most common forms of cancer.

Chromosome abnormalities are genetic disorders caused by changes in the number or the structure of the chromosomes. These conditions usually entail the presence of several dozens to hundreds of extra genes (called "chromosome duplication") or the absence of such genes (called "chromosome deletion"). One of the most well-known chromosome abnormalities is Down syndrome, also called trisomy 21. Chromosome abnormalities may or may not be inherited.

Complex disorders result from the additive effect or interaction of a number of genetic factors and a number of non-genetic factors.[6] The sum of these factors determines an individual's susceptibility to develop the disease. Examples of such disorders include diabetes, high blood pressure and obesity. An individual's risk for these conditions increases with the increased number of close relatives and earlier age of onset of disease.[7] For example, if one of your parents had a heart attack at age 40, you are at increased risk of developing early-onset heart disease. Recent advances in genomics medicine have permitted us to look at multiple areas of our genetic information (called "genetic loci") to try to decipher how these suspected genetic loci have an impact on disease. The risk of disease will change depending on which and how many genetic variants are present.

3.2 Genetic Testing and Genetic Screening

Some genetic tests permit geneticists to confirm a clinical diagnosis in an individual who presents with signs and symptoms of a specific disease. The results of the genetic test can then be used to inform family members of their risks of developing the disease.

Other genetic tests are said to be 'predictive'. Predictive genetic testing is used to identify individuals who do not have symptoms but who will develop signs or symptoms of a disease sometime in the future. This testing is usually offered in the context of a positive family history. For example, members of a family affected by Huntington disease might want to know whether they carry the gene for this devastating neurodegenerative disease that becomes apparent most often in the third to fourth decade of life. Huntington's is an autosomal dominant condition; therefore a person whose parent has Huntington disease has a 50% chance of inheriting the condition from his or her parent.

Genetic screening is a population-based method to identify persons with certain DNA sequences known to be associated with a genetic disease or predisposition to a genetic disease.[8] The objective of genetic screening is to examine all members of a designated population, regardless of the presence of disease in the family. Systematic screening programmes are offered to a specified population of asymptomatic individuals and allows for identification of individuals with a disease for which early treatment significantly improves outcomes. It may also determine the risk of transmitting a disease to an offspring.

One of the best known genetic screening initiatives is newborn screening. It is premised on the understanding that babies born with certain genetic conditions can avoid suffering devastating harm if the genetic condition is detected and treated early.

Genetic screening programs have also been developed to determine carrier status in the context of an autosomal recessive condition. Individuals who are "carriers" of an autosomal recessive condition are asymptomatic and are not at risk of developing disease. But they can pass on the disease to their children. Current carrier screening programs focus on particular ethnic groups in which the frequency of the disorder is high enough to justify population screening. For example, individuals of Ashkenazi Jewish descent are at-risk for several genetic conditions such as Tay-Sachs disease and Canavan disease – two severe childhood-onset neurodegenerative conditions. Screening programs for this population have been available since the late 1960s worldwide.[9]

3.3 Genomics

The "genome" refers to the entire genetic information found in an individual. Genomics testing involves evaluating "thousands of DNA markers, spanning genes throughout the genome and their interrelationships".[10] The concept of surveying the entire DNA sequence for important disease-causing variants has been applied to the evaluation of complex traits. Genomic medicine can be disease-specific or population-based. The vast majority of results are said to be "predisposing" or "predictive", meaning that the individual in question is at risk or has a higher chance of developing a specific disease. Rarely is this risk absolute. For some conditions, an individual at risk can choose to pursue preventative measures either through lifestyle modifications or clinical screening programs to reduce the risk of developing the disease. But for many conditions, there are no effective preventative measures to reduce risk. Much has yet to be learned about interpreting and applying this information to assess disease risk at the individual level.

4. The Importance of Family History

Because biological parents give genes to their children, knowledge of one's parents' medical history is, in an importance sense, knowledge of one's own medical history. To promote the health and well being of children, it is important to know what health risks they might face and to use the knowledge to work to prevent or reduce such risks. Despite the promise of recent technological developments in genetic testing, some "low tech" strategies (i.e. obtaining a family medical history) to gain knowledge of genetic risk remain useful and indeed indispensible. Because no existing genetic test can determine and accurately quantify risk for all diseases, a 'good old-fashioned' family history remains the best way to screen for genetically linked health problems.[11]

Yet not everyone is in a position to give a family history. These include people created by anonymous donor gametes. From the perspective of caring for these children and providing them prevention and/or screening strategies based on possible inherited or genetic disease risk, the lack of a family history raises problems that are not in the interests of the patient. In other words, it is not to the medical advantage of persons conceived by gamete donation not to know their family medical histories. This section describes how such lack of knowledge is a detriment and how, in some cases, it can be life-threatening.

4.1. The Advantages of a Family History

The importance of knowing your family medical history is well recognized.[12] Through a family history, physicians can learn about the various diseases that affect family members and the environmental and social factors that can influence health and disease. There are many components to a family history that can reveal risk factors for disease, most of which are shared by family members.

4.1.1 Family History Promotes Diagnosis, Screening, Prevention and Treatment

Obtaining a family history is considered a standard element of good medical care. Primary care practitioners use the family history as a tool to identify the known genetic diseases present in their patients' relatives and to identify any other non-genetic risk factors that may exist. Depending upon what the history reveals, physicians can take further steps in terms of screening and prevention strategies.

The presence of specific symptoms of disease in family members can guide diagnosis in a patient. For example, a child who faints and whose parent has also experienced fainting episodes prompts us to consider the diagnosis of long QT syndrome.[13] In reviewing the family history, physicians can gain insight also into patients' experiences of disease within the family, which are relevant to framing preventive advice.[14]

Likewise information obtained in a family history can lead to preventative measures. The U.S. Preventive Services Task Force requires that physicians consider relevant family history in recommending preventative measures for certain asymptomatic patients.[15] For example, general screening for colon colorectal cancer is recommended for people aged 50 years of age and older. Such screening should be initiated at an earlier age in individuals at higher risk including individuals with a first degree relative (parent or sibling) who was diagnosed with colorectal cancer before the age of 60.[16] Therefore a family history can lead to early disease screening. It can also prompt physician-patient discussion about family disease risks. This discussion can motivate a patient to change behaviour that can exacerbate the risk.[17]

It is important that physicians update their patients' family history to identify newly diagnosed medical conditions within the family.[18] They should also review information about pregnancies and learning issues. In certain situations, it may be important to obtain medical records on family members to confirm a diagnosis that can then influence medical management options for their relatives to ensure the accuracy of the information.

4.1.2. Family History Helps Determine Reproductive Risk

Family history is also extensively used in the preconception and prenatal care setting. The American College of Obstetrics and Gynaecology recommends that patient encounters include a review of a three-generation family medical history, "ideally with both members of the couple."[19] Benjamin Solomon *et al.* state that such a history is indispensible:

> A complete 3 generation family medical history that includes ethnicity information from both sides of the family is arguably the best genetic "test" that is applicable to preconception care ... family history and other historic data provide an inexpensive and non invasive assessment of conditions that might affect pregnancy.[20]

It is, of course, best to learn about these risks before conception because such information can help guide reproductive decision-making and improve prenatal care by minimizing risks to the pregnant woman and the child. For example, individuals with a genetic condition called Marfan syndrome have an increased risk for aortic root dissection and subsequent sudden death. This risk is further increased during pregnancy. If a woman has Marfan syndrome then close monitoring of her cardiac status will be most important during pregnancy. If a woman has a positive family history of Marfan syndrome then it will be important to assess whether she has subtle features of this condition and thus guide management. If she is found to have Marfan syndrome, her biological children are at 50% risk of also having Marfan syndrome. Questions about the presence of stillbirths, recurrent miscarriages, birth defects and mental handicap in biological family members can help identify further genetic risks.

It is also recommended to offer preconception and prenatal carrier screening for genetic disorders based on a couple's ethnic background. Couples at increased risk for any genetic condition based on either family history or ethnic background are eligible for prenatal diagnosis in addition to general prenatal screening testing available for common genetic conditions in the general population.

4.1.3 Family History Helps Physicians Care for Children

Most pediatric primary care physicians collect family history information without a disease in mind.[21] They seek to learn about the health of the child and their family members as well as the various factors influencing health and disease in their familial context.[22] Information gained through a family history can provide clues regarding the underlying cause of the disease when caring for a sick child and can expedite diagnosis and treatment. Often, a paediatrician may see children and their parents more frequently than their primary care provider in the first year of life and can play an important role in providing preconception care by raising "familial awareness of increased risk and motivate behaviour modification and decision-making to reduce risk and improve obstetric and subsequent pediatric outcome."[23] If a severe autosomal recessive disease is diagnosed in a young infant, then the biological parents are usually found to be carriers of this condition. They have a 25% risk of having another affected child. Genetic counselling can be offered to the couple to discuss family planning issues and reproductive options, which may include prenatal diagnosis and adoption. It is the current practice also to discuss gamete donation.

When physicians know the family history, they are in a better position to recommend participation in a health initiative to attempt to prevent complex trait conditions such as the 'Healthy Eating and Activity Together' program on obesity[24] and 'Keep Your Children/Yourself Safe and Secure', a program for families with mental health issues.[25]

4.1.4 Family History is the Foundation of Genetic Counselling

The family history is a key component of every medical genetics clinical assessment. Medical geneticists perform a family history in every patient encounter. Geneticists are trained accurately to obtain and to interpret a three generation pedigree to help diagnose medical conditions and identify genetic risk factors present in families. Not knowing half or all the family history is a serious limiting factor.

Knowing that there is a family history of a disease and who is affected can help us to determine which conditions to test for. A family history can also tell us about the mode of inheritance to enable us to identify at-risk family members, offer genetic testing (if available) and recommend treatment, screening and/or prevention strategies to at-risk individuals.

Sometimes, there is an important need for genetic testing to prevent harm in more than one member of a family. For example, a child who presents with multiple light brown birthmarks and learning difficulties needs to be investigated for a condition called Neurofibromatosis type 1 (NF-1). These children are at risk of developing brain tumours and bone malformations.[26] Clinical assessment of the parents is necessary to determine if they may also have NF-1 because 50% of children inherit the gene change from an affected parent. Often parents are unaware that they have NF-1. It is important that they also be screened for complications related to this condition to enable early detection and treatment. (A sperm donor has passed this condition to five children.)[27]

When a family appears to have a genetic condition, then a family history can be vital to ensure that we are testing for the correct genetic disease. This is important because various genetic diseases can generate the same clinical presentation. Often a disease can be caused by many different genes. If we order the wrong genetic test, then we might falsely reassure patients. For example, Charcot Marie Tooth (CMT) is a disease whose cause could be misstated without a proper family history. CMT is a hereditary neuropathy that causes individuals to develop muscle weakness and sensory abnormalities in their limbs.[28] CMT has many causes, both genetic and non-genetic. Genetic forms can be inherited in an autosomal dominant, autosomal recessive or X-linked fashion. Family history is the best way to determine which form of CMT the patient may have and to help decide which CMT genes should be studied. Confirming the diagnosis in the patient and the proper mode of inheritance in the family is important to ensure that we are offering the right genetic test to the correctly-identified at-risk family members. A complicating factor is that we cannot yet test for all forms of CMT. Our clinical diagnosis must, therefore, be based on both the specific clinical features seen in the affected individuals and the presence or absence of disease in family members. To assess whether the disease is present in family members, we may need to examine and perform neurological tests on them. It is important to know who the family members are so that they may be tested.

Genetic counsellors spend much time reviewing with the family what genetic testing can and cannot offer: its limitations, the type of testing, the information that testing can yield and who ought to be offered genetic testing. In addition, some results are difficult to interpret. The significance of some changes in genetic information are not clear. In other words, we may not know if the change is disease-causing or not (because it may be a normal benign variant in the genetic sequence). In such cases, family genetic studies are warranted because they can help us understand the significance of the test results.

4.1.5 Family History Can Help Predict Medical Issues

Most conditions have a wide range of presenting features and complications. In certain cases, it is impossible to predict which medical issues will arise in an affected individual. In these circumstances, screening and preventive strategies are tailored to address all of the possible complications that can be seen in that condition. Sometimes, knowing which specific change in which specific gene is present in the family can help us delineate which complications to expect and which ones will not occur. Long-term management is thus tailored specifically for that family. For example, Autosomal Dominant Polycystic Kidney disease (ADPKD) is a condition that causes affected individuals to develop multiple cysts in their kidneys that can lead to renal failure. A small proportion of families with this condition suffer brain aneurysms that are abnormal blood vessels in the brain that can bleed and cause a stroke. If brain aneurysms have not been described in other affected family members, then the risk of brain aneurysm in that family is minimal and screening for this complication is not necessary.[29] It is, therefore, important to understand the disease in the context of the family history to minimize risk, optimize treatment and protect health.

4.1.5.1 Family History Helps Assess Magnitude of Risk

Sometimes, family history is essential in quantifying genetic risk. This is true, for example, when screening for cancer syndromes such as inherited forms of breast and ovarian cancer. About 5-10% of all cases of breast cancer are caused by a change in either the BRCA1 or BRCA2 gene. Individuals who carry a change in their BRCA1 or BRCA2 gene have a significantly increased risk of developing breast and ovarian cancer in their lifetime (lifetime risk of approximately 85% of developing breast cancer and a 27-63% lifetime risk for ovarian cancer).[30] In addition, these individuals have a 50% chance of passing on this significant cancer predisposition to their off-spring, because it is inherited in an autosomal dominant fashion. Individuals who have a genetic form of breast cancer are offered counselling and the opportunity to discuss preventive strategies including earlier and more frequent screening (i.e. mammograms, magnetic resonance imaging) because earlier detection permits prompt treatment with higher success rate and better overall prognosis. Physicians also discuss preventative strategies such as surgery to remove breast and ovarian tissue. Genetic testing can be offered to those individuals who are at-risk based on family history in an attempt to predict whether they are at risk of breast cancer.[31] People who do not know half or all their family history might be at risk of breast cancer but, because of their lack of knowledge, may not be in a position to engage in such preventative strategies.

4.1.5.2 Family History Can Reveal Consanguinity Which Can Help Assess Risk

Consanguinity, the marriage or union between closely related individuals, is frequent in many cultures.[32] This possibility, in conjunction with the specific ethnic background, needs to be considered when a patient is found to have unusual symptoms that suggest the individual has a rare genetic condition. Individuals who are related share a greater proportion of their genes and are therefore at increased risk of being carriers for the same rare autosomal recessive conditions and are at slightly higher risk than the general population to have a child with a birth defect or handicapping condition. This chance is increased from 2-3% to 4-6%.[33] There is also an increased risk for complex genetic disorders. People who do not know their family history might not know their ethnic background and are at risk of mating with a blood relative and therefore unwittingly creating the risks of consanguinity.

4.1.6 Family History Can Reveal Misconceptions and Provide Opportunity for Clarification

Family history can also be used to clarify misconceptions that families may have about a genetic condition present in their family.[34] Often "families erroneously assume that certain genetic diseases affect only one gender, because thus far, for example, only men have been affected in their family."[35] Another common misconception is that a disease "skips" generations. This is often a result of incomplete penetrance, variability of expression, or misdiagnosis. Sometimes family members can believe that their family has a disease when it is more probable that the disease's cause is environmental. Correcting these misunderstandings by simply drawing out a family history can help all the family members and can lead to expanded opportunities to explore levels of understanding and facilitate patient and family education.[36]

4.1.7 Summary of Health Advantages to Individuals in Obtaining a Family History

In summary, family history is indispensible in genetic counselling. It can help physicians recognize that a condition may be genetic; guide diagnostic testing and treatment; identify at-risk family members and offer genetic testing if available; implement screening strategies in affected or at-risk individuals; provide education, understanding and support to families; and discuss reproductive options and family planning. People who do not know half or all of their family history are disadvantaged because such ignorance limits the ways in which physicians and other healthcare providers can work with the patient to promote his or her health and well being. In some cases where there is an unknown history of serious disease, such as Marfan's syndrome, ignorance of this family history can prove lethal.

4.2 The Role of Family History in an Era of Increasingly Sophisticated Genetic Testing

It might be argued that obtaining a family history, which is time consuming and subject to error based on patient knowledge and recall, might be outdated. Some ask, "Can't we just do a genetic test to assess disease risk?" This is a common misunderstanding. As Steven Galston, Acting U.S. Surgeon General lamented.[37]

> You ask some people about the age of personalized medicine and they think, 'Take a drop of blood and put it in the machine and it's going to tell me everything' ... That's really science fiction. Today [...] and for the foreseeable future, the best way to inform your health care practitioners about your genetic predisposition is through old-fashioned family history.

Even in the four per cent of genetic disorders in which a single gene is responsible, access to the determinative genetic test depends on a family history.[38] Personal and family history characteristics are crucial to identifying many genetic disorders. While it is true that testing is available for single gene disorders, geneticists and other physicians need to know what test to order because there are so many available. Approximately 1,820 genetic conditions can be identified by testing; clinical genetic laboratories offer 1,563 tests and research laboratories offer 268 additional tests.[39] Individuals are not tested for all genetic disorders because the cost is prohibitive. Prudent use of patient time and resources requires that genetic testing for the single gene disorders occurs on a case-by-case basis after a thorough medical evaluation looking for specific signs and symptoms of disease in an individual, review of the family history and possibly evaluation of family members.

Genetic testing is even less likely to be the only method to identify a person who is at risk for multi-factorial disorders. Common diseases like obesity, Alzheimer's disease and diabetes are caused by a set of several genetic variations in each person and non-genetic factors. In an attempt to predict whether individuals are susceptible to such diseases, many studies called, "genome-wide association studies (GWAS)" have been undertaken over the last decade. These studies examine several genetic variants. Most of these studies have found that, for many common conditions, these gene variants account for only a small to moderate effect on an individual's total disease risk susceptibility.[40] A meta-analysis conducted by the Human Genome Epidemiology Network (HuGENet) reviewed the data from GWAS studies and concluded that the "scientific evidence for most associations between genetic variants and disease risk is insufficient to support useful applications."[41] The Network predicts that "it will be many years to decades before lifestyle and medical interventions can be responsibly and effectively tailored to individuals' genomic profiles."[42] In other words, genetic tests are not able to predict susceptibility to multi-factorial disorders like obesity and asthma. Family history remains vital.

Nevertheless, people are being encouraged to believe that genetic testing can give them conclusive information. For example, the development of "direct-to-consumer" genetic testing could lead people to believe that such testing can tell them all they need to know. These companies have capitalized on the information learned from GWAS studies offering genetic testing for these common disorders via the internet.[43] Some of the information that the tests offer could be helpful. For example, most companies test for disorders such as cystic fibrosis and hemochromatosis and evaluate several genetic variants for common genetic conditions including diabetes and asthma. They might also offer individual information about ancestry or ethnic background. But these tests are not comprehensive nor are they targeted to the individual. A family history could reveal the need for a specific genetic test that is not available from the direct-to-consumer company. For example, Counsyl, a US-based genetic testing company offers a genetic test that screens for 100 genetic disorders; this test is called the "Universal Genetic Test" and includes mostly single gene disorders.[44] This test is marketed to people who wish to start a family and to patients being seen in fertility clinics. But there has been no independent study of the Universal Genetic Test to address the possibility that false reassurance might be given to people because the testing is for only 100 of the thousands of known genetic conditions.[45]

Whole genome sequencing looking at the DNA in its entirety is now being performed on a research basis and has been conducted for a few individuals including James Watson and Craig Venter. This technology looks at an individual's whole DNA sequence rather than only selective genetic variants.[46] Such comprehensive examination permits the discovery of gene mutations causing known genetic disorders and common disease susceptibility gene variants. This test has the potential to be very promising. We can envision a future where we will have a single comprehensive screening test for all genetic disorders that is routinely assessed to guide both prevention and clinical care. But at present, the cost is still prohibitive and our knowledge of how all the genetic variants affect health is limited.

Thus despite our technological advances in understanding the genetic basis of common diseases, it remains true that "the clinical utility of DNA-based testing for disease susceptibility compared to other risk assessment strategies, including familial risk assessment and assessment of biochemical risks factors, must be proven."[47] Blood testing alone is not yet a practical initial approach for genetic risk assessment. Further studies are required to evaluate the prevalence, the degree of risk that genetic variants confer and the effect of other genes and environmental factors on disease susceptibility.[48] The new genetic technologies have allowed us to generate vast amounts of genetic data but we have not yet determined and understood the "benefits and harms associated with this testing including related clinical interventions, effectiveness and social consequences."[49] Therefore, an "old-fashioned family history is more predictive than all the new gene tests we identified."[50] Moreover, and as discussed, "genetic tests are most often ordered and best interpreted in the context of family history."[51] Not knowing half or all of one's family history is a disadvantage to one's health and well being.

5. Implications of Ignorance of Family History in the Context of Gamete Donation and Genetic Disorders

This chapter has emphasized that genetic information is at once personal *and* familial. It can reveal medical information about both the individual and about other individuals with whom they share the genetic information. In the context of gamete donation, the genetic information of a donor is therefore relevant to the possible health in a resulting child. The possibility of genetic disorders being passed to a large group of children can occur because gametes from donors can be used in the conceptions of dozens of children.

The inter-generational nature of genetic information is obvious in gamete donation. Infertility clinics might seek to eliminate a possible donor who could pass on a genetic disease to a child. Likewise a child born could develop symptoms that reveal that one of the biological parents has a genetic condition.

5.1 Gamete Donors as Carriers of Genetic Conditions

The genetic disease of a donor might not be known to the donor but can be revealed by his or her offspring. Maron *et al* recently reported that a 23-year-old man who was found to have a serious genetic heart condition called Hypertrophy Cardiomyopathy (HCM) after one of his donor offspring was diagnosed with HCM.[52] There was no suspicion of heart disease in the gamete donor prior to the news about the child and then genetic testing of the donor. HCM is an autosomal dominant condition. Individuals with HCM can be asymptomatic, develop progressive heart failure or present with sudden cardiac death. These symptoms vary from individual to individual even within the same family. The fertility clinic which obtained the man's semen had screened him by reviewing his personal and family history, conducted a physical exam and laboratory investigations for infectious diseases. They deemed him to be in good health. The diagnosis of HCM in the child triggered notification to the sperm bank and initiated evaluation of this man's 22 children and donor offspring. Sixteen children were tested and eight were found to have the genetic defect, including one of his children with his wife. The majority of the children were asymptomatic but one donor offspring died of HCM-related heart failure at age 2.5 years and two children had cardiac symptoms.

Likewise, another donor offspring developed symptoms that suggested she had inherited a disease from her donor. The young girl was found to be a premutation carrier for Fragile X syndrome.[53] Fragile X syndrome, in the full mutation state, is one of the most common causes of mental retardation and autism in boys. Recently girls have been found also to have symptoms of this X-linked condition. Individuals who have a Fragile X premutation do not have cognitive disabilities but women are at increased risk of developing early onset of menopause and both men and women are at risk of having Fragile X Associated Tremor and Ataxia (FXTAS) in the 4th to 7th decade of life. The young girl's mother was found not to carry the gene mutation but the male sperm donor was found to have a Fragile X premutation. Such medical information about the child is important to the sperm donor because he is at risk of developing a neurologic disorder later in life and will transmit this genetic defect to all his daughters. His extended family members are also at-risk of being carriers of a Fragile X premutation and may potentially have children with Fragile X syndrome in the full mutation form which is associated with mental handicap and autism.[54] Such information is relevant to reproductive decision-making.

Similarly a man who donated his sperm at a clinic in Denmark has passed on a genetic disease to five children. It is known that 43 children have been born as a result of his donation and that his sperm has been exported to 10 countries both in and outside Europe. Five of the children have been diagnosed with Neurofibromatosis-1 (NF-1). As mentioned above, the symptoms of NF-1 can vary from mild skin pigmentation changes to brain and nerve sheath tumours.[55]

Gamete donors have been linked to transmission of Autosomal Dominant Polycystic Kidney Disease and Cystic Fibrosis.[56] The lay press reported on a case in which four children were found to have congenital neutropenia, an immune disorder with increased risk of severe infections.[57] All four children appear to have inherited the genetic defect from the same gamete donor because they all had the same version of the genetic defect and their families had each used the same sperm bank.[58] A sophisticated and immediate response system of record keeping might have prevented subsequent use of those gametes after the first child was diagnosed with the disease.

These cases illustrate the implications for gamete donors and their offspring when either party is diagnosed with a well-recognized genetic condition. If a genetic disease is highlighted during the process of recruitment, then appropriate investigations and counselling can be undertaken.[59] As is true with more traditional conceptions, the potential parent might not have any symptoms of a genetically transmissible disease and yet be at risk of passing it to one of his or her children. In the case of HCM, the family history of the gamete donor did not suggest any genetic condition. But it is not uncommon for parents to be diagnosed with a mild form of a genetic disease after the birth of a severely-affected child. Currently, there is no established method to inform the gamete donor or the donor offspring of this risk.[60] Risks can potentially be substantial for the health of the child, the donor and their biological relatives. Access to the medical and family histories of the gamete donor could expedite diagnosis of genetic diseases and permit earlier screening and potential preventive strategies to be pursued. In addition, it "may not be the donor alone that holds a vital key in the health puzzle, but any one of his or her relatives."[61]

Another problem presented to children of donor offspring who do not know their family history, is that they might wish to be able to choose predictive genetic testing but do not know that they could be at risk of a serious disease.

For example, a gamete donor might show symptoms of Huntington disease later in life. There is no cure for this neurodegenerative condition and unlike HCM, all individuals with the Huntington disease gene defect develop signs and symptoms of the disease. Offspring of anonymous gametes would not be aware that this condition is present in the family and yet they would be at 50% risk of also having Huntington disease. Although predictive genetic testing would be available for children of parents with Huntington's, there is no established mechanism to inform donor offspring of this risk.[62] (Genetic counselling prior to predictive testing ought to be available to donor offspring to discuss the advantages and disadvantages of genetic testing including employment and insurance discrimination and the medical and psychosocial impact this testing may have on family members (both biological and non biological).)

Extensive and comprehensive screening of donor gametes for all genetic conditions is not possible. Genetic diseases will be diagnosed in both gamete donors and donor offspring and this will have health implications for both parties and their biological relatives. The challenge remains to develop systems of record keeping and immediate response to communicate these risks whilst respecting the privacy and confidentiality of donor offspring and gamete donors.

5.2 Secrecy Can Lead to Harms of Incest and Accidental Discovery

"A single donor may make a large contribution to a local ethnic community ... intra-marriage within such a community would result in increased inbreeding due to artificial insemination."[63]

As discussed, assessment of the family history includes information about possible consanguinity (marriage or union between closely genetically related individuals). If the biological parents are related, then they are at slightly higher risk over the general population to have a child with a birth defect or handicapping condition. For first cousins, who share one-eighth of their genes, this chance is increased from 2-3% to 4-6%. This is because the more closely related a couple is, the higher the chance they share the same genes. There is also an increased risk for multifactorial conditions or complex traits and autosomal recessive conditions. People who do not know that they are related are at risk of reproducing with each other and increasing genetic risk to their child. Consanguinity at the level of third cousins or more is not believed to be genetically significant.[64] A brother and sister share half their genes and half siblings share one quarter of genes. Given that these individuals share a greater proportion of their genes, a child from these unions would be at significantly increased risk of a major birth defect or handicapping condition.

Many people who have conceived children through gamete donation have not disclosed to their children their biological parentage.[65] As more genetic tests become part of routine medical care, more cases of non-paternity will be discovered. Such discoveries may take place increasingly in the classroom. Many schoolroom activities involve learning about genetics and patterns of inheritance revealing that parentage may not quite fit with what a child was led to believe. As Barry Stevens, a Canadian film maker and donor offspring predicts, "It won't be long before a child in biology class will be able to take a epithelial swab of his mom or dad and very quickly be able to determine if he is or is not the biological child of his parents."[66]

5.3 Secrecy Can Also Lead to Harm to Individuals Who Wrongly Believe That They Know Their Family History

Individuals can be harmed by the clinical consequences of falsely assuming that the genetic history of your non-biological parent is their own.[67] False family history can lead to misdiagnosis of a genetic condition and perhaps to screening for a condition for which the individual is not at-risk. Such error can have serious consequences to the health and well being of the individual. For example, screening guidelines for Familial Adenomatous Polyposis, an autosomal dominant colon cancer predisposition syndrome, recommend regular abdominal ultrasounds and blood measurements of serum alpha-fetoprotein concentration until age five years; annual colonoscopy beginning at age ten to 12 years until colectomy; and removal of the esophagus and/or stomach by age 25 years among other regular medical examinations.[68] If this condition is present in the non-biological parent and the donor-offspring is unaware that this individual is not his biological relative, this child will undergo screening from birth and will be subject to invasive clinical examinations in early adolescence. Alternatively, the child's parent may choose to have the child undergo genetic testing for FAP to determine that she/he is not at-risk for this condition all the while still presuming that he/she was at 50% risk for this condition. There have been documented cases of "survivor guilt "and a sense of "not belonging to the family" in sib-ships where some siblings have been found to carry the familial mutation for a serious genetic disease while others have not.[69] Conversely, if the gamete donor has FAP and the donor offspring is unaware of his or her risks for this condition, there is a significant risk for colon cancer by means of colonoscopy if screening is not implemented at a young age. Ninety-five percent of individuals carrying the gene change will develop polyps in their colon by age 35; colon cancer is inevitable without colectomy.[70]

6. Conclusion

Advocates of anonymous donation argue that parents' privacy concerns and the intended benefits of the child's life for the parents and for the child supercede the negative consequences of holding such family secrets and by the individual's right to, and medical need for, information about his/her origins.[71]

But knowledge is empowering – in both health and disease. Knowing our family medical history is important and can lead to improved medical care permitting early detection of disease, improved treatment, and optimal health promotion with targeted prevention and screening strategies. In the context of gamete donation, family history ought to be available to donor-offspring. When the donor offspring is a child, "parents should be encouraged to use the health history of the gamete donor in all encounters pertaining to the health of the child and to tell the child about the use of donor gametes, beginning at the time of the child's earliest understanding of reproduction in general."[72] At adulthood, it is not in the patient's medical interest to deny him or her information regarding family medical history.

Currently, knowledge of genetic predisposition to disease is best obtained by family medical history which takes into account both genetic and non-genetic influences on health. Although this method of obtaining important health information may be superceded by new genetic technologies such as whole genome sequencing, there is still much to be learned about the effects of numerous factors important in modifying disease risk including gene-gene interactions and gene-environment interactions.

Genetic counselling and support is available to gamete donors and donor offspring to help interpret and understand the potential benefits but also the limitations of what genetic testing can tell us.

While donors and others who participate in conceiving a child have a general right to privacy, adults who participate in the conception of a child ought to be informed of the importance to the child of their family history and understand that the child has a moral right to it. Ultimately, the first duty of adults who bring a child into being is to the health of the child.

Bibliography

Andermann A. and I. Blancquaert. "Genetic Screening: A Primer for Primary Care." *Can Fam Physician*. 2010; 56: 333-339.

Berg, A.O., M.A. Baird, J.R. Botkin, D.A. Driscoll, P.A. Fishman, P.D. Guarino, R.A. Hiatt, G.P. Jarvik, S. Millon-Underwood, T.M. Morgan, J.J. Mulvihill, T.I. Pollin,

S.R. Schimmel, M.E. Stefanek, W.M. Vollmer and J.K. Williams. National Institutes of Health State-of-the-Science Conference Statement Family History and Improving Health: 26-29 August 2009. *NIH Consens State Sci Statements*. 2009; 26(1): 1-19.

Boxer, L.A., S. Stein, D. Buckley, A.A. Bolyard and D.C. Dale. "Strong evidence for autosomal dominant inheritance of severe congenital neutropenia associated with ELA2 mutations." *J Pediatr* 2006; 148(5): 633-636.

Caulfield, T., N.M. Ries, C. Shuman and B. Wilson. "Direct-to-Consumer Genetic Testing: Good, Bad or Benign." *Clin Genet*. 2010; 77(2):101-5. Epub, 21 November 2009.

Clarke, A.J. "Musings on Genome Medicine: The Value of Family History." *Genome Med*. 2009; 1:75.

Cohen, George J. "The Prenatal Visit." *Pediatrics*. 2009; 124(4):1227-1232.

Daar, J.F. and R.G. Brzyski. "Genetic Screening of Sperm and Oocyte Donors: Ethical and Policy Implications." *JAMA*. 2009; 302(15): 1702-1704.

Dolan, S.M. and C. Moore. "Linking Family History in Obstetric and Pediatric Care: Assessing Risk for Genetic Disease and Birth Defects." *Pediatrics*. 2007; 120:S66-70.

Evans, D.M., P.M. Visscher and N.R. Wray. "Harnessing the Information Contained Within the Genome-Wide Association Studies to Improve Individual Prediction of Complex Disease Risk." *Human Molecular Genetics*. 2009;18(18): 3525-3531.

F:\gamete donation\donor gamete\Sperm donor passes rare dangerous disease on to four children.mht.

Gazvani, R., M.P.R. Hamilton, S.A. Simpson and A. Templeton. "New Challenges for Gamete Donation Programmes: Change in Guidelines are Needed." *Human Fertil*. 2002;5: 183-184.

Green, R.F. "Summary of Workgroup Meeting on Use of Family History Information in Pediatric Primary Care and Public Health." *Pediatrics*. 2007; 120:S87-100.

Hampton, T. "Anonymity of Gamete Donations Debated." *JAMA*. 2005;294(212): 681-3.

Harper, P.S. *Practical Genetic Counselling*. 2001. 5th Edition. Oxford University Press, New York.

http://www.napnap.org/ProgramsAndInitiatives/HEAT/AboutHEAT.aspx.

http://www.napnap.org/ProgramsAndInitiatives/KySS/AboutKySS.aspx.

Jenkins, M.M., S.A. Rasmussen, C.A. Moore, M.A. Honein. "Ethical Issues Raised by Incorporation of Genetics into the National Birth Defects Prevention Study." *Am J Med Genet* 2008;148C: 40-6.

Jett, K. and J.M. Friedman. "Clinical and Genetics Aspects of Neurofibromatosis 1." *Genet Med*. 2010;12(1):1-11.

Laberge, A. and Burke W. "Clinical and Public Health Implications of Emerging Genetic Technologies." *Semin Nephrol*. 2010;30(2): 185-94.

Levenson, D. "New Test Could Make Carrier Screening More Accessible." *Am J Med Genet A*. 2010;152A(4): vii-iii.

Lupski, J.R., J.G. Reid, C. Gonzaga-Jauregui, D. Rio Deiros, D.C.Y. Chen, L. Nazareth, M. Bainbridge, H. Dinh, C. Jing, D.A. Wheeler, A.L. McGuire, F. Zhang, P. Stankiewicz, J.J. Halperin, C. Yang, C. Gehman, D. Guo, R.K. Irikat, W. Tom, N.J. Fantin, D.M. Muzny and R.A. Gibbs. "Whole Genome Sequencing in a Patient with Charcot-Marie-Tooth Neuropathy." *N Engl J Med*.2010; 362: 1181.

Maron, B.J., J.R. Lesser, N.B. Schiller, K.M. Harris, C. Brown and H.L. Rehm HL. "Implications of Hypertrophic Cardiomyopathy Transmitted by Sperm Donation." *JAMA.* 2009; 302(15): 1681-1972.

McGee, G., S.V. Brakman, A.D. Gurmankin. "Gamete Donation and Anomnymity." *Human Reprod.* 2001;16(10): 2033-2038.

Nussbaum, R.L., R.R. McInnes, H.F.Willard. *Thompson and Thompson Genetics in Medicine*, 6th Edition. Philadelphia: Saunders, 2004.

Patrizio, P., A.C. Mastroianni, L. Mastroianni. "Disclosure to Children Conceived with Donor Gametes Should be Optional." *Human Reprod.* 2001;16(10): 2033-2036.

Rimoin, D.L., J.M. Connor, R.E. Pyeritz, B.R. Korf. *Emory and Rimoin's Principles and Practice of Medical Genetics.* 2007. 5th edition. Elsevier, Philadelphia.

Solomon, B.D., B.W. Jack and W.G. Feero. "The Clinical Content of Preconception Care: Genetics and Genomics." *Am J Obstet Gynecol.* 2008;199(6 suppl 2):S340-4.

"Sperm Donor Secrecy Seen Risking Incest." *The Washington Post*, 16 March 1979: ProQuest Historical Newspapers the Washington Post (1887-1991) pg A24.

Trotter, T.L. and H.M. Martin. "Family History in Pediatric Primary Care." *Pediatrics.* 2007; 120:S60-65.

US Preventive Services Task Force. "Screening for colorectal cancer: recommendations and rationale." *Ann Intern Med* 2002;137: 129-31.

Valdez, R., K.J. Greenlund, J.K. Muin, and P.W. Yoon. "Is Family History a Useful Tool for Detecting Children at Risk for Diabetes and Cardiovascular Diseases? A Public Health Perspective." *Pediatrics.* 2007; 120:S78-86.

Wattendorf, D.J. and D.W. Hadley. "Family History: The Three Generation Pedigree." *Am Fam Physician.* 2005;72(3): 441-448.

Wilfond, B. and L.F. Ross. "From Genetics to Genomics: Ethics, Policy and Parental Decision-Making." *J Pediatr Psychol.* 2009;34(6):639-47. Epub, 22 July 2008.

Wilson, B.J., N. Qureshi, P. Santaguida, J. Little, J.C. Carroll, J. Allanson and P. Raina. "Systematic review: family history in risk assessment for common diseases." *Ann Intern Med.* 2009;151(12): 878-85.

Wirojanan, J., K. Angkustsiri, F. Tassone, L.W. Gane and R.J. Hagerman. "A Girl with Fragile X Premutation from Sperm Donation." *Am J Med Genet A.* 2008;146(7): 888-92.

Woodward, C. "United States Government Grows a Family Health Tree, Helping People Trace Hand-Me-Down Genetic Risks." *CMAJ.* 2009;180(2): 707.

www.23andme.com.
www.acmg.net (family history day).
www.counsyl.com.
www.decode.com.
www.financialpost.com/related/topics/story.html?id=2743890.
www.geneclinics.org.
www.hhs.gov/familyhistory.
www.navigenics.com.

Notes

1. McGee, Brakman and Gurmankin, "Gamete Donation and Anonymity, 2033-2038.
2. Patrizio, Mastroianni and Mastroianni, "Dislosure to Children Conceived with Donor Gametes Should be Optional," 2033-2036.
3. Nussbaum, McInnes and Willard, *Thompson and Thompson Genetics in Medicine*, 2004.
4. *Ibid.*
5. Jenkins, Rasmussen, Moore, and Honein, "Ethical Issues Raised by Incorporation of Genetics into the National Birth Defects Prevention Study," 40-6.
6. Ibid; Harper, *Practical Genetic Counselling*, 2001.
7. Rimoin, Connor, Pyeritz and Korf, *Emory and Rimoin's Principles and Practice of Medical Genetics*, 2007.
8. Nussbaum and others, see note 3 above.
9. Nussbaum and others, see note 3 above.
10. Wilfond and Ross, "From Genetics to Genomics: Ethics, Policy and Parental Decision-Making," 639-47.
11. www.financialpost.com/related/topics/story.html?id=2743890.
12. Nussbaum and others, see note 3 above; Rimoin and others, see note 7 above; Green, "Summary of Workgroup Meeting on Use of Family History Information in Pediatric Primary Care and Public Health," 2007; Berg, Baird, Botkin, Driscoll, Fishman, Guarino, Hiatt, Jarvik, Millon-Underwood, Morgan, Mulvihill, Pollin, Schimmel, Stefanek, Vollmer and Williams, National Institutes of Health State-of-the-Science Conference Statement Family History and Improving Health: 26-29. *NIH Consens State Sci Statements*, 1-19; www.hhs.gov/familyhistory; www.acmg.net; Wilson, Qureshi, Santaguida, Little, Carroll, Allanson and Raina, "Systematic review: family history in risk assessment for common diseases," 878-85; Clarke, "Musings on Genome Medicine: The Value of Family History," 75.
13. Geneclinics, http://www.ncbi.nlm.nih.gov/sites/GeneTests/.
14. Wilson and others, see note 12 above.
15. Wattendorf and Hadley, "Family History: The Three Generation Pedigree," 441-448.
16. US Preventive Services Task Force, "Screening for colorectal cancer: recommendations and rationale," 129-31.
17. Wilson and others, *supra*, note 12; Dolan and Moore, "Linking Family History in Obstetric and Pediatric Care: Assessing Risk for Genetic Disease and Birth Defects," S66-70.
18. Wattendorf and Hadley, *supra*, note 15.
19. Cohen, "The Prenatal Visit," 1227-1232.
20. Solomon, Jack and Feero, "The Clinical Content of Preconception Care: Genetics and Genomics," S340-4.
21. Green, "Summary of Workgroup Meeting on Use of Family History Information in Pediatric Primary Care and Public Health," S87-100.
22. Trotter and Martin, "Family History in Pediatric Primary Care," S60-65; Valdez, Greenlund, Muin and Yoon, "Is Family History a Useful Tool for Detecting Children at Risk for Diabetes and Cardiovascular Diseases? A Public Health Perspective," S78-86.
23. *Ibid.*
24. http://www.napnap.org/ProgramsAndInitiatives/HEAT/AboutHEAT.aspx.
25. http://www.napnap.org/ProgramsAndInitiatives/KySS/AboutKySS.aspx.
26. Jett and Friedman, "Clinical and Genetics Aspects of Neurofibromatosis," 1-11.
27. http://www.hfea.gov.uk/7532.html.
28. Geneclinics, *supra*, 13.
29. *Ibid.*
30. *Ibid.*
31. *Ibid.*
32. Nussbaum and others, see note 3 above; Wattendorf and Hadley, *supra*, note 15.
33. Harper, *Practical Genetic Counselling*.
34. Rimoin and others, *supra*, note 7 above.
35. Trotter and Martin, *supra*, note 22.
36. *Ibid.*

37 Woodward, "United States Government Grows a Family Health Tree, Helping People Trace Hand-Me-Down Genetic Risks," 707.
38 Rimoin and others, *supra*, note 7 above.
39 Geneclinics, *supra*, note 13.
40 Evans, Visscher and Wray, "Harnessing the Information Contained Within the Genome-Wide Association Studies to Improve Individual Prediction of Complex Disease Risk," 3525-3531.
41 Caulfield, Ries, Shuman and Wilson, "Direct-to-Consumer Genetic Testing: Good, Bad or Benign," 101-5.
42 *Ibid*.
43 www.23andme.com, www.decode.com and www.navigenics.com.
44 www.counsyl.com.
45 Levenson, "New test Could Make Carrier Screening More Accessible," vii-iii.
46 Lupski and others, "Whole Genome Sequencing in a Patient with Charcot-Marie-Tooth Neuropathy," 1181.
47 Rimoin and others, see note 7 above.
48 Clarke, *supra*, note 12 above.
49 Laberge and Burke, see note 13 above.
50 Woodward, see note 39 above.
51 www.acmg.net.
52 Maron and others, "Implications of Hypertrophic Cardiomyopathy Transmitted by Sperm Donation," 1681-1972.
53 Wirojanan and others, "A Girl with Fragile X Premutation from Sperm Donation," 888-92.
54 *Ibid*.
55 United Kingdom Human Fertilisation and Embryology Authority, September 2012, http://www.hfea.gov.uk/7532.html.
56 Daar and Brzyski, "Genetic Screening of Sperm and Oocyte Donors: Ethical and Policy Implications," 1702-1704.
57 F:\gamete donation\donor gamete\Sperm donor passes rare dangerous disease on to four children.mht.
58 Boxer and others, "Strong evidence for autosomal dominant inheritance of severe congenital neutropenia associated with ELA2 mutations," 633-636.
59 Gazvani and others, "New Challenges for Gamete Donation Programmes: Change in Guidelines are Needed," 183-184.
60 *Ibid*.
61 *Ibid*.
62 *Ibid*.
63 "Sperm Donor Secrecy Seen Risking Incest," *The Washington Post*, A24.
64 Nussbaum and others, see note 3 above.
65 McGee and others, see note 1 above; Patrizio and others, see note 2 above.
66 Hampton, "Anonymity of Gamete Donations Debated," 681-3.
67 McGee and others, see note 1 above.
68 www.geneclinics.org.
69 Rimoin and others, see note 7 above.
70 www.geneclinics.org.
71 McGee and others, see note 1 above.
72 *Ibid*.

PART FOUR

COMPETING ARGUMENTS FOR DONOR ANONYMITY: LEGISLATIVE EFFECTS AND ETHICAL ASSESSMENT

The most frequently cited barrier to removing anonymity is that the supply of donor gametes will cause a decline in supply.[1] The claim that an anonymity ban will have this effect has been made frequently. But in the United Kingdom, where anonymity was banned in 2005, the evidence does not support the conclusion. New donor registrations increased in 2005 from 272 males and 1,023 females, to 480 males and 1,258 females in 2010.[2]

Clearly, some people *will* donate in the knowledge that their identity may be disclosed to any offspring. If the practice is to continue and if anonymity is banned, then service providers face the challenge of devising recruitment strategies that effectively encourage gamete donation from individuals willing to be known to their offspring.

Despite the absence of clear evidence that an anonymity ban would cause supply to decrease, the fear that it might was a central reason that Canada's Parliament shifted from focusing on the health and well-being interests of the donor-conceived to the interests of the adults who wished to have children.

In her chapter, "Donor Anonymity in the Assisted Human Reproduction Act: the back story", journalist, *Alison Motluk,* investigates a pivotal time in the Canadian federal legislative history of donor anonymity: the three-year period May 2001 to April 2004. In December 2001, the Health Standing Committee recommended that donor anonymity be abolished. Despite that recommendation, on March 29, 2004, the *Assisted Human Reproduction Act* was passed, protecting donor anonymity. Motluk's investigation, which includes extensive interviews with Parliamentarians and parties influential in the debate, reveals that legislation ultimately was based on the belief that an anonymity ban would decrease the supply of donor gametes thus making it even more difficult for people who wish to have children to fulfill their desires. Motluk's interviews and report insightfully reveal that some of those who participated in the Parliamentary process still engage in introspection, wondering if the legislative outcome that placed adult interests first, was indeed best.

Thus, even though a decline in supply is not an inevitable result of an anonymity ban, many Canadian legislators acted as though it was. Independently of the supply concern, are there good moral reasons to maintain a system that prevents the donor-conceived from knowing the identity of their progenitors?

Philosopher, *Laura Shanner*, canvasses a range of moral theories and finds none that justifies the current practice of donor anonymity. She argues that assisted conception must be understood as entailing profound ethical responsibilities to protect the resulting offspring's interests. Secrets and lies do not provide strong foundations for healthy children, functional families, and social justice. Adults are free to avoid participating in donor conception but the offspring have no choice; the most basic notions of respect require that we at least tell them the truth about matters so intimately important to them. Having canvassed the matter from a variety of ethical theories including theories of justice and of virtue, the ethic of care, and utilitarianism, she states that no plausible account of ethics justifies anonymity in donor conception; the tradition of secrecy was clearly born of shame and embarrassment rather than of virtuous intent. Shanner concludes that if we cannot admit what we are doing and be held accountable for it, then we should not be doing it at all.

Notes

1 See for example, S. Blakemore, "Couples 'Facing Donor Trauma,'" *Birmingham Post*, 22 January 2004; Mark Henderson, "Egg Shortage Threatens Baby Hopes of Thousands," *The Times*, 22 January 2004.
2 Human Fertilisation and Embryology Authority, "New donor registrations", 1992 – 2010, http://www.hfea.gov.uk/3411.html, accessed November 12, 2012.

Chapter Fifteen

Donor Anonymity in the *Assisted Human Reproduction Act*: The Back Story

Alison Motluk

1. Introduction

Now that the Supreme Court has decided that the issue of donor anonymity is a provincial matter,[1] it is instructive to examine how legislative policy outcomes can be influenced. This chapter considers how, when the ill-fated *Assisted Human Reproduction Act* was being created, shifting slates of committee members caused policy also to shift, and that fear that anonymity would reduce gamete supply was a significant factor in the legislative outcome.

For a short time, in December 2001, it looked as though Canada might ban the use of anonymous sperm and egg donors. An all-party Committee of Members of Parliament had just made such a recommendation in their report, after having considered proposals for a new law on assisted human reproduction.

They did not mince words. The Committee wrote,

> We feel that, where there is a conflict between the privacy rights of a donor and the rights of a resulting child to know its heritage, the rights of the child should prevail. ... We want to end the current system of anonymous donation.[2]

The Committee made clear recommendations regarding how this change should be implemented. They argued that sperm, egg or embryo donors should consent, as a condition of being donors, to having their identities known to offspring and their families. They believed strongly that offspring and legal guardians should have access not only to a snapshot of their donor's family health, but also to updated medical histories. The Committee urged that connections between genetic siblings be facilitated, if for no other reason than to avoid incest. And the Committee recommended that counseling should be provided to donors both before they actually donate and before a donor-conceived person contacts them. In return, donors should be legally protected from the financial and other responsibilities that normally accompany genetic parenthood.[3]

These ideas were progressive for the time. Only Sweden, Austria, Switzerland, and the state of Victoria in Australia had, at that point, abolished the practice of using anonymous gamete donors. The United Kingdom had yet to face its High Court challenge on the issue,[4] let alone amend its law.

But when Canada's *Assisted Human Reproduction Act*[5] finally received royal assent on 29 March 2004, it contained none of these proposed elements. On the contrary, donor anonymity was fully protected. The Act contained no provisions to require current medical histories or to facilitate contact between siblings. All that remained of the Committee's concern for the rights of the child was the declaration, still given top billing, that "the health and well-being of children born through the application of assisted human reproductive technologies must be given priority in all decisions respecting their use." In the new context, the words rang hollow.

What happened?

2. Legislative History

Attempts at regulating assisted human reproduction in Canada have been fraught since they began. In the 1980s, it became clear that reproductive technology was developing rapidly and there were calls from various quarters, including women's groups and religious organizations, for laws to guide it.

In response, Prime Minister Brian Mulroney in 1989 created a *Royal Commission on New Reproductive Technologies*, led by University of British Columbia geneticist, Patricia Baird. Enduring four years and costing $28 million, the Commission held public hearings across the country, initiated independent research, and heard the views of thousands of Canadians.[6]

The Commission's difficult experience of agreeing upon recommendations made it abundantly clear, if it wasn't so already, that assisted human reproduction was a highly contentious and emotional issue.[7] In many ways, the same controversies that hindered the commission continue to dog efforts to regulate reproductive technology today.

On 15 November 1993, the Commission released its final report, *Proceed with Care*.[8] Among numerous other issues, the report addressed the question of donor anonymity. Four of the five commissioners recommended that anonymity be allowed. In their opinion, a donor's identity should be revealed only in cases of serious medical need, and even then, that need would have to be established in court.[9]

There was a single dissenting opinion by Suzanne Rosell Scorsone, a social anthropologist and Catholic theologian, who wrote:[10]

> The assumption that the rights of an adult child of gamete donation to information on the specifics of his or her heritage can be negated rests upon

definitions of the parent-child bond which would deny the importance of the perduring genetic link, that aspect of his or her identity which is genetically based. ... The determination of these social definitions has been set solely on the wishes of the engendering or receiving adults ... [T]his nullification of the rights of the offspring appears to me to be unjustified on any social or empirical ground.

The first federal legislative attempt in Canada to tackle assisted human reproduction was Bill C-47, introduced in June 1996, by then Minister of Health, David Dingwall. It did not address the issue of donor anonymity and died on the Order Paper when a federal election was called on 27 April 1997.[11]

It would be almost four more years before the next health minister, Allan Rock, would take the plunge. When Rock finally did bring forward legislation, he did so in an unusual fashion. Ordinarily, a bill is sent to committee for review only after Parliament has already given it second reading. By that time, the bill is nearly in the form the government would like it to be when it becomes law; the committee's job is just to make minor amendments.

In this case, however, Rock chose to submit a bill in a preliminary form to the Committee as a series of "draft legislative proposals and accompanying documents" – before a proper bill had even been drawn up. Rock's decision signaled that, though the government had an idea of the legislation's general aim, it wanted the Committee to test the public mood and help shape the law's direction.

Rock met with the Commons Health Standing Committee[12] on 3 May 2001 and explained why he was not tabling the legislation directly in Parliament. "This legislation is like no other," he told the Committee members. "These issues are like no others. The issues are at once extremely personal for individuals and their families, yet at the same time of profound interest to all of society."[13]

On the issue of donor anonymity, in particular, Rock sided with the donors. He told the Committee that his draft legislation would "ensure that men and women who chose to help others build their families or to advance science would be assured of their privacy."[14]

Rock emphasized the importance of the Committee's work and asked the Committee to report by 31 January 2002.[15] Over the course of its inquiry, the Committee called numerous witnesses to give testimony on this question. And, in the end, the Committee members disagreed with Rock on anonymity: they came down on the side of banning it.

3. The Commons Standing Committee on Health, May 3 – December, 2001

The Commons Standing Committee on Health had 16 members, from all parties in the House of Commons. At the time, Parliament consisted of Liberals (172), Canadian Reform/Conservative Alliance (66), Bloc Québécois (38), New Democratic Party (13) and Progressive Conservatives (12).[16] The Committee[17] was chaired by Bonnie Brown, a Liberal MP who represented Oakville, Ontario.

When asked to recollect their experience of serving on the Committee, many members still recalled the moving testimony from the then19-year-old Olivia Pratten,[18] who had been conceived with donor sperm. She told them:[19]

> Sometimes when I'm in Vancouver I wonder whether I pass him on the street. When I meet someone who was a UBC student around the time I was conceived, I look him over and wonder, could he be my biological father? ... What I do know is that there is an undeniable piece missing that I'm always subconsciously trying to find.

Olivia Pratten rejected the idea that offspring should be satisfied with a portfolio of non-identifying information. "I'd call it taunting information," she told the committee. "Basically, the message is, we know who he is but we will not tell you." She wanted to know who the man was, not just his answers to a sperm bank questionnaire. She concluded by asking the Committee members if they honestly thought they could be satisfied not knowing half their identity.

The Committee heard from others, too, including a second donor-conceived person, Barry Stevens; from bioethicists such as Laura Shanner and Margaret Somerville; and from representatives of various groups advocating more openness. Jean Haase, a social worker at the London Health Sciences fertility clinic told the Committee:[20]

> The aspect of regulation about which I'm most concerned relates to an apparent contradiction that I see inherent in placing the rights of children born from reproductive technology above all others and yet proposing the establishment of a system that is potentially discriminatory against them in terms of access to the identifying information about their gamete donors.

Haase said that, given the tendency of the medical world to take into account only the rights of the adults, she expected there would be problems applying the principle of the best interests of the child.[21]

Proponents of anonymity argued that without it, the supply of donor sperm and eggs would plummet, leaving infertile couples, as well as lesbians and single women, without this option.[22]

Arthur Leader, a founding physician at the Ottawa Fertility Centre, told the Committee that though many children may grow up wanting to know their donors, many parents, in fact, prefer anonymous donors. "The problem is... the fetus is not a person and certainly the sperm is not a person. So the child who is yet to be created and the child who is yet to be born can't speak on its behalf."[23] Further, he did not think banning anonymous donation would change the situation. In countries where anonymity had been banned, he told the Committee, many parents simply go elsewhere. "People will do what they think is necessary."[24]

Committee members were feeling overwhelmed. The issues they were grappling with – stem cells, cloning, the fate of surplus embryos, payment for gametes and other reproductive services, as well as donor anonymity – were not only technically complex, they were also extremely divisive.

Standing Committee Chair, Bonnie Brown, recalls Judy Sgro, a Toronto Liberal MP, saying she was having trouble sleeping. Brown was feeling at sea herself and one night found herself scribbling down her thoughts, trying to sort them out. "We were trying to make several groups happy," says Brown. "But we had no principle underpinning our work."[25]

As it happened, Brown's husband had been director of the Halton Region Children's Aid Society. "Every single thing he did was built around the best interests of the child," says Brown. "Here we had a situation where we were going to produce new children through unorthodox means. And, of course, the principle should be the best interest of the child."[26]

Brown proposed to the Committee that they assess evidence first and foremost according to how it would affect the children created. Whereas Rock had listed the welfare of children as the ninth item of twelve in the preamble, the Committee members now agreed to give it top rank. Although not formally a part of the law, the preamble is important because it gives guidance to the judges who would eventually interpret it.[27]

Early in December, Sgro told reporters that she and others were working to ensure that donor offspring would be able to learn their donor's identity at age 18. "There should be no anonymous donors, period," she declared.[28] On 12 December 2001, the Commons Standing Committee on Health submitted its report, *Building Families*.[29] It was the culmination of months of research and thoughtful consideration and it offered bold advice to the Minister. Under the heading "Our Priorities", the Report stated:[30]

> Overall, our thinking is directed by the feeling that children conceived though assisted human reproduction warrant even greater consideration than the adults seeking to build families or the physicians or researchers seeking new knowledge.

Everyone felt a sense of urgency. The Committee had worked hard to meet the timeline Rock suggested of January 2002, and even though the committee members knew the bill was a political hot potato, they anticipated the Minister's response to their report early in the new year. "We had the expectation," says Brown, "that we'd have the whole bill through Senate by June."[31]

4. A New Minister of Health

It was not to be. In January, 2002, when Parliament reconvened after Christmas break, there had been a cabinet shuffle. Allan Rock was no longer Health Minister and had been succeeded by Anne McLellan. Whereas Rock had been keen on getting the bill through, McLellan waited until May before even responding. Moreover, her Bill, C-56, rejected the recommendation by the Committee that donor anonymity be abolished.

Indeed, when McLellan moved on 21 May 2002, that the bill be read for a second time, she put an original spin on the word "anonymous". She told the House:[32]

> I would like to make it clear that there will be no anonymous donors. All donors will have to provide their names to clinics before they can donate. However, the release of donor names would require the donor's consent. This approach is similar to that used by the provinces and territories for adopted children.

The Minister neglected to mention the evolving trend to permit birth parents' names to be given to adoptees provided birth parents do not take positive steps to prevent disclosure, and in future adoptions to remove altogether birth parents rights to object to such disclosure.[33] Nor was she correct to suggest that there was a provincial consensus on how to handle the issue in the context of adoption.[34] Perhaps not surprisingly, during the four days of parliamentary debate that followed, several parliamentarians gently opposed the Minister's position on anonymity. Then, as is the norm, the bill was returned to the Health Committee for review.

The first Health Committee meeting following the reading of the bill in the House was a heated one. Several government officials had been asked in to explain the bill. The very first question raised was about the fact that donor anonymity had been protected. Carol Skelton, a Canadian Alliance MP from Saskatoon, said, "One of the clearest recommendations from the Health Committee was that children conceived through AHR procedures should have the right to know who their parents are ... Why did you ignore the Committee recommendation and the pleas of the donor offspring?"[35]

Several MPs were clearly angry. James Lunney, a Canadian Alliance MP from Nanaimo, said, "We felt the interests of the children needed to be placed first, then the interests of the parents involved ... We notice that emphasis is dropped in the bill. Would you care to comment on why you didn't choose to include that?"[36] Réal Ménard, a Bloc Quebecois MP from Montreal was even more incensed: "I don't see why we should work for months as a Committee if after that we are saying exactly the opposite of what the witnesses have told us ... I think the Government has shown a total lack of sensitivity by not listening to the members of the Committee."[37]

Caroline Weber, from Health Canada, replied that the decision came down to trying to balance the interests of the child with the interests of the would-be parents. She argued that the double whammy of banning payment and banning anonymity might restrict too severely the number of donors who would be willing to come forward. "We are prohibiting commercialization here, and that's going to have an impact on donation," she said. "Mandatory release of identifying information would have a further impact."[38]

Preston Manning, who was not a member of the Committee but attended most of the early meetings regarding the legislation, recalls that Committee members accepted there was a straight trade-off between the desire of would-be parents to have an adequate pool of donors and the desire of children to know their identity. "It came down to a contest between these two positions," says Manning. "Supply versus the rights of children."[39]

The Committee had clearly decided the trade-off should favour the children. But the new Minister did not agree. "I was sympathetic that they should have health information," says Anne McLellan. "But did they need to know who these guys were? I didn't see why that was necessary."[40]

And there was another thorny issue: provincial family law. Some other jurisdictions that had banned anonymous gamete donations had been able to rewrite family law simultaneously to protect identified donors from claims from offspring.[41] But in Canada, where power is divided between the federal government, on the one hand, and the provinces and territories on the other, a genetic parent's rights and responsibilities are determined by the provinces.[42] Glenn Rivard, senior legal counsel from Justice Canada, reminded the Committee that only the provinces could protect identified donors from legal responsibility for offspring, and though the provinces had been asked to do so, most had not yet legislated. "Therefore there is the potential that until the provinces have addressed it, a child of this procedure could claim, for example, support against the biological parent, or could claim an interest under the estate of the biological parent," said Rivard. "Only the provinces can regulate those matters."[43]

5. A Shift in Focus

Matters grew even more complicated after the summer recess. Shortly after the new parliamentary session began on 30 September 2002, two new members, Carolyn Bennett and Hedy Fry, joined the Health Committee who would change its course.[44] Significantly, both Bennett and Fry were physicians. Like Jeannot Castonguay, a returning member of the Committee, they had both been in general practice, where they encountered patients struggling to have families. Now, instead of viewing evidence through the lens of how a potential child might be affected, the doctors encouraged Committee members to see things through the eyes of the would-be parents.

Both Bennett and Fry believed that many original members showed disdain for the infertile. Bennett recalls members arguing there were plenty of "cute disabled children" that infertile people could adopt.[45] Fry says some seemed to think infertility was "God's will" and that people who couldn't have children should "get a dog" or "get over it."[46]

Yet Brown also saw herself as an advocate of the infertile. "I was on the side of the couples – trying to protect them," she says. "We were concerned about a certain chicanery within the fertility industry," recalls Brown. She says Committee members had heard of instances where it was fairly clear a couple would never conceive, but the clinics kept asking them back and taking their money. "It was costing every cent of their savings," she says, "and their marriage."[47] She and others were also concerned about the long-term effects of fertility drugs on women, which had not been rigorously studied. She was also worried that would-be parents might inadvertently cause harm to the children they were bringing into the world, by cutting them off from their genetic connections.

The Committee decided to hear further from witnesses only on issues where the proposed bill had disagreed with their report.[48] One of those areas, clearly, was anonymity. Bennett and Fry believed that the views of the infertile in this debate had not been adequately represented during the initial gathering of testimony. "They really did need to hear more from the infertile," says Bennett. "Stories weren't well told on that side. They didn't look into the faces of these people."[49]

Both Bennett and Fry worked hard to get more infertile patients to relate their personal stories to the Committee. Fry telephoned physicians to see if they could convince patients to speak.[50] As a consequence, the Committee heard from moving witnesses such as Kate Acs, who learned at age 35 that she was going into menopause, and Tanya Constantine, who suffered premature menopause at age 28, both of whom subsequently used egg donors to conceive.[51]

Another witness, Dara Roth Edney, told the Committee:[52]

> It has been four years since Peter and I started trying to have a baby, and our arms are still empty ... We rarely see friends, as it is too painful to watch them with their growing families. I have had to hold back tears as people I love, voices breaking, say they are sorry to tell me the news of their own pregnancies. We have gone from enjoying holiday celebrations to avoiding them. As a social worker, I used to enjoy working with the elderly, but their concerned prodding about when I was going to have children became too painful.

The couple had recently asked a woman to be a "surrogate mother", that is, to carry their child for them. Patients like these pleaded with the Committee not to create law that would further constrain their reproductive options.

One MP who made a complete about-face as a result of the new testimony was Judy Sgro. "When we first started to listen to stories, it seemed to be sensible to know who the donor is," she recalls. "But when we listened to other people, it got less and less clear." She no longer felt it was fair for donors to face the uncertainty of being confronted by offspring in the future, and she worried that banning anonymity would put a chill on assisted reproduction. "Wonderful things are happening today," she says.[53]

There were ideological tensions within the Committee as well. On one side was a great faith in the power of science and medicine while on the other, there was some distrust of it. The former thought they could smell the influence of religion and the latter sniffed the foul odour of commerce.

To be sure, many physicians and scientists felt under attack. Arthur Leader, a witness and fertility physician, recalls feeling an underlying hostility towards the entire fertility industry, not only among MPs on the Health Committee, but also within Health Canada and the Department of Justice. "It was not latent – it was expressed," he says. "There was a fundamental belief that what we do is unnatural, unnecessary and not in the best interest of infertile Canadians."[54]

Bennett says that physicians like her were considered part of the medical model and therefore part of the problem. "I found it extraordinarily difficult," she says, referring to the blanket distrust of physicians.[55] Recalls Fry: "It became personal – vicious, mean."[56] The non-physicians on the Committee, however, found it tiresome to hear the doctors preface every comment with "After thirty years in practice, I think I know about this...". Brown readily acknowledges that the physician Committee members did know more about the science. "But this is politics," she says. "We were trying to find that sweet spot where the majority of Canadians would be comfortable."[57]

The new Committee viewed differently not only the plight of the infertile but also the situation of donors. Whereas previously Bonnie Brown had spoken of protecting donors from exploitation by the industry, the new Committee focused more on protecting them from the consequences of their own actions. Of sperm donors, Fry said, "He could have sired I-don't-know-how-many babies around Canada. It could be difficult to have all these kids seeking your parentage."[58]

This was especially a problem, thought Fry, if legislation banning anonymity led to fewer donors: "It would bring about reluctance."[59] Concern about a possible diminished supply of gametes was shared by McLellan. "For me the primary motivation was that we didn't want to put up barriers to prevent people from making a donation," she says. As Minister of Health, she heard directly from interested parties, including MPs, officials, and infertile individuals. "I've never encountered a more desperate group of people than those who want to be moms and dads," she says.[60]

6. The New Committee's Vote

After the second round of witnesses had been heard, the Committee had to agree on recommended changes to the proposed law, now known as Bill C-13. Any MP who wanted to table an amendment had to submit the proposed change to the legislative clerk. Then, the Committee dealt with the proposed amendments one by one, in what is known as a "clause-by-clause" reading, and decided on each change with a vote.

On 9 December 2002, the clause protecting the anonymity of donors came up for discussion and some Committee members were still intent on changing it. As it happens, the two strongest proponents of the system of anonymity were not able to be present: Carolyn Bennett was at her dying mother's bedside, and Hedy Fry was in Vancouver. Though they had replacements, it was not clear how those MPs would cast their votes.

Rob Merrifield, a Canadian Alliance member from Alberta, recommended the following change to bill C-13:[61]

> The Agency shall disclose on request the identity of a donor to a person conceived by means of an assisted reproduction procedure using that donor's

human reproductive material or in vitro embryo, or to their descendant, if the person or their descendant ... is at least 18 years of age.

But when a vote was taken, six people voted against the proposed amendment and only five in favour. Two members, Brenda Chamberlain and Réal Ménard, both of whom had previously supported a ban on anonymity, had unexpectedly abstained.[62]

The following day, Ménard raised a point of order, arguing that because Merrifield's amendment had not been available in French, it should be reconsidered. But later that day, after consulting expert staff, the Chair ruled against the point of order.

After the vote on Merrifield's proposed amendment, Chamberlain, who had revealed during Committee hearings that she was an adoptee,[63] told Brown that she'd had personal reasons for abstaining, but was now having second thoughts. She asked Brown if they could reintroduce the amendment after all. Procedurally, this was not possible. "Unfortunately," says Brown, "if an amendment fails, you can't have a second kick at the can."[64]

There ended the Commons discussion about donor anonymity in the current law. The Bill went back to the House, passed, and moved on to the Senate. The Senate heard more testimony on anonymity and many senators reacted sympathetically[65] not only to the offspring, but to parents of donor-conceived children who were pleading for an end to anonymity. However, by this time, another election seemed imminent and if one were called, all this work would have been for naught: the legislation would die on the Order Paper yet again. As a result, there was a general feeling among Senators that, however imperfect, this Bill had to get through.[66]

In its report,[67] the Senate Committee made several "Observations" including the following:

> Some of the most compelling testimony given to the Committee addressed identifiable gamete donation. Several witnesses, including ethicists, the offspring of these reproductive techniques, as well as individuals who had been through the fertility process, spoke eloquently and passionately about the need for mandatory donor identification. It was their position that offspring are entitled to identifying information regarding their biological origins.

Medical professionals, gamete collectors and other individuals who struggle with infertility expressed equally passionate positions that mandatory donor identification would effectively eliminate all gamete donations, especially in the absence of reasonable compensation for the donations. These witnesses testified that currently under family law in all but two provinces and one territory, a non-anonymous sperm donor is deemed to be the father of any child(ren) born as the consequence of his sperm. The Committee was told that the anonymity provision cannot change until family law is changed in all jurisdictions. Additionally, family law does not assign maternity to egg donors currently in any Canadian jurisdiction. The position was clearly expressed that Canada should not make donor identification mandatory before family law has been appropriately addressed to protect the donors.[68]

> The Committee understands the difficulty in requiring donor identification at this time. However, we would observe that this issue should be carefully examined when this legislation is reviewed within three years.

In the end, the clause preferred by Minister Anne McLellan[69] was accepted: "... the identity of the donor – or information that can reasonably be expected to be used in the identification of the donor – shall not be disclosed without the donor's written consent."

7. Conclusion

The *Assisted Human Reproduction Act* was so controversial that it contained a provision requiring it be reviewed three years after the establishment of the agency that would administer it.[70] The goal of this provision was to persuade disparate parties to reach agreement, at least temporarily. It also allowed everyone time to see how well the law worked and what might need to be tweaked. "We made it plain to people," says McLellan, "it's going to be reviewed. The state of knowledge will change. We'll be able to see the results and judge them."[71]

In fact, there are no results to judge. Although the review should technically have begun no later than 12 January 2009,[72] only one regulation had been enacted, concerning consent by donors.[73] It is impossible to weigh the impact of banning payment for gametes, because sperm from paid donors is routinely imported from the United States,[74] an arrangement that was supposed to be temporary while Canada developed an altruistic system.[75] "Compensation" for Canadian donors continues to be unregulated.[76]

Questions surrounding a donor's legal liability have still not been resolved in many provinces. "Our laws really haven't identified what the obligations of a donor might be and what the rights of offspring might be," says McLellan. "The courts are free agents in that sense. They are motivated by a sense of compassion. Legislation can only go so far."[77] Other countries' experiences have not yet been fully studied. Will someone win a court challenge against this legislation? Will the law devised by Canada's Parliament become irrelevant as women simply travel abroad for assisted reproduction, to avoid Canadian legal constraints?

Many of the MPs who served on the Health Committee during the crafting of the law continue to ruminate about the issue. Bonnie Brown, the chair, who was outspoken about the right of offspring to know their progenitors, acknowledges today that perhaps the outcome accurately represented the views of Canadians. "If the majority of the Committee voted against it," she says, "that probably means the majority of Canadians would not have been comfortable."[78]

On the other side, Carolyn Bennett, who fought hard to retain anonymity, recognizes that there are competing interests. "I don't know what the right answer is in terms of weighing the rights of the offspring," she admits. In addition to infertile patients in her practice, Bennett also recalls those who were searching for birth parents. "There's something about not knowing," she says. She is still deeply concerned that the supply of donated gametes would dry up as a result. But she confesses: "The pros and cons of anonymity, we really didn't do a proper piece of work on this."[79]

McLellan, now out of politics, argues that the law can and should change with new knowledge. "There may be a growing and overwhelming consensus that anonymity is bad," she says. "Maybe we'll better understand how big a barrier this is to people donating – maybe it's not so big. And are there court cases? Maybe there won't be any. If not, maybe you move down the road like adoption. Maybe it wouldn't be bad."[80]

Bibliography

Anonymous. *A Short History of the Royal Commission on New Reproductive Technologies*; [Final Edition] The Hamilton Spectator. Hamilton, Ont.: 1 December 1993, A.9.

Freedman, Benjamin. "Commission picks way through a minefield," *The Vancouver Sun*, Vancouver, B.C.; 12 March 1991, A.9.

Greenaway, Norma. "Group may suggest end of anonymity for sperm donors," *National Post*, 3 December 2001.

Graham, Randy N. *Statutory Interpretation: Cases, Texts and Materials*. Toronto: Emond Montgomery Publications Ltd., 2002.

Mironowicz, Margaret. "The Human Side of Reproductive Technology: It gives us hope, woman explains," *Kitchener-Waterloo Record*, 29 November 1990, F.1.

Motluk, Alison. "The Human Egg Trade." *The Walrus*, April 2010.

Royal Commission on New Reproductive Technologies. *Proceed with Care*. Ottawa: Minister of Government Services Canada, 1993.

Standing Committee on Health. *Assisted Human Reproduction: Building Families*. Ottawa: Public Works and Government Services Canada, December, 2001.

Notes

1 2010 SCC 61, [2010] 3 SCR 457.
2 *Assisted Human Reproduction: Building Families*, Report by the Commons Standing Committee on Health, Bonnie Brown, Chair, (Ottawa: Public Works and Government Services Canada, December 2001), 21.
3 *Ibid*, Recommendation 19.
4 *Rose & Another v. Secretary of State for Health Human Fertilisation and Embryology Authority* [2002] EWHC 1593 (Admin) (26 July 2002) (England and Wales High Court).
5 *Assisted Human Reproduction Act* S.C. 2004, c.2.
6 Anonymous, A short *history* of the *Royal Commission on New Reproductive Technologies*; [Final Edition] The Hamilton Spectator, Hamilton, Ont. 1 December 1993, A.9.
7 See, for example, Benjamin Freedman, "Commission picks way through a minefield", 12 March 1991, *The Vancouver Sun*, A9; and Margaret Mironowicz, "The Human Side of Reproductive Technology: It gives us hope, woman explains," 29 November 1990, *Kitchener-Waterloo Record*, F1.
8 *Proceed with Care*, Final Report of the Royal Commission on New Reproductive Technologies, (Ottawa: Minister of Government Services Canada, 1993).
9 *Ibid*., 483.
10 *Ibid*., 1063.
11 Elections Canada, "Appendix 3: Canadian parliaments, 1867-2006," The Electoral System of Canada," http://www.elections.ca/content.aspx?section=res&dir=ces&document=part4&lang=e#49.
12 Chaired by Bonnie Brown.
13 Allan Rock, evidence to Standing Committee on Health, 3 May 2001, http://cmte.parl.gc.ca/cmte/CommitteePublication.aspx?SourceId=54849.
14 *Ibid*.
15 *Ibid*.
16 Robert Marleau and Camille Montpetit eds., "Appendices: General Election Results Since 1867", *House of Commons Procedure and Practice*, November 2005, http://www2.parl.gc.ca/MarleauMontpetit/DocumentViewer.aspx?DocId=1001&Sec=Ch25&Seq=11&Lang=E.
17 Members of the Commons Standing Committee on Health between 3 May 2001, when Allan Rock initiated legislation until 9 December 2002, when the committee's final attempt to remove the anonymity clause failed: Diane Ablonczy [until 22 April 2002], Reg Alcock [from 27 September 2001 until 5 November 2002], Andre Bachand [until 5 November 2002], Raymond Bonin [until 27 September 2001], Colleen Baumier [from 2 October 2001 until 2 March 2002], Carolyn Bennett [from 5 November 2002], Diane Bourgeois, Bonnie Brown, Jeannot Castonguay, Brenda Chamberlain [from 27 September 2001], Yvon Charbonneau [until 27 September 2001], Stan Dromisky, Hedy Fry [from 5 November 2002], James Lunney, Real Menard, Rob Merrifield, Stephen Owen [until 27 September 2001], Carolyn Parrish [until 2 October 2001], Helene Scherrer, Judy Sgro, Carol Skelton [from 23 April 2002], Bob Speller [from 4 March 2002 until 5 November 2002], Yolande Thibeault [from 27 September 2001], Greg Francis Thompson [from 5 November 2002], Judy Wasylycia-Leis; see "Membership", House of Commons Committees, Parliament of Canada Web Site, http://www2.parl.gc.ca/CommitteeBusiness/CommitteeMembership.aspx?Cmte=HEAL&Language=E&Mode=1&Parl=37&Ses=1.
18 See *infra*, Olivia Pratten, Chapter 6.
19 Olivia Pratten, evidence to Standing Committee on Health, 25 October 2001, http://cmte.parl.gc.ca/cmte/CommitteePublication.aspx?Sourceid=55522#T1110.
20 Jean Haase, evidence to Standing Committee on Health, 8 November 2001, http://www2.parl.gc.ca/HousePublications/Publication.aspx?Language=E&Mode=1&Parl=37&Ses=1&DocId=1041144&File=0.
21 *Ibid*.
22 Preston Manning, telephone conversation with author, 10 April 2008.

23 Arthur Leader, evidence to Standing Committee on Health, 23 October 2001, (http://www2.parl.gc.ca/HousePublications/Publication.aspx?DocId=1041030&Language=E&Mode=1&Parl=37&Ses=1).
24 Arthur Leader, telephone conversation with author, 3 April 2008.
25 Bonnie Brown, telephone conversation with author, 19 March 2008.
26 *Ibid.*
27 Randy Graham, *Statutory Interpretation*, 150.
28 Norma Greenaway, "Group may suggest end of anonymity for sperm donors," *National Post*, 3 December 2001.
29 *Assisted Human Reproduction: Building Families*, Report by the Commons Standing Committee on Health, (Ottawa, Public Works and Government Services Canada, December 2001).
30 *Ibid.*, 4. On the specific issue of donor anonymity, there was one dissent from André Bachand, then a Progressive Conservative for the Quebec riding of Richmond-Athabasca. He wrote that he had "strong reservations about doing away with anonymity. What will the consequences be for the number of donors?" (*Ibid.*, 93).
31 Bonnie Brown, telephone conversation with author, 6 June 2008.
32 Canada, *House of Commons Debates,* 21 May 2002, http://www2.parl.gc.ca/HousePublications/Publication.aspx?Language=E&Mode=1&Parl=37&Ses=1&DocId=1385277#SOB-239150.
33 See Guichon, infra, "A Comparison of the Law in Canada Related to the Disclosure of Information Regarding Biological Parents of Adoptees and the Donor-Conceived".
34 *Ibid.*
35 Carol Skelton, evidence to the Standing Committee on Health, 30 May 2002, HEAL 37-1 Edited Evidence 85, Parliament of Canada, http://www2.parl.gc.ca/HousePublications/Publication.aspx?DocId=606622&Language=E&Mode=1&Parl=37&Ses=1.
36 James Lunney, evidence to the Standing Committee on Health, 30 May 2002, HEAL 37-1 Edited Evidence 85, Parliament of Canada, http://www2.parl.gc.ca/HousePublications/Publication.aspx?DocId=606622&Language=E&Mode=1&Parl=37&Ses=1.
37 Réal Ménard, evidence to the Standing Committee on Health, 30 May 2002, HEAL 37-1 Edited Evidence 85, Parliament of Canada, http://www2.parl.gc.ca/HousePublications/Publication.aspx?DocId=606622&Language=E&Mode=1&Parl=37&Ses=1.
38 Caroline Weber, evidence to Standing Committee on Health, 30 May 2002, HEAL 37-1 Edited Evidence 85, Parliament of Canada, http://www2.parl.gc.ca/HousePublications/Publication.aspx?DocId=606622&Language=E&Mode=1&Parl=37&Ses=1.
39 Preston Manning, telephone conversation with author, 10 April 2008.
40 Anne McLellan, telephone conversation with author, 9 April 2001.
41 The United Kingdom, for example is a unitary jurisdiction which perhaps makes it easier for legislation to be enacted than in the Canadian federation.
42 Ss. 91 and 92, *Constitution Act, 1867* (U.K.), 30 & 31 Vict., c. 3, reprinted in R.S.C. 1985, App. II, No. 5 [*Constitution Act*]. See also http://laws.justice.gc.ca/en/const/c1867_e.html.
43 Glenn Rivard, evidence to Standing Committee on Health, 30 May 2002, HEAL 37-1 Edited Evidence 85, Parliament of Canada, http://www2.parl.gc.ca/HousePublications/Publication.aspx?DocId=606622&Language=E&Mode=1&Parl=37&Ses=1.
44 See note 17 above.
45 Carolyn Bennett, telephone conversation with author, 27 March 2008.
46 Hedy Fry, telephone conversation with author, 4 April 2008.
47 Bonnie Brown, telephone conversation with author, 6 June 2008.
48 *Ibid.*
49 Carolyn Bennett, telephone conversation with author, 27 March 2008.
50 Hedy Fry, telephone conversation with author, 4 April 2008.
51 Kate Acs, Tanya Constantine, evidence to Standing Committee on Health, 26 November 2002, HEAL 37-2 Edited Evidence 5, Parliament of Canada,http://www2.parl.gc.ca/HousePublications/Publication.aspx?DocId=588336&Language=E&Mode=1&Parl=37&Ses=2.

52 Dara Roth Edney, evidence to Standing Committee on Health, 26 November 2002, HEAL 37-2 Edited Evidence 5, Parliament of Canada, http://www2.parl.gc.ca/HousePublications/Publication.aspx?DocId=588336&Language=E&Mode=1&Parl=37&Ses=2.
53 Judy Sgro, telephone conversation with author, 6 June 2008.
54 Arthur Leader, telephone conversation with author, 3 April 2008.
55 Carolyn Bennett, telephone conversation with author, 27 March 2008.
56 Hedy Fry, telephone conversation with author, 4 April 2008.
57 Bonnie Brown, telephone conversation with author, 6 June 2008.
58 Hedy Fry, telephone conversation with author, 4 April 2008.
59 *Ibid.*
60 Anne McLellan, telephone conversation with author, 9 April 2008.
61 Rob Merrifield, evidence to the Standing Committee on Health, 9 December 2002, HEAL 37-2 Edited Evidence 14, Parliament of Canada, http://www2.parl.gc.ca/HousePublications/Publication.aspx?DocId=1037149&Language=E&Mode=1&Parl=37&Ses=2.
62 Réal Ménard, telephone conversation with author, 6 August 2008. Ménard does not remember why he abstained, nor does he recall the events surrounding the point of order. The author made repeated attempts to reach Brenda Chamberlain. Ms. Chamberlain did not respond to these attempts.
63 Brenda Chamberlain, evidence to the Standing Committee on Health, 7 November 2001, Parliament of Canada, http://www2.parl.gc.ca/HousePublications/Publication.aspx?DocId=1041143&Language=E#T1725.
64 Bonnie Brown, telephone conversation with author, 6 June 2008.
65 Standing Senate Committee on Social Affairs, Science and Technology, Third Session, Thirty-seventh Parliament, 2004, 25 February 2004, http://www.parl.gc.ca/37/3/parlbus/commbus/senate/Com-e/soci-e/02eva-e.htm?Language=E&Parl=37&Ses=3&comm_id=47.
66 Proceedings of the Standing Senate Committee on Social Affairs, Science and Technology, 3 March 2004, http://www.parl.gc.ca/37/3/parlbus/commbus/senate/Com-e/soci-e/03ev-e.htm?Language=E&Parl=37&Ses=3&comm_id=47.
67 Proceedings of the Standing Senate Committee on Social Affairs, Science and Technology, Issue 3 – Second Report of the Committee, 9 March 2004, http://www.parl.gc.ca/37/3/parlbus/commbus/senate/Com-e/soci-e/03rp-e.htm?Language=E&Parl=37&Ses=3&comm_id=47.
68 *Ibid.*
69 By the time the bill became law, Pierre Pettigrew had replaced Anne McLellan as Health Minister. Pettigrew served from 12 December 2003 until 19 July 2004.
70 Section 70, *Assisted Human Reproduction Act*, 2004, S.C. c. 2.
71 Anne McLellan, telephone conversation with author, 9 April 2008.
72 S. 70 of the Assisted Human Reproduction Act (Canada) 2004, requires Parliament to review the Act within three years of the coming into force of section 21 of the Act. Section 21 came into force on 12 January 2006, Canada Gazette, Vol. 139, No. 10 -SI/2005-42 18 May 2005, http://canadagazette.gc.ca/partII/2005/20050518/html/si42-e.html.
73 Section 8 came into force 1 December 2007.
74 "Brave New Family", Ideas, *CBC Radio*, 15 October 2007.
75 "Health Canada announces project to explore altruistic (not for payment) donation of sperm and eggs in Canada", news release, Health Canada, 2 May 2005,http://www.hc-sc.gc.ca/english/media/releases/2005/2005_34.html.
76 See Motluk, "The Human Egg Trade".
77 Anne McLellan, telephone conversation with author, 9 April 2008.
78 Bonnie Brown, telephone conversation with author, 6 June 2008.
79 Carolyn Bennett, telephone conversation with author, 27 March 2008.
80 Anne McLellan, telephone conversation with author, 9 April 2008.

Chapter Sixteen

When Is a Secret Justified? Ethics and Donor Anonymity

Laura Shanner

1. Introduction

Ethics is the systematic evaluation of our choices and policies in light of our most important values. Core principles such as fairness, respect for persons, and avoiding harm to others are central to our best choices. Virtues such as honesty, compassion and accountability offer further guidance, while the promotion of caring relationships and beneficial outcomes help us to create the better world that we seek. All ethical theories extend equal regard to the interests of everyone affected by a decision. We must therefore consider individual cases and policy applications, localized and ripple effects, and immediate and long-term implications, all at the same time. This challenging process of robust ethical assessment has been compared to looking out of both lenses of bifocal glasses simultaneously.[1]

The ethics of assisted reproductive technologies (ARTs) have been debated for three decades. Yet, while the rights of embryos[2] and of infertile and childless persons[3] have been discussed extensively, the perspectives of *living children and adults* from assisted reproduction – and in particular, from donor conception ("Offspring") – are only beginning to be taken seriously. One might argue that, because these people do not exist when ART decisions are made, they have no morally relevant interests to consider. Our bifocal lenses, however, reveal that the practical, social and ethical implications of assisted conception do not end in the infertility clinic.

Joel Feinberg offers a helpful analogy for understanding ethical obligations to people who do not yet exist. Setting a time bomb to explode tomorrow, injuring whoever is nearby, would clearly be unethical. Setting it to go off in 100 years – when nobody alive today would be hurt – is not ethically better: we anticipate that *somebody* will be here then, and these future-persons will have interests that are just as compelling as our interests are today.[4] The moral issue is not *when* someone is affected, but *that* someone is affected, by today's decision.

Because the point of assisted human reproduction is to bring children into the world, the interests of the resulting people are essential components of procreative ethics. We cannot reach appropriate conclusions from a lopsided analysis that considers only the reproductive collaborators.[5] When we integrate the issues raised by Offspring into our ethical analysis of donor conception, it becomes clear that donor anonymity cannot be justified.

2. Privacy, Secrets and Lies

Secrecy historically shrouds even the fact of donor conception, not just the identity of donors. Secrecy isn't always a bad thing. Sissela Bok explains that this complex phenomenon has both positive and negative aspects.[6] We all require a sphere of privacy, she claims, to maintain our identities and even our sanity. Some secrets, such as passwords, can prevent privacy violations, while withholding incomplete data can promote more reliable research results. Secrecy is therefore not *prima facie* wrong, in the way that lying, promise-breaking and violence are inherently difficult to justify.

Privacy is distinguishable from *secrecy*. Privacy rightly protects matters that do not affect another person's interests; a secret involves withholding information that *does* affect another's interests. Who rightly "owns" the fact of donor involvement in a person's conception? Quite reasonably, donors and recipients may each insist upon standard medical confidentiality. But as Bok observes, children also require privacy in order to develop and protect their emerging identities. If other people have more control over your own personal information than you do, then your privacy has effectively been breached. This is the case for Offspring. Donor anonymity is thus a matter of secrecy toward the Offspring, not mere privacy for the parents.

While all deceptions require secrecy, not all secrets require deception. Because lying is *prima facie* wrong, we must ensure that secrecy about genetic origins does not entail any deception about them. The challenge for donor conception is that a child's normal questions about "where I came from" may make silence impossible. If comments on family resemblances remain uncorrected, deception has been allowed even if no one intended to deceive. In doctors' offices, parents must either reveal the truth or deliberately mislead the child and clinicians about relevant family medical history. As a result, recipient parents who expected to put the circumstances of conception behind them typically find it quite difficult to maintain this secret without lying. As one Offspring wrote:

> Apparently they'd matched the donor with my 'father's' hair and eye colour, and that was that. Then the lies began. The man listed as my father on my birth certificate, isn't. No one knew, or even guessed, the truth. The little lies my mother told helped the deception. ... What I have only just realised is that

> *these lies even extend to what colour eyes I think I have.* Mark and I have a long-running joke/argument: he says I've got green eyes, I say they're brown. When I look in the mirror, I do see that the nearest they get to brown is hazel. Maybe. But the reason I think they're brown is that my mother always said I had brown eyes like Dad. So all along, in school essays entitled 'Myself' or letters to penpals or anything, I have said I have brown eyes.[7]

It can be embarrassing if private matters (e.g., details of one's sexual life) gain public attention, but embarrassment is not the same thing as shame at wrongdoing. Genuine concern to hide one's behaviour (such as an extramarital affair), usually indicates a problem with the activity. To recall an old adage, "If you don't want anyone to know what you're doing, then you probably shouldn't be doing it."

The historical stigma of infertility is an important contributor to the culture of secrecy surrounding donor conception. Two-part birth records, similar to those issued in adoption, could publicly name the social parents to protect their privacy (as well as that of donors and offspring) from public scrutiny, while ensuring accurate genetic information for the offspring.[8] However, if social parents are truly unprepared to admit the involvement of a donor, then perhaps they are unprepared at an important level for the practical consequences of assisted reproduction. Some Offspring claim that their social parents were unable to accept them:

> [M]y father could not stand looking at me because every time he did, he was reminded that he was not really my father.[9]
>
> I had always felt that my mother viewed me as second best – not the baby she really wanted. Now I understood why. When she looked at me she saw a stranger and it affected our relationship until she died. At 41, I had to reassess my life. I felt like a sordid secret transaction, something my mother would have been ashamed of.[10]

Do donors have interests that require secrecy? Accessing confidential health records should require the donor's consent and/or case-specific court orders to protect the Offspring's health. Legal protection from custody or financial responsibility for one's Offspring can be ensured separately from identity release. Choosing to interact (or not) with Offspring who seek contact would be similar to interaction with any relative tracing the family tree. It can be embarrassing to discuss matters such as masturbation to provide sperm samples, but strong emotions of fear or anger at the notion of being identified to the Offspring indicate something more worrisome than embarrassment is in play.

Secrets are not always maintained by individuals, and the bifocal lens shows how laws and policies related to ARTs, birth certificates, and medical records influence (dis)honesty within families. Many more social parents would likely tell their children about using donor conception if they could answer the questions about the donor that naturally follow. Offspring often express anger not only toward their parents for lying and withholding information, but also toward the medical community and government[11] for "setting up the situation" and "washing its hands of responsibility."[12] One donor-conceived person characterized his inaccurate birth certificate as "statutorily sanctioned fraud."[13] Policies intended to protect privacy have thus, instead, created and entrenched systemic deception.

3. Justice

Although we can rarely ensure fair outcomes, justice requires that we protect equal opportunities, liberties and rights, and give equal consideration to all interests at stake regardless of whose interests they happen to be. In anonymous donor conception, none of these conditions of justice are met. A donor-conceived teenager vividly expressed anonymity's essential inequity:

> So you want a biologically related child because it's important to you, but we are not allowed to feel grief that one or both of our biological parents are not raising us?! ... Parents need to realize that their feelings towards their infertility, no matter how painful they may be, are in no way shape or form any more important or more validated than the feelings of their child towards [the parents'] deliberate severing of kinship.[14]

In practical terms, unequal access to personal information that most of us take for granted denies Offspring equal opportunities to interact with their relatives and to explore the familial historical roots that many people find profoundly meaningful. More dangerously, Offspring face unequal risks and benefit from health care. One's family medical history significantly influences accurate diagnosis, pre-symptomatic monitoring, effective preventative health measures and informed choice among treatment options. Anonymity ensures that Offsprings' inadequate medical records can never be corrected or updated.

The injustices created by donor anonymity are of constitutional importance in Canada. According to Section 15(1) of the Charter of Rights and Freedoms, "Every individual is equal before and under the law and has the right to the equal protection and equal benefit of the law without discrimination."[15] However, the former anonymity provisions of the *Assisted Human Reproduction Act*[16] created two categories of Canadians: the majority, whose birth certificates are required to be as accurate as possible, and Offspring, whose genetic parentage is required to be falsified. A donor-conceived Australian observes the unique exclusion her international cohort faces:

> Adoptees have had their rights recognized ... With the Stolen Generation [of Australian Aboriginal children], we recognise that state wards and child migrants have a need to feel connected to their past; and yet donor-conceived adults and adolescents' rights haven't been recognised. In fact we have no rights.[17]

The nondiscrimination rights of Offspring require that the records of their genetic parentage be equally accurate and available.

4. Respect for Persons

Informed consent, a key application of the principle of autonomy[18] or respect for persons, is a cornerstone of contemporary North American bioethics.[19] These principles arise from concepts of essential human dignity, the profound importance of our capacity to make thoughtful choices, and the protection of individual liberties to live as one chooses.

Because people obviously cannot consent to the circumstances of their conception, we tend to assume that issues of respect and choice reside solely with the gamete donors and recipients. However, respect is owed to all persons affected by a decision, not just the decision-makers.

Onora O'Neil helpfully explains what it means to respect human dignity and autonomy: we must treat others only in ways to which they could, *in principle*, give consent.[20] Lies are unethical because consenting to deception is inherently contradictory. Suppose that Stan wants to lie to Betty. Betty's consent for such treatment would require her being informed of the truth, the lie, and the implications of each. Because Betty knows the truth, though, Stan's lie would be foiled. Thus, it is *logically impossible* to consent to be deceived. Accordingly, Offspring cannot consent to deception about their parentage; every implied or explicit falsehood denies their autonomy and human dignity.

The cumulative impact of familial secrets, officially sanctioned misinformation, emphasis on adults' interests in ARTs, and marginalizing of Offsprings' concerns creates a dehumanizing effect that some offspring feel intensely.

> When I read some of the mothers' thoughts about their choice for conception, it made me feel degraded to nothing more than a vial of frozen sperm. It seemed to me that most of the mothers and donors give little thought to the feelings of the children who would result from their actions.[21]

> The fact that there are children being born who have one or even two fake biological parents recorded, as fact, in their original birth certificate is … appalling, as it has completely nullified the authenticity of birth certificates to a mere question of ownership. They have become property rights instead of birth certificates, declaring those who shelled out the money for the child are hereby declared owners [-] oops, I meant parents![22]

Rights-based ethical theories offer a different angle on respect for persons and autonomy, but *justified* rights are fewer than commonly claimed. The legitimate exercise of individual liberties ends whenever one's action causes harm to another or constrains the equal liberty of others. Exercising a right to engage in assisted reproduction, therefore, must not injure Offspring or impede their rights to make their own life choices. As above, Offspring are articulating a range of problems caused by donor anonymity, and secrecy clearly fails the equal liberties test. As lamented by one Offspring:

> Other kids have the right to know their biological parents. My mom may have signed away her rights, but I didn't.[23]

If Offspring are to be bound in perpetuity by the terms of donor conception agreements to which they could not consent, then respect for the *persons they will be when the agreement is enforced against them* requires fair representation of their (future) interests during the initial negotiations. On the other hand, if future persons have no standing in the infertility clinic, then how can they logically be bound by contracts made there? To be ethically binding upon stakeholders who arrive later, new anonymity agreements would have to be negotiated with their participation.[24]

The principles of fundamental equality and respect for persons ground international human rights law as well as ethical rights theories. Governments – not just individual moral agents – have a duty to protect basic, universal human needs and promote physical, emotional and social wellbeing. As Veronica Pinero discusses elsewhere in this volume, the *United Nations Convention on the Rights of the Child*[25] seems particularly clear that donor anonymity fails to respect the human rights of Offspring.

5. Relationships

Two concerns at the heart of an ethic of care[26] are highly relevant to donor conception: interconnection and power dynamics. Human relationships are viewed as central both to the context that gives rise to ethical questions in the first place, and to the appropriate resolution of ethical concerns. Fractured relationships and hurtful interactions are ethical failures, according to this approach; our primary moral guides should be compassion, responsiveness to need, attentiveness to unique individual circumstances, and cultivation of mutual trust and respect.

Assisted conception using third-party gametes, *by definition,* involves creating and expanding complex familial relationships that evolve over lifetimes and generations. Donor anonymity automatically fractures relationships between donors and their genetic-related children, as well as among half-siblings and extended families, causing problems for the Offspring.

Construction of a healthy self-image prompts questions about genetic origins at several life stages. Young children ask, "How was I made?" and seek reassurance that they belong in their families. Adolescents struggle to construct their adult identity, while dating, marriage and parenting all prompt questions about kinship across multiple generations.

Those who learn that they are not genetically related to one or both parents frequently experience feelings of "genetic bewilderment."[27] Wondering which of their physical characteristics and personality traits are inherited from the donor, Offspring often use metaphors to describe feelings of incompleteness: "missing links,"[28] "puzzles,"[29] and "the pain of not knowing who you are."[30]

> The mirror is a monster, it's my worst enemy; I see questions instead of answers. I don't see a whole person; I see a fragmented piece of art that is yet to be signed. I see a stranger who is strangely familiar.[31]

> Getting hold of the truth has done a lot to make being donor-conceived palatable. Not knowing donor identity is like being lost in the middle of a great, featureless ocean.[32]

Donor-conceived individuals frequently express feelings of profound loss related to gaps in their sense of identity, damaged relationships with their social parents, estrangement from others who do not share their experience, disconnection from genetic relatives, and the inability to trust others when they have been systematically deceived.

Some challenge whether "genetic bewilderment" is truly harmful; indeed, not all Offspring are curious, let alone driven, to identify their donor progenitors. People do assign varying levels of importance to kinship, genealogy and family histories. The problem with a policy of anonymity is that it summarily denies that genetic kinship can ever be of great value, or that its disruption can be damaging. As another donor-conceived adult explains:

> There is a saying that there are two lasting bequests we can give our children: one is roots and the other is wings. I think donor-conception denies a child both of these. I feel like a tree that has half of its roots missing. And without them, I can hardly stand up.[33]

Bok observes that secrets create barriers between those who know the truth and those who do not,[34] straining personal relationships in ways that an ethic of care would find unacceptable. Offspring often report such obstacles:

> The lack of openness in our family is evident ... I hope this is not irreversible, as I want to overcome the biggest hurdle – to talk about it with my dad ... I have wasted years trying to protect myself and my dad from this topic; I wish I knew whether talking to him would provide the answers that I want – to help me to reach an acceptance and to lose the restlessness and anger that I have.[35]

The ethic of care also calls attention to the moral implications of power dynamics within each relationship, emphasizing duties of care that the more powerful have toward the weaker party. While all people retain equal moral worth in an abstract sense, practical equality is usually lacking among individuals and groups.[36] Children are always more vulnerable than adults, creating strong parental obligations to protect their interests and nurture them to healthy adulthood. The challenge is to distinguish the necessary exercise of parental power *to take care of* children, from inappropriate exertions of adult power *over* children who cannot defend their own interests. Secrets rarely empower those kept in the dark, and hiding the truth about donor conception clearly benefits the adult reproductive collaborators more than the resulting Offspring.

Donor anonymity thus does more than fracture kinship connections. Secrecy amounts to a misuse of power in which adults place their own interests ahead of their duties as parents – whether social or genetic – to protect and support their vulnerable children. From an ethic of care perspective, donor anonymity is disruptive and dangerous.

6. Virtue

Are any ethical traits of character uniquely represented, or embodied more fully, by donor anonymity rather than openness? It is difficult to imagine what they might be, when core virtues such as honesty and taking responsibility for one's choices clearly favor openness. Virtues are embodied not just by individuals, but also by communities. Falsifying official documents and denying common opportunities for a minority group would not seem to promote an accountable and just population.

Virtuous role models are also central to psychological development toward moral maturity. How precisely are we to teach our children to be truthful and responsible, when we create fictions and deny the consequences of major decisions in their most intimate and trusting relationships? If we want our children to be honest, then adults must be honest, too.

7. Outcomes

Benefits and harms can be explored various ways in ethics. A utilitarian seeks "the greatest good for the greatest number"[37] by adding up the anticipated benefits and harms of each option for everyone affected, and choosing the course that results in the greatest net benefit over harm.

Contrary to the utilitarian approach, the principle of *nonmaleficence*[38] – captured in the Hippocratic Oath's "above all, do no harm" – warns us to avoid causing injury even when doing so might maximize the overall benefits. While the principle of *beneficence* leads us to promote individual and collective goods, nonmaleficence reminds us that the road to Hell is often paved with our good intentions.

Basing ethical decisions on anticipated outcomes requires evidence about the nature, extent and likelihood of various consequences. Since anonymity has historically been the only available donor conception option, little evidence exists to determine whether anonymity is actually the best approach. Evidence of many previously unrecognized negative outcomes is coming to light as Offspring speak out. Showing that benefits outweigh these harms would not satisfy a utilitarian; one must demonstrate that, despite these harms, anonymity offers the *best possible* net results of all available options. The principle of nonmaleficence is more direct: if avoiding harm is possible, then we should do so regardless of the benefits.

A common fear is that identity release would lead to a shortage of sperm donors, preventing the beneficent relief of infertility; many clinics have documented reduced donations after shifting to identity-release. On the other hand, the Human Fertilisation And Embryology Authority in the United Kingdom, Sperm Bank of California[39] and some other clinics around the world[40] demonstrate that openness does not necessarily create donor shortages, and/or that shortages might be temporary. Oddly, the role of anonymity is rarely mentioned regarding the supply of ova or embryos.

7.1 Whose Outcomes?

The preceding discussion of practical, emotional, and relational implications of anonymous donor conception has been limited to effects for donors, recipients and resulting offspring, but ethics requires a broader scope still. What might be at stake for other parties?

Perhaps most obviously, medical and social consequences of donor conception may be passed to Offspring's children and subsequent descendants. Genetic bewilderment and the loss of extended family relationships, for example, echo through multiple generations who are missing limbs of their family tree.

While donors often wish to prevent contact between their social families and their Offspring, it is virtually unheard of to ask what the donor's family might actually find beneficial. Are the donor's "own" children truly better off never knowing about their half-siblings, when many people find the discovery of additional relatives to be a positive experience? Is the donor's secrecy more likely to strengthen marriage and family relationships, or to create the barriers common to recipient families within the donor's own family?

Children conceived by close genetic relatives face significantly greater risks of serious genetic anomalies. Accidental consanguinity thus concerns later generations and society as a whole. Some sperm donors are known to have given hundreds of samples over many years, and the Donor Sibling Registry records multiple donors with over 60 known offspring.[41] Offspring who later use donor conception themselves might even receive stored gametes from their own genetic parent. Consanguinity is especially worrisome among ethnic minorities with few available donors, or in smaller communities where offspring from the same clinic are likely to cross paths.

Rarely noticed is that health information about Offspring may have implications for the wellbeing of the donor and his or her other children, the half-siblings conceived from the same donor, and perhaps for the descendants of all of these people. Entire networks of relatives can thus be placed at unnecessary risk by impeding the exchange of medical histories. The resulting treatment errors add unnecessary costs to the health care system, extending the ripples of negative outcomes across entire communities.

7.2 Revealing the Truth

Because parents can lack social support for assisted conception, answers to questions about anonymous donors, and practical guidance for revealing the nature of the conception to their children, many who wish to tell the truth about donor conception may find themselves unable to do so. The resulting secrets, and especially lies, are a lot like time bombs. Adolescent and adult offspring commonly respond to the revelation of donor conception with feelings of shock, betrayal,[42] and distrust.[43] If their parents lied about genetic relationships, what else had they lied about?

> Another feature of the ensuing years [after donor conception was revealed] was the strain in my relationship with Dad. … So I had to work hard to ensure everything looked OK. But the fact was that I was angry and horrified. I felt in many ways as if I had been raped … something precious (my trust and unguarded affection) had been taken from me under false pretences. I became much more aware of the ways in which he ignored or belittled [me, and the] ways in which I am different from him.[44]

(The problem of secrecy regarding the nature of the conception is, of course, not typically a feature of homosexual relationships because it is obvious to everyone that third parties participated in the conception.)

Donors who were promised anonymity may understandably feel betrayed if their names are revealed without their consent. Emotional upheaval and challenges within the donor's close relationships may commonly follow unsealing donor records. On the other hand, these injuries seem to be balanced by the feelings of betrayal and fractured familial relationships reported by Offspring who are denied the donor's identity. Openness from the outset of *future* donations would prevent such harms to either party.

If currently anonymous donors were legally protected from financial and practical responsibilities toward Offspring, and supportive counselling were available to help donors, Offspring, and their families navigate the situation as it evolves, then would identity disclosure cause other significant injuries? We should consider whether the manner of revelation may do as much harm as the revelation itself. Some donors protective of anonymity might consent to identity release after all if they are not simply forced to comply, but have support to reflect on the deeper meanings of the donor relationship for themselves, their offspring and others. Historically, encouragement for such reflection has been lacking when donations are given.

Genetic secrets are becoming increasingly difficult to protect in any event. Tissue typing for transplantation, genetic counseling in pregnancy, and diagnostic and predictive genetic tests can reveal discrepancies among presumed relationships. Internet donor conception databases are linking relatives at a dizzying rate.[45] Even basic education can reveal the truth:

> In a biology lesson we learnt about genetics and inheritance. The exercises that we were to try on our parents to demonstrate dominance suggested that one of my parents was not genetically related. Luckily, I knew the truth already. Had I not, my parents and teachers would have had some tricky questions to answer.[46]

Clearly, it would be safer to defuse donor conception secrets sooner than later, and best never to establish them in the first place. Given the increasing risks of inadvertent discovery, a structured and sensitive process of disclosure would likely cause fewer injuries overall.

7.3 Verdicts on Outcomes

If we include perspectives of Offspring, a utilitarian assessment must conclude that the sometimes-profound injuries to Offspring from donor anonymity, and the rippling risks and concerns for future generations and the wider community, tend to outweigh benefits that accrue primarily to the social and genetic parents – many of which can be achieved without anonymity. It might be argued in response that, while donor anonymity may create some complications in a child's life, surely the benefits of being alive at all outweigh such harms. However, this is not the correct comparison; the issue is not anonymity vs. non-existence, but anonymity vs. openness. Never existing is not a loss, as nobody exists to perceive his or her own non-existence. The utilitarian question is about benefits and harms to those who experience them.

Donor anonymity is also sometimes compared to other family arrangements with fractured lineage, such as step-families, adoption or fostering, in which many children thrive. Why should we be so concerned about anonymous donor conception? The principle of Nonmaleficence explains why this approach misses the moral point. Although people do carry on despite challenges and difficult circumstances, what justifies *intentionally creating* additional burdens for someone to bear? By analogy, many victims of violence manage to thrive, but this fact does not justify committing physical assault. Further, many of the "non-standard" family arrangements compared to donor conception are chosen as a least-worst solution for the care of existing children; *purposely* creating children to fit into difficult social arrangements is far less defensible. Finally, some challenging or fractured family situations result from irresponsible behaviour in the first place, such as abandonment, which hardly makes them appropriate justification for causing predictable harms via other choices. Thus it will not do to justify the harms of anonymity by noting that other possible harms to offspring are worse; *this* imposition of harm, when a less painful option is possible, must be justified.

8. Conclusions

Assisted conception is a process of building families, and must be understood as entailing profound ethical responsibilities to protect the resulting Offsprings' interests. Secrets and lies simply do not provide strong foundations for healthy children, functional families, and social justice. Adults are free to avoid participating in donor conception, but the Offspring have no choice; the most basic notions of respect require that we at least tell them the truth about matters so intimately important to them. Reproductive practices and policies have largely failed so far to give equal weight to the interests of the Offspring as to the adults; fairness demands that we make amends.

No plausible account of ethics justifies anonymity in donor conception; the tradition of secrecy was clearly born of shame and embarrassment rather than of virtuous intent. If we cannot admit what we are doing and be held accountable for it, then we should not be doing it at all.

Bibliography

Anonymous. "Personal Views: How it Feels to be a Child of Donor Insemination," *British Medical Journal* 324, no. 7340, 30 March 2002, http://www.bmj.com/cgi/content/full/324/7340/797/DONOR CONCEPTION1.

Baier, Annette. "The Need for More than Justice," *Canadian Journal of Philosophy*, Supp. 13, December (1987): 41-56.

Baran, Annette and Reuben Pannor. "Lethal Secrets: The Psychology of Donor Insemination," New York, Amistad Publications (1993): p. 58.

Beauchamp, Tom L. and James Childress. *Principles of Biomedical Ethics*, 5th ed. NY: Oxford (2001); first ed. 1979.

Beauchamp, Tom L. and Ruth R. Faden. *A History and Theory of Informed Consent*, NY: Oxford.

Bok, Sissela. *Secrets: On the Ethics of Concealment and Revelation*, NY: Vintage (1984).

Cordray, Bill. "Is DI Another Form of Adoption?" *Report to Health Canada on The Offspring Speak: An International Conference of Donor Offspring*, eds. Sherry Franz and Diane Allen, Toronto: Infertility Network (2001): pp. 32-33.

Elizabeth, "Brown-eyed Girl." Frabjous Days Blog, comment posted 14 January 2007, http://frabjousdays.blogspot.com/2007/01/brown-eyed-girl.html. Italics in original.

Feinberg, Joel. "The Rights of Animals and Unborn Generations," ed., William T. Blackstone, *Philosophy and Environmental Crisis,* Athens, GA: University of Georgia Press (1974): pp 43-68.

Gilligan, Carol. *In a Different Voice,* Harvard University Press, (1982).

Gollancz, David. "Donor Insemination: A Question of Rights," *Human Fertility* 4 (2001): 164-167, p 164.

Henderson, Mark. "Sperm Donor Figures Rising Despite Loss of Anonymity," *The Times* (London), 4 May 2007, http://www.timesonline.co.uk/tol/news/uk/science/article1744309.ece.

Hewitt, Geraldine. "Missing Links: Identity Issues of Donor-Conceived People," *Journal of Fertility Counselling* 9, (2002): 14-20.

Australia) Four Corners "Secrets of the Fathers," aired 24 October 2005 [Edited transcript of Janine Cohen's interview with Geraldine Hewitt], http://www.abc.net.au/4corners/content/2005/s1488988.htm.

Kreutz, Shelley, "Controversy Over Sperm-donor Anonymity," ed. Susan McClelland, Maclean's, 20 May 2002, http://www.thecanadianencyclopedia.com/index.cfm?PgNm=TCE&Params=M1ARTM0012412.

Lindsay. "All you need is...love??," Confessions of a Cryokid, Blog, comment posted 15 March 2008, http://cryokidonor conceptiononfessions.blogspot.com/2008/03/all-you-need-islove_15.html.

-- "Legal Deceptions," Confessions of a Cryokid, Blog, comment posted 13 March 2008, http://cryokidonor conceptiononfessions.blogspot.com/2008/03/legal-deceptions.html.

Louise, "Louise's Story," [no posting date]. TangledWebs UK, http://www.tangledwebs.org.uk/tw/Stories/Louise.

Mill, John Stuart. *Utilitarianism,* (1861) [many reprinted versions are available].

O'Neill, Onora. A Simplified Account of Kant's Ethics. *Matters of Life and Death,* ed. Tom Regan, McGraw-Hill (1986).

Priday, L. Open Letter to the Minister for Public Health, *Journal of Fertility Counselling*, 7(1) (2000): 25-26, p. 26.

Rel. "Rel's Story," TangledWebs UK. http://www.tangledwebs.org.uk/tw/Stories/Rel.

Rose, Joanna. "Kinship: Are Some More Equal Than Others?" in *Who Am I? Experiences of Donor Conception*, ed. Alexina McWhinnie, UK: Idreos Education Trust (2006): p. 1-13; p. 2.

Turner, A.J. and A. Coyle. "What Does it Mean to be a Donor Offspring? The Identity Experiences of Adults Conceived by Donor Insemination and the Implications for Counselling and Therapy," *Human Reproduction* 15(9) (2000): 2041-2051.

Whipp, Christine. *"My Daddy's Name is Donor,"* ed. Catherine Bruton, The Times (London), 13 December 2007, http://women.timesonline.co.uk/tol/life_and_style/women/families/article3041127.ece?token=null&offset=12.

Notes

1. Carol Gilligan, *In a Different Voice,* Harvard University Press (1982).
2. Extensive ethics literature on the status and rights of embryos in the contexts of abortion, contraception and prenatal intervention predates the emergence of IVF and embryo research.
3. See, for example, John A. Robertson, *Children of Choice: Freedom and the New Reproductive Technologies,* (Princeton, NJ: Princeton University Press, 1994).
4. Joel Feinberg, "The Rights of Animals and Unborn Generations," William T. Blackstone, ed. of *Philosophy and Environmental Crisis,* Athens, GA: University of Georgia Press, (1974): pp 43-68. For a lengthier discussion of Feinberg's analogy for reproductive ethics, see Laura Shanner, "The Right to Procreate: When Rights Claims Have Gone Wrong," *McGill Law Journal* Vol. 40, No. 4, (August 1995), pp. 823-87.
5. Some argue that *clinicians* have role-specific, fiduciary responsibilities to their patients only, not to future persons, although this distinction is challenged by obstetric medicine, sustainable health care access, and anticipated benefits for future patients from clinical research on current patients. Laws and policies always presume future applications and society-wide implications, however, while prospective parents and reproductive collaborators shoulder standard responsibility for the consequences of our individual choices.
6. Sissela Bok, *Secrets: On the Ethics of Concealment and Revelation,* NY: Vintage (1984).
7. Elizabeth, comment on "Brown-eyed Girl." Frabjous Days Blog, comment posted 14 January 2007, http://frabjousdays.blogspot.com/2007/01/brown-eyed-girl.html. Italics in original.
8. International Donor Offspring Alliance (IDOA) http://web.jaguarpaw.co.uk/idoa.
9. Annette Baran and Reuben Pannor, *Lethal Secrets: The Psychology of Donor Insemination.* New York: Amistad Publications (1993): p. 58.
10. Christine Whipp, "*My Daddy's Name is Donor,*" ed. Catherine Bruton, The Times (London). 13 December 2007. http://women.timesonline.co.uk/tol/life_and_style/women/families/article3041127.ece?token=null&offset=12.
11. Geraldine Hewitt, "Missing Links: Identity Issues of Donor-Conceived People," *Journal of Fertility Counselling* 9, (2002): 14-20.
12. Louise, "Louise's Story," [no posting date]. TangledWebs UK, http://www.tangledwebs.org.uk/tw/Stories/Louise.
13. David Gollancz, "Donor Insemination: A Question of Rights," *Human Fertility* 4 (2001): 164-167, p 164.
14. Lindsay, "All you need is...love??," Confessions of a Cryokid, Blog, comment posted 15 March 2008, http://cryokidonorconceptiononfessions.blogspot.com/2008/03/all-you-need-islove_15.html.
15. *Canadian Charter of Rights and Freedoms,* being Part I of the *Constitution Act, 1982,* which is itself Schedule B of the *Canada Act 1982,* c. 11 (U.K.).
16. Canada. Assisted Human Reproduction Act, (2004, c.2) (assented to March 29, 2004).
17. Geraldine Hewitt, on ABC (Australia) Four Corners "Secrets of the Fathers," aired 24 October 2005 [Edited transcript of Janine Cohen's interview with Geraldine Hewitt], http://www.abc.net.au/4corners/content/2005/s1488988.htm.
18. Tom L. Beauchamp and James Childress, *Principles of Biomedical Ethics,* 5th ed. NY: Oxford 2001; first ed. 1979.
19. Tom L. Beauchamp and Ruth R. Faden, *A History and Theory of Informed Consent.* NY: Oxford.
20. Onora O'Neill (1986) A Simplified Account of Kant's Ethics. *Matters of Life and Death,* ed. Tom Regan, McGraw-Hill.
21. Clark, 2006.
22. Lindsay, "Legal Deceptions," Confessions of a Cryokid, Blog, comment posted 13 March 2008, http://cryokidonor conceptiononfessions.blogspot.com/2008/03/legal-deceptions.html.
23. Shelley Kreutz, "Controversy Over Sperm-donor Anonymity," ed. Susan McClelland, Maclean's, 20 May 2002, http://www.thecanadianencyclopedia.com/index.cfm?PgNm=TCE&Params=M1ARTM0012412.
24. Anonymity advocates might at this point appeal to social contract theory, in which we imagine that representatives of society make agreements necessary to promote a functional community, which are then binding upon all of us. However, since the social norm is to keep accurate

records of lineage, donor anonymity would violate plausible elements of a hypothetical social contract.

25 United Nations, *Convention on the Rights of the Child*, Can. T.S. 1992, No. 3. Article 8 commits States Parties "to respect the right of the child to preserve his or her identity" and to provide "assistance and protection" when a child is deprived of "some or all of the elements of his or her identity". Other relevant articles prevent discrimination (Art. 2), separation from parents except where necessary for the child's best interest (Art. 9), and interference with privacy, family and home (Art. 16).
26 See, for example, Carol Gilligan *In a Different Voice* Boston: Harvard 1982; Sara Ruddick *Maternal Thinking* NY: Ballantine 1989; Alisa Carse "The Voice of Care: Implications for Bioethics Education" *Journal of Medicine and Philosophy* 16, (1991) 5-28; Virginia Held *Justice and Care: Essential Readings in Feminist Ethics* Boulder: Westview 1995.
27 Joanna Rose, "Kinship: Are Some More Equal Than Others?" ed. Alexina McWhinnie, *Who Am I? Experiences of Donor Conception*, UK: Idreos Education Trust (2006): p. 1-13; p. 2.
28 Hewitt, 2002.
29 Clark, 2006.
30 L. Priday, Open Letter to the Minister for Public Health, *Journal of Fertility Counselling*, 7(1) (2000): 25-26, p. 26.
31 Rel, "Rel's Story," TangledWebs UK. http://www.tangledwebs.org.uk/tw/Stories/Rel.
32 Louise, TangledWebs UK.
33 Ellis, 2006.
34 Bok.
35 Anonymous, "Personal Views: How it Feels to be a Child of Donor Insemination." *British Medical Journal* 324, no. 7340, 30 March 2002, http://www.bmj.com/cgi/content/full/324/7340/797/DONOR CONCEPTION1.
36 Annette Baier, "The Need for More than Justice," *Canadian Journal of Philosophy*, Supp.13, December 1987: 41-56.
37 John Stuart Mill, *Utilitarianism, (1861)* [many reprinted versions are available].
38 Beauchamp and Childress.
39 The Sperm Bank of California: http://www.thespermbankofca.org/. Also see M. Riordan and J. Scheib (2001) The Sperm Bank of California: A Sperm Bank Prepares for Donor IdentityRrelease, *Report to Health Canada on The Offspring Speak: An International Conference of Donor Offspring*, Sherry Franz and Diane Allen (eds.) Toronto: Infertility Network, pp. 34-37.
40 Mark Henderson, "Sperm Donor Figures Rising Despite Loss of Anonymity," *The Times* (London), 4 May 2007, http://www.timesonline.co.uk/tol/news/uk/science/article1744309.ece.
41 Donor Sibling Registry www.donorsiblingregistry.com. Also see: Oprah. "The Ultimate Reunion: When Dad is a Sperm Donor / Anonymous fathers," aired February 8, 2008,http://www.oprah.com/relationships/slide/20080208/rel_20080208_117.jhtml and CBS News, 60 Minutes "Sperm donor siblings find family ties" 2007.
42 Bill Cordray, "Is DI Another Form of Adoption?" *Report to Health Canada on The Offspring Speak: An International Conference of Donor Offspring*, eds. Sherry Franz and Diane Allen, Toronto: Infertility Network (2001): pp. 32-33.
43 A.J. Turner and A. Coyle, "What Does it Mean to be a Donor Offspring? The Identity Experiences of Adults Conceived by Donor Insemination and the Implications for Counselling and Therapy," *Human Reproduction* 15(9) (2000): 2041-2051.
44 Louise, "Louise's Story," [no posting date]. TangledWebs UK, http://www.tangledwebs.org.uk/tw/Stories/Louise.
45 See chapter 7, infra, Harris and Shanner.
46 Anonymous, "Personal Views: How it Feels to be a Child of Donor Insemination," *British Medical Journal* 324, no. 7340, 30 March 2002, http://www.bmj.com/cgi/content/full/324/7340/797/DONOR CONCEPTION1.

PART FIVE

THE CURRENT STATE OF THE LAW: INTERNATIONAL LAW AND ANALOGOUS DOMESTIC LAW

In her examination of international law, *Veronica Piñero* argues that Canada has international obligations to respect rights to health, identity, and family relations. Yet Canada has given priority to the donor's right to privacy, despite the compelling – and compulsory – international legal framework on children's rights to identity, health and family relations. In other words, Canadian law violates international law because it is adult-orientated rather than child-centred in failing to observe and protect the child's rights to health, identity, and family. She concludes that Canada must alter its domestic law to accord with its international legal obligations and its domestic principles; therefore law in Canada should be modified to permit Offspring to know their origins.

Within Canadian domestic law, the *Canadian Charter of Rights and Freedoms* protects a right to know one's identity, according to the British Columbia Supreme Court in *Pratten* v. *A.G. Canada*. There, the Court found that the Province of British Columbia unjustifiably discriminated against donor-conceived people, who are similarly situated to adoptees, when it enacted the British Columbia *Adoption Act* in 1996. This is the first decision in North America to hold government accountable for failing to create, preserve, make current and disclose identifying medical, social and cultural history records of the donor-conceived and their progenitors.

Accepting the judicial determination that donor-conceived people are similarly situated to adoptees for the purpose of equality protection, *Juliet Guichon* considers what legal protections and benefits adoptees receive that donor-conceived people do not. She describes the law concerning disclosure of adoption records in all provinces and territories of Canada. Generally speaking, information concerning the biological parents of adoptees is collected, preserved and disclosed by government officials. The law in Canada distinguishes between non-identifying information, to which adoptees tend to have access as of right; and identifying information, to which adoptees have rights limited by those of birth parents: either active consent by birth parents is necessary, or birth parents must actively oppose release of identifying information and may file a no-contact veto. Most birth parents do not oppose release of their records or contact with the adoptee. (Legislation that failed to provide a disclosure veto was struck down for violating the Charter.) The legislative trend is toward increasing rights of access to both adoptees and birth parents. Adoption history and such examples of legislative policy are instructive in designing a regime to permit the donor-conceived to access records regarding their biological parents. But the initial hurdle to overcome is that there are no state-created records for the donor-conceived. At the moment, existing records, if any, are considered the medical records of the fertility patient to be preserved for a limited period under rules created by physician-licensing bodies, rather than a civil status document regarding the parentage of the intended child to be preserved permanently under provincial or territorial vital statistics legislation. Despite the British Columbia Supreme Court decision in *Pratten* requiring legislative adoption records and disclosure schemes to include the donor-conceived, there are no such procedures in place to create, preserve and disclose vital information.

Yet it is possible for the state to initiate a record keeping system of Offspring to keep records on donor conception. Using a novel approach to demonstrate this fact, journalist *Alison Motluk* examines the procedure of registering other mammals – purebred cattle in Canada. Her report makes clear that for cattle conceived by assisted insemination or embryo transfer, the Government of Canada requires that progenitor information be collected, preserved, verified and disclosed. But Canadian governments have no similar requirements for obtaining, maintaining and revealing progenitor information for donor-conceived humans.

Chapter Seventeen

This Is Not Baby Talk: Canadian International Human Rights Obligations Regarding the Rights to Health, Identity and Family Relations

Verónica B. Piñero

> *If we want to see our visions of children's rights prevail across communities, some of which currently lack our judgment, we must engage in dialogue. Our aim must be the enlargement of a shared common sense. Children's rights discourse must not be seen, as it frequently is, as a foreign imposition, rather as an element of shared common sense.*[1]

1. Introduction

In 1986, an Argentinean movie won the Academy Award for Best Foreign Film. *The Official Story* tells the tale of an Argentinean middle-class married woman, Alicia, who discovers that her adopted daughter, Gaby, is the child of a "disappeared" political prisoner. Her husband knows that the girl's parents did not surrender her voluntarily. Indeed, he obtained Gaby through his political connections. During this period (1976-1983), Alicia refused to see what was going on; she had never questioned Gaby's origins. Yet one day, Alicia awakens to the horrors being perpetrated by the Argentinean military government and decides to inquire about Gaby's biological origins. Eventually, she meets Gaby's grandmother, who wants Gaby to be returned to her biological family. In the ensuing marital argument, Alicia's husband states that he and Alicia are Gaby's family. He rhetorically asks, "who cares" about the biological family? Alicia defiantly replies, "I do care. I do not want to do this to Gaby."[2] Alicia's response is evidence not just of a mother's unconditional love for her child, but also of her recognition that Gaby needs to know who she is. Alicia, at least, acknowledges that Gaby is entitled to know her identity.

This chapter accepts the moral correctness of Alicia's anguished response. Yet the context of this paper is not the Argentinean "dirty war", but rather the legal regulation in Canada of assisted human reproduction.[3] Canada's Parliament did not accept that children have a right to know the identity of their progenitors. With its 2004 statute, the *Assisted Human Reproduction Act*, Parliament prohibited the disclosure of the donor's identity or of identifying information to the recipient(s) of reproductive materials without the donor's written consent.[4,5] This paper argues that Canada's national response to a child's right to know the identity of his or her progenitor(s) was inconsistent with international law on health, identity and family rights.

2. Relevant International Law Binding on Canada

Canada is an active member of the international community: it joined the *United Nations* in 1948 and the *Organization of American States* in 1990, the latter being a multinational organization that operates within a regional geographic area. As a member of the *United Nations*, Canada is a State Party to numerous international human rights instruments, among them the *Universal Declaration on Human Rights* (UDHR),[6] the *International Covenant on Civil and Political Rights* (ICCPR),[7] the *International Covenant on Economic, Social and Cultural Rights* (ICESCR),[8] and the *Convention on the Rights of the Child* (CRC).[9] The Supreme Court of Canada, the Senate of Canada and Canadian scholars agree that these international human rights instruments are part of the Canadian legal system and consequently, they bind Canada today.[10] The *Organization of American States* (OAS) has adopted a number of human rights documents, of which Canada has signed only the *American Declaration on the Rights and Duties of Man* (ADRDM).[11] Even though the *ADRDM* was originally adopted by the OAS as a non-binding declaration (rather than a binding convention), both the Inter-American Court and the Inter-American Commission on Human Rights have held that the *ADRDM* is a source of international obligation for the OAS Member States.[12] Indeed, the Inter-American Commission specifically decided that Canada is subject to the Commission's jurisdiction regarding the observance of the human rights guaranteed in the *ADRDM*.[13]

These documents contain relevant international human rights law that binds Canada. This chapter examines the content of this law on health, identity, and family relations to demonstrate that were the provinces and territories to prohibit the disclosure of the donor's identity or identifying information to Offspring without the donor's written consent, then they would be in violation of these rights.

3. International Human Rights Law on Identity, Health, and Family Rights[14]

In considering the extent to which international law guarantees rights to health, identity, and family, this section addresses two questions: (1) What is the content of these rights under international human rights law?; and (2) Are the interests that Offspring have in health, identity, and family properly considered "rights" under international law?

3.1. International Obligations Regarding Health Rights

The protection of the right to health is a core human right indispensable to the exercise of other human rights. The right to health was first recognized by the *International Convention on the Elimination of All Forms of Racial Discrimination* in 1965. Article 5(e)(iv) of that convention guarantees to everyone, "without distinction as to race, colour, or national or ethnic origin ... the right to public health, medical care, social security and social services."[15] The most comprehensive protection of the right to health followed one year later with the adoption of the *ICESCR* in 1966. It reads, in part, "[t]he States Parties to the present Covenant recognize the right of everyone to the enjoyment of the highest attainable standard of physical and mental health."[16] A new dimension to the right to health came with the 1979 *Convention on the Elimination of All Forms of Discrimination against Women*. That convention specifically requires that health rights be granted to women and men equally:[17]

> States parties shall take all appropriate measures to eliminate discrimination against women in the field of health care in order to ensure, on a basis of equality of men and women, access to health care services, including those related to family planning.

Recognition of the right to health applied to children as well. This recognition became more explicit with the adoption of the *CRC* in 1989:[18]

> States Parties recognize the right of the child to the enjoyment of the highest attainable standards of health and to facilities for the treatment of illness and rehabilitation of health. States Parties shall strive to ensure that no child is deprived of his or her right of access to such health care services.

Although none of these conventions makes explicit reference to the right to health in the context of assisted human reproduction, none of the conventions explicitly refers to any health-related context.[19] Each of the conventions requires States Parties to grant persons under their jurisdictions the right to the highest attainable standards of health without discrimination.

States Parties must give broad effect to the right to health in an expeditious manner. The *ICESCR* requires States Parties to take steps "to achieve the full realization" of the right to health.[20] Accordingly, the Committee on Economic, Social and Cultural Rights recognizes that States Parties should adopt legislation because this is an "indispensable element" for implementing the right to health domestically.[21]

Legislation should ensue quickly. Article 2(1) of the *ICESCR* stipulates the general legal obligations of States Parties to observe those rights that they have recognized, and states:

> [E]ach State Party to the present Covenant undertakes to take steps, individually and through international assistance and co-operation, especially economic and technical, to the maximum of its available resources, *with a view to achieving progressively the full realization of the rights recognized in the present Covenant* by all appropriate means, including particularly the adoption of legislation measures. [Emphasis added]

The Committee on Economic, Social and Cultural Rights notes that the term "progressive realization" imposes an obligation to move as expeditiously and effectively as possible towards that goal. Moreover, any deliberately retrogressive measures in that regard would require the most careful consideration and would need to be fully justified by reference to the totality of the rights provided for in the Covenant and in the context of the full use of the maximum available resources.[22] In other words, States Parties must justify a failure to move quickly to give effect to a broad right to health. As the Covenant and Committee commentary make clear, the "right to the highest attainable standard of health" is a compelling obligation for State Parties.

Such implementation may not discriminate against any group. The *ICESCR* stipulates:[23]

> [T]he States Parties to the present Covenant undertake to guarantee that the rights enunciated in the present Covenant will be exercised without discrimination of any kind as to race, colour, sex, language, religion, political or other opinion, national or social origin, property, *birth or other status* [Emphasis added]

Thus the right to health under international law is comprehensive in nature, and State Parties are required to grant it expeditiously and without discrimination against any group. By unlawfully discriminating against Offspring in refusing to grant them access to their progenitors' identifying information without progenitor consent, Canada violates its international legal obligations to recognize the right to health.

Consider this hypothetical case: Marie decides to donate her eggs anonymously to another woman. Having successfully met the screening criteria, Marie undergoes egg extraction. The eggs are fertilized in vitro and transferred to the waiting woman who eventually gives birth to a baby girl, Camille. Around the time of the birth, Marie is diagnosed with breast cancer, which fortunately responds well to treatment. Physicians advise Marie to tell her daughters about her diagnosis and treatment so that the girls can be diligent in seeking breast cancer screening if they have inherited this condition. Marie's cancer diagnosis does not appear in her egg donation file at the fertility clinic because the diagnosis was received after her eggs were extracted. Canadian law under s.15 of the *Assisted Human Reproduction Act* did not provide for the cataloguing and transmission of donors' current health information. Under that regime, Camille would not have known about the latent risks of developing breast cancer. There is no provincial or territorial mandate requiring that such information be transmitted to Offspring. The failure to transmit this important health information regarding Camille's genetic mother violates Camille's right to health under international law.

This is because an important aspect of the right to health is the right to knowledge to engage in (among other things) preventative health measures. The Committee on Economic, Social and Cultural Rights has explicitly described the content of the *ICESCR* "right to the highest attainable standard of health," the Committee said:[24]

> [T]he right to health is not to be understood as a right to be *healthy*. The right to health contains both freedoms and entitlements. *The freedoms include the right to control one's health and body.* [Emphasis added]

The Committee continued:[25]

> [T]he Committee interprets the right to health, as defined in article 12.1, *as an inclusive right extending not only to timely and appropriate health care but also to the underlying determinants of health, such as ... access to health-related education and information.* [Emphasis added]

Moreover, when highlighting the "interrelated and essential elements" that belong to the full implementation of the right to health, the Committee identifies "information accessibility" as a core requirement and defines it as including "the right to seek, receive and impart information and ideas concerning health issues."[26] Because, in the hypothetical example, Camille is denied access to health-related information and education that can lead her to "timely and appropriate health care," Canada has unlawfully denied Camille the "right to the highest attainable standard of health"[27] as guaranteed by the *ICESCR*.

Canadian provinces and territories could not justifiably hide behind a claim of the gamete providers' "confidentiality" in failing to grant Camille the right to health. Although the right to health explicitly recognizes the importance of confidentiality,[28] such recognition does not require people who have a valid interest in health information to be denied access. The Committee on the Rights of the Child[29] in its *General Comment No. 4* also requires States Parties to implement the principle of accessibility: "[h]ealth facilities, goods and services should be known and easily accessible (economically, physically and socially) to all adolescents, without discrimination."[30] With regard to "confidentiality", the Committee on the Rights of the Child notes: "[c]onfidentiality should be guaranteed, when necessary."[31] It seems that the Committee's intention in regulating the notion of "confidentiality" was to protect the individuals' privacy without limiting access to information to people who have a legitimate interest. On this, article 9 of the *Universal Declaration on the Human Genome and Human Rights* states that:[32]

> [I]n order to protect human rights and fundamental freedoms, limitations to the principles of consent and confidentiality may only be prescribed by law, *for compelling reasons within the bounds of public international law and the international law of human rights.* [Emphasis added]

In other words, the information an individual wants to have access to may be confidential information; nevertheless, the private nature of the information should not be an absolute bar to its transmission to people who have a legitimate interest in it. People can have a legitimate interest in another's private health information because it is about them and is significant to their health and wellbeing. Under international human rights law, such persons must be able to access this information; compelling reasons under international human rights law, such as the full observance of the right to health, must be read in to understand the proper limits of the principle of confidentiality.[33]

It is difficult to justify limiting access to information for reasons of confidentiality, when one considers the relative status of the parties and the vulnerability of children. The *CRC* considers the child's best interest to be a core principle that should guide the enactment of legislation to implement the right to health. Referring to the *CRC*, the Committee on Economic, Social and Cultural Rights notes that "[i]n all policies and programmes aimed at guaranteeing the right to health of children and adolescents their best interest shall be a primary consideration."[34] Indeed, some of the obligations for States Parties to the

CRC are to pass legislation that observes the *CRC* rights: "States Parties shall undertake all appropriate legislative, administrative, and other measures for the implementation of the rights recognized in the present Convention."[35] This means that States Parties assume the obligation to make the rights regulated in the *CRC* effective in their jurisdictions, among them the right to health. According to Eide and Eide, when a State becomes a Party to the *CRC*, it assumes obligations to respect, protect and fulfill the right to health. The obligation "to fulfill" entails the duty to "to adopt appropriate legislative, administrative, budgetary, judicial, promotional and other measures towards the full realization of the right of the child to health."[36]

The obligation "to fulfill" the right to health is, according to the Committee on Economic, Social and Cultural Rights, a "positive measure": "[t]he obligation to *fulfill* requires States Parties, *inter alia*, to give sufficient recognition to the right to health in the national political and legal systems."[37] Similar views have been expressed by the Committee on the Rights of the Child with regard to States Parties' legal obligations in relation to the health and development of adolescents under the *CRC*:[38]

> States Parties must take all appropriate legislative, administrative and other measures for the realization and monitoring of the rights of adolescents to health and development as recognized in the Convention. *To this end, States Parties must notably fulfill the following obligations ... (b) To ensure that adolescents have access to the information that is essential for their health and development ...* [emphasis added]

Thus, when a Canadian province or territory denies Camille "access to the information that is essential for her health and development", it violates her health rights as established by the *CRC*.

In sum, the right to health under international law is a comprehensive right which includes the right of access to health-related information. Canada has accepted a positive obligation to facilitate, provide, and promote without discrimination in its jurisdiction the highest attainable standards of health, primarily through the enactment of legislation that both implements and observes the international requirements. "Access to health information" is considered a core element in evaluating whether international obligations on health rights have been successfully implemented. In enacting s. 15 of the *AHRA*, however, Canada failed to meet its positive obligations, but has implemented legislation in direct contravention of them. The fact that the provinces and territories are not creating, preserving and disclosing health information for Offspring is also a failure to meet positive international law obligations to provide access to health information.

3.2. International Obligations on Identity Rights

For the donor-conceived, the right to identity is argued to be the most important of the three rights under discussion. According to one scholar, Freeman, the right to identity has received the most attention.[39] The importance that the *CRC* places on this right is evidenced by how Articles 7 and 8 are positioned at the beginning of the Convention, directly after the child's inherent right to life.[40] The importance of identity rights for all human beings has also been recognized by a prestigious Australian state commission. The Waller Committee stated that:[41]

> [W]hether or not a person pursues her or his origins; it should be possible for everyone to discover them. In this sense everyone has a strong interest in being able to discover some information about her or his origin.

Yet despite the recognised importance of this right, surprisingly, the only international regulation on the right to identity is contained in Article 8 of the *CRC*:[42]

> (1) States Parties undertake to respect the right of the child to preserve his or her identity, including nationality, name and family relations as recognized by law without unlawful interference.
> (2) Where a child is illegally deprived of some or all of the elements of his or her identity, States Parties shall provide appropriate assistance and protection, with a view to reestablishing speedily his or her identity.

The international recognition of the right to identity has been a recent development. A clear understanding of the history of this article is vital to its proper interpretation. Article 8 did not exist in the first draft to the *CRC* (1978) – also known as the Polish draft because of the leading role of the government of Poland in drafting the *CRC*. It was not until 1985 that the draft article was presented to the Working Group by the Argentinean Government.[43] Argentina had elected a democratic government in December 1983; the proposed article reflected the problems with identity and discovering one's origins that Argentina was attempting to address locally. As dramatized by *The Official Story*, the children of political prisoners, who had been abducted along with their parents, and children born to political prisoners while illegally detained had been "stolen" by individuals connected to the militia or the police and their biological families were now looking for them.⁴⁴ Fearing that this problem could arise in other nations, the representative of Argentina introduced the following article to address it:⁴⁵

> The child has the inalienable right to retain his true and genuine personal, legal and family identity. In the event that a child has been fraudulently deprived of some or all of the elements of his identity; the State must give him special protection and assistance with a view to re-establishing his true and genuine identity as soon as possible. In particular, this obligation of the State includes restoring the child to his blood relation to be brought up.

Even though the Argentinean draft was accepted by the *CRC* working group, the notion of "family identity" created much discussion because such a concept was not known in every State. The Dutch delegation asked to introduce the phrase "as recognized by law" after the words "family identity."⁴⁶ As well, the Norwegian delegation asked that the phrase "family identity" be replaced by the words "family relations."⁴⁷ The draft article was modified accordingly. During the second reading of this article (1988-1989), the representative of Mexico unsuccessfully attempted to modify the wording to make more explicit the commitments of the States Parties, as well as to include the biological elements of identity.⁴⁸

As noted above, this article was originally drafted having in mind the situation of the Argentinean "disappeared" children and not to address the case of children conceived by use of third party gametes. Indeed, Jaap Doek, the chairperson of the Committee on the Rights of the Child for the period 2001-2007, accepts this point. Nevertheless, he notes that⁴⁹

> In the light of the present day developments and a dynamic interpretation of the CRC, it [article 8.1 of the *CRC*] can be considered to include in the right to preserve your identity, the right to be informed about your (biological) origins.

Considering the high regard in which Doek is held in the field of international human rights law and his understanding of the legal implications of article 8 of the *CRC*, his views ought to be taken seriously. Moreover, many international law scholars note that the list of elements fundamental to the preservation of identity enumerated in Article 8.1 (nationality, name and family relations) is not exhaustive.⁵⁰ Therefore, the biological origins of a child are also included within the notion of identity. Indeed, Doek argues that it is not clear whether the limiting qualification "as recognized by law" in the first paragraph of the article should be linked to "identity" or "to family relations." As noted above, the original iteration of the article referred to the notion of "family identity", and because this was an unknown concept for many domestic legal systems, the representative from the Netherlands requested that the phrase "as recognized by law" be added. The limitation of "as recognized by law" was not meant to restrict the notion of identity, but the notion of "family identity", which now reads "family relations."

The protection afforded to the right to identity by the CRC should be read in light of current international human rights law. Doek notes that paragraph 2 of Article 8 of the CRC has not been written with artificial procreation in mind. But the obligation to respect the right of the child to preserve her or his identity, requires the State Party to undertake all legislative, administrative or other measures (Article 4 of the CRC) to implement that right, interpreting it in a dynamic manner and with present day conditions in mind.[51] In addition, the notion of "illegally" in the second paragraph of article 8, as Van Bueren highlights:[52]

> Applies both when the deprivation is illegal under domestic law and when the deprivation of identity is contrary to international law. To interpret article 8 only to include the former would open up a dangerous loophole.

According to this author, the elements of identity are regulated both by domestic law and international law.

Finally, current interpretation of article 8 of the CRC protects Offspring's identity rights. As noted above, Doek states that even though this article was intended to address a specific situation – the abduction and return of children of Argentinean political prisoners – a dynamic interpretation must include children who were artificially conceived through anonymous donors' genetic material and who are interested in knowing their progenitors' identity. Therefore, under international law, information related to a child's biological origins is part of his or her identity, and consequently protected by CRC Article 8. Canadian domestic interference with this right proposed by section 15 of the AHRA was a violation of a donor-conceived person's right to identity under international law; as a result this interference was "illegal" under the second paragraph of Article 8 of the CRC to which Canada is a signatory.

3.3. International Obligations on Family Rights

International law recognizes the importance of the family as the basic unit upon which society is organized, and, for that reason, requires that States protect the family. However, neither the notion of "family" nor who are to be considered as "family members" has been defined under international law. In 1948, the *ADRDM* recognized that "[e]very person has the right to the protection of the law against abusive attacks upon his honor, reputation, and his private and family life,"[53] and provided it with protection accordingly: "[e]very person has the right to establish a family, the basic element of society, and to receive protection therefore."[54] The *UDHR* was adopted also in 1948; it recognized an analogous protection:[55]

> [N]o one shall be subjected to arbitrary interference with his privacy, family, home or correspondence, nor to attacks upon his honour and reputation. Everyone has the right to the protection of the law against such interference or attacks.

As well, this declaration states that "[t]he family is the natural and fundamental group unit of society and is entitled to protection by society and the State."[56] Similar protection was brought by the two international covenants adopted in 1966: the *ICESCR* states that "[t]he widest possible protection and assistance should be accorded to the family, which is the natural and fundamental group unit of society, particularly for its establishment and while it is responsible for the care and education of dependent children."[57] The *ICCPR* brought a civil rights perspective to the right to family relations and provided for proper protection as well. First, Article 17(1) notes that "[n]o one shall be subjected to arbitrary or unlawful interference with his privacy, family, or correspondence, nor to unlawful attacks on his honour and reputation."[58] Second, Article 23(1) states that "[t]he family is the natural and fundamental group unit of society and is entitled to protection by society and the State."[59]

The protection of the right to family received a child-focused perspective with the enactment of the *CRC*. Indeed, this convention introduced three new articles on the subject: Article 16(1), with an almost identical formulation to that contained in the *ICCPR*, states that "[n]o child shall be subjected to arbitrary or unlawful interference with his or her privacy, family, or correspondence, nor to unlawful attacks on his or her honour and reputation."[60] Article 20(1) regulates the child's right to a family environment:[61]

> [A] child temporarily or permanently deprived of his or her family environment, or in whose own best interests cannot be allowed to remain in that environment, shall be entitled to special protection and assistance provided by the State.

Finally, Article 7(1) regulates children's right to know their parents:[62]

> [T]he child shall be registered immediately after birth and shall have the right from birth to a name, the right to acquire a nationality and, as far as possible, the right to know and be cared for by his or her parents.

As noted above, the right to family is recognized by many international human rights documents. The following question thus arises: How does the recognition of the right to family affect Offspring's legal entitlements with respect to their half or full siblings and their progenitor(s)? In answering this question, this subsection first addresses Offspring's relationship rights to their half or full siblings, and then their relationship rights to their progenitors.

A person's relationship to his or her half or full siblings is increasingly being recognised as an important interest. In a 2009 study, Cambridge University researchers found that parents of Offspring reported positive experiences of contacting and meeting their child's donor siblings.[63] Likewise, Blyth reports that Offspring are interested in and willing to know about the existence of half-siblings: how many half-siblings they have, their age, sex, and whereabouts.[64] This should come as no surprise:[65]

> Dwyer argues that siblings' relationships are the most important relationships in the lives of some children and central to the life of most, typically entailing emotional ties stronger than those with any other nonparent relatives, such as grandparents, aunts, uncles, and cousins.

Unlike parents who usually have lived at least two decades before children arrive and who tend to predecease their children, siblings are usually part of one's life from beginning to end.

Astonishingly, under international law there is no express provision regarding the importance to children of access and contact with their siblings. Nevertheless, one can find implicit recognition of this interest. Van Bueren argues that children's right "to access and contact with siblings falls within article 16 of the *CRC* as amounting to unlawful interference with the family."[66] Paraphrasing this author, any obstruction (either material or legal) of siblings' relationship will violate the *CRC*. Moreover, both the *UDHR* and the *ICCPR* recognize the right to protection against "arbitrary interference" and "arbitrary or unlawful interference" (respectively) with the family to every human being, therefore expanding the legal protection beyond children.[67] Any distinction regarding "siblings' relationships" could be contrary to Article 2(1) of the *CRC*, which stipulates that rights should be implemented "without discrimination of any kind",[68] including "birth or other status."[69] Similar protection against discrimination is accorded by both the *UDHR* and the *ICCPR* concerning the rights regulated therein: "without distinction of any kind, such as … birth or other status."[70] Therefore, the lack of access to information regarding Offspring's siblings amount to "arbitrary or unlawful interference with his or her privacy [and] family"[71]

To date, the interest in establishing and preserving one's relationship with siblings has been addressed only by Van Bueren, and not in the context of assisted human reproduction. Following Doek's dynamic interpretation of the *CRC*, Article 16(1) should be interpreted to protect one's relationships to siblings against arbitrary or illegal intrusions in the context of assisted human reproduction.[72] This view is supported also by Articles 12 of the *UDHR* which provides protection against arbitrary interference, and 17(1) of the *ICCPR* which protects against arbitrary or illegal interference with his or her family. Moreover, as noted in the previous subsection, the notion of "illegal intrusion" refers to any conduct that can be considered contrary to domestic law, to international human rights law or to both.[73] Referring to *ICCPR* Article 17, the Human Rights Committee – the monitoring body to the *ICCPR* – held that[74]

> [T]he term 'unlawful' means that no interference can take place except in cases envisaged by the law. Interference authorized by States can only take place on the basis of law, *which itself must comply with the provisions, aims and objectives of the Covenant [ICCPR]*. [emphasis added]

With regard to the term, "arbitrary interference", which appears in *ICCPR* article 17, the Human Rights Committee understood that this expression[75]

> Can also extend to interference provided for under the law. The introduction of the concept of arbitrariness is intended to guarantee that even interference provided for by law should be in accordance with the provisions, aims and objectives of the Covenant and should be, in any event, reasonable in the particular circumstances.

The "right to family" grants a donor-conceived person the right to know his or her progenitor(s). The current practice of using third party gametes envisions that the child conceived through the donor's genetic material will be born in a family and that the donor will not be considered a member of that family. So it might be argued that a right to family cannot establish a right of Offspring to know their progenitors. Yet, under international law, every child is granted "as far as possible, the right to know and be cared for by his or her parents."[76] Ziemele notes that:[77]

> [S]ome exchanges between the CRC Committee and States in the framework of the State reports suggest that the CRC Committee takes the view that the term "parents" in the context of Article 7 and the aims of the CRC *includes biological parents* and that the child has the right to know, as far as possible, who they are. This right is both part of Article 7 and Article 3 of the CRC since *it is considered to be in the best interest of the child to know, as far as possible, the child's birth parents.* [emphasis added]

The phrase "as far as possible" should not be understood to limit a child's rights. This conclusion in evident in an examination of the legislative history of the CRC. Article 7, as regulated in the first draft to the CRC (1978), stated only that "[t]he child shall be entitled from his birth to a name and a nationality."[78] During the period 1979-1988, most of the discussion surrounding this article focused on how to implement the child's right to a nationality, which was then a controversial topic amongst negotiating States. It was not until the 1988 technical review, that UNESCO proposed that a new paragraph be added to this article; it read:[79]

> [T]he child shall have the right from birth to respect for his/her human, racial, national and cultural identity and dignity, as well as have the duty to respect the human, racial, national and cultural identity and dignity of others.

This text was adopted by the Working Group, but during the second reading (1989), the delegation of Egypt, on behalf of nine Arab countries, proposed an amendment to it: "[t]he child shall have the right from his birth to know and belong to his parents, as well as the right to a name and to acquire a nationality."[80] As the delegation of Egypt explained:[81]

> The purpose of the first amendment was that of ensuring the psychological stability of the child, which was of equal importance to his physical and mental growth and helped to form his personality. *In most cases the right to know his parents was quite essential to the child* and equal to his right to a name or a nationality, which were only important to him at a certain age. [emphasis added]

The delegations of the German Democratic Republic, the Union of Soviet Socialist Republics and the United States of America expressed some concerns about this proposal because their legislation regulated the right of "secret adoptions" and the right to know one's parents would jeopardize such secrecy.[82] Therefore, the representative of the United States of America introduced a new proposal: "[t]he child shall have the right from birth to a name and registration and to acquire a nationality, and, as far as possible, to know and be cared for by his or her parents."[83] To accord with the legislative history of the *CRC*, the phrase "as far as possible" should be interpreted in a manner that takes into consideration the best interests of the child. Moreover, as the legislative history reveals, the phrase was added only to take into consideration the "secret" adoption procedures, and for no other reason.

This amendment was greeted with doubt by some participants who viewed the words "as far as possible" as giving rise to an arbitrary interpretation of this article.[84] Consequently, a new discussion arose in which the observers for New Zealand and Sweden proposed that the phrase "as far as possible" should be replaced by the phrases, "subject to the provisions of this Convention" or "as far as possible and subject to the provisions of the Convention", respectively.[85] In addition, the representative of the United States of America suggested adding the words "in the best interests of the child."[86] Once the final text was adopted, the representative of Sweden stated that "his delegation was able to join in the consensus on article 2 [current article 7] on the understanding that the provisions of this article should be interpreted in the best interests of the child."[87] Therefore, the words 'as far as possible' cannot be interpreted to limit the child's rights. According to Ziemele:[88]

> [T]he limitation 'as far as' possible presupposes that there might be circumstances which may limit the right of the child to know the biological parents. In any event, often there will be a need to weigh all the circumstances, *but an absolute prohibition on the right to know biological parents is contrary to the CRC*. [emphasis added]

In conclusion, a complete prohibition on the right to know biological parents is contrary to the *CRC*. Moreover, any limitation on the exercise of this right – for instance, recognition of this right only in the context of adoption procedures and not in the context of assisted human reproduction – is contrary to *CRC* Article 2(1) (prohibition against discrimination).[89] Such an understanding has been accepted by the Austrian government. As Blyth and Farrand report, that government has interpreted Article 7 of the *CRC* as giving Offspring the right to know about their genetic father when they reach the age of 14 years old (Austria does not regulate the right to know one's genetic mother because egg and embryo donation are illegal in Austria).[90] Thus, with section 15 of the *AHRA*, Canada also violates the international human right of the donor-conceived to family.

4. Implementing the Rights to Health, Identity and Family in Canadian Domestic Law

The amendment of Canadian domestic law to permit donor-conceived people to know their origins is possible. At the moment, there is concern about whether legislation to ban anonymity should operate both prospectively and retrospectively, or just prospectively. In other words, should past promises of anonymity to donors be overridden in the interests of providing their Offspring information, should they seek it? Prospective legislation does not raise issues of breach of promise. In this regard, Canada might follow the Australian state of Victoria; its legislation states:[91]

> [A]t the time at which a donor gives consent under section 12, he or she ... must be advised, in writing – (i) of the rights of any person born as a result of a donor treatment procedure ... to information under Division 3 of Part 7.

Part 7 refers to the information that can lead an Offspring to identify a donor. In addition, Victoria's legislation grants donors the right to be informed about the children who were born as a result of donor treatment procedures.[92]

Should Canadian provinces and territories enact legislation that would have retrospective effect? This is more difficult. Victoria has said no. The Victorian statute stipulates that the right of persons born from donor treatment procedures to have access to donors' identifying information applies only to procedures undertaken after January 1, 1998 with gametes and embryos also donated after that time.[93] Access to donors' identifying information before that date requires the donor's written consent.[94] Such consent can, in practice, be obtained. As Waller and Mortimer report, "[l]icensed hospitals and clinics have, in some instances, obtained post-1998 consents from donors whose sperm was not used successfully before 1 January 1998."[95]

Nevertheless, Victoria's decision to honour past promises of anonymity made to donors does not meet the needs of many donor-conceived persons and violates their international rights. Under the Victoria legislation, a donor-conceived cannot know his or her identity if the donor has died or is unwilling to be identified to the donor-conceived person. Victorian legislation concerning the pre-1998 period focuses on the donor's privacy rights and not on the donor-conceived person's health, identity, and family relations rights.[96] Such regulation violates international human rights law by wrongly discriminating against donor-conceived persons whose conceptions occurred before the revision of the statute.[97] If Canadian jurisdictions grant future Offspring the right to know their progenitors but does not grant that right to persons in existence, such a law will breach the international human rights of donor-conceived people to health, identity and family.[98]

5. Conclusion

Canada is a party to numerous international human rights instruments, and consequently must observe international rights to health, identity, and family relations. Canada's Assisted Human Reproduction Act gave priority to the donor's right to privacy, despite the compelling – and compulsory – international legal framework on children's rights to identity, health and family relations. No province or territory has required the creation, preservation and disclosure of a child's medial, social and cultural history. In other words, law in Canada is adult-orientated rather than child-centered, in violation of international law. Although adults obviously have rights, rights that conflict must be prioritized.[99] Canadian legislators must ask themselves the fundamental question: "Whose rights should prevail?" To abide by international law, Canadian jurisdictions should give priority to the child's rights to health, identity and family rather than to the donor's right to privacy.[100] In Canada, the donor's right to privacy has not been adequately interpreted in a manner that also observes and protects the child's rights to health, identity, and family.[101]

Not only do Canadian jurisdictions fail to honour international law, they violate the nation's own domestic law principles. The *AHRA*'s first principle, which remains in force, states:[102]

> The health and well-being of children born through the application of the assisted human reproductive technology *must be given priority in all decisions respecting their use.* [emphasis added]

Therefore, jurisdictions in Canada must alter domestic law to accord with its international legal obligations and its domestic principles. Current legislation in Canada regarding assisted human reproduction ought to be modified to permit Offspring to know their origins.

Acknowledgments

I am very thankful to Juliet Guichon for her excellent comments and suggestions, and her commitment as main editor of this collaborative project. Danilo D'Addio Chammas, Mariana De Lorenzi, Michelle Giroux and Angela Long provided me with insightful comments on some parts of this paper, and John Cecchetti kindly assisted me in editing this article. The Social Sciences and Humanities Research Council of Canada generously funded my research through a CGS Doctoral Scholarship. An extended version of this article was published in the *Canadian Yearbook on International Law*. I am thankful to Donald McRae, editor of the journal, for facilitating this publication. As always, this article is dedicated to my mum, Nilda Di Croche.

Bibliography

Act respecting assisted human reproduction and related research, S.C. 2004, c. 2.
Baker v. Canada (Minister of Citizenship and Immigration), 2 S.C.R. 1999, 817.
Blyth, Eric. "Donor assisted conception and donor offspring rights to genetic origins information," *The International Journal of Children's Rights* 6 (1998): 237-253.
-- "Information on genetic origins in donor-assisted conception: is knowing who you are a human rights issue?" *Human Fertility* 5 (2002) 4:185-192.
-- and Abigail Farrand. "Anonymity in donor-assisted conception and the UN Convention on the Rights of the Child," (2004) 12 *The International Journal on Children's Right* 12 (2004): 89-104.
Bortnik, Aida, and Luis Puenzo. *La Historia Oficial*[*The Official Story*]. DVD directed by Luis Puenzo. Port Washington, NY: Koch Lorber, 1985.
Cerda, Jaime Sergio. "The Draft Convention on the Rights of the Child: New Rights," *Human Rights Quarterly* 12 (1990) 1: 115-119.
Canada. Standing Committee on Health. "Canadian Alliance Minority Report. Regulating Assisted Human Reproduction and Related Research." In *Assisted Human Reproduction: Building Families*, chaired by Bonnie Brown, M.P., 2001, 77-83.
-- "Children: The Silenced Citizens. Effective Implementation of Canada's International Obligations with Respect to the Rights of Children. Final Report of the Standing Senate Committee on Human Rights." April 2007. Parliament of Canada, http://www.parl.gc.ca/39/1/parlbus/commbus/senate/Com-e/huma-e/rep-e/rep10apr07-e.htm.
-- "Who's in charge here? Effective Implementation of Canada's International Obligations with Respect to the Rights of Children." November 2005. Parliament of Canada. http://www.parl.gc.ca/38/1/parlbus/commbus/senate/com-e/huma-e/rep-e/rep19nov05-e.htm.
Canadian Foundation for Children, Youth and the Law v. Canada (Attorney General), [2004] 1 S.C.R. 76.
Cantwell, Nigel and Anna Holzscheiter. "Article 20: Children Deprived of Their Family Environment." In *A Commentary on the United Nations Conventions on the Rights of the Child*, André Alen, Johan VandeLanotte, Eugeen Verhellen, Fiona Ang, Eva

Berghmans, and Mieke Verheyde, eds. Leiden: Martinus Nijhoff Publishers 2008, 1-68.

Chapman, Audrey. "A 'Violation Approach' for Monitoring the International Covenant on Economic, Social and Cultural Rights," *Human Rights Quarterly* 18 (1996):23-66.

Comisión Nacional sobre la Desaparición de Personas. *Nunca Más*. Buenos Aires: EUDEBA 1984. Proyecto Desaparecidos, http://www.desaparecidos.org/arg/conadep/nuncamas/nuncamas.html.

Comité Consultatif National d'Éthique pour les sciences de la vie et de la santé. *Avis no. 90. Accès aux origines, anonymat et secret de la filiation* (2005). Comité Consultatif National d'Éthique pour les sciences de la vie et de la santé. http://www.ccne-ethique.fr/docs/fr/avis090.pdf.

Committee on Economic, Social and Cultural Rights, *General Comment No. 14 (2000). The right to the highest attainable standard of health (article 12 of the ICESCR)* (11 May 2000). Office of the High Commissioner for Human Rights, http://daccessdds.un.org/doc/UNDOC/GEN/G00/439/34/PDF/G0043934.pdf?OpenElement.

-- *CESCR General Comment 3. The nature of State Parties Obligations (Art. 2, part. 1)* (14 December 1990). Office of the High Commissioner for Human Rights, http://www.unhchr.ch/tbs/doc.nsf/(Symbol)/94bdbaf59b43a424c12563ed0052b664?Opendocument.

Committee on the Rights of the Child, *General Comment No. 4 (2003). Adolescent health and development in the context of the Convention on the Rights of the Child* (1 July 2003). Office of the High Commissioner for Human Rights, http://www.unhchr.ch/tbs/doc.nsf/898586b1dc7b4043c1256a450044f331/309e8c3807aa8cb7c1256d2d0038caaa/$FILE/G0340816.pdf.

Convention on the Elimination of All Forms of Discrimination against Women, 18 December 1979, 1249 U.N.T.S. 13, Can. T.S. 1982 No. 31.

Convention on the Prevention and Punishment of the Crime of Genocide, 9 December 1948, 78 U.N.T.S. 277, Can. T.S. 1949 No. 27.

Convention on the Rights of the Child, 20 November 1989, 1577 U.N.T.S. 3, Can. T.S. 1992 No. 3 (entered into force 2 September 1990, entered into force for Canada 12 January 1992).

Declaration of the Rights of the Child, GA Res. 1386 (XIV), UNGAOR, 14th Sess., 20 November 20 1959.

Doek, Jaap E. "Article 8: The Right to Preservation of Identity, and Article 9: the Right Not to Be Separated from His or Her Parents." In *A Commentary on the United Nations Conventions on the Rights of the Child*, André Alen, Johan Vande Lanotte, Eugeen Verhellen, Fiona Ang, Eva Berghmans, and Mieke Verheyde, eds. 1-31. Leiden: Martinus Nijhoff Publishers 2006.

Dwyer, James. *The Relationship Rights of Children*. Cambridge: Cambridge University Press 2006.

Eide, Elisabeth. "Interaction between International and Domestic Human Rights Law: A Canadian Perspective", *Sino-Canadian International Conference on the Ratification and Implementation of Human Rights Covenants: Beijing, China, October 2001*. International Centre for Criminal Law Reform and Criminal Justice Policy, http://www.icclr.law.ubc.ca/Publications/Reports/E-Eid.PDF.

-- Eide, E., Asbjørn and Wenche Barth Eide. "Article 24 The Right to Health." In *A Commentary on the United Nations Conventions on the Rights of the Child*, André Alen, Johan Vande Lanotte, Eugeen Verhellen, Fiona Ang, Eva Berghmans, and Mieke Verheyde, eds. 1-51. Leiden: Martinus Nijhoff Publishers 2006.

Fleeming, Donald J. and John P. McEvoy. "Domestic Implementation of Canada's International Human Rights Obligations." In *The Globalized Rule of Law. Relationships between International and Domestic Law*, Oonagh E. Fitzgerald, ed., 521-547. Toronto: Irwin Law 2006.

Freeman, Mark and Gibran Van Ert, *International Human Rights Law*. Toronto: Irwin Law 2004.

Freeman, Michael. "Book Review: A. Eide and W.B. Eide 'Article 24. The Right to Health'," *The International Journal of Children's Rights* 15 (2007): 315-318.

-- "Article 3. The Best Interest of the Child." In *A Commentary on the United Nations Conventions on the Rights of the Child*, André Alen, Johan Vande Lanotte, Eugeen Verhellen, Fiona Ang, Eva Berghmans, and Mieke Verheyde, eds., 1-79. Leiden: Martinus Nijhoff Publishers 2007.

-- "The Rights of the Artificially Procreated Child." In *The Moral Status of Children. Essays on the Rights of the Child*, 185-212. The Hague: Kluwer Law International 1997.

-- "The new birth right? Identity and the child of the reproduction revolution," *The International Journal of Children's Rights* 4 (1996): 273-297.

Freeman, T., V. Jadva, W. Kramer, S. Golombok. "Gamete donation: parents' experiences of searching for their child's donor siblings and donor," *Human Reproduction* 23:4 (2009): 505-516.

Giroux, Michelle. "Le droit fondamental de connaître ses origines biologiques." In *Droits de l'enfant. Actes de la Conférence internationale / Ottawa 2007. Rights of the Child. Proceedings of the International Conference / Ottawa 2007*, Tara Collins, Rachel Grondin, Verónica Piñero, Marie Pratte and Marie-Claude Roberge, eds., 355-390. Montreal: Wilson &Lafleur 2008.

Hodgson, Douglas. "The International Legal Protection of the Child's Right to a Legal Identity and the Problem of Statelessness," *International Journal of Law and the Family* 7 (1993): 255-270.

Howe, Brian R. "Implementing children's rights in a federal state: The case of Canada's child protection system," *The International Journal of Children's Rights* 9 (2001): 361-382.

Human Rights Committee, *General Comment No. 16: The right to respect of privacy, family, and home and correspondence, and protection of honour and reputation (Art. 17)*, 8 April 1988. Office of the High Commissioner for Human Rights, http://www2.ohchr.org/english/bodies/hrc/comments.htm.

Infertility Treatment Act 1995. Act No. 63/1995.

International Covenant on Civil and Political Rights, 19 December 1966, 999 U.N.T.S. 171, Can. T.S. 1976 No. 47.

International Covenant on Economic, Social, and Cultural Rights, 16 December 1966, 999 U.N.T.S. 3, Can. T.S. 1976 No. 46.

International Convention on the Elimination of All Forms of Racial Discrimination, 21 December 1965, 660 U.N.T.S. 195, Can. T.S. 1970 No. 28.

Ninth International Conference of American States, American Declaration on the Rights and Duties of Man, 1948.

-- General Assembly, *Statute of the Inter-American Commission on Human Rights,* Res. 447, 1979.

-- Inter-American Commission on Human Rights, *Grand Chief Michael Mitchell (Canada),* Report No. 74/03, Petition 790/01, 2003.

-- Inter-American Commission on Human Rights, *James Terry Roach and Jay Pinkerton (United States),* Res. no. 3/87, case 9647, 1987.

-- Inter-American Commission on Human Rights, *Rafael Ferrer-Mazorra et al. (United States),* Report 51/01, Case 9903, 2001.

-- OAS, Inter-American Court on Human Rights, *Interpretation of the American Declaration of the Rights and Duties of Man Within the Framework of Article 64 of the American Convention on Human Rights.* Advisory Opinion OC-10/89, 1989.

O'Donovan, Katherine. "A Right to Know One's Parentage?" *International Journal of Law and the Family* 2 (1988): 27-45.

Office of the United Nations High Commissioner for Human Rights, *Legislative History of the Convention on the Rights of the Child.* 2 vols. United Nations: New York and Geneva, 2007, http://www.ohchr.org/EN/PublicationsResources/Pages/ReferenceMaterial.aspx.

Rose & Anor v. Secretary of State for Health Human Fertilisation and Embryology Authority, 2002, EWHC 1593 (Admin).

Stewart, George. "Interpreting the Child's Right to Identity in the U.N. Convention on the Rights of the Child," *Family Law Quarterly* 26 (1992) 3: 221-233.

Universal Declaration of Human Rights, GA Res. 217 (III), UNGAOR, 3d.Sess., Supp. No. 13, UN Doc. A/810, 1948.

Universal Declaration on the Human Genome and Human Rights, UNESCO, 29th Sess. (1997), GA Res. 53/152, 1998.

Van Bueren, Geraldine. *The International Law on the Rights of the Child.* The Hague: Martinus Nijhoff Publishers 1998.

Van Ert, Gib. *Using International Law in Canadian Courts.* 2nd ed. Toronto: Irwin Law 2008.

Vienna Declaration and Programme of Action, World Conference on Human Rights, 1993.

Waller, Louis and Debbie Mortimer. "The Gifts of Life-Donating Gametes and the Consequences." In, *Law and Medicine. Current Legal Issues,* Michael Freeman and Andrew D.E. Lewis, eds. 303-316. Vol 3. New York: Oxford University Press, 2000.

Wilson, Sara. "Identity, Genealogy and the Social Family: The Case of Donor Insemination," *International Journal of Law, Policy and the Family* 11 (1997): 270-297.

Ziemele, Ineta. "Article 7: The Right to Birth Registration, Name and Nationality, and the Right to Know and Be Cared for by Parents." In *A Commentary on the United Nations Conventions on the Rights of the Child,* André Alen, Johan Vande Lanotte, EugeenVerhellen, Fiona Ang, Eva Berghmans, and MiekeVerheyde, eds., 1-30. Leiden: Martinus Nijhoff Publishers 2007.

Notes

1 Freeman, "Article 3", 39.
2 *La Historia Oficial* [*The Official Story*], VHS, directed by Luis Puenzo (Port Washington, NY: Koch Lorber Films, 1985).
3 Wilson, "Identity", 279. Sara Wilson's research compared the disclosure of the biological parents' identity in the case of the children of the disappeared (Argentina), with adoption and donor insemination regulation (United Kingdom). She justifies her methodology from a child's rights standpoint: "from the perspective of the children, on which I concentrate in this paper, there are marked similarities between the situation of the children in all three cases: many of them have had very little or no contact with their biological 'genitors', and have very little or no information about them, or even that they exist".
4 *Assisted Human Reproduction Act*, 18(3).
5 In a constitutional reference, the Supreme Court of Canada rendered its opinion that that section among many others were not within federal jurisidiction, *Reference re Assisted Human Reproduction Act*, 2010 SCC 61, [2010] 3 S.C.R. 457.
6 *Universal Declaration of Human Rights*.
7 *International Covenant on Civil and Political Rights*.
8 *International Covenant on Economic, Social, and Cultural Rights*.
9 *Convention on the Rights of the Child*.
10 *Baker*, S.C.R. 80; *Canadian Foundation*, S.C.R. 9; Canada. Standing Senate Committee on Human Rights, *Who's in charge here?*, 4, see also 43-44, 62-62; Canada. Standing Senate Committee on Human Rights, *Children: The Silenced Citizens*, 113; Freeman and Van Ert, *International Human Rights Law*; Fleeming and McEvoy, "Domestic Implementation"; Eid, "Interaction", 4-5; Howe, "Implementing children's rights", 365; Van Ert, *Using International Law*. Accordingly, the Standing Senate Committee recommended that:
> the federal-provincial-territorial negotiations on adoption proposed in Recommendation 10 should include consideration of access to a biological parent's identity and of the benefits of identity disclosure vetos. The Committee also recommends that Assisted Human Reproduction Canada review the legal and regulatory regime surrounding sperm donor identity and access to a donor's medical history to determine how the best interests of the child can better be served.

> The status of the Universal Declaration on Human Rights is a contentious issue: while some argue that it is a declaration that does not have binding effects on signatory States, others argue that its wording has become customary international law, and therefore compulsory to signatory States.

11 *American Declaration on Rights and Duties of Man*.
12 OAS, Inter-American Court on Human Rights, *Interpretation of the American Declaration*, 35-45; OAS, Inter-American Commission on Human Rights, *James Terry Roach*, 46-49; OAS, Inter-American Commission on Human Rights, *Rafael Ferrer-Mazorra*, 171; OAS, *Statute of the Inter-American Commission on Human Rights*, 20.
13 Ibid., *Grand Chief*, 30.
14 Since Canada is neither a State Party to the European nor the African regional human rights systems, the study of these systems is beyond the scope of this paper.
15 *International Convention on the Elimination of All Forms of Racial Discrimination*. Early attempts to regulate this right can be found in the *Universal Declaration of Human Rights*, article 25(1): "[e]veryone has the right to a standard of living adequate for the health and well-being of himself and of his family, including food, clothing, housing and medical care and necessary social services…"; in the *American Declaration on the Rights and Duties of Man*, article XI: "[e]very person has the right to the preservation of his health through sanitary and social measures relating to food, clothing, housing and medical care, to the extent permitted by public and community resources", and in the *Declaration of the Rights of the Child*, principle 4: "[t]he child shall enjoy the benefits of social security. He shall be entitled to grow and develop in health; to this end, special care and protection shall be provided both to him and to his mother, including adequate pre-natal and post-natal care."
16 *International Covenant on Economic, Social, and Cultural Rights*, 12(1).

17 *Convention on the Elimination of Al Forms of Discrimination against Women,* 12(1). With regard to health rights in the work environment, see article 11(1)(f).
18 *Convention on the Rights of the Child,* 24(1).
19 Office of the United Nations High Commissioner for Human Rights, *Legislative History,* vol. II, 898-899. During the negotiations of the text of the *Convention on the Rights of the Child,* there were two unsuccessful attempts to regulate genetic engineering. One was brought by the Government of Colombia, as a comment to the first Polish draft to the Convention (1978). The second attempt was a proposal submitted to the Commission on Human Rights by the World Association of Children's Friends (NGO) following the second reading of the Convention (1989).
20 *International Covenant on Economic, Social, and Cultural Rights,* 12(2).
21 Committee on Economic, Social and Cultural Rights, *CESCR General Comment 3,* 3. This committee monitors the implementation and observance of the *International Covenant on Economic, Social and Cultural Rights* by States Parties.
22 Committee on Economic, Social and Cultural Rights, *CESCR General Comment 3,* 9; Chapman, "A Violation Approach", 23. Chapman is against the notion of "progressive realization" for assessing State Parties' compliance with economic, social, and cultural rights since, as she argues, this "is inexact and renders these rights difficult to monitor."
23 *International Covenant on Economic, Social, and Cultural Rights,* 2(2).
24 Committee on Economic, Social and Cultural Rights, *General Comment 14,* 8.
25 *Ibid.,*11.
26 *Ibid.,* 12(b) (iv).
27 Comité Consultatif, *Avis no. 90,* 4. Eric Blyth reports how donor-conceived people have identified the lack of updated information about donors as a health issue: "[w]ith increasing awareness of the importance of genetics and of personal genetic biographies, donor-conceived people have begun to itemize the information they want about their genetic and social heritage and to emphasize the need for this information to be updated and not to cease at the point of donation.", "Information", 187 [emphasis added]. See also Ms. Joanna Rose's and E.M.'s personal accounts on the relevance of the subject in *Rose & Anor,* EWHC, 7 and 12, respectively.
28 Committee on Economic, Social and Cultural Rights, *General Comment 14,* 12(b) (iv).
29 The Committee on the Rights of the Child is the monitoring body of the *Convention on the Rights of the Child*; *Convention on the Rights of the Child,* Part II.
30 Committee on the Rights of the Child, *General Comment No. 4,* 41(b). See as well para. 24: "[a]dolescents have the right to access adequate information essential for their health and development and for their ability to participate meaningfully in society."
31 *Ibid.*
32 *Universal Declaration on the Human Genome and Human Rights,* adopted by the General Conference of the United Nations Educational, Scientific and Cultural Organisation in its 29th session on 11 November 1997, endorsed by United Nations General Assembly resolution 53/152 of 9 December 1998.
33 For a similar perspective, see Eide and Eide, "Article 24", 22. Michael Freeman, also writing for this series of volumes intended to discuss the "scope" of different articles of the *CRC,* has critically commented about the authors' lack of discussion of children's health rights in the assisted reproduction domain: "What obligations are there [article 24 of the *CRC*] to the children of reproductive technology?"; Freeman, "Book Review", 317.
34 Committee on Economic, Social and Cultural Rights, *General Comment 14,* 24. See also Eide and Eide, "Article 24", 5.
35 *Convention on the Rights of the Child,* article 4 (1).
36 Eide and Eide, "Article 24", 6-7.
37 See note 33 above, 36.
38 Committee on the Rights of the Child, *General Comment No. 4,* 39. See as well Eide and Eide:
[The *CRC*] does not provide a right of the child to be healthy – no legal instrument can do that – but it spells out obligations of States Parties to adopt measures which, if implemented, will ensure the highest attainable standard of health taking into account the genetic and other biological predispositions of the individual child and the risks that children are exposed to. "Article 24", 1.

39 Freeman, "The new birth right?", 277. See also O'Donovan, "A Right to Know"; Wilson, "Identity".
40 Hodgson, "The International Legal Protection", 256.
41 The Committee to Consider the Social, Ethical and Legal Issues Arising from In Vitro Fertilization (Professor Louis Waller, Chair), *Report on the Disposition of Embryos Produced by In Vitro Fertilization* (Melbourne, 1984), para. 3.30, 26; cited in Waller and Mortimer, "The Gifts", 304.
42 *Convention on the Rights of the Child*, 8. A different attempt to regulate identity rights can be found in the *Convention on the Prevention and Punishment of the Crime of Genocide*, article II (e): "In the present Convention, genocide means any of the following acts committed with intent to destroy, in whole or in part, a national, ethnical, racial or religious group, as such: ... Forcibly transferring children of the group to another group".
43 Office of the United Nations High Commissioner for Human Rights, *Legislative History*, vol. I, 383.
44 Comisión Nacional, *Nunca Más*. The partial relocation of these children has been an extremely difficult task since many of them had been registered as having been born in the families who had really adopted them. During the Argentinean military government, individuals associated to the militia or the police forces had access to the official registries, and were able to falsify the information related to the kidnapped child. Up to present, many children (adults) do not know their biological origins; neither are they aware that their parents are not their progenitors.
45 Office of the United Nations High Commissioner for Human Rights, *Legislative History*, vol. I, 383.
46 *Ibid*, 385.
47 *Ibid*.
48 *Ibid*, 387.
49 Doek, "Article 8", 12. Freeman understands the right to identity in a negative – and maybe broader – fashion: he argues "that the right to identity is a right not to be deceived about ones true origins." Freeman, "The new birth right?" 291.
50 Van Bueren, *The International Law*, 119; Doek, "Article 8", 8; Cerda, "The Draft Convention", 116 [Cerda was the Argentinean sponsor of article 8 of the *CRC*]; Stewart, "Interpreting the Child's Right", 224.
51 Doek, "Article 8", 13.
52 Van Bueren, *The International Law*, 119.
53 *American Declaration on the Rights and Duties of Man*, V.
54 *Ibid.*,VI.
55 *Universal Declaration of Human Rights*, 12.
56 *Ibid.*,16(3).
57 *International Covenant on Economic, Social, and Cultural Rights*, 10(1).
58 *International Covenant on Civil and Political Rights*, 17(1).
59 *Ibid.*, 23(1).
60 *Convention on the Rights of the Child*, 16(1). See as well the preamble to the *Convention on the Rights of the Child*.
61 *Ibid.*,20(1).
62 *Ibid.*, 7(1).
63 Freeman et al., "Gamete Donation".
64 Blyth, "Donor assisted", 244-245; Blyth, "Information", 188.
65 Dwyer, *The Relationship Rights*, 59-60.
66 Van Bueren, *The International Law*, 83.
67 *Universal Declaration of Human Rights*, 12 and *International Covenant on Civil and Political Rights*, 17(1), respectively.
68 *Convention on the Rights of the Child*, 2(1).
69 *Ibid*.
70 *Universal Declaration of Human Rights*, 2(1); *International Covenant on Civil and Political Rights*, 2(1).
71 *Convention on the Rights of the Child*, 16(1); *Universal Declaration of Human Rights*, 12; and *International Covenant on Civil and Political Rights*, 17(1).

72 Doek, "Article 8", 12.
73 For example, the enactment of legislation by a State Party to the *CRC* that does not observe the human rights law recognized to individuals therein.
74 Human Rights Committee, *General Comment No. 16*, 3.
75 *Ibid.*, 4.
76 *Convention on the Rights of the Child*, 7(1). Cantwell and Holzscheiter understand that articles 7(1) and 20 of the *CRC* are closely related; Cantwell and Holzscheiter, "Article 20", 5.
77 Ziemele, "Article 7", 26.
78 Office of the United Nations High Commissioner for Human Rights, *Legislative History*, vol. I, 370.
79 *Ibid.*, 376.
80 *Ibid.*, 378.
81 *Ibid.*
82 *Ibid.*
83 *Ibid.*,379.
84 *Ibid.*
85 *Ibid.*
86 *Ibid.*
87 *Ibid.*, 380.
88 Ziemele, "Article 7", 27.
89 *Convention on the Rights of the Child*, 2(1).
90 Blyth and Farrand, "Anonymity", 94-95.
91 *Infertility Treatment Act*, 17 (b)(i).
92 *Ibid.*, 76.
93 Waller and Mortimer, "The Gifts", 307.
94 Blyth, "Donor assisted", 238.
95 See note 92 above.
96 Professor Louis Waller, personal communication, 22 March 2009. Moreover, there are more legal questions associated to access to information in Victoria (Australia): what is the situation of the individuals who were artificially procreated before 1 July 1988? What is the situation of those artificially procreated between 1 July 1988 and 1 January 1998?
97 *Universal Declaration of Human Rights*, 7; *American Declaration on the Rights and Duties of Man*, II; *International Covenant on Economic, Social, and Cultural Rights*, 2(2); *International Covenant on Civil and Political Rights*, 2(1), 3 and 26; *Convention on the Rights of the Child*, 2.
98 The problem associated to this sort of "distinction" in the regulation was brought in *Rose & Anor*, EWHC, 15. There the claimants argued, among other matters, that the regulation was contrary to article 14 (protection against discrimination) of the European Convention on Human Rights. However, this was not discussed by the court. Worth noting, the wording of article 14 of the European Convention on Human Rights is similar to international human rights law that Canada has ratified: *International Covenant on Economic, Social, and Cultural Rights*, 2(2) and *International Covenant on Civil and Political Rights*, 2(1).
99 Freeman and Van Ert, *International Human Rights Law*, 35. See as well *Vienna Declaration*, 5: "[a]ll human rights are universal, indivisible and interdependent and interrelated. The international community must treat human rights globally in a fair and equal manner, on the same footing, and with the same emphasis."
100 Giroux, "Le droit fondamental", 371.
101 Committee on Health, "Canadian Alliance Minority Report", 81. Interesting to note, the Canadian Alliance recommended that "the final legislation [*Assisted Human Reproduction* draft bill] contain a clear statement to the effect that where the privacy rights of the donors of human reproductive materials conflict with the rights of children to know their genetic and social heritage, that the rights of the children shall prevail."
102 *Assisted Human Reproduction Act*, 2 (a).

Chapter Eighteen

A Comparison of the Law in Canada Related to the Disclosure of Information Regarding Biological Parents of Adoptees and the Donor-Conceived

Juliet R. Guichon

1. Introduction

The practices of donor conception and adoption have much in common. They both entail the creation of a family in which the child is not genetically related to one or both parents. The two practices each attempt to balance the rights and interests of adults with those of the resulting child.

There are differences, of course. For example, adoption addresses the needs of an existing child whereas donor conception is a practice that aims to cause a child to come into being; in other words, one practice is about an existing child and the other about a potential child. A second difference is that, in most cases of adoption, the adoptive parents who rear the child share the fact that they are not genetically related to the child, whereas in donor conception, often one rearing parent is genetically related.

But these differences are not as significant as the central fact that both adoptees and the donor-conceived are raised by at least one person who is not genetically related to them and that both adoptees and the donor-conceived may wish to know the identity of that parent and to come to meet him or her.

Indeed, the British Columbia Supreme Court has decided[1] that adoptees and donor-conceived people are relevantly similar for constitutional human rights purposes. A donor-conceived person, Olivia Pratten (who contributed a chapter to this volume), claimed that the British Columbia *Adoption Act*[2] violates the s. 15 equality provisions of the *Canadian Charter of Rights and Freedoms*.[3] The Court agreed with Pratten that British Columbia violated the rights of donor-conceived people to equality by failing to provide them a right or opportunity to obtain information about their biological parents similar to that which the Province provided to adoptees. In so doing, Madame Justice Adair held that it was appropriate to compare the donor-conceived with adoptees because they were in fact similarly situated in not being reared by one or both of their biological parents and yet they share similar needs to information about their progenitors.[4] She wrote:[5]

> There is much to learn from the adoption experience in considering the needs, circumstances and best interests of donor offspring, that there are many points of similarity between the two groups, that donor offspring share with adoptees many of the same social, psychological and medical needs for information about biological parents, and that, even if well-intentioned, serious harm can be caused by cutting off a child from his or her biological roots.

There are other reasons that the social practice of adoption can offer lessons to regulators of donor conception. Adoption is older and more established than donor conception, adult adoptees are more numerous than adult donor-conceived people, and adult adoptees have been expressing their views about secrecy and withholding information for a longer period than donor-conceived people.[6] Adult adoptees have helped to frame current and developing adoption law in Canada.

This chapter considers law in Canada from the perspective of the adoptee in relation to disclosure of adoption records. Because the practice of adoption in Canada is regulated under provincial and territorial jurisdiction, adoption information law is distinct to each province and territory.[7] Examination of this law reveals a stated legislated aim to focus on the best interests of the child and an evolving trend toward disclosure of medical and other background information and the identities of all those involved whilst protecting the expectation of privacy of the parties.[8] Analysis of law related to disclosure of adoption records also suggests that the law grants adoptees rights of *state-supervised* creation, retention and disclosure of records, which is not the case with donor conception.

2. Canadian Legislative Response Regarding Release of Identifying Information in Adoption Records

Every provincial and territorial adoption regime states that the paramount consideration is the "best interests of the child."[9] There are a range of provincial and territorial responses to the desires of people separated by adoption to learn the identities of the other and to seek reunion. These shall be discussed in order – moving from most government and individual restrictions on disclosure, to least restrictions on disclosure.

2.1 Release of Non-Identifying Information

Non-identifying information is typically social, cultural and medical information provided prior to the adoption and placed in the adoption file. Such information may be limited to descriptive details about an adopted person and the adopted person's birth relatives and tends to be sought by the adoption agency from the person or persons who place the child for adoption. In turn, the adoption agency gives the information to the adopting parents at the time of the adoption. Non-identifying information may include the following: date and place of the adopted person's birth; age of the birth parents and general physical description, such as eye and hair colour; race, ethnicity, religion, and medical history of the birth parents; educational level of the birth parents and their occupation at the time of the adoption; reason for placing the child for adoption; and existence of other children born to each birth parent.[10]

The value of non-identifying information is perhaps most clear when the information is medical and the consequences of withholding medical and social background information from adoptive parents proves serious. In the United States in the 1980s, for example, an adopted boy suffered "permanent and irreversible" brain damage and would "need special help for the balance of his life" because the medical information in the file given to the adopted parents was incomplete.[11] (The boy had not been tested for phenylketonuria, a condition that can cause brain damage if the child is not immediately placed on a special diet.). Similarly, an adopted girl whose biological father had bipolar disorder and schizophrenia suffered throughout her childhood before being diagnosed herself. Her adoptive mother lamented that she did not have medical information sooner about the biological father, "Laura had so much pain and went undiagnosed for so long. She didn't just need family therapy, she needed lithium."[12] These sorts of experiences helped to change U.S. adoption practice:[13]

> At many adoption agencies, a child is no longer passed from one family to another like a closely held secret. Instead, birth parents fill out lengthy questionnaires that probe not only their medical histories, but also their interests, talents and goals; that information is presented to the adoptive parents as a part of the child's birthright.

In Canada, the practice throughout the nation is to collect or to attempt to collect such important information. Prior to placing a child for adoption, parents are required[14] or requested[15] to provide medical, social and cultural information about themselves. For example in Prince Edward Island, the law states that[16]

> Any person placing a child shall provide in writing to the person receiving the child a summary of non-identifying information concerning the background and circumstances of the child including cultural heritage, medical history, family history as it might affect the child's rearing, reasons for the placement, and such other information as may be prescribed in the regulations.

In British Columbia, the information required is specified in great detail and the person placing the child for adoption must provide as much of the specified information as is reasonably practicable.[17]

Such information can be very important to the adoptee but it can become dated. An opportunity for the state to make the information current can come when a party begins an adoption search, for example, when the adoptee reaches the age of majority. In provinces where identifying information can be disclosed with permission, the government representative has authority to ask parties who refuse permission to disclose identifying information or to permit contact, if they will provide current medical, social and cultural information about themselves. The government official must give any information thus provided to the adoptee.[18]

Such non-identifying medical, social or cultural information is available in all provinces and territories to adoptees when they reach the age of majority or shortly thereafter,[19] (or with permission of their adoptive parents earlier[20]) and in Quebec, at the age of 14.[21]

2.1.1 Disclosure for Health and Safety Reasons

In unusual cases of medical severity, information may be released regarding the identity of the biological parents without their consent or ability to prevent disclosure. Saskatchewan,[22] Ontario,[23] Quebec,[24] New Brunswick,[25] Prince Edward Island,[26] Newfoundland and Labrador,[27] the Northwest Territories[28] and Nunavut[29] have specific statutory provisions to permit access to adoption records in cases of medical severity or to address the health, safety or welfare of the child. Other jurisdictions would likely entertain court applications for access in the interests of the child.

2.2 Release of Identifying Information

Even though non-identifying information is relatively easy for adoptees to obtain, it is typically not enough to satisfy adoptees. According to the Ontario Superior Court in the recent *Cheskes* decision, "Most adoptees want to know something about their birth parents and even make contact with them."[30] Often they wish to know the names of their biological parents. Indeed, according to the Ontario Court, such seekers are in the majority.[31] Adoptees often seek identifying information because of the "extraordinary level of grief, anxiety, and stress" caused by their "lack of personal and family information."[32] Studies of search motives among adoptees state the following reasons most frequently:[33]

> They were curious about their genealogical background; they wanted medical history; they wanted to answer the question, "who do I look like?" they wanted more detailed information about their 'roots'; and they felt 'out of place' in their adoptive family.

Non-identifying information is not typically sufficient for medical practitioners who are attempting to treat the adult-onset genetic disease of an adult, as is discussed by medical geneticist Julie Lauzon in this volume.

2.2.1 Registries Requiring Explicit Consent to Disclosure

2.2.1.1 Mutual Consent Registries with Passive Government Involvement

To the "compelling and heartfelt"[34] wish for more openness in the disclosure of identifying adoption information, Canadian legislatures have, since the 1980s, reacted variously. The least intrusive and most common legislative response is a "mutual consent registry" in which the government plays a passive role. All Canadian jurisdictions have registries that can operate with mutual consent to release identifying information.[35] These registries seem to be popular. For example, some 75,000 Ontario people have registered with the province's voluntary Adoption Disclosure Register since 1979.[36]

Under such a system, identifying information is revealed when both the adoptee and the birth relative have filed consents with the registry. Yet the passive role of the government means that the registry is not always successful in permitting adoptees and parents to gain identifying information. Both the party seeking and the one sought must choose to contact the registry without knowledge that the one is seeking the other.[37] Passive registries, by definition, do not grant administrators the authority to contact the person whom the registrant is seeking to ask for consent. Thus, if a daughter registers to know the identity of her birth mother, she will not receive that information unless the birth mother also registers. An administrator will not contact the birth mother to tell her that her daughter would like to know her identity, even though the birth mother may wish to see her daughter but not know about the existence of the passive registry.

2.2.2.1 Mutual Consent Registries with Government Search Authority

Consequently, many Canadian provinces improve the effectiveness of their registries by granting administrators authority to look into the file to find the name of the person sought and then to conduct a search themselves. The goal of the administrator's search is discretely to advise the person sought that an adoptee (or other biologically related person) is attempting to find the person. Provinces and territories that grant government agents the authority to engage in active searches at the request of an adoptee are: British Columbia, Saskatchewan, Manitoba, Quebec, New Brunswick, Prince Edward Island, Newfoundland and Labrador, the Yukon, the Northwest Territories and Nunavut.[38] These jurisdictions have varying stated waiting times before which searchers may expect a reply. According to the Adoption Council of Canada, the wait for a search to be completed can, in Manitoba and New Brunswick, take up to one year; in the Yukon, 2 years; in Newfoundland and Labrador, 5 years; and in Quebec, 10 years.[39]

Even with search powers granted to administrators, registries can be ineffective in conveying identifying information also because Canada has a mobile populace and adoptees do not always know the province or territory in which they were adopted and therefore where they should register. There is no federal registry, which would circumvent this problem.

More fundamentally, these mutual consent registries can provide information only with the active consent of the other party, which requirement can create a serious barrier to access. Mutual consent registries, whether government plays a passive or active intermediary role, do not address the need for that self-affirmation which advocates claim attaches to the ability to receive an original birth certificate. Such an experience of self-affirmation is unremarkably enjoyed by non-adopted persons.

Four provinces continue to maintain the system that requires mutual consent before identifying information can be released: Quebec,[40] Nova Scotia, New Brunswick and P.E.I.[41] Other jurisdictions, however, have moved beyond a mutual consent system to consider how best to permit adoptees to receive their original birth certificate whilst protecting the expectation of privacy of the birth parents.

2.2.2 Registry Requiring Consent to Disclose Identifying Information Regarding Past Adoptions. Disclosure Regarding Future Adoptions Limited by Disclosure Veto

In Saskatchewan, the adoption disclosure law retained the mutual consent registry for those adoptions that took place prior to the new adoption act.[42] In other words, if the adoption was finalized before 1 April 1997, then disclosure of identifying information requires mutual consent. For adoptions that took place after 31 March 1997, identifying information is available to the adoptee at age 18 years 6 months,[43] provided that the birth parents have not filed a disclosure veto.[44]

2.2.3 Registries Where Disclosure of Identifying Information and/or Contact is Available for Past Adoptions but Capable of Limitation by Veto. No Veto is Permitted Regarding Future Adoptions

Four provinces and one territory have reformed their adoption information disclosure rules since the 1990s, making it is easier for adoptees to receive identifying information. In B.C., Alberta, Ontario, Newfoundland and Labrador, and the Yukon, adult adoptees may access identifying information even on a retroactive basis subject to some constraints. For an adoption finalized before the passing of the new legislation, birth parents and adoptees may file "a written veto prohibiting the disclosure of a birth registration or other record"[45] and a no-contact veto which is a notice filed with the government adoption registrar "that he or she wishes not to be contacted" by the other party to the adoption.[46] A disclosure veto prevents the Registrar of Adoptions (or equivalent official) from revealing identifying information.[47] A "no-contact veto" prevents a person from attempting to make contact with the person who files the veto on pain of a fine, in one case up to $50,000 for an individual or $250,000 for a corporation.[48] Unusually, in Alberta, the adoptive parents may prevent the adult adoptee from having access to information about their biological parents.[49] In each of these provinces' cases and in the Yukon, no veto is permitted regarding future adoptions.[50]

Thus, four provinces and one territory have decided that the right of adoptees to know the identity of their birth parents is a *prima facie* entitlement which should be superceded only by a privacy expectation created and encouraged by the state and asserted by the relevant party. Such a privacy expectation was defined by an Ontario court judge as "a reasonable expectation that their adoption or birth registration information, absent health or safety reasons, would remain private and would not be disclosed without their permission."[51] The judgement appears to have held that the expectation may exist in the birth parent, the adopted parent and even the adoptee (who would not typically have been aware of any government promises of privacy).[52]

From the perspective of adoptees, this system of open records – provided that no disclosure veto has been filed – permits adoptees to obtain their original birth certificate as long as the parent has not taken active steps to oppose. Such a system is better than a registry alone because the point of departure is that the adoptee will have the information if the parent has not acted to prevent this result.

For prospective adoptions, that is for adoptions after the law comes into effect, there is no expectation of privacy. In other words, because the parents are not promised that their identifying information would remain secret, it would not be a breach of any right regarding their privacy to disclose identifying information at the age of majority to the adoptee.

2.2.4 Registries Where Disclosure of Past Adoption is Unlimited by Veto

2.2.4.1 The Ontario Legislative Attempt and Constitutional Challenge

Releasing identifying information about birth parents retroactively is the least restrictive means by which government guards adoption records. There was an Ontario attempt to adopt this least restrictive hold on adoption records which attempt failed.

In 2005, the Ontario legislature attempted unsuccessfully to make adoption records almost fully open – both with respect to past and future adoptions. In November of that year, the Ontario Legislative Assembly enacted the *Adoption Information Disclosure Act*,[53] which amended the *Vital Statistics Act* to allow adopted children and birth parents to apply for the release of previously confidential details. The amendment would have transformed Ontario from a closed records system to an almost completely open system. The ability to veto disclosure of retrospective adoption information lay not in the hands of one of the parties to the adoption but in a government body. The Child and Family Services Review Board could grant a "non-disclosure order" upon application by an affected party but only if the Board was satisfied that "because of exceptional circumstances, the order is appropriate to prevent sexual harm or significant physical or emotional harm to [the adopted person or birth parent]."[54] If the application was not granted, then that person could nevertheless file a "no-contact" notice with the Registrar General. Once filed, the no-contact notice would require anyone requesting adoption or birth information to sign, before receipt of the information, an agreement of no-contact, the breach of which would result in criminal prosecution and a fine.

On 17 September 2007, this new legislation came into effect.[55] Two days later,[56] in its decision in the case of *Cheskes v. Ontario (Attorney General)*,[57] the Ontario

Superior Court of Justice struck down the *Adoption Information Disclosure Act* and its amendments to the *Vital Statistics Act* relating to disclosure of information in adoption registries.

In the *Cheskes* case, three adoptees and a putative birth father had brought a constitutional challenge against the new law. They alleged that their lives would be seriously affected by the stress such threatened disclosure of their identifying information had caused and would cause them. Plaintiff adoptee, Denbigh Patton, stated in her affidavit,

> My present decision is that I do not want my personal information that is in my adoption file to be disclosed to my birth parents. I am not currently willing to risk trauma to my life as it is, to my family, to my loving aging parents, to my identity. This is a weighty decision that I have carried all my adult life and will continue to ponder. But it is for me to ponder and it is I who will suffer or benefit as a consequence of this decision.

The prospect of having to apply to the Board to prevent disclosure was also stated to be upsetting. As plaintiff adoptee Joy Cheskes wrote,

> My reasons for not wishing to seek out my birth family and wanting to keep my family information private are my own ... I do not see why I should be forced to reveal this information or go through the stress and emotional turmoil of having to divulge these feelings to a board in the hope of then being allowed to keep my personal information private.

Applicants also argued that the possibility of filing a no-contact veto was unhelpful in addressing their concerns. "C.M." stated in her affidavit:[58]

> The no-contact is totally irrelevant to me, because no contact will not mean that they cannot watch me, they can't drive past my house. This person could get my name and give this to children that she has, to other friends, to relatives. It ... does not provide me any comfort whatsoever – whatsoever [sic], other than I could be stalked.

These arguments opposing the new law had been challenged when the legislation was being considered. In a public hearing on the draft bill in May 2005, witnesses testified that birth mothers neither sought nor valued the privacy imposed by the state:[59]

> I was never offered confidentiality; I had it imposed upon me by a system. I never signed anything, I never requested it and I've never met a single birth mother, in the 18 years that I've worked in this, who asked for this kind of imposed confidentiality. No one wants his washing out on the public lawn. Everyone would like some level of privacy, but most people would like to know what happened to their children.
>
> I was forced through this system to have to crawl and grovel to get information and find my daughter on my own. She knew nothing about adoption registries and all the other government systems. She would never have come looking for us.

Another testified that the concern that the birth parent would stalk the child was not relevant because stalking is already a prohibited activity:[60]

> The large fine imposed in the bill implies the government views those adopted and their natural families as deviants and potential stalkers. Surely current stalking laws will encompass the unfounded concern that adopted adults and natural families will routinely violate this existing law.

Similarly, another said that the demonization of biological family members is beside the point. The point is to have access to information:[61]

> We're always warned by well-intentioned family and friends, "What if it's rape? What if it's incest? What if it's this and that?" or my favourite: The birth father is always an axe murderer coming to get you. We expect the worst. That is what we are told. So whatever little bit of information we get, whether it's just our name, whether it's just a little bit of background information, we're so pitifully grateful for every little bit we get, and then when we finally do get the truth, it's very fulfilling and very revealing.
>
> I'm here today to ask you to help right a very social wrong. The system has been set to default to secrecy, and I'm asking that you switch that over to openness. That's where it has to be. Thank you.

Nevertheless, the court struck down the impugned new provisions of Ontario law. Mr. Justice Belobaba ruled that the provisions violated the liberty interest in section 7 of the Canadian Charter of Rights and Freedoms[62] in a manner not in accordance with the principles of fundamental justice. He held that section 7 contains an "informational privacy interest"; in other words, control over private information is a key component of what it means to be free. Where there is a reasonable expectation of privacy, a breach of that privacy is an invasion of the dignity and self-worth of the individual and of an essential aspect of that person's liberty. Such a violation of the expectation of privacy constituted a violation of section 7 and contravened a principle of fundamental justice which Mr. Justice Belobaba defined as the expectation of privacy: "Where an individual has a reasonable expectation of privacy in personal and confidential information, that information may not be disclosed to third parties without his or her consent."

Mr. Justice Belobaba held that the impugned sections could not be saved by section 1 of the *Charter* because the disclosure of the adoption information was not a minimal impairment of the *Charter*-protected right to privacy, but rather was its "total obliteration."[63] This conclusion was not saved by the affected parties' ability to apply for a non-disclosure order, which the applicants testified would be humiliating and would in any event not guarantee their privacy. Further, the beneficial effects of disclosure for most adoptees and birth parents did not outweigh the harms to those who wanted their identifying information to remain sealed.

The judge commented that the impugned law could easily comply with the *Charter*. Quoting the Ontario privacy commission, Mr. Justice Belobaba wrote:[64]

> A disclosure veto for past adoptions is imperative to ease the transition to an open disclosure scheme and to preserve the privacy rights of those who were assured that their confidentiality would be protected. To do less than introduce a retroactive disclosure veto would be to ignore the wishes of an entire segment of society: birth parents and adopted persons who were once promised privacy, who still want it and who have governed their entire lives according to that assurance.

The province did not appeal the decision and instead passed legislation[65] that allowed birth parents and adopted children to access birth and adoption records only after the adopted children or birth parents have foregone an opportunity to block access by filing a disclosure veto.

Thus, the current law in Ontario allows for adopted people to learn their birth parents' identities if the birth parents do not activily oppose such attempts. The first instance decision in *Cheskes v. Ontario (Attorney General)* held that adoptees (and birth parents) do not have a right protected by the constitution to obtain identifying information about their birth parents. With respect to adoptions finalized prior to September 2008, because of a state-created expectation of privacy, adoptees (and birth parents) may access information only if no disclosure veto has been filed. On 1 September 2008, the Province of

Ontario made it possible for adopted adults and birth parents to file disclosure and no-contact vetoes if their adoption order was made before that date. After an 18-month period elapsed, adoptees and birth parents could begin, on 1 June 2009, to seek identifying information about each other provided that vetoes had not been filed.

It appears that those who seek to file disclosure and no contact vetoes are very much in the minority – about 1% of those eligible to do so; as of 1 May 2009, fewer than 2,500 people filed vetos regarding a total of about 250,000 adoptions that had taken place in Ontario since 1921.[66]

2.2.4.2 Northwest Territories and Nunavut: Retroactive Release of Identifying Information Permitted after One Year

Given the successful and prominent constitutional challenge to Ontario's attempt to open records to adoptees and birth parents, it is worth noting that two territories effectively have a system of retroactive release of identifying adoption information that has not gained similar public attention. If an adoptee or birth parent seeks identifying information about the other party to the adoption, the seeker may have the information without consent if one year passes without the Registrar being able to locate the relevant person from whom to seek consent.

In both the Northwest Territories and Nunavut, the family information that governments seek to offer the adoptee and birth parents might be described as both deep and wide. It is 'deep' in the sense that government encourages parties affected by an adoption to deposit with the government a significant amount of information about themselves including a "personal history."[67] It is 'wide' in that the people encouraged to file personal histories include grandparents of the adoptee provided that the relevant child of the grandparent consents. A "grandparent" is defined broadly to means the parent of a person who was a natural parent, a former adoptive parent or an adoptive parent of an adoptee.[68] If persons who are eligible to deposit a personal history choose not to do so, the reason that they declined must be recorded in the registry.[69] In short, these two territories attempt to collect a great deal of information for transmission to the adoptee and birth parent(s).

For an adoption completed after 1 November 1998, parties may apply for original birth certificates as of right; they do not need the consent of the other party. But if the adoption was completed prior to 1 November 1998,[70] transmission of identifying information generally requires consent. The adopted person who has attained the age of majority and the "natural parent" must each consent before the Registrar will release information to them about each other. To facilitate the obtaining of consent, these territories require the Registrar to conduct "a discreet and reasonable search for the person whose consent to disclosure is required in order to request his or her consent."[71] Yet the government will waive the requirement of consent "if the person cannot be found after the search has continued for at least one year."[72] In other words, passing information to the affected party (the adoptee or the "natural parent") is the aim of the Act. And failure to consent is not an absolute bar to the transmission of information to a party to adoption. (Information concerning children adopted in customary adoptions must be filed with the Registrar and apparently is subject to the same rules of disclosure in Nunavut as other adoptions.[73] In the Northwest Territories, however, it is unclear how information concerning customary adoption is stored and transmitted.[74])

Thus, the two territories, the Northwest Territories and Nunavut appear to be the most willing to permit the disclosure of identifying information. Adoptees and birth parents adopted prior to the passing of legislation that makes disclosure routine, may have access to identifying information including personal histories of their genetically related family and former adoptive families without their consent after a one-year delay.

3. Law Regarding Disclosure of Information Regarding Biological Parents in Donor Conception in Canada

All Canadian provinces and territories attentively, if variously, regulate the collection, storage and disclosure of identifying and non-identifying information concerning the parentage and social and medical history of children who were adopted. By contrast, there is no similar and effective government-regulated system operating in Canada for children created by donor gametes.

The federal *Assisted Human Reproduction Act* (the "AHR Act")[75] contemplated the collection and storage and disclosure of information about donors and created an agency on January 2006 to undertake these tasks.[76] The Supreme Court of Canada held in 2010 that those provisions are invalid.[77] Those sections were repealed.

There is one other federal statute that requires the collection of identifying information about donors, in this case, donors of sperm only. The semen regulations[78] under the *Food and Drugs Act*[79] were enacted to address the possibility of transmitting infectious disease to people by sperm donation. Whilst sections 12 and 13 of the regulations require processors and distributors of human semen to maintain a system that would permit tracing of the donor, there are no provisions to permit or require processors and distributors to divulge that information to people conceived by the semen they have processed or distributed.

There appear to be no provincial or territorial statutes or regulations that stipulate what information, if any, a donor-conceived person may receive about his or her genetic parent(s) who donated the reproductive material.

4. Comparison of Disclosure of Information Regarding Biological Parents in Adoption and Donor Conception in Canada

The foregoing discussion of law in Canada related to adoption records has revealed these points of comparison.

4.1 Existence of Effective State Regulation

The disparities in government regulation of the two practices is striking: Adoption is strictly and carefully regulated by provinces and territories, and managed by social workers with the avowed aim of focusing on the best interests of the child. By contrast, donor conception has no effective regulation in Canada and is managed by physicians, fertility clinics, sperm banks and ovum donor agencies in the best interests of the adult patient – and perhaps also the physician, fertility clinic and operators of the sperm bank and ovum donor agencies.

4.2 State Response to Change in Social Mores

Like donor conception, the practice of adoption occurred in an atmosphere of stigma, shame and secrecy, which has tended to dissipate.[80] But whereas, in adoption, governments have responded to the needs and wishes of adoptees to know their genetic families, federal law created as late as 2004[81] appeared indifferent to the lessons learned in adoption about the need to know one's origins. Such law did not grant a right of access to identifying information[82] and effectively provided no means to gain access to non-identifying information because it permitted its destruction.[83] Since its repeal, no provincial or territorial law has created registries for information about donor-conceived people.

4.3 The Collection and Documentation of Data to Create Accurate Certificates of Parentage

Records of the birth and the original parentage of an adopted child are created and preserved by the state. The accuracy of such documents depends upon the willingness of the birth mother to disclose the identity of the father and to offer her own name truthfully. Social workers actively seek to ensure that the documents are accurate. By contrast, no level of government in Canada is effectively required to preserve accurate records of the biological parents of the donor-conceived.

4.4 The Collection and Creation of Accurate Medical, Social and Cultural Information

In adoption, biological parents are typically requested or required to provide social and cultural information identifying and non-identifying information to the agency placing the child for adoption. No government agency currently requires the transmission of such information about donors, recipients and the donor-conceived to a government registry for storage for the purpose of disclosure to the donor-conceived.

4.5 State Collection and Storage of Medical Information

Government officials or adoption agency workers attempt to obtain extensive identifying and non-identifying medical information about birth parents in adoption. For the donor-conceived, the state is not collecting or storing information except for the purpose of preventing infectious disease,[84] or, as in Quebec, without permitting disclosure of identifying information.[85]

4.6 Disclosure of Medical Information in Cases of Medical Severity

There tends to be a statutory right for adoptees in cases of medical severity to learn details about the biological parents and to share with them important medical information. There is no statutory provision in Canada for the transmission of information in similar circumstances.

4.7 Mutual Consent Registries

All provinces and territories permit adoptees and birth parents to exchange identifying information if they mutually consent. Provinces and territories fund the mutual consent registries. No level of government in Canada has created a mutual consent registry for donors, recipients and Offspring.

4.8 State Search Facilities

Some provinces and territories will go further than merely to provide passive registries for adoption. Once a person registers, some jurisdictions will make an active effort to contact the other party or parties to let them know about the registration so that they, too, can register if they desire to reunite with their biological family members. There is no government search service available for the donor-conceived, let alone government workers engaged in facilitating reunions.

4.9 Right to Know if Proposed Sexual Partner is Genetically Related

It is likely that adoptees may successfully apply to court to open sealed adoption records in an attempt to learn whether a prospective sexual partner is biologically related. At the moment, governments do not collect information upon which to make such a disclosure to donor-conceived persons.

4.10 Prospective Right to Know

There is trend in adoption legislation to permit people to receive, as a right, all information that the state has about their adoption. Adoption reform has uniformly moved in the direction of opening formerly sealed adoption records. In the most progressive provinces – British Columbia, Ontario, Newfoundland and Labrador – and in the Yukon, the North West Territories and Nunavut, the adoptee may obtain the original birth certificate, which typically contains identifying information about the birth parents, unless, in cases where the adoption took place prior to the enactment of the legislation, the birth parent has actually filed a disclosure veto. In Alberta, adoptees have a similar right (though, unusually, the adoptive parents may apply to waive that right without notice to the adoptee as though it were waived by the adult adoptee).[86] The Northwest Territories and Nunavut appear to have moved toward even greater openness; no matter when adopted, adoptees may receive state-held information about their progenitors provided that the biological parents have not registered an objection and if the Registrar fails to find their birth parents within one year of searching. By contrast, in donor-conception, there is no state recognition of Offspring's right to know their origins.

5. Conclusion

At the moment, in Canada, there appears to be no effective legal mechanism by which donor-conceived people may obtain the entitlements concerning records of their progenitors that adoptees themselves have obtained. Accurate records of the identities of the biological parents of donor-conceived people are not created by the state. Government officials in Canada do not request or require gamete donors to provide social, cultural or medical histories. There is no established government mechanism to exchange important non-identifying and identifying information in cases of medical severity, or to prevent the possibility of incest. Commercial gamete provider agencies might collect and store such information but such agencies tend to be in the United States where[87]

> No central registry exists to record and safely retain information that would allow possible future linkage of donors and Offspring or Offspring related through their donor (and raised in different families). Compliance of donor insemination programs, sperm banks, and fertility clinics with professional guidelines regarding recordkeeping is voluntary.

Canada has imposed no statutory obligations on importers of human reproductive material that would permit the collection, storage and disclosure of identifying and non-identifying social, cultural and medical information of the gamete providers to the people created by the imported gametes. Moreover, there is no government registry to which Offspring may apply for identifying information about their progenitors.

It might be argued that donors have an expectation of privacy created by reproductive physicians. Yet it is important to question whether adult, non-governmental parties, may collude to deprive children of information regarding their biological parents. In other words, even if adult donors expect privacy, is it reasonable for the state to protect that desire? If it is reasonable to expect government to protect it, what steps can government take to permit those who wish to be known to each other to reunite?

Donor-conceived people have much in common with typical adoptees. They did not agree to be separated from one or both of their biological parents. Many of the arguments they make for the right to know their origins are the same. Members of both groups of people have been subject to disenfranchised grief. But whereas adoptees have succeeded in many Canadian jurisdictions in easing access to government adoption records, Canadian governments do not even collect or store identifying records regarding Offspring. No independent third party body creates, preserves and discloses these records, which, in any event, are considered the private medical record of the adult who initiated the conception, rather than the biological parentage record of the resulting child.

This Chapter began by stating that the disparity in legal treatment of these similarly situated groups has been decided by the Supreme Court of British Columbia to be a violation of the constitutional right to equality and not demonstrably justifiable in a free and democratic state.[88] This decision is now on appeal and will perhaps encourage legislators in other provinces to reconsider why a growing number of Canadian children are not accorded even the limited rights of Canadian adoptees to know their origins.

Bibliography

Adoption Agency Manual, quoted by E. Wayne Carp, *Family Matters: Secrecy and Disclosure In the History of Adoption*, Cambridge, Harvard University Press (1998) at 120 cited by Elizabeth J. Samuels, "*The Idea of Adoption: An Inquiry into the History of Adult Adoptee Access to Birth Records*", 53 *Rutgers L. Rev.* 367-437 (2001) at 410.

The Adoption Council of Canada. *About Adoption, Search and Reunion*, http://www.adoption.ca/AboutAdoption.html.

Anderson, C. Wilson. The Sealed Record in Adoption Controversy, *The Social Service Review* (1977), 51:1 141 at 142.

Baldassi, Cindy L. The Quest to Access Closed Adoption Files in Canada: Understanding Social Context and Legal Resistance to Change, 2004 21, *Canadian Journal of Family Law*, 211 at 230.

Blyth, Eric and Ruth Moore. "Involuntary Childlessness and Stigma", in *Stigma and Social Exclusion in Health Care*, Tom Mason, Caroline Carlisle, Caroline Watkins, Elizabeth Whitehead, eds. (London: Routledge, 2001): p. 218.

Brower Blair, D. Marianne. "The Impact of Family Paradigms, Domestic Constitutions, and International Conventions on Disclosure of an Adopted Person's Identities and Heritage: A Comparative Examination", 2001 *Michigan Journal of International Law*, 589 at 603.

The Canadian Press. "Adoptees have option to learn identity of birth parents come Monday", Toronto: 31 May 2009.

-- "Canada not doing enough to open adoption records, U.N. says", *The Globe and Mail*, Tuesday, 14 October 2003, http://www.globeandmail.com/servlet/story/RTGAM.20031013.wadopt1013/BNStory/National/?query=adoption.

Chambers, Lori. Adoption, Unwed Mothers and the Powers of the Children's Aid Society in Ontario, 1921-1969, Ontario History. Autumn 2006. Vol. 98, Iss. 2; at 161.

Daley, Timothy T. Adoption and Access: Recent Developments, 23 R.F.L. 257 1976.

Donaldson, Evan B. Adoption Institute: Old Lessons for a New World: Applying Adoption Research and Experience to Assisted Reproductive Technology, New York: February 2009, at 3.

Franklin, Deborah. What a Child is Given, *New York Times Magazine*, 8 September 1989.

Gillespie, Kerry. "Adoptee urges flexibility in *Ontario* legislation", *Toronto Star.* Toronto, Ont.: 2 November 2007: pg. A.17.

Jowett, Sandi. Ontario Adoption Reform History, http://www.cuckoografik.org/trained_tales/orp_pages/news/news35.html.

Lettner, Margot. Closing the Door on Disclosure: The Adoption Records Provisions of The Child and Family Services Act, 1984.44 R.F.L. (2d) 28 Reports of Family Law (Articles) 2nd series 1985.

Murdoch, Ron. Bill 183 to open adoption records in Ontario, Canada (29 July 2005), Child Rights Information Network, http://www.crin.org/resources/infoDetail.asp?ID=5969&flag=news.

O'Malley, Martin, Owen Wood and Amy Foulkes. *Indepth: Genetics and Reproduction,* The Birth Control Pill, CBC News Online, 3 July 2001, http://www.cbc.ca/news/background/genetics_reproduction/birthcontrol_pill.html.

Parent Finders. http://www.parentfindersottawa.ca/aboutus.html.

Patton, Jean M. *Orphan Voyage,* New York: Vantage Press, 1968.

Petrie, Anne. *Gone to an Aunt's: Remembering Canada's Homes for Unwed Mothers,* Toronto: McClelland & Stewart, Toronto, Canada, 1998.

Ravitsky, Vardit and Joanna E. Scheib. "Donor-Conceived Individuals' Right to Know", 20 July 2010, *Human Reproduction,* http://www.thehastingscenter.org/Bioethicsforum/Post.aspx?id=4811&blogid=140&terms=ravitsky+and+%23filename+*.html.

Reiniger, Anne. Adoption Searches: Ethical Considerations, Practising Law Institute: Litigation and Administrative Practice Course Handbook Series, Criminal Law and Urban Problems, 14 December 2007.

Rook, Katie. "No appeal of adoption record ruling", [National Edition] *National Post,* Don Mills, Ont.: 14 November 2007: pg. A.6.

Samuels, Elizabeth J. *"The Idea of Adoption: An Inquiry into the History of Adult Adoptee Access to Birth Records",* 53 *Rutgers L. Rev.* 367-437 (2001) at 370.

Sokoloff, Heather. "A national policy on adoption remains elusive: Provinces keep track of adopted babies in their own ways," *National Post,* 9 June 2005.

Sorosky, A., A. Baran and R. Pannor. The Adoption Triangle. New York: Doubleday. (1984) (rev. ed.).

Thompson, Janette. *Roots and Rights – A Challenge for Adoption,* Social Worker 13, 13 (1979) (reporting a study by the Children's Aid Society of Metro Toronto, Canada) cited by Elizabeth J. Samuels, *The Idea of Adoption: An Inquiry into the History of the Adult Adoptee,* Rutgers Law Review, Winter, 2001 at 404.

Triseliotis, John. *In Search of Origins: the Experiences of Adopted People* (1973).

Tyler May, Elaine. *Barren in the promised land: childless Americans and the pursuit of happiness,* (Cambridge: Harvard University Press, 1997) at 127.

United Nations. *Convention on the Rights of the Child,* 20 November 1989, 1577 U.N.T.S. 3, Can. T.S. 1992 No. 3 (entered into force 2 September 1990, entered into force in Canada 12 January 1992). Article 7.

Notes

1 Pratten v. British Columbia (Attorney General), 2011 BCSC 656, 219. May 19, 2011 [Hereinafter "*Pratten Judgement*"] currently on appeal before the British Columbia Court of Appeal.
2 *Adoption Act [RSBC 1996] Ch. 5.*
3 Part I of *The Constitution Act, 1982*, being Schedule B to the *Canada Act 1982* (UK), 1982, c 11 [hereinafter, "The *Charter*"].
4 *Pratten Judgement*, Paragraph 268.
5 *Pratten Judgement*, Paragraph 207.
6 Evan B. Donaldson, Adoption Institute: Old Lessons for a New World: Applying Adoption Research and Experience to Assisted Reproductive Technology, New York: February 2009, at 3.
7 Although the Federal government has enacted the Privacy Act, Privacy Act, R. S. C. 1985, c. P-21, and the Access to Information R. S. C. 1985, c. A-1 which grant Canadians access to government-held information about that citizen, these Acts are unlikely to overrule the confidentiality protection legislated in the provincial adoption Acts. Such statutes clearly state that no provincial statute granting access to information may override the confidentiality of adoption information.
8 Donaldson, see note 1 above.
9 Adoption Act, R. S. B. C. 1996, c. 5., s. 2; Child, Youth and Family Enhancement Act, R. S. A. 2000, c. C-12, s.58.1; Adoption Act, S. S. 1998, c. A-5.2, s. 3; Adoption Act, C. C. S. M. c. F20, s. 2; Child and Family Services Act, R. S. O. 1990, c. C. 11, s. 1.(1); Civil Code of Quebec, S. Q. 1991, c. 64 (C. C. Q.), s. 543; Family Services Act, S. N. B. 1980, c. F-2.2, 71(1); Children and Family Services Act, S.N.S. 1990, c. 5, s. 2 (1); Adoption Act, R. S. P. E. I. 1988, c. A-4. 1, s.2; Adoption Act, S. N. L. 1999, c. A-2. 1, s.3; Child and Family Services Act, S.Y. 2008, c. 1, s. 2(a); Adoption Act, S. N. W. T. 1998, c. 9, s. 2(a), Adoption Act, S. N. W. T. (Nu.) 1998, c. 9, s. 2(a).
10 Anne Reiniger, Adoption Searches: Ethical Considerations, Practising Law Institute: Litigation and Administrative Practice Course Handbook Series, Criminal Law and Urban Problems, 14 December 2007.
11 *Foster v. Bass, 575 So. 2d 967 (Sup. Crt. Miss. 1990) at 971.*
12 Deborah Franklin, What a Child is Given, *New York Times Magazine*, 8 September 1989.
13 *Ibid.*
14 Adoption Regulation, B.C. Reg. 291/96, s. 4; Adoption Regulation, Alta. Reg. 187/2004 187/2004, s 13(3); Adoption Regulations, 2003, R.R.S. c. A-5.2 Reg. 1, s. 18; Adoption Regulation, Man. Reg. 19/99, s. 10(1); General, R.R.O. 1990, Reg. 70, s. 54(1); Youth Protection Act, R.S.Q. c. P-34.1, s. 71; Adoption Act, R.S.P.E.I. 1988, c. A-4.1, s. 7(1).
15 In Nova Scotia, parents are not obligated to provide medical, social or cultural information but it is the routine practice of social workers to seek it, telephone conversation with Ms. Janet Nearing, Department of Department of Community Services, PO Box 696, Halifax NS B3J 2T7, Telephone: (902) 424-2755; New Brunswick, "Birth Family Medical And Social History", 20-page form sent to birth families prior to placement for adoption, as received from Tracey Burkhardt, Director, Communications New Brunswick, (Social Development Unit), 22 September 2010; in Newfoundland and Labrador, and in the Yukon Territory, the Director of Adoptions has a duty to obtain as much information as possible about the medical and social history of the child's birth family and preserve the information for the child, Adoption Act, S.N.L. 1999, c. A-2.1, s.97(c); Child and Family Services Act, S.Y. 2008, c. 1, s. 7(1)(b); in the Northwest Territories and in Nunavut, the Director has a duty to record and preserve whatever medical, social and cultural information that has been obtained by the social worker, Adoption Regulations, N.W.T. Reg. 141-98, 41; and Adoption Regulations, N.W.T. Reg. (Nu.) 141-98, s. 41.
16 Adoption Act, R.S.P.E.I. 1988, c. A-4.1, s. 7(1).
17 Adoption Regulation, B.C. Reg. 291/96, s. 4.
18 Adoption Act, R. S. B. C. 1996, c. 5. s. 65(3) and 66(5); Adoption Act, C. C. S. M. c. F20, s. 112(4) and 113(3); Vital Statistics Act, R.S.O. 1990, c. V.4, s. 48.5(7);, s. 1.(1); Adoption Information Act. 1996, c. 3, s.19(5) Adoption Act, R. S. P. E. I. 1988, c. A-4. 1, s.2; Adoption Act, S. N. L. 1999, c. A-2. 1, s.3; Child and Family Services Act, S.Y. 2008, c. 1, s. 143(3); Adoption Act, S. N. W. T. 1998, c. 9, s. 62; Adoption Act, S. N. W. T. (Nu.) 1998, c. 9, s. 62.
19 Adoption Act, R. S. B. C. 1996, c. 5, s. 65(4), 66(7); Child, Youth and Family Enhancement Act,

R. S. A. 2000, c. C-12, s. 74.2(2) – adoptive parents may apply to block transmission of non-identifying information if the adult adoptee does not know of the adoption and the Minister finds that conveying information would be extremely detrimental to the adopted person, s. 74.2(9); Adoption Act, S. S. 1998, c. A-5.2, s. 26(1) (c) and (e); Adoption Act, C. C. S. M. c. F20, s. 112(4) and 113(4); Adoption Information Disclosure, O. Reg. 464/07, s. 11(2); Family Services Act, S. N. B. 1980, c. F-2.2, 92(1); Adoption Information Act, S.N.S. 1996, c. 3 s. 11(1); Adoption Act, R. S. P. E. I. 1988, c. A-4. 1, s. 48(1); Adoption Act, S. N. L. 1999, c. A-2. 1, s. 48; Child and Family Services Act, S.Y. 2008, c. 1, s. 143(4) and (6); Adoption Act, S. N. W. T. 1998, c. 9, ss. 63 – 64; Adoption Act, S. N. W. T. (Nu.) 1998, c. 9, ss. 63 – 64.

20 Adoption Act, C. C. S. M. c. F20, s. 111(b).
21 Article 583. C.C.Q.; Origins Canada: Quebec Adoption Records: http://www.originscanada.org/quebec-adoption-records.
22 Adoption Regulations, 2003, R.R.S. c. A-5.2 Reg. 1, s. 33.
23 Adoption Information Disclosure, O. Reg. 464/07, ss. 16-21.
24 Article 584, C.C.Q.
25 Family Services Act, S.N.B. 1980, c. F-2.2, s. 92(2)(h).
26 Adoption Act, R.S.P.E.I. 1988, c. A-4.1, s. 48(2).
27 Adoption Act, S.N.L. 1999, c. A-2., s. 45(1).
28 Adoption Act, S.N.W.T. 1998, c. 9, s. 67(1).
29 Adoption Act, S.N.W.T. (Nu.) 1998, c. 9, s. 67(1).
30 Cheskes v. Ontario (Attorney General), 2007 CanLII 38387 (ON S.C), at para. 68. Per Balobaba J.
31 *Ibid*.
32 *Ibid*.
33 *Ibid*., see case note 37.
34 *Ibid*.
35 Adoption Act, R.S.B.C. 1996, c. 5, s. 69; Child, Youth and Family Enhancement Act, R. S. A. 2000, c. C-12, s. 75; Adoption Regulations, 2003, R.R.S. c. A-5.2 Reg. 1, ss. 27-32; Adoption Act, C. C. S. M. c. F20, s. 108, Post-Adoption Registry; Adoption Information Disclosure, O. Reg. 464/07, s. 9-10; Article 583 C.C.Q.; Family Services Act, S.N.B. 1980, c. F-2.2, s. 92(5); Adoption Information Act, S.N.S. 1996, c. 3, s. 9(1); Adoption Act, R. S. P. E. I. 1988, c. A-4. 1, ss.49-50.; Adoption Act, S. N. L. 1999, c. A-2. 1, s.44; Child and Family Services Act, S.Y. 2008, c. 1, s. 146; Adoption Act, S. N. W. T. 1998, c. 9, s. 66; and Adoption Act, S. N. W. T. (Nu.) 1998, c. 9, s. 66.
36 The Canadian Press, Adoptees have option to learn identity of birth parents come Monday, Toronto: 31 May 2009.
37 Blair at 602 quoting Joan Heifetz Hollinger, *Aftermath of Adoption: Legal and Social Consequences*, in 2 Adoption Law and Practice 13-5 (Joan Heifetz Hollinger, ed. 2000).
38 Adoption Act, R. S. B. C. 1996, c. 5., s. 71(1); Adoption Regulations, 2003, R.R.S. c. A-5.2 Reg. 1, s. 31(1); Post-Adoption Registry Regulation, Man. Reg. 22/99, s. 5; Adoption Council of Canada, About Adoption, Search and Reunion: Quebec, http://www.adoption.ca/AboutAdoption.html; Family Services Act, S. N. B. 1980, c. F-2.2, 92(3); Adoption Council of Canada, About Adoption, Search and Reunion: Nova Scotia: http://www.adoption.ca/AboutAdoption.html; Adoption Act, R. S. P. E. I. 1988, c. A-4. 1, s. 50(3); Adoption Act, S. N. L. 1999, c. A-2. 1, s. 56; Child and Family Services Act, S.Y. 2008, c. 1, s. 147(1) Adoption Act, S. N. W. T. 1998, c. 9, ss. 66(4); Adoption Act, S. N. W. T. (Nu.) 1998, c. 9, ss. 66(2). In both the Northwest Territories and Nunavut, if the person is not found within one year, the Registrar of the Adoption Registry may release identifying information.
39 The Adoption Council of Canada, *About Adoption, Search and Reunion*, http://www.adoption.ca/AboutAdoption.html.
40 Quebec considered the rights of persons adopted in Quebec to seek identifying information about their progenitors. The proposed law would distinguish between adoptions that took place before and after the law comes into force. For adoptions that precede the new law, the adoptees could, among other things, receive information if the person has been deceased 2 years and did not file a disclosure veto. For adoptions after the law comes into force, the accessibility of identifying information would be the norm unless one of the parties had taken steps to prevent transmission of that information by filing vetos. See: *Avant-projet de loi, Loi modifiant*

le *Code civil et d'autres dispositions législatives en matière d'adoption et d'autorité parentale*, 1ère session, 39ᵉ législature, déposé par Mme Kathleen Weil, Ministre de la Justice le 30-10-2009. Carmen Lavallée: Groupe de travail sur le régime québécois de l'adoption, *Pour une Adoption Québécoise a la Mesure de Chaque Enfant: Rapport du groupe de travail sur le régime québécois de l'adoption* (Carmen Lavallée, Chair), online Justice Québec, http://www.justice.gouv.qc.ca/francais/publications/rapports/pdf/adoption-rap.pdf.

41 Articles 582-3, C.C.Q.; Family Services Act, S. N. B. 1980, c. F-2.2; Adoption Information Act, S.N.S. 1996, c. 3, s. 19; ss. 91-2; Adoption Act, R. S. P. E. I. 1988, c. A-4.1, s. 5.
42 The Adoption Act, 1998, S. S. 1998, c. A-5.2, Reg 1, s. 28.
43 *Ibid.*, s. 29(3).
44 *Ibid.*, s 30(2).
45 *Adoption Act*, R.S.B.C. 1996, c. 5, s. 65(1).
46 Vital Statistics Act, R.S.O. 1990, c. V.4, s. 48.4(1).
47 See for example, Vital Statistics Act, R.S.O. 1990, c. V.4 s. 48.1(9).
48 See note 88 above, s. 56(5).
49 Child, Youth and Family Enhancement Act, R. S. A. 2000, c. C-12, s. 74.2(4) and 74.2(9).
50 *Adoption Act*, R.S.B.C. 1996, c. 5, s. 65(1); Child, Youth and Family Enhancement Act, R. S. A. 2000, c. C-12, s. 74.2; Vital Statistics Act, R.S.O. 1990, c. V.4, 48.5(1); Adoption Act, S. N. L. 1999, c. A-2. 1, s. 50(1). Child and Family Services Act, S.Y. 2008, c., 143.
51 Cheskes v. Ontario (Attorney General), 2007 CanLII 38387 (ON S.C), at case note 37 at para. 69 per Belobaba J.
52 Cheskes v. Ontario (Attorney General), 2007 CanLII 38387 (ON S.C), at para. 132.
53 S.O. 2005, c.25.
54 Vital Statistics Act, as amended by S.O. 2005, c.25.Sections 48.5(7) and 48.7(3).
55 Information from the Ministry of Community and Social Services website maintained by the Government of Ontario, last modified December 10, 2007.
56 *Kerry Gillespie,* Adoptee urges flexibility in *Ontario* legislation, *Toronto Star*. Toronto, Ont.: 2 November 2007. pg. A.17.
57 Cheskes v. Ontario (Attorney General), 2007 CanLII 38387 (ON S. C.).
58 Ibid., at para. 41.
59 Ms. Monica Bryne, Birth Mother, testifying before the Ontario Standing Committee on Social Policy: Adoption Information Disclosure Act, 2005 Loi de 2005 sur la Divulgation de Renseignements sur les Adoptions, http://www.ontla.on.ca/committee-proceedings/transcripts/files_html/18-MAY-2005_SP032.htm.
60 Ms. Leslie Wagner, see note 101 above.
61 Ms. Patricia McCarron, see note 101 above.
62 Canadian Charter of Rights and *Freedoms* as in *The Constitution Act*, 1982, being Schedule B to the *Canada Act* 1982 (U. K.), 1982, c. 11.
63 Cheskes v. Ontario (Attorney General), 2007 CanLII 38387 (ON S.C), at para. 153.
64 Cheskes v. Ontario (Attorney General), 2007 CanLII 38387 (ON S.C), at para. 172. per Balobaba J., quoting Ann Cavoukian, Ontario, Standing Committee on Social Policy, *Official Reports of Debate (Hansard)* (11 May 2005) at SP-1074.
65 Katie Rook, "No appeal of adoption record ruling"; [National Edition] *National Post*. Don Mills, Ont.: 14 November 2007: pg. A.6.
66 The Canadian Press, "Adoptees have option to learn identity of birth parents come Monday", Toronto, 31 May 2009.
67 Adoption Act, S.N.W.T. 1998, c. 9, s. 53; Adoption Act, S.N.W.T. (Nu.) 1998, c. 9, s. 60.
68 Adoption Act, S.N.W.T. 1998, c. 9, s. 54(1); Adoption Act, S.N.W.T. (Nu.) 1998, c. 9, s. 57(1).
69 Adoption Act, S.N.W.T. 1998, c. 9, s. 54(5); Adoption Act, S.N.W.T. (Nu.) 1998, c. 9, s. 57(5).
70 Adoption Act, NWT, s. 66(1); Adoption Act, Nu. S. 66(1).
71 Adoption Act, NWT, 66(4); Adoption Act, Nu.s. 66(2).
72 *Ibid.*
73 Aboriginal Custom Adoption Recognition Act, S.N.W.T. (Nu.) 1994, c. 26. s. 5.
74 Aboriginal Custom Adoption Recognition Act, S.N.W.T. 1994, c. 26.
75 Assisted Human Reproduction Act, S.C. 2004, c. 2.
76 AHRA, s. 21.

77 *Reference re Assisted Human Reproduction Act*, 2010 SCC 61. The relevant provisions (Sections 13 to 19) were repealed by *Jobs, Growth and Long-term Prosperity Act*, S.C. 2012, c. 19, Consequential Amendment to the Department of Public Works and Government Services Act, 2012, Division 56, Assisted Human Reproduction Act, Section 720.
78 Processing and Distribution of Semen for Assisted Conception Regulations, SOR/96-254.
79 R.S.C. 1985, c. F-27.
80 See, for example, Ferguson v. Director of Child Welfare for Ontario 40 O.R. (2d) 294, 142 D.L.R. (3d) 609, per Killeen Co. Ct. J.; Ferguson v. Ontario (Director of Child Welfare) 1983, 44 O.R. (2d) 78, 3 D.L.R. (4th) 178 (Ont. C.A.) Zuber, Thorson and Robins JJ.A; and Margot Lettner, Closing the Door on Disclosure: The Adoption Records Provisions of The Child and Family Services Act, 1984.44 R.F.L. (2d) 28 Reports of Family Law (Articles)2nd series 1985.
81 Assisted Human Reproduction Act, S.C. 2004, c. 2.
82 *Ibid*. s. 15(1)(a), and s. 18(2).
83 *Ibid*. S. 16(2).
84 Processing and Distribution of Semen for Assisted Conception Regulations, SOR/96-254
85 An Act respecting clinical and research activities relating to assisted procreation, R.S.Q. c. A-5.01, s. 42.
86 Adoptive parents may apply to the minister for a disclosure veto on the grounds that the adoptee does not know that he or she has been adopted and that the release of personal information "would be extremely detrimental" to the adopted person. If the Minister is satisfied, based on the information provided to the Minister by the adoptive parents, then the Minister may consider that a disclosure veto has been registered by the adoptee. Child, Youth and Family Enhancement Act, R.S.A. 2000, c. C-12, s. 72(1). 74(2)(b)(9).
87 Vardit Ravitsky and Joanna E. Scheib, "Donor-Conceived Individuals' Right to Know", 20 July 2010, Human Reproduction, http://www.thehastingscenter.org/Bioethicsforum/Post.aspx?id=4811&blogid=140&terms=ravitsky+and+%23filename+*.html.
88 *Pratten, supra,* note 1.

Chapter Nineteen

A Tale of Two Embryos: Record Keeping after Gamete or Embryo Donation in Cattle and Humans

Alison Motluk[1]

1. Introduction

"Daisy" was born just north of Calgary, Alberta, Canada, in the spring of 2010 from donated sperm and egg. No one need ever wonder about her health history, her complete heritage and all the details surrounding her conception – they are all carefully documented and available for scrutiny. "Rose" will always be less certain about her background. Rose's mother has detailed profiles of the sperm and egg donors and some information about their family backgrounds, but none of these data have been verified. Rose's mother cannot even be completely certain that her child was conceived from the donors she selected.

Why the difference? Daisy is a calf.[2] Rose is a little girl.[3] And for calves in this country, but not children, there is legislation and regulation that stipulates how such important information must be collected, verified, stored and disclosed.

Fertility specialists and regulators who balk at the challenge of keeping complete, accurate and accessible records for humans created through assisted reproduction need only look to the cattle industry for a solid template. The underlying motives for good record keeping in the cattle industry are completely different – commerce as opposed to self-knowledge – but the practicalities of doing so are largely the same.

2. Origins of Daisy and Rose

Daisy's conception took place on April 6, 2009 by artificial insemination. Her biological father is "Red Fine Line Mulberry 26P", a purebred Red Angus. His sperm was collected and frozen on October 15, 2007 and thawed just before the insemination. Daisy's biological mother is "Red KBJ Miss Power 0890P", also a Red Angus.

In cattle, assisted reproduction usually involves fertilizing the eggs *in vivo*, that is, inside the donor animal's body. For humans, this takes place *in vitro*, in a glass petri dish. Before the insemination, a veterinarian gave hormonal injections to Miss Power. These injections are not unlike the ones taken by human egg donors. They prompted Miss Power's ovaries to ripen more than the customary one egg per cycle. Then the cow was artificially inseminated with the bull's semen. As a result, multiple conceptions took place within Miss Power's body. After seven days, on April 13, the cow embryos were "flushed" out using a special saline solution, and then recovered from the ejected fluid.

A total of 33 embryos were recovered from Miss Power that day by veterinarian and embryo transfer practitioner, Dr Roger Davis, of Davis-Rairdan ET Ltd., based in Crossfield, Alberta, Canada. Twelve of the embryos were top quality, four were of fair quality, and seventeen were "degenerated". All twelve grade 1 embryos were frozen on the day of recovery and placed into individual storage "straws".

Then, on May 14, the embryo that became Daisy, a.k.a. embryo DT21, was transferred by Dr. Davis into a cow, HO 5291, that would act as surrogate mother, gestating the embryo for approximately nine months. Early the following year, Daisy was born.

Rose's conception also took place in April 2009 – but in a petri dish in Toronto. Her biological father is Xytex donor AFL 9821 and her egg donor is donor DEB823004. The date when the semen was collected is clear from the batch number on the vial. The eggs were removed from the ovum donor in early April by Rose's mother's fertility doctor.

Notes in Rose's mother's medical file show that ten eggs were retrieved from DEB823004 and that all of them were fertilized later the same day. For each day thereafter for five days, there is a report noting the quality of each embryo and whether and why it was discarded. By the fifth day following the day of fertilization, there were seven embryos remaining: three of them were grade 1. Two of these were transferred into Rose's mother's uterus that day, and the other top-grade embryo was frozen. Within weeks, it was clear that only one *in utero* embryo had survived. Rose was born in January 2010.

3. Differences in Documenting Assisted Reproduction in Cattle and Humans

In comparing the assisted creation of Daisy and Rose, important differences in record keeping come to light. In cows but not humans:

1. The progenitors' history is carefully documented and the accuracy of that documentation is subject to Canadian federal law;
2. Information about health and family history is available through a registry;
3. The genetic identity of the offspring is confirmed through DNA analysis;

4. Misrepresenting the identity of offspring is a serious offence; and
5. The records follow the progeny.

Let us examine each of these differences in turn.

3.1 The Progenitors' History is Carefully Documented and the Accuracy of that Documentation is Subject to Canadian Federal Law

The documentation for Daisy says that her biological father is Fine Line Mulberry, and her biological mother, Miss Power. The official Canadian Angus online Herdbook shows the history of both her biological mother and her biological father, back multiple generations on each side.[4]

For Fine Line Mulberry himself, a single click reveals his registration number, colour, sex, birth date, identification by ear tatoo, that he is free of a number of genetic defects and who his parents were.[5]

Another click shows his immediate family tree, with links to each member. His sire, for instance, was Red Compass Mulberry 449M. Fifteen previous progeny of Fine Line, all searchable, are also listed, along with an analysis of the growth and performance qualities of those offspring.

There is good reason to trust that the information about Daisy's family background is accurate. *The Animal Pedigree Act*,[6] formed in part to "protect persons who raise and purchase animals", makes it a federal offence to misrepresent an animal's identity on a registration, subject to a fine of up to $50,000.[7]

The job of policing accuracy in animal lineages falls to breed associations, such as, in Daisy's case, the Canadian Angus Association.[8] Under the Act, these associations are empowered to be the sole keepers of detailed historical pedigrees of their breeds, and to register and identify all animals whose owners claim they belong to the breed.

But whereas in cattle, there is a federal law requiring accurate reporting of family history, no such protection is extended to "persons who raise" a human child born through in vitro fertilization (IVF). Indeed, the *Assisted Human Reproduction Act*[9] says nothing at all about ensuring accuracy of information about donors. Though children are conceived for completely different reasons than are cows, concerns about the progenitors' identities are just as valid – if not more so.

Like Daisy, Rose's conception is documented. Her paperwork states that her biological father was Xytex donor AFL9821 and her biological mother DEB823004. According to information contained in the donor profile, AFL9821 is a Caucasian male with dark brown eyes and thick, dark brown hair. His parents are reportedly both still alive and in good health, as are his two female siblings; three of his grandparents are deceased, two of "old age" and one from emphysema. AFL9821 claims to have three male offspring of his own, a singleton plus twins.

Unlike Daisy's biological father, Fine Line Mulberry, whose precise heritage is documented and openly available for scrutiny, little about Rose's donors is really certain. Indeed, the Xytex website carries the disclaimer that "the medical and social history was provided by the donor and cannot be verified for accuracy." He says he is of German, Irish and Scottish extraction, but neither Rose's mother nor the fertility doctor can know for sure. (AFL9821 may not even be certain himself.)

Rose's sperm donor lists various conditions in the elder family members, including asthma, cataracts, diabetes, heart disease, stroke and skin cancer. Records indicate that no one in the family has suffered any mental illness, but as with the other information, this has not been confirmed. It is not possible to verify these claims because no information about the identities of the donor's progenitors is provided at all. The same discrepancy exists between the egg donors: Miss Power's background is carefully documented, but human egg donor DEB823004 – of alleged Greek and Canadian ancestry, with a family history of alcoholism, type 2 diabetes and ulcers – must be taken at her word.

3.2 Information about Health and Family History is Available through a Registry

In time, Daisy will be registered with the Canadian Angus Association. To complete the registration, her owner must provide Daisy's birth date, her ear tattoo number and the names of her sperm and egg donors, known as the sire and the dam. Most Canadian breed associations require that official documents pertaining to the retrieval, freezing and transfer of embryos be filed with them in order to complete the identification process, though the Canadian Angus Association does not. But even breed associations that do not keep those records on file retain the right under the law to audit the owners of all registered animals, and at that time may demand to see the certificates.

Provided that all conditions are met, the Canadian Angus Association will enter Daisy into the Official Herdbook and issue her owner an individual registration certificate. The records of her parentage and ancestry will be kept indefinitely in an online open-access database.[10]

Rose will also be registered with the province of Ontario. According to the *Vital Statistics Act*, all human offspring born in the province must be officially registered.[11] Information about Rose's weight, sex, date of birth, place of birth and birth attendant must all be recorded.[12] It is also noted whether she was a singleton or a multiple.[13] Information about her mother – defined as the person from whose body she is born – is also collected, including the woman's legal surnames (any she has ever had), given names, her place of birth, her age at the time of Rose's birth, her address, the total number of children to whom she has given birth and whether or not they were live births. Details about the "other parent" are also collected. No information is collected specifically about the biological progenitors and no inquiries are made about whether or not they are different people from those already registered. Nowhere in the official record of Rose's birth will there be information pertaining to or alluding to those progenitors.

Obviously, neither Rose nor her parents would want this information about her identity freely available to the public the way Daisy's information is. And indeed no information about Rose's identity is freely available; only people with a demonstrated right to view the information, such as Rose and her parents, can gain access.

In time, the province will issue Rose an official birth certificate. But that legal document will make no mention of her biological progenitors. Indeed, the Vital Statistics Office will remain unaware of them. Only her legal parents will be named. Rose may someday be interested in the information about her genetic background, but at present, she has no legal right to any of it. Her parents may choose to share that information with her – or not. They might keep from her even the fact that she was donor-conceived.

The Assisted Human Reproduction Act called for a "health information registry", which was to have collected and maintained health data about the parties involved in reproductive procedures.[14] Under the statute, the Agency had an obligation to give people conceived through assisted reproductive technology (ART) or their descendants the right and practical ability to discover whether they had been conceived using donor gametes and, if so, to learn about the health of their progenitors. The registry would also have given donor offspring a way to ensure that a mate was not a genetic relative.[15] But the relevant portions of the Act were not declared to be in force and then they were repealed,[16] so there is no official registry of donor-conceived human offspring in Canada.

3.3 The Genetic Identity of the Offspring is Confirmed through DNA Analysis

The cattle industry recognizes that, even when a detailed pedigree is maintained, and even when embryos are retrieved and transferred by professionals, sometimes the offspring are not who you think they are. A stray bull could inseminate the donor female during the seven days of embryo development prior to flushing, for instance, or a surrogate cow might produce her own egg that is then accidentally fertilized. For that reason, many breed associations require a calf's identity to be confirmed through DNA testing after birth.

As soon as Daisy's owner applies to register Daisy officially as a member of the herd, the Canadian Angus Association will send out a "DNA parentage kit", so that a sample of hair can be taken from Daisy (and from Miss Power, if that isn't already on file). The hair sample must be sent to a specific lab that will analyze its DNA to confirm – or dispute – that Fine Line and Miss Power are in fact Daisy's genetic parents.

All Angus animals created through embryo transfer must be DNA tested. For those calves conceived naturally, the Canadian Angus Association does spot tests on roughly one in every 200 animals born. (According to the association, about 8 per cent of animals who are spot-tested turn out to be the biological offspring of animals other than those whom the owner stated were the parents.)

Such routine DNA confirmation does not occur in human fertility clinics. Obviously, DNA testing on humans after birth would have enormous ethical and social ramifications. Those effects must be weighed against the possibility of learning the same information later in life. But even before conception, there is no routine or random verification that the sperm in a vial is, in fact, sperm belonging to the man in the donor profile. Further, there is no DNA confirmation that the sperm intended for use – even when provided by an intended parent – is the sperm that is ultimately used for fertilization.

As in veterinary IVF, in human IVF errors occasionally occur.[17] How frequently they occur is unknown, because no one audits human fertility clinics in Canada for accuracy.[18] The *Assisted Human Reproduction Act* did not call for data collection regarding errors of this kind.

The reason people seek accuracy in the use of donor gametes in the cattle industry is commerce. Purebred heifers with known pedigrees can fetch $3000 to $5000 in the marketplace, whereas regular young cows are sold for approximately $1000.

The need for accuracy in human offspring is much more complex – and arguably, even more important. Often, one of the intended parents wants to be genetically related to the offspring; there is no book value for such a relationship. Sometimes parents have painstakingly selected donors for very specific attributes that they feel are important to them, for instance, ethnicity, health history or appearance. Yet, unlike ranchers, intended parents have no means to ensure that they received what they asked for.

3.4 Misrepresenting the Identity of an Offspring is a Serious Offence

In most provinces, only licensed veterinarians can perform embryo transfer in cattle. Vets, like doctors, are licensed by their provincial professional body and subject to provincial law. In Ontario, for instance, vets must adhere to the *Veterinarians Act*, which states that failing to make or keep proper records could bring a charge of professional misconduct.[19] Even accidental errors can be considered misconduct, according to the College of Veterinarians of Ontario.[20] One item that must be accurate is the individual animal's identity.[21] The College can, at any time, inspect the records.[22]

Similarly, only licensed doctors can perform embryo transfer in humans in Canada. Doctors are also expected to accurately identify patients. But whereas in veterinary medicine, the veterinarian identifies the embryo or animal created, in human medicine, the only individual identified by the fertility doctor is the commissioning parent. Because formal identification of the human embryo is not required, there are no specific penalties for getting it wrong.[23]

Nonetheless, parents who discover an error can take their case to the College governing physicians in their province, which has the power to limit or remove their license to practice medicine.[24] They might also have gone to the Assisted Human Reproduction Agency or to Health Canada. But there is no evidence that anyone did so, though lawsuits have been recently launched about sperm mix-ups during straightforward insemination.[25]

The rules regarding cattle identity are even more strict in cases where embryos will be exported. Errors in embryo identification can result in the permanent loss of not only the license to export but also the license to practice veterinary medicine.[26] All vets who create embryos for export must be licensed by the Canadian Food Inspection Agency and be certified by the Canadian Embryo Transfer Association (CETA), a non-profit body based in Kemptville, Ontario.

Among other things, CETA helps promote practice standards established through its international counterpart, the International Embryo Transfer Society, based in Champaign, Illinois. Like their parallel bodies in the world of assisted human reproduction – the Canadian Fertility and Andrology Society and the International Federation of Fertility Societies – neither CETA nor IETS has powers of enforcement.

3.5 The Records Follow the Progeny

In Canada, typically an animal's veterinarian is required by law to keep the records of that animal's conception, along with other records about its health, for a minimum of five years after the last entry on its chart. Most importantly, the documentation of a cow's conception – the "certificate of embryo recovery", "certificate of freezing", "certificate of transfer" – are considered part of the veterinary history of that animal, and as such, are kept in the file of that animal and in the possession of its owner.

In human medicine, records about a conception are kept in the file of the commissioning parent. They are not considered to be documents pertaining to the offspring. Records about the means of conception and the genetic parents are not placed into the child's pediatric medical file at birth and the person created through that conception has no legal right ever to possess them or even to view them.[27]

4. Conclusion

When cattle are conceived by assisted insemination or embryo transfer for registration as purebred, the state requires progenitors' information to be collected, preserved, verified and disclosed. The same is not true for donor-conceived humans. Even though information regarding the progenitors of humans created through assisted human reproduction is an important part of the child's record of health or identity, it is not a part of the child's record at all. It should be.

The experience of record keeping in the cattle industry demonstrates that with the right combination of legislation and practice standards, it is possible to create and maintain accurate records, ones which can follow the individual created. There is no practical or scientific reason why human offspring cannot have access to complete, accurate and verified records about their origins.

Bibliography

Animal Pedigree Act, R.S.C. 1985, c. 8 (4th Supp.), http://www.canlii.org/en/ca/laws/stat/rsc-1985-c-8-4th-supp/latest/rsc-1985-c-8-4th-supp.html.http://laws.justice.gc.ca/en/A-11.2/index.htmlhttp://laws.justice.gc.ca/en/A-11.2/index.html
Assisted Human Reproduction Act, 2004 S.C., ch. 2, s. 18(3), Canada.
-- s. 18(4).
-- s. 78.
Canadian Angus Association, http://www.cdnangus.ca.
-- "CAA Online Herdbook", http://www.cdnangus.ca/registry/online_herdbook.htm.
-- "Canadian Angus Animal Inquiry", http://abri.une.edu.au/online/cgi-bin/i4.dll?1=20213329&2=2431&3=56&5=2B3C2B3C3A.

-- "Red Fine Line Mulberry 26", Canadian Angus Animal Details, http://abri.une.edu.au/online/cgi-bin/i4.dll?1=20213329&2=2420&3=56&5=2B3C2B3C3A&6=5A5D5C222222272F23&9=5A5B5058.

Fischer, Martin. Investigator, College of Veterinarians of Ontario, personal communication with author, April 19-26, 2010.

Motluk, Alison. "Who's the Daddy?", http://www.newscientist.com/article/mg19526164.100-whos-the-daddy-us-sperm-banks-must-be-better-regulated.htmlhttp://www.newscientist.com/article/mg19526164.100-whos-the-daddy-us-sperm-banks-must-be-better-regulated.html.

Ontario Newborn Registration Service, https://www.orgforms.gov.on.ca/IBR/start.do.

Veterinarians Act, R.R.O 1990, c,V.3, s. 17. (1) 27.

-- 1990 R.R.O., c.V.3, s. 22 (2) 1, Ontario.

-- s. 50 (1).

Vital Statistics Act, R.S.O. 1990, c. V.4, ss. 8-9.

Notes

1 I wish to acknowledge and thank Dr. Jay Cross, Associate Dean Research & Graduate Education, Faculty of Veterinary Medicine and Professor, Department of Comparative Biology and Experimental Medicine, University of Calgary; and Dr. Roger Davis, of Davis-Rairdan ET Ltd., Crossfield, Alberta, Canada, for their expertise and insight.

2 All the details about this animal's provenance come from actual records. The author has invented the name and guessed at the gender.

3 Rose's sperm and egg donors are real, and the details come from actual records, but as far as I know, no child was conceived from their union. The details about the date of conception and birth were contrived. Details about what records might have existed come from interviews with fertility doctors.

4 Canadian Angus Association, "CAA Online Herdbook", http://www.cdnangus.ca/registry/online_herdbook.htm.

5 Canadian Angus Association, "Red Fine Line Mulberry 26", Canadian Angus Animal Details,http://abri.une.edu.au/online/cgi-bin/i4.dll?1=20213329&2=2420&3=56&5=2B3C2B3C3A&6=5A5D5C222222272F23&9=5A5B5058.

6 Animal Pedigree Act, R.S.C. 1985, c. 8 (4th Supp.) http://www.canlii.org/en/ca/laws/stat/rsc-1985-c-8-4th-supp/latest/rsc-1985-c-8-4th-supp.html.

7 *Ibid.*, s. 66.

8 Canadian Angus Association, "Canadian Angus Association Website", http://www.cdnangus.ca.

9 Assisted Human Reproduction Act, S.C. 2004, c. 2.

10 Canadian Angus Association, "Canadian Angus Animal Inquiry", http://abri.une.edu.au/online/cgi-bin/i4.dll?1=20213329&2=2431&3=56&5=2B3C2B3C3A.

11 Vital Statistics Act, R.S.O. 1990, c. V.4, ss. 8-9.

12 Ontario Newborn Registration Service, https://www.orgforms.gov.on.ca/IBR/start.do.

13 No attempt is made to ascertain whether, as in Rose's case, she shared a womb at any point during the pregnancy unless the other conceptus died after the twentieth week of pregnancy or after it attained the weight of 500 grams or more. "Missing twins" are a well-documented phenomenon: Ainsworth, "And then there was one", http://www.newscientist.com/article/mg17223134.600-and-then-there-was-one.html.

14 *Assisted Human Reproduction Act,* 2004 S.C., ch. 2, s. 18(3), Canada.

15 *Ibid.*, s. 18(4).
16 *Ibid.*, s. 78 and *Jobs, Growth and Long-term Prosperity Act*, S.C. 2012, c. 19, Consequential Amendment to the Department of Public Works and Government Services Act, 2012, Division 56, Assisted Human Reproduction Act, Section 720.
17 Alison Motluk, "Who's the Daddy?", http://www.newscientist.com/article/mg19526164.100-whos-the-daddy-us-sperm-banks-must-be-better-regulated.html.
18 In the UK, where they do check, there were apparently eight "serious incidents" in UK clinics in 2009, some of which may have involved sperm or embryo mixups. The Human Fertilisation and Embryology Authority, the UK equivalent of AHRC, has now agreed to post inspection reports on its website, outlining the incident, its seriousness and the consequences. Michael Cook, "UK watchdog to disclose IVF errors", *BioEdge*, October 6, 2009, http://www.bioedge.org/index.php/bioethics/bioethics_article/uk_watchdog_to_disclose_ivf_errors/.
19 *Veterinarians Act*, R.R.O 1990, c,V.3, s. 17. (1) 27.
20 Martin Fischer, Investigator, College of Veterinarians of Ontario, personal communication with author, April 19-26, 2010.
21 *Veterinarians Act*, 1990 R.R.O., c.V.3, s. 22 (2) 1, Ontario.
22 *Ibid.*, s. 50. (1).
23 There are no known cases in Canada where a physician has knowingly and deliberately misrepresented the identity of a donor. In the US, however, in 2009, a US physician was fined $10,000 and ordered to stop performing artificial inseminations by the Connecticut Public Health Department when it was discovered he used his own sperm rather than that of the intended father to impregnate a patient. A separate civil suit filed by the couple was settled out of court. There was no criminal inquiry and the doctor retained his licence.
24 Each College has the legislated responsibility to regulate the medical profession in its province. For example, in Alberta, responsibility is delegated to the Alberta College of Physicians and Surgeons under Section 3(1) Health Professions Act, R.S.A. 2000, c. H-7, Current version in force since Dec 17, 2008.
25 Journalist, Amber Kanwar, investigated the case of an Ottawa fertility doctor who allegedly used sperm that was not that agreed upon. In the first case. a woman named Trudy Moore alleges that her husband's sperm did not participate in their daughter Samantha's conception as they had intended. In the second case, Jacqueline Slinn alleges that she learned in April 2010 that her five-year-old daughter, Bridget, is not a genetic match to her intended sperm donor. Amber Kanwar, "Doctor sued over allegedly mixing up sperm samples" Globe and Mail, Saturday, September 11, 2010, http://www.theglobeandmail.com/news/national/ontario/doctor-sued-over-allegedly-mixing-up-sperm-samples/article1703585.
26 In an extraordinary case, Ontario veterinarian, Brian Hill was charged in 2009 with falsifying the identities of over 6000 exported bovine embryos. Bryce Urquhart, "Oxford vet charged with cattle embryo fraud", *Sentinel-Review*, September 3, 2009, http://www.oxfordreview.com/ArticleDisplay.aspx?archive=true&e=1373851. He lost his veterinary licence, his accreditations and was placed under house arrest for 9 months. The case illustrates both that such incidents concerning non-human animals are taken very seriously and that the monitoring of transgressions is extremely poor.
27 *Assisted Human Reproduction Act*, s. 18(3).

PART SIX

WHAT CHANGES WOULD BE NECESSARY IN PROVINCIAL LAW TO FACILITATE A BAN ON DONOR ANONYMITY?

In their chapter, "The recognition of the right to identity of children born of assisted procreation: a provincial responsibility", *Michelle Giroux* and *Mariana De Lorenzi* consider the nature of the right to identity and how it has been established by international law to which Canada is a signatory. Giroux and De Lorenzi argue that the right to identity is multi-faceted and requires both establishment and protection. They describe how current law in Quebec fails to protect the right by making it impossible for the donor-conceived to know their origins and the identity of their donors. They recommend that Quebec exercise its responsibility urgently and offer suggestions as to how Quebec law ought to change to guarantee the donor-conceived's right to identity.

Likewise common law provinces and territories should recognize the rights of donor offspring to know that they were donor-conceived, and the identity and medical, social and cultural history of their donors. Further, provincial and territorial law ought to clarify the legal parentage of gamete donors. The chapter by *Juliet Guichon* discusses how, in Canadian common law jurisdictions, those rights might be respected and, using the template of the *Uniform Child Status Act*, makes suggestions for provincial law reform to clarify the parentage of the donor-conceived.

Chapter Twenty

The Recognition of the Right to Identity of Children Born of Assisted Procreation: A Provincial Responsibility

Michelle Giroux and Mariana De Lorenzi

This chapter considers the responsibilities of the provinces and more specifically of Quebec to guarantee the right to identity as protected by section 7.1 and 8.1 of the *UN Convention on the Rights of the Child* (CRC) and how it might implement such guarantees.

1. The Absence of Recognition of the Right to Identity in Québec Civil Law

In Québec, the filiation of children born of assisted procreation is addressed in Chapter I.1 of Title two (Filiation) of the Civil Code ("C.C.Q."). The Code must be interpreted in accordance with some general rules. Among others, decisions about children must be made with central regard to the child's best interests.[1] Parents have the prerogative to decide whether to tell the child that he or she has been donor-conceived.[2] Despite this parental prerogative the state duty to recognize the right to identity remains. Parents have an obligation to respect this fundamental right. Public policies ought to help parents become more conscious of the importance of the right of offspring to know their progenitors.

Regarding assisted reproductive technologies, ("ART") more specifically, Article 538.2 C.C.Q. states,

> The contribution of genetic material for the purposes of a third-party parental project does not create any bond of filiation between the contributor and the child born of the parental project [...]

So, donations of gametes and embryos are included in the definition of "genetic material", provided the donations are unpaid, as stated in Article 25 C.C.Q. Also, under Québec civil law, the donor bears no legal or financial responsibility for a child born through his or her gamete donation. Article 541 C.C.Q. stipulates that surrogacy arrangements are contrary to public order and void.

Article 542 C.C.Q. recognizes confidentiality of donor identity as a guiding principle.[3] It is thus impossible for the donor-conceived, under current Québec law, to obtain information relating to their progenitors' identity. Nevertheless, there is a limited exception to this rule. At 542 C.C.Q. *in fine* allows a person born of ART (or descendant of such a person) to receive health information to prevent a serious threat to his or her health. In that situation, non-identifying information may be transmitted to medical authorities and only through a tribunal.[4]

So, although Quebec grants offspring[5] a very limited opportunity to obtain some information concerning the donor, it does so as a consequence of the right to health, not the right to identity. In fact, according to the strict wording of paragraph 2 of Article 542 C.C.Q., no information relating to the identity of the donor should ever be divulged to the Offspring.

In 2009, Quebec legislation was modified concerning collection and retention of information related to ART.[6] Nevertheless, the policy of anonymity was maintained and, therefore, Offspring may still not have access to information about their identity and their medical, social and cultural history.

Legislators have discussed the question of one's origins in both the contexts of adoption and ART.[7] Generally speaking, the interest of Offspring to know their origins is of less legislative concern than the interests of donors and parents. Further, in cases where information has been disclosed, the disclosure was justified on the basis of ensuring the protection of one's health.

Neither Quebec nor Canada has expressly recognized the right to identity, as an autonomous[8] and fundamental right.[9] Even if offspring were to win a court challenge asserting a right to know one's origins, a right to health (not just physical but also psychological) or a recognition through the principle of non-discrimination, it would be preferable to have a clear legislative policy on the matter.[10] Governments should not wait until a court challenge is decided to react. They should be proactive and legislate on the question as soon as possible. It is the responsibility of the state to do so under international law.

2. The Responsibility of Canada Under the International Convention on the Rights of the Child

As discussed by Veronica Pinero in this volume, the right to identity is recognized in Articles 7 and 8 of the *CRC*. It is the first international instrument expressly recognising such a right.[11] It is binding in Canada.

Therefore, Canada must take all measures that allow people to know their origins and form their identity. The right also entails the obligation of states to respect and guarantee it.¹² This responsibility is both *passive* and *active*. It is *passive* in not interrupting, hiding or denying any licit act made in favour of the right to identity and not hiding or falsifying any information in relation to it. The responsibility is *active*, in removing obstacles and facilitating the means to make the right effective.¹³

Article 4 of the CRC states that Canada has a duty to undertake "… all appropriate legislative, administrative, and other measures for the implementation of the rights recognized in the present Convention …" Having ratified it, Canada has accepted three obligations: to supervise the application of the right to identity, to respect it and to remedy any illegal deprivation of it. The first is imposed by Article 7.2;¹⁴ the latter two later are stipulated by Article 8, paragraphs 1 and 2,¹⁵ respectively.

The importance of the CRC in the development and implementation of children's rights in Canada has been underlined by the Second Report of Canada to the United Nations on the CRC (2001).¹⁶ Canada's failure to implement the CRC in domestic law and the existence of gaps in its implementation have been noted in the *Interim Report* of the Senate Human Rights Committee (2005). Tellingly, it states, "… Canada must begin to take its international human rights treaty obligations more seriously."¹⁷

The U.N. Committee on the Right of the Child (2003) has also expressed concern that the right to know one's origins cannot be respected in Canada as long as it permits anonymous birth, secret adoption and medically assisted reproduction with anonymous donors. Consequently the Committee recommended that Canada adopt legislation that would respect Articles 7 and 8 of the CRC.¹⁸ The Canadian Senate Committee on Human Rights agrees with the UN Committee. In its Report, that Committee said that "[c]hildren have a right to their own identity – to know who they are – and this right is not always being effectively protected in Canada"¹⁹ and "… that the best interests of the child are not being served by current adoption and donor insemination policies across the country."²⁰ The donor-conceived in Canada are entitled to the creation, preservation and disclosure of their genetic origins and their donors' identities. It is imperative that provincial governments in Canada give effect to this right.

3. Reform is Needed to Put the Child's Rights First

The Supreme Court of Canada has decided that action must take place at the provincial level.²¹ Hence, provincial legislation²² should be modified to ban anonymity in the context of gamete donation in Québec. Thus, Article 542 C.C.Q. must be amended to recognize the right to identity.

The recognition of this right requires that information be created, preserved and then disclosed. As a practical matter, this entails the establishment of a Registry as a repository of information[23] and the collection of current information about the donor, not only on the ultimate recipients of the donated gametes and those who are born from them, (which the declared invalid federal legislation aimed to do).[24] Law must also empower and require Registry personnel to advise people that they might be genetically related.[25] Such information can help people avoid incest, especially in the present context where the number of times a person can donate is unregulated and where there could be "overuse" of one particular donor's gametes. Proper regulation would also limit the number of children conceived by the same donor.[26]

Other matters under provincial jurisdiction, such as parental authority and birth registration, must also be addressed. Québec has legislated on the issue regarding whether donors have parental rights and has established that they do not have parental rights and responsibilities toward the offspring and vice versa (it would be a reciprocal duty) (see Article 538.2 C.C.Q.). But not all provinces have yet done so and should act urgently.[27] Also, despite the fact that it is the prerogative of parents to tell their children the truth about their conception, other methods, like the child's birth certificate and counselling[28] could be used to facilitate transparency and truth.

Will those conceived by donor gametes under a past regime of anonymity have a right to access information concerning their origins? At first glance, it seems legally difficult to recognize such a right retroactively because of the effect it would have on those who either donated or used donated gametes under the regime where anonymity is the default. Nevertheless, more thought should be given to the creation of a voluntary registration system[29] for those who were conceived prior to the establishment of the registry. A registry could ensure that medical information would be continually updated.

If Canada and Québec value fundamental rights, then the fundamental right to identity appears not to have been effectively recognized. Given the international tendency to recognize such a right, Quebec must insist upon explicit recognition of this very fundamental right from the children's rights perspective.[30]

4. Conclusion

The international CRC recognizes a right to identity. One important aspect of this right is the right to know one's origins. Over the past several years, the number of nations that have banned the anonymous character of gamete donations has increased, including nations that had once strongly supported such a position.[31] This shift in national legislative policy worldwide has aided a growing recognition of the right to know one's origins in international law and gives a wider effect to this fundamental right.

The current Canadian legal system grants donors and parents a choice while giving children none. Arguments of confidentiality and privacy favoured the former, and adults rights are buttressed by the established ART regime. While donors can take measures to protect their own best interests, children cannot.[32] Given the rise in the right to know one's origins in the international sphere, Quebec law reform is required to explicitly recognize this right. This is the time to put the child first.

Bibliography

Annas, George J. "Fathers Anonymous: Beyond the Best Interests of the Sperm Donor." *Family Law Quarterly* 14, no. 1 (1980): 1-13.

Australian Health Ethics Committee, *Ethical Guidelines on the Use of Assisted Reproductive Technology in Clinical Practice and Research*, September 2004.

Blyth, Eric and Abigail Farrand. "Anonymity in Donor-Assisted Conception and the UN Convention on the Rights of the Child." *International Journal of Children's Rights* 12, no. 2 (2004), 89-104.

Blyth, Eric, and Lucy Frith. "Donor-conceived People's Access to Genetic and Biographical History: An Analysis of Provisions in Different Jurisdictions Permitting Disclosure of Donor Identity." *International Journal of Law, Policy and the Family* 23 (2009): 174-191.

Blyth, Eric, Frith, Lucy, Jones, Caroline and Speirs, Jennifer M., "The Role of Birth Certificates in Relation to Access to Biographical and Genetic History in Donor Conception" (2009) *International Journal of Children's Rights*, 17(2), pp. 207-233.

Canada, House of Commons, Standing Committee on Health. *Assisted Human Reproduction: Building Families*. Ottawa: House of Commons Canada, 2001.

Canada, Senate, Standing Senate Committee on Human Rights. *Children: The Silenced Citizens. Effective Implementation Of Canada's International Obligations With Respect To The Rights Of Children*. Ottawa: Senate, 2007.

Canadian Heritage, *Canada's Second Report on the Convention on the Rights of the Child*, April 26, 2001, http://www.pch.gc.ca/pgm/pdp-hrp/docs/crc-2001/index-eng.cfm.

Canadian Heritage, *Canada's Third and Fourth Reports on the Convention on the Rights of the Child*, November 2011, on line: http://www.pch.gc.ca/ddp-hrd/docs/pdf/canada3-4-crc-reports-nov2009-eng.pdf.

Canadian Law Reform Commission. *Medically assisted reproduction. Working Paper 65*. Ottawa: Law Reform Commission, 1992.

Cerda, Jaime Sergio. "The Draft Convention on the Rights of the Child: New Rights." *Human Rights Quarterly* 12, no. 1 (1990): 115-119.

Committee on the Rights of the Child, *Concluding observations: Canada*, CRC/C/15/Add.215, 27 October 2003.

Committee on the Rights of the Child, *Concluding observations: France*, CRC/C/15/Add.240, 30 June 2004.

Conseil de la famille et de l'enfance. *Avis. Prendre en compte la diversité des familles.* Québec: Conseil de la famille et de l'enfance, 2005.

Freeman, Michael. "The New Birth Right? Identity and the Child of the Reproduction Revolution." *The International Journal of Children's Rights* 4, no. 3, (1996): 273-297.

Giroux, Michelle. "Le droit fondamental de connaître ses origines biologiques." in Tara Collins *et al.* eds. *Rights of the Child. Proceedings of the International Conference / Ottawa 2007.* Montréal: Wilson & Lafleur, 2008.

Harvison Young. Alison, "Reconceiving the Family: Challenging the Paradigm of the Exclusive Family", (1998) *Journal of Gender & the Law.* 6, 505-555.

Howe, R. Brian. "Implementing Children's Rights in a Federal State: The Case of Canada's Child Protection System." *The International Journal of Children's Rights* 9 (2001): 361-382.

Klibanoff, Elton B. "Genealogical Information in Adoption: The Adoptees Quest and the Law." *Family Law Quarterly* 11, no. 2 (1977): 185-198.

Oscapella, Eugene Leon. "Overview of Canadian laws relating to privacy and confidentiality in the medical context." In *Overview of Legal Issues in New Reproductive Technologies*, edited by the Research Studies of the Royal Commission on New Reproductive Technologies, Ottawa: Minister of Supply and Services Canada, 1993.

Ouellette, Françoise-Romaine. "Le droit aux origines des enfants adoptés à l'étranger." In *Rights of the Child. Proceedings of the International Conference, Ottawa 2007,* Tara Collins and others eds. Montréal: Wilson & Lafleur, 2008.

"The civil code of Quebec and new reproductive technologies." In *Overview of Legal Issues in New Reproductive Technologies*, edited by the Research Studies of the Royal Commission on New Reproductive Technologies, Ottawa, Minister of Supply and Services Canada, 1993.

Québec, National Assembly, *Journal des débats,* 7 (5 September 1991).

Québec, National Assembly, *Journal des débats,* 30 (5 December 1991).

Québec, National Assembly, *Journal des débats,* 33 (10 December 1991).

Sloss, E. and R. Mykitiuk. "The Challenge of the New Reproductive Technologies to Family Law", in Royal Commission on New Reproductive Technologies. *Legal and Ethical Issues in New Reproductive Technologies: Pregnancy and Parenthood.* Research Studies of the Royal Commission on New Reproductive Technologies, Ottawa: Minister of Supply and Services Canada, 1993.

Trahan, Anne-Marie. "Les droits de l'enfant, la Convention des Nations Unies et l'arrêt Baker: une trilogie porteuse d'espoir." in Benoît Moore, ed. *Mélanges Jean Pineau.* Montréal: Thémis, 2003.

Wallbank, Julie. "The Role of Rights and Utility in Instituting a Child's Right to Know her Genetic History." *Social Legal Studies* 13, no. 2 (2004): 245-264.

Notes

1 Article 33 states:
 Every decision concerning a child shall be taken in light of the child's interests and the respect of his rights.
 --- Consideration is given, in addition to the moral, intellectual, emotional and physical needs of the child, to the child's age, health, personality and family environment, and to the other aspects of his situation."
2 Article 597ss C.C.Q. See also Ouellette, "Le droit aux origines", 710. According to the Canadian Law Reform Commission, *Medically assisted reproduction*, 169, one can't impose to the parents the duty to divulge the details of his/her child's origins, as it might be considered an unconstitutional infringement on the fundamental right of parents to make decisions concerning their children. In any case, the respect of such a rule could remain utopian. In a case dealing with adoption, the Court insisted that the adoptive parents have the implicit duty (even if article 632 CCQ (1980) does not force it) to reveal his/her adoptive status to the child, *Droit de la famille 657*, [1989] R.J.Q. 1693 (C.Q.).
3 Article 542 C.C.Q.: "Nominative information relating to medically assisted procreation is confidential."
4 Article 542, 2 C.C.Q. states:
 However, where the health of a person born of medically assisted procreation or of any descendant of that person could be seriously harmed if the person were deprived of the information requested, the court may allow the information to be transmitted confidentially to the medical authorities concerned. A descendant of such a person may also exercise this right where the health of that descendant of a close relative could be seriously harmed if the descendant were deprived of the information requested. A reform proposal suggests to remove the condition of serious harm to allow transmission of information, *Loi modifiant le Code civil et d'autres dispositions législatives en matière d'adoption et d'autorité parentale*, Bill 81, (2nd Sess., 39th Leg.)
5 Offspring is defined as: "people conceived through reproductive technology which used gametes other than those of social parents and includes people conceived by embryo transfer".
6 *An Act respecting clinical and research activities relating to assisted procreation*, R.S.Q., c. A-5.01. art. 42 to 45.
7 For more details in the province of Québec, see National Assembly, *Journal des débats*, 254-261, 271, 273; National Assembly, *Journal des débats*, 1231-1242; National Assembly, *Journal des débats*, 1333-1335. See discussions on Bill 125, before the Québec National Assembly, where it is assumed that there is such a right in matter of adoption or ART. See also the recent shift, a proposal for a ban on anonymity, in matter of adoption, *Loi modifiant le Code civil et d'autres dispositions législatives en matière d'adoption et d'autorité parentale*, Bill 81, 2nd Sess., 39th Leg.). For a discussion on the same phenomenon in the common law provinces, see Juliet Guichon's chapter in this book.
8 Because of its complexity, typical of the sphere that it regulates, the right to identity has points of contact with several other rights (e.g.: the rights to privacy, to health, to physical integrity, honour, name, etc.) and principles (such as, the dignity, the free development of the personality, etc.). Some of those rights have obtained legal recognition before the right to identity; and their gradual recognition led to a system consisting of all of them as aspects of a specific right that we nowadays call right to identity. A violation of the right to identity can thus implicate the violation of other rights.
9 Klibanoff, "Genealogical Information", 191. On the qualification of the right to identity as a fundamental right, see as early as 1977.
10 This is what we have argued in the past, see Giroux "Origines biologiques", 353.
11 See Freeman, "The New Birth Right?" 283.
12 Cerda, "Draft Convention", 116, states that:
 ... under Article 8 it is mandatory for states to respect the right of the child to preserve his or her identity. The purpose of this obligation is to establish an explicit safeguard against the unlawful intervention of the state.
13 Howe, "Children's rights," 364; Cerda, "Draft Convention," 116. The responsibility of the States, as Howe shows, is different after the new concepts of the child as existing person (not any more

as object of protection) and of children's fundamental rights (instead of the paternalistic notion of children's welfare). "Such a concept of children's rights is much more demanding of state and parental action than the traditional concept of child welfare ... The language of rights works to make the protection of children a more imperative undertaking", or, as Cerda maintains, it is a new obligation for the States to provide " ... a legal mechanism for the reestablishment of the child's identity".

14 Article 7.2 states:
States Parties shall ensure the implementation of these rights in accordance with their national law and their obligations under the relevant international instruments in this field, in particular where the child would otherwise be stateless.

15 Article 8.2 states:
Where a child is illegally deprived of some or all of the elements of identity, States Parties shall provide appropriate assistance and protection, with a view to re-establishing speedily identity.

16 Canadian Heritage, *Second, Third and Fourth Reports.*

17 "Canada, "The Silenced Citizens.", ix.

18 Committee on the Rights of the Child, *Concluding observations: Canada*, 7. It is possible to find some examples in the Concluding observations that the Committee on the Rights of the Child made to several countries; like France (Committee on the Rights of the Child, *Concluding observations: France*, 6.) Of the eleven countries that the UNCRC's Concluding Observations (2003) published as revealing specific reference to donor anonymity in ART, only four forbid the disclosure of the donors (Denmark, France, Greece and Spain), the other seven (Austria, the Netherlands, New Zealand, Norway, Sweden, Switzerland and the United Kingdom) have abolished the concealing of donor's identities. We could also mention Australia (in Victoria in 1998 and in Western Australia in 2004) and Finland (2006). For more information, see Blyth and Farrand, "Donor-assisted Conception", 96ss.

19 Canada, "The Silenced Citizens.", 113.

20 Canada, "The Silenced Citizens.", 110-114. To arrive to this last conclusion, the Canadian Senate Committee collected specialized-technical information which suggests several disadvantages for the child health and wellbeing of the lack of access to donors' identities.

21 *Reference re Assisted Human Reproduction Act*, 2010 SCC 61, [2010] 3 SCR 457.

22 For an example of the Quebec provincial legislation of the regulation of assisted reproduction, see *An Act respecting clinical and research activities relating to assisted procreation*, R.S.Q., c. A-5.01. See also the existing uniform legislation *Uniform Child Status Act* of April 1992, <http://www.ulcc.ca/en/us/index.cfm?sec=1&sub=1u9>. However, the statute would need to be amended to provide for provinces and territories, namely to record accurately the facts of conceptions and all participants; to insure a mechanism is put in place for offspring to have access to all documents relevant to their conception and genetic parentage including medical information and to provide for mental health counselling.

23 House of Commons Canada, *Assisted Human Reproduction*, 21. The House of Commons Standing Committee on Health, in its report on a draft of the *AHRA* was astonished by the fact that there was no proof that sperm banks in Canada hold detailed information on donor and on the use of the gametes. This situation has been often criticized, see Ouellette, "New Reproductive Technologies", 707; Canadian Law Reform Commission, *Medically Assisted Procreation*, 168ss; Sloss and Mykitiuk "New Reproductive Technologies", 431, 432. For more details on the privacy issues with person born of ART, see Oscapella, "Overview of Canadian laws", 231, 232. The Canadian Law Reform Commission, (*Medically Assisted Procreation*, 158) was of the opinion that information relating to identity of the parties should be kept separately from the medical file.

24 Repealed section 17 stated:
The Agency shall maintain a personal health information registry containing health reporting information about donors of human reproductive material and *in vitro* embryos, persons who undergo assisted reproduction procedures and persons conceived by means of those procedures.

25 It might prove useful to look at now repealed section 18(4) *AHRA* on that point.

26 Guideline 6.3.1 of Australia's *Ethical Guidelines on the Use of Assisted Reproductive Technology in Clinical Practice and Research* (Australian Health Ethics Committee, *Ethical guidelines*, 18) recommends that:

Gametes from one donor should be used in a limited number of families. In deciding the number of families, clinicians should take account of: the number of genetic relatives that the persons conceived using the donation will have; the risk of a person conceived with donor gametes inadvertently having a sexual relationship with a close genetic relative (with particular reference to the population and ethnic group in which the donation will be used); the consent of the donor for the number of families to be created; and whether the donor has already donated gametes at another clinic.

27 Canada, "The Silenced Citizens.", 110-115. In finishing their report, the Committee provided Recommendation 11, which states:
Pursuant to articles 7 and 8 of the *Convention on the Right of the Child*, the Committee recommends that the federal-provincial-territorial negotiations on adoption proposed in Recommendation 10 should include consideration of access to a biological parent's identity and of the benefits of identity disclosure vetos. The Committee also recommends that Assisted Human Reproduction Canada review the legal and regulatory regime surrounding sperm donor identity and access to a donor's medical history to determine how the best interests of the child can better be served. (At 109, 115).

28 Blyth, Eric, Frith, Lucy, Jones, Caroline and Speirs, Jennifer M., "The Role of Birth Certificates", 207-233.The Australian *Ethical Guidelines on the Use of Assisted Reproductive Technology in Clinical Practice and Research* states at Guideline 9.1 (Australian Health Ethics Committee, *Ethical guidelines*, 29) that:
To make informed decisions about their treatment, participants in ART need to understand all the procedures involved, including any health risks and psychosocial consequences associated with them. Clinics must give up-to-date, objective, accurate information about treatment options and the procedures involved to all potential participants in ART procedures and discuss it with them…
These rules also take into account the fact that:
Donors and recipients in gamete or embryo donor programs (see Sections 6 and 7) each have complex information needs. Clinics must consider the information needs of both donors and recipients … (Guideline 9.2).
Furthermore, because:
ART involves complex decision making … participants may find it an emotional and stressful experience,
that is why:
[c]linics must provide readily accessible services from accredited counsellors to support participants in making decisions about their treatment, before, during and after the procedures … (Guideline 9.3).
Section 18.1 of the *The Infertility Treatment Act 1995* (Vic.) will only allow donor gametes to be used if, before the procedure takes place:
(c) the woman and her husband, the donor and the spouse of the donor (if any) have received counselling as to its use from a counsellor approved under Part 8 to give counselling about the use of sperm, ovocytes or embryos from named donors.
Counseling is also required by the UK *Human Fertilisation and Embryology Act 1990*, (U.K.) 1990, c. 37, to the woman (and, if she is being treated together with a partner, also to him/her) who is using donated gametes or embryos (Section 13-6); and to the offspring who want to obtain information about their donors (Section 31-3) or the specific person whom s/he proposes to marry (Section 31-6). It is also required for the providers of gametes or embryos (Schedule 3, Section 3-1 of the UK Act, and by s. 46 of the *Human Assisted Reproduction Act 2004*.)

29 *Human Assisted Reproduction Act 2004*, (N.Z.), 2004/92, s. 63, and *Human Fertilisation and Embryology Act 2008* (U.K.), 2008, c. 22, s. 24, and Québec *Bill 81, supra*, note 7 are good examples. See also Blyth and Frith, "Donor-conceived People", 10-11.

30 On the necessity on moving towards effective recognition of the rights of the child, see namely Trahan, "Les droits de l'enfant", 151. See also Howe, "Children's Rights", 361-382; Harvison Young, "Reconceiving the Family", 551; and Wallbank, "Child's Right", 262.

31 Giroux, "Origines biologiques", 353.

32 Annas, "Fathers Anonymous", 11.

Chapter Twenty-One

How Canadian Common Law Might Change to Facilitate Legislation to Permit the Donor-Conceived to Access Information Regarding Their Progenitors

Juliet R. Guichon

1. Introduction

Legislation in Canada regarding assisted human reproduction should be based on the ethically correct decision of the Parliament of Canada to recognize and declare that:[1]

> [T]he health and well-being of children born through the application of assisted human reproductive technologies must be given priority in all decisions respecting their use.

Benward and Lauzon, in this volume, have argued that the health and wellbeing of donor offspring would almost certainly be advanced if there were no secrecy regarding the fact that donor gametes participated in their conception, and if donors were not statutorily permitted to be anonymous to their biological children. This chapter considers what new legislation or law reform in common law provinces is needed to give effect to the primacy of this understanding of the health and wellbeing interests of offspring.

2. A Framework for Law Reform or New Legislation to Advance Offspring Interests

In 2010, the Supreme Court of Canada held that the provinces have jurisdiction to govern the collection, storage and dissemination of health and vital statistics information about donors and the donor–conceived.[2] Now the provinces (and possibly the territories[3]) must choose to legislate, or to continue to fail to create registries of donor gametes. The latter strategy is not in the interests of the donor-conceived. Yet, to date, no common law province has passed legislation to protect the interests of offspring in knowing their progenitors' identity and their medical, social and cultural history.

The provinces have a number of examples to follow. They could collaborate with the Uniform Conference of Canada. That organization aims to promote harmonization of law in Canada.[4] Its civil section develops uniform statutes on a variety of subjects that provinces may choose to follow when developing and enacting their own statutes. (The Uniform Conference of Canada has developed relevant draft legislation discussed below at note 32.)

Provinces might also choose to adopt the objectives of the *Assisted Human Reproduction Act*.[5] Misconduct under the new provincial law would be a provincial offence. The provinces could also choose to follow the examples of international jurisdictions (for example, Sweden, Australia, New Zealand, Japan and the United Kingdom).[6]

Whatever template common law legislators adopt, they ought to accept that the health and well-being of offspring are the highest priority and that offspring have the legal right to know: 1. That they were conceived by donor gametes; 2. The current medical[7] history of the gamete provider; 3. The identity of the gamete provider; and 4. Their legal relation to the donor.

2.1. Rights

The right to know one's identity has been commonly referred to as one single, all-encompassing right: the right of the person to know the identity of their gamete donor.[8] But the right to know one's identity consists of two rights: (1) the right to know the circumstances of one's conception, to be 'told' about the donor conception; and (2) the right to identifying information about the gamete donor. Both rights must be addressed when considering how legislation or law reform should address the interests of the donor-conceived.[9]

2.1.1 Right to Know Fact of Donor-Conception

The first right, the right to be told about the donor conception, tends to be disregarded. Most parents do not tell their children the truth about how they used donor gametes to have the children. According to Ken Daniels, a New Zealand-based researcher:[10]

The majority of studies that have examined parents' views about sharing the DI [donor insemination] family building history with their children show that most parents have not, or do not intend to tell their offspring. In one particular study covering four European countries (UK, The Netherlands, Italy and Spain), families who had children via IVF [in vitro fertilization], DI [donor insemination,] adoption and natural conception were studied. Not one of the 111 DI families had told their 4-8 year olds and 75% said that they had no plans to do so.

In other words, even if the state were to provide offspring access to records, most would not know they have reason to seek such access, thus they would not seek the identifying and medical, social and cultural information contained in the records to which they would be entitled. The second right, the right of access, is therefore wholly contingent upon the protection of the first – the right to know.

The issue of the right to know that one has been donor-conceived has become prominent in the United Kingdom. There, the Joint Committee of the House of Lords and House of Commons recognized the force of the argument that "the fact of donor conception should be registered on a person's birth certificate."[11] As Blyth et al. have elucidated,[12] the case for this reform is based on three arguments.

First, as just stated, most parents have not and do not intend to tell children the truth about their donor conception. The law's attempts to offer donor-conceived people information about their identity will be thwarted if the law does not provide the donor-conceived person a means independent from their social parents to know the truth about their conception.

The second argument for law reform is based on the important principle that the state should not be party to deception. According to this argument, not only are donor-conceived people possibly deceived by their parents, but the state currently colludes with this deception.[13]

The third argument for some form of annotated birth certificate is the claimed need for an accurate record of one's genetic history. As Alison Motluk has demonstrated in this volume, such a record is created when donor gametes are used in the conception of cattle. Donor-conceived people have argued that the fact that the state creates no similar record for humans is a denial of a basic right. According to David Gollancz:[14]

> No one is entitled deliberately to deceive other people, or deprive them of essential information, about their personal history. Our stories belong to us and we are entitled to the truth.

The argument that having an accurate record of one's genetic lineage is a fundamental human right is supported by Article 7(1) and Article 8 of the United Nations *Convention on the Rights of the Child*[15] as has been discussed in this volume by Veronica Pinero, Michelle Giroux and Mariana De Lorenzi. Donor-conceived people are denied their internationally-protected rights to identity when they are denied an accurate record of their parentage. Therefore, birth certificates ought to record both genetic and social parentage.

Knowledge of the fact of assisted conception by donor gametes can be protected and transmitted only if it is recorded. Physicians who used donor gametes to create a conception should, as discussed above, be under an obligation to record this fact and to submit such records to the appropriate provincial or territorial agency that would record the matter. That information would then inform the annotation of a birth certificate because the chief instrument to record the truth about one's conception and birth is the birth certificate. An appendix to the birth certificate recording the fact of donor conception should be created at birth and made available to the person at majority.

It might be contended that such a system would invade the parents' privacy but as the International Donor Offspring Alliance argues:

> It is not open to recipient parents or anyone else to decide on a child's behalf that it does not need to know or [that the child] can justifiably be deceived or deprived of information. Requiring that birth certificates record the truth does not impinge on recipient parents' lives in any way but it safeguards information that properly belongs to the offspring. Including the name of the donor as well as the fact of donor conception is the only means by which donor offsprings' rights and their dignity as people can be honoured. The principal legal instrumentality of this should be the person's birth certificate, which should make it clear that donor conception has taken place. The genetic parentage should be recorded on the certificate itself or associated documentation available to the donor-conceived person concerned.[16]

The International Donor Offspring Alliance makes a cogent case for the establishment of a system to create accurate birth certificates. Because government is involved in regulating donor conception in Canada,[17] it must not cause, promote or collude in deceiving people or depriving them of information about their own origins; nor may it discriminate against particular groups in terms of the provision of significant information about their own lives.

Consequently, the birth certificates of donor-conceived persons must enable them to know that they have been donor-conceived.

2.1.2 Right to Know One's Identity

Donor-conceived people ought to be in a position to know the identity of their progenitors and their medical, social and cultural history. Such information ought to be collected by clinics and sent by them to be stored in the provincial or territorial registry to be made available to the donor-conceived person at the age of majority, with or without the consent of the donor or the person who received the gametes.

Given that such prospective legislation would prevent anonymous donation, future donors will donate gametes in the expectation that they will be identified and contacted by their offspring. Nevertheless, there ought to be a state-run agency with counselling services available to facilitate the initial meeting between donor and the donor-conceived person to meet one another, as is offered to adoptees and birth parents.[18]

2.2 Principles and Suggestions for Implementation in Law Reform or New Legislation

As provinces develop legislation, the following principles should guide them.

2.2.1 The Interests of Offspring Should Have Priority

The "health and well-being" of people conceived by assisted human reproduction has not been legislatively defined. Some argue that the donor-conceived do not need to know their origins.[19] But the very premise of adoption disclosure law throughout Canada is that, at minimum, the state should assist people to come to know their progenitors if they mutually agree. Law reform or legislation giving effect to the principle that the health and well-being of the children should have the highest priority could be modeled after sections 3 and 4 of New Zealand's *Human Assisted Reproductive Technology Act 2004*[20] which, specifically declares, amongst other things, that "donor offspring should be made aware of their genetic origins and be able to access information about those origins."[21]

To reinforce this principle, such provisions might also state that, in the event of a conflict between the rights of donor offspring to know their genetic heritage and the privacy interests of gamete and embryo donors, the rights of the donor offspring conceived after the promulgation of the law will prevail.

2.2.2 Accurate, Comprehensive Records Should be Made and Retained

The provincial and territorial statutes should establish a comprehensive framework for collecting, verifying, preserving, updating and disclosing health and personal information (both identifying and non-identifying) about gamete donors, women who agree to gestate a child, persons who have undergone an assisted reproduction procedure or persons conceived by means of such procedures. Like provincial adoption registries,[22] there ought to be statutorily-established registries to preserve and update records to be disclosed in accordance with the principle that the interests of the offspring are the priority.

The legislation ought to require the collection, verification, retention and updating of specific information about each donor. The task of collecting information should be a statutory duty required of physicians, a provincial or territorial agency and social workers.

2.2.2.1 Obligations of Physicians

The Uniform Law Conference of Canada in its *Uniform Child Status Act*[23] has contemplated that physicians have certain obligations to create and maintain records.

> 11.6 (1) Every duly qualified medical practitioner who carries out procedures that are intended to result in an assisted conception shall maintain, in the form and manner prescribed in the regulations, records indicating the donor and recipient of every egg or sperm used in the assisted conception procedures.

The statute would require physicians to submit such records to a government agency.

> 11.6 (2) Every duly qualified medical practitioner who carries out procedures that are intended to result in assisted conceptions shall submit information within the knowledge of the practitioner with respect to:
> (a) assisted conceptions that result from procedures carried out by the practitioner,
> (b) births resulting from assisted conceptions that result from procedures carried out by the practitioner, and
> (c) procedures carried out by the practitioner that are intended to result in assisted conception, where the practitioner does not know whether conception was or was not achieved.
> (3) Every duly qualified medical practitioner shall submit information within the knowledge of the practitioner with respect to births of children delivered by the practitioner that result from assisted conceptions.
> (4) The information mentioned in subsection (2) or (3) is to be submitted to the agency designated in the regulations in the form and manner and at the times prescribed in the regulations.

2.2.2.2 Obligations of an Agency

The agency would then be required to maintain the records.

> (5) The agency that receives information pursuant to subsection (4)
> (a) shall maintain a permanent registry of the information

Legislators should then develop procedures for disclosure of the records that physicians send to the Agency to offspring, recipients and donors.

2.2.2.3 Obligations of Social Workers

Such physician records would not, however, be sufficient. They would not include all categories of information that are created for other children who are separated from their genetic parents. Because children of gamete donation and children of adoption are alike in this regard, a government social worker should be required to collect the same information about donors as they are required to collect about parents who surrender a child for adoption. Specifically, and to paraphrase the requirements in British Columbia,[24] social workers should, with respect to each donor, be required by law to obtain information about the medical and social history of the donor and the donor's biological family that includes, as practicable, all of the following:

> (1) (a) a physical description of the donor, and information about
> (i) his or her personality and personal interests,
> (ii) his or her cultural, racial and linguistic heritage, and
> (iii) his or her religious and spiritual values and beliefs;
> (b) a detailed health history of the donor, including
> (i) the lifestyle of the donor respecting usage of tobacco, alcohol and prescription and non-prescription drugs,
> (ii) in cases of "surrogate motherhood" the prenatal information respecting the birth mother, and
> (iii) any medical condition and other health information about the donor that may be relevant to the child;
> (c) a detailed social history of the donor, including
> (i) the relationship between the donor and the recipient, if any,
> (ii) details about any other child born to either of the donor or the recipient,
> (iii) educational background and, if applicable, future educational plans,
> (iv) particulars respecting past, present and future employment, and
> (v) family background information about the donor and the sisters and brothers (both by birth and adoption) of the donor;

(d) the reason that the donor has decided to surrender gametes to conceive a child

(2) The foregoing information must be in the form of a written report.

2.2.3 Authorization of Identifying and Medical/Social/Cultural Information

Provisions in either federal law reform or provincial legislation should specifically authorize the disclosure (in enumerated circumstances and to specified persons) of *both* non-identifying medical, social and cultural information *and* identifying background, demographic, and contact information regarding gamete donors, gestational carriers, persons who have undergone an assisted reproduction procedure or persons conceived by means of such procedures.

2.2.4 Independent Counselling Services

Provincial legislation should recognize the short and long-term psychological, emotional and practical effects of gamete donation and use, and mandate that counseling and other types of professional support independent of fertility clinics be offered throughout the process, to gamete donors, gestational carriers, persons who have undergone an assisted reproduction procedure or persons conceived by means of such procedures.

2.2.5 Provisions to Establish the Supremacy of Legislation

Provincial legislation should also stipulate that the rights, rules and procedures established in relation to the collection, verification, retention, updating and disclosure of gamete donor information (both identifying and non-identifying) must prevail in the event of a conflict or an inconsistency with any other enactment. Such provisions ought also to confirm that any regulation promulgated under the statute will prevail over any other bylaw, rule, order or regulation with which it conflicts.

2.3 Application of Law Reform or New Legislation: Retroactive or only Prospective?

In legislating, government ought to establish principled policy regarding whether such participant and Offspring rights would obtain retrospectively or prospectively only, or if some compromise between the two might be achieved.

Arguments have been advanced that past gamete donors and users of assisted human reproduction services entered into relationships with each other on the understanding that their privacy and confidentiality would be protected.[25] Such arguments attend to the interests only of adults and, in effect, hold that their interests in privacy and confidentiality are morally superior to the Offsprings' interest in health and wellbeing. Irrespective of the merits of these arguments, government efforts that aim retrospectively to override adults' interests might find such efforts politically impracticable.[26]

Therefore, provinces should, at minimum, establish reunion registers to permit meetings of willing people who were participants to donor conceptions that occurred *prior to* the enactment of legislation banning donor anonymity. Such registries would require that infertility practitioners send patient records with donor identification to the provincial registry. The registrar would then be required to correlate those records accurately with birth records, given that not all assisted human reproduction participants report pregnancies to the infertility service providers. The registrar should have power and a statutory duty discretely to inform parties that a related person is searching for them.

Some might argue that it would be futile to create mutual consent registries because donors would not want contact with their offspring. This conclusion is probably incorrect. A United Kingdom study of men who donated semen considered the donors' attitudes and views about a proposed contact register concluded that many respondents would agree to a contact registry provided that they had some control over the information released and whether they would be contacted, and they had access to ongoing information, advice or support from professionals who are skilled and experienced in search and reunion services.[27] Another UK study reported that it is possible to recruit semen donors who are required to be identifiable.[28] So it is probable that at least some people who donated semen in the past would be willing to join a registry to facilitate meetings among donors, participants and Offspring.

3. Provincial Legislation to Clarify Legal Parentage Where Children are born of Donor Gametes

If government requires that donor-conceived people be in a position to know the truth about their conception and that gamete donation no longer be permitted to be anonymous, then law and regulation must address not just the practice itself but also the legal outcome of the practice, that is, the legal status of all the parties in relation to one another.

3.1 History of Call for Legislative Action To Clarify Parentage Status

The need to provide certain legal status to participants in, and offspring of, assisted human reproduction has been an issue in Canada for at least 19 years. As long ago as 1993, the Royal Commission on New Reproductive Technologies lamented the fact that the provinces and territories in general had not acted to make clear the status under family law of gamete providers.[29] It called upon government to act with alacrity to resolve outstanding issues *before* individual families found themselves in situations that could be resolved only through recourse to the courts.[30]

A year earlier, the Uniform Law Conference of Canada had actually addressed the problem by creating draft legislation that it made available for adoption by provinces to address this issue. The *Uniform Child Status Act*,[31] discussed above, aimed, *inter alia*, to help legislatures create legislation to clarify the legal status of children conceived by assisted human reproduction.

But only four of thirteen jurisdictions have taken steps to do so. The Yukon,[32] Alberta,[33] Newfoundland and Labrador[34] and Quebec[35] have amended their legislation to make clear the parental rights and responsibilities of male gamete providers. Alberta[36] and Quebec[37] have done so also with respect to ovum providers. But in many other parts of the country, the rights and duties of gamete donors to the children of their gametes have not been established.[38]

Indeed, fourteen years after the Royal Commission called on provinces to act with alacrity, the Attorney General of British Columbia's office noted that such action had not yet occurred there. In a discussion paper, it stated that:

> The law can best protect the parent-child relationship through a legal framework that provides clarity and certainty of legal parentage for all children at the earliest possible time. All children born in British Columbia are entitled to equal treatment regardless of the circumstances of their conception and birth. They all should have the benefit of the stability and certainty about their family relationships that could be provided by clear rules for determining legal parentage at birth.

3.2 Proposed Legislation to Clarify Parentage of the Donor-Conceived

The establishment of rules to determine legal parentage is a matter of family law that (apart from marriage and divorce) is the jurisdiction of the provinces. They have power and responsibility to regulate parental status, rights and duties.[39]

Provinces could act quickly by considering the adoption of the provisions created by the Uniform Law Conference of Canada.[40] These provisions apply with respect to people conceived by assisted conception:

> 11. In sections 11.1 to 11.6, "assisted conception" means a conception resulting
> (a) by means other than sexual intercourse, or
> (b) by removal and implantation of an embryo after sexual intercourse.

The provisions address parental status concisely in stating that with respect to egg providers:

> 11.4 (1) A woman whose egg is used in an assisted conception and who does not give birth to the child conceived using her egg is deemed not to be the mother of the child.

Likewise, draft legislation is available to state that a sperm donor who is not the partner of the birth mother would not have legal paternal obligations toward the child:

> 11.4 (2) A man whose sperm is used in an assisted conception and who is not presumed to be the father of a child pursuant to section 9 is deemed not to be the father of the child.

All participants in, and offspring of, assisted reproduction would benefit if the legal status of the resulting families were clarified and standardized across the country.

In addition, such clarification would have the pragmatic effect of ensuring a supply of gametes in an era when donors must agree to be known to their offspring. Potential gamete providers are more likely to agree to donate in an identified manner if they can be assured that they will have no financial obligations toward the children so created. Likewise, users of assisted human reproduction will be more likely to accept gametes from identified donors if they know in advance that donors may make no legal claim to the child. As one commentator argued:[41]

> Whether a woman is married or single, she ordinarily chooses insemination only on the condition that the donors not demand any of the rights and responsibilities of fatherhood. In both cases, when the sperm donor is a complete stranger, the prospect of sharing parenting of the child would be an effective deterrent to choosing this technique.

Thus, to permit donor offspring to obtain identifying information about their progenitors while ensuring that these progenitors will not have the responsibilities and entitlements of parenthood requires the provinces to legislate in the manner exemplified by the *Uniform Child Status Act*.

The Uniform Law Conference of Canada specifically states, however, that jurisdictions that use the *Uniform Child Status Act* as a precedent should check their relevant statutes and amend them accordingly to ensure that they are compatible with the *Uniform Act*. Numerous existing provincial statutes and regulations would require amending to stipulate that donors are not included within the legal definitions assigned to terms such as "mother", "father", "parent" or "guardian". The list of statutes and regulations requiring some sort of amendment is potentially long. What follows below is an attempt to consider what legislation might require attention in the most populous common law provinces of Ontario and British Columbia to specify the legal relatedness of donor to offspring, to protect donor assets and estates, and to address privacy law that might otherwise prevent donor identification.

3.3.1 Ontario

3.3.1.1 Acts To Be Amended To Specify The Relatedness Amongst Donors And Their Offspring

Ontario statutory definitions assigned to the terms "birth father", "birth mother", "birth parents", "father", "mother", "parent", "stepparent", "guardian", "next of kin", and "relative" would require amendment so that donors of eggs, sperm or embryos are not included within these definitions. A list of potentially affected Acts includes:

1. *Children's Law Reform Act*, R.S.O. 1990, Chapter C. 12 – definitions could be specified in section 1.
2. *Change of Name Act*, R.S.O. 1990, c. C. 7 – definitions could be specified in section 1.
3. *Child and Family Services Act*, R.S.O. 1990, c. C. 11 – definitions could be specified in section 3.
4. *Compensation for Victims of Crime Act*, R.S.O. 1990, c. C. 24 – definitions could be specified in section 1.
5. *Conveyancing and Law of Property Act*, R.S.O. 1990, c. C. 34 – definitions could be specified in sections 1 or 45.
6. *Credit Unions and Caisses Populaires Act, 1994*, S.O. 1994, c. 11 – definitions could be specified in section 1.

7. *Education Act*, R.S.O. 1990, c. E. 2 – definitions could be specified in sections 1 or 18.
8. *Estates Administration Act*, R.S.O. 1990, Chapter E.22 – definitions could be specified in section 1.
9. *Fairness for Parents and Employees Act (Teachers' Withdrawal of Services), 1997*, S.O. 1997, Chapter 32 – definitions could be specified in section 1.
10. *Family Benefits Act*, R.S.O. 1990, c. F. 2 – definitions could be specified in section 1.
11. *Family Responsibility and Support Arrears Enforcement Act, 1996*, S.O. 1996, c. 31 – definitions could be specified in section 1.
12. *Freedom of Information and Protection of Privacy Act*, R.S.O. 1990, c. F. 31 – definitions could be specified in section 2.
13. *Parental Responsibility Act, 2000*, S.O. 2000, c. 4 – definitions could be specified in section 1.
14. *Personal Health Information Protection Act, 2004*, S.O. 2004, c. 3, Schedule A – definitions could be specified in section 2, but may not be necessary for this Act.
15. *Succession Law Reform Act*, R.S.O. 1990, c. S. 26 definitions could be specified in section 1.
16. *Trillium Gift of Life Network Act*, R.S.O. 1990, c. H. 20 – definitions could be specified in section 5.
17. *Victims' Bill of Rights, 1995*, S.O. 1995, c. 6 – definitions could be specified in section 1.
18. *Vital Statistics Act*, R.S.O. 1990, c. V. 4 – definitions could be specified in section 1. Specific categories for information collected about donor offspring might be necessary.
19. *Workplace Safety and Insurance Act, 1997*, S.O. 1997, c. 16, Schedule A – definitions could be specified in section 2, however, changes to the *Family Law Act* may cover potential problems under this Act since this Act uses the *Family Law Act* to define terms such as "parent".
20. *Adoption Information Disclosure*, O. Reg. 464/07 – definitions could be specified in section 1.

Article 16 of the *Intercountry Adoption Act, 1998*, S.O. 1998, c. 29, should be amended to include donor history if applicable.

3.3.2 British Columbia

3.3.2.1 Acts to Be Amended To Specify the Relatedness Amongst Donors and Their Offspring

1. *Adoption Act*, R.S.B.C. 1996, c. 5, ss. 1, 13(2) – In addition to section 1, section 13(2) requires clarification so that gamete donors are not statutorily deemed to be 'the child's father' for the purposes of consenting to adoption.
2. *Child Care BC Act*, S.B.C. 2001, c. 4, s. 1.
3. *Child Care Subsidy Act*, R.S.B.C. 1996, c. 26, s. 1.
4. *Child, Family and Community Service Act*, R.S.B.C. 1996, c. 46, s. 1 – Amendments to section 1 definitions of the term 'parent' would preclude difficulties that might otherwise arise in respect of guardianship under Part 3, Division 5 – Continuing Custody Hearings and Orders.
5. *Family Compensation Act*, R.S.B.C. 1996, c. 126, s. 1.
6. *Family Relations Act*, R.S.B.C. 1996, c. 128, ss. 1, 95, 121.
   Amendments to these sections and the definitions assigned to the terms 'parent' and 'father' would ensure that gamete donors were not unwittingly implicated in conflicts over custody, access or guardianship as governed by Part 2 of the Act. This holds true for obligations relating to child support established in section 88 of the Act.
7. *Law and Equity Act*, R.S.B.C. 1996, c. 253, s. 61(1) – As this provision outlines how 'child status' is typically established under British Columbia law, it would be prudent for this subsection to state, specifically, that a person is not, in law, to be deemed the child of a donor of eggs, sperm or embryos in the process of assisted reproduction.
8. *Parental Responsibility Act*, S.B.C. 2001, c. 45, s. 1.
9. *School Act*, R.S.B.C. 1996, c. 412, c. 1.
10. *Victims of Crime Act*, R.S.B.C. 1996, c. 478, s. 1.
11. *Vital Statistics Act*, R.S.B.C. 1996, c. 479, s. 3.
12. *Youth Justice Act*, S.B.C. 2003, c. 85, s. 1.

3.3.2.2 Amendments to Statutes Governing Wills, Wills Variation and the Administration of Estates to Protect Donor Estates from Claims from Offspring

1. *Estate Administration Act*, R.S.B.C. 1996, c. 122, ss. 2, 81, 89 and 91 – Section 2, which outlines the application of the Act, might be amended to state that nothing in the Act should be taken to create testamentary entitlements in favour of donor offspring who have not otherwise been specifically named and provided for in a gamete donor's will.

To ensure that donor offspring are not statutorily entitled to distribution of the estate of an intestate donor, sections 81 and 89 would likely need to be amended to stipulate that donor offspring are not included within the definitions of 'issue' or 'next of kin' for the purposes of Part 10 of the Act. Because Section 91 permits descendants and relatives of the deceased, who were conceived before the person's death but born afterwards, to inherit as if they had been born in the lifetime of the intestate and had survived the intestate, section 91 would probably need amendment to ensure that its application was specified *not* to extend to donor offspring.

2. *Wills Variation Act*, R.S.B.C. 1996, c. 490, s. 2 – Section 2 would require amending to state that donor offspring are not to be included within the term 'children' (as employed therein) so as to be eligible to initiate an action seeking adequate provision for proper maintenance and support from the deceased gamete donor's estate.

3.3.2.3 Amendments to Prevent Privacy Legislation from Being Used to Limit Exercise of Offspring's Right to Know the Identity of Their Progenitors

1. *Freedom of Information and Protection of Privacy Act*, R.S.B.C. 1996, c. 165, ss. 2, 22, 26, 33 – Potentially, a simple amendment to section 2 might suffice to ensure the primacy of the information collection, retention and disclosure mechanisms established in any provincial legislation enacted to address assisted human reproduction. For instance, section 2 might read:

> (2) This Act does not replace or derogate from other procedures for access to information, including those established in the [name of provincial assisted human reproduction statute], or limit in any way access to information that is not personal information and is available to the public.

Notably, it might be argued that subsection 22(4)(c) of the Act,[42] as presently drafted, is sufficient to ensure that the disclosure of identifying information and medical, social and cultural information regarding participants and offspring, would not be deemed to be a "disclosure harmful to personal privacy."

Further, section 79 of the Act (which outlines the relationship of the Act to other Acts) already states as follows:

If a provision of this Act is inconsistent or in conflict with a provision of another Act, the provision of this Act prevails unless the other Act expressly provides that it, or a provision of it, applies despite this Act.

Consequently, statutes regulating assisted human reproduction ought to state that their provisions regarding the collection, retention, updating and disclosure of *both* identifying and non-identifying information about participants and offspring prevail if they conflict with other statutes.

2. *Personal Information Protection Act*, S.B.C. 2003, c. 63, s. 3 – If this Act were to have application in relation to the disclosure of gamete donor information (both identifying and non-identifying), section 3 might need to be amended to ensure that a statute permitting donor disclosure prevails over the *Personal Information Protection Act*.

3. *Privacy Act*, R.S.B.C. 1996, c. 373, s. 2 – Significantly, subsection 2(2)(c) of this statute states, in part, that "[a]n act or conduct is not a violation of privacy if … the act or conduct was authorized or required under a law in force in British Columbia …"

   Consequently, it appears that donor disclosure authorized by statute would not constitute a statutory violation of privacy under this Act.

4. *E-Health (Personal Health Information Access and Protection of Privacy) Act*, S.B.C. 2008, c. 38 – A simple amendment to section 2 of this Act (the interpretation section) might be enough to ensure that a donor disclosure statute prevails over this statute.[43]

3.3.2.4 Amendments to Rules and Procedures Regarding Patient Records Promulgated by the College of Physicians and Surgeons of British Columbia

1. *Health Professions Act*, R.S.B.C. 1996, c. 183, s. 19 – Bylaws (and rules) promulgated by the British Columbia College of Physicians and Surgeons under section 19 of this Act would require amendment to enable the collection, retention, updating or disclosure of identifying or non-identifying personal health information, particularly in relation to the practice of assisted human reproduction. The rules regarding Medical Records in Private Physicians Offices should be amended to require that such records may be held by an independent authority.[44]

3.3.3 Summary

The foregoing list of suggested amendments to Ontario and British Columbia legislation, prompted by the Consequential Amendments notation in Section 11.6 of the *Uniform Child Status Act*, is preliminary and focuses on those statutes and regulations that require amendment to clarify the rights and responsibilities toward offspring of donors and recipients in gamete donation.

4. Conclusion

The goal of promoting the interests of the children of assisted human reproduction tends to receive universal support in the abstract. But when it comes to operationalizing this principle, disagreement abounds.[45] Some physicians, parents and commentators do not believe that the interests of future children in knowing their progenitors should be permitted to limit the choice of adults to agree to donor anonymity.[46] On the assumption, however, that health and well-being of children of donor gametes ought to be the highest concern and that a ban on anonymity promotes those interests, this chapter has considered what legislative changes ought to occur in Canadian common law jurisdictions (using the most populous two provinces as examples) to promote the health and well-being interests of donor-conceived people. Provincial and territorial governments have the constitutional authority and the moral obligation to act in the interests of Offspring by making it possible for them to know: (1) that they were conceived by donor gametes; (2) the identity of their gamete providers; (3) the current medical history of their gamete providers; and (4) their legal relation to their progenitor.

Bibliography

Baird, Patricia A. "Reproductive Technology and the Evolution of Family Law", *Canadian Family Law Quarterly*, Volume 15 (1997): 103.

Blyth, Eric. "The Role of Birth Certificates in Relation to Access to Biographical and Genetic History in Donor Conception," *International Journal of Children's Rights*, 17 (2009): 207-233, at 216.

Crawshaw M.A., E.D. Blyth and K.D. Daniels. "Past Semen Donors' Views about the Use of a Voluntary Contact Register," *Reproductive Biomed Online*, 2007 April, 14(4): 411-7.

Frith, Lucy. "Telling is More Important than Ever: Rights and Donor Conception," Comment, *BioNews*, 542, 19 January 2010.

Daniels, Ken. "Donor Gametes: Anonymous or Identified?" *Clinical Obstetrics & Gynaecology*, Volume 21, Issue 1, February 2007: 113-128.

-- "Anonymity and Openness and the Recruitment of Gamete Donors. Part I: Semen Donors," Human Fertility (Cambridge, England). September 2007, 10(3):151-8.

Daniels, Ken R., Eric Blyth, Darrel Hall, and Kathy M. Hanson. "The Best Interests of the Child in Assisted Human Reproduction: The Interplay between the State, Professionals, and Parents," *Politics and the Life Sciences* 19, 1 (March 2000): 33-45.

Gollancz, David. "Time to Stop Lying," *The Guardian*, Thursday, 2 August 2007, http://www.guardian.co.uk/society/2007/aug/02/childrensservices.humanrights.

Hyder, Nishat. "Lawsuit Against US Clinic Reignites Sperm Donor Debate", quoting Sean Tipton of the American Society of Reproductive Medicine. *BioNews*, 12 October 2009.

Samuels, Elizabeth J. "The Idea of Adoption: An Inquiry into the History of Adult Adoptee Access to Birth Records", *Rutgers Law Review*, 53 (2000-2001) 367.

Sloss, E. and R. Mykitiuk. "The Challenge of the New Reproductive Technologies to Family Law," *Royal Commission on New Reproductive Technologies (RCNRT), Research Volume 4*, c. 3. Ottawa: Canada Communications Group, 1993.

Wikler, Daniel. "Policy Issues in Donor Insemination," *Stanford Law and Policy Review*, 6:2 (1995): 47.

Notes

1 Assisted Human Reproduction Act, (Canada 2004), c. 2, A-13.4, s. 2.
2 *Reference re Assisted Human Reproduction Act*, 2010 SCC 61. On 18 December 2007, Quebec had brought a reference to the Quebec Court Appeal regarding the constitutionality of many provisions of the *Assisted Human Reproduction Act*, S.C. 2004, c.2.
3 This chapter does not purport to discuss the role of the territories given that they do not have assisted human reproduction clinics and have relatively very small populations.
4 Uniform Law Conference of Canada, "What We Do", http://www.ulcc.ca/en/about.
5 *Supra*, note 1.
6 For discussion, please see, Eric Blyth and Lucy Frith, "Donor-Conceived People's Access to Genetic and Biographical History: An Analysis of Provisions in Different Jurisdictions Permitting Disclosure of Donor Identity" International Journal of Law, Policy and the Family Volume23, Issue 2, pp. 174-191.
7 The medical history of the donor needs to be made current to take into account the onset of hereditary diseases and conditions.
8 Lucy Frith, "Telling is More Important Than Ever: Rights and Donor Conception," *Comment, BioNews*, 542, 19 January 2010.
9 *Ibid*.
10 Ken Daniels, "Donor Gametes: Anonymous or Identified?" *Clinical Obstetrics & Gynaecology*, Volume 21, Issue 1, February 2007: 113-128.
11 House of Lords House of Commons, Joint Committee on the Human Tissue and Embryos (Draft) Bill, 2006-2007, Session 2006-2007,
http://www.publications.parliament.uk/pa/jt200607/jtselect/jtembryos/169/169.pdf.
12 Eric Blyth, "The Role of Birth Certificates in Relation to Access to Biographical and Genetic History in Donor Conception," *International Journal of Children's Rights*, 17 (2009): 207-233, at 216.
13 *Ibid*.
14 David Gollancz, "Time to Stop Lying", *The Guardian*, Thursday, 2 August 2007, http://www.guardian.co.uk/society/2007/aug/02/childrensservices.humanrights.
15 United Nations Convention on the Rights of the Child, Adopted and opened for signature, ratification and accession by General Assembly resolution 44/25 of 20 November 1989 entry into force 2 September 1990, in accordance with article 49. http://www.crin.org/docs/resources/treaties/uncrc.asp#Seven.
16 These are the proposals of the International Donor Offspring Alliance. http://www.idoalliance.org.
17 International Donor Offspring Alliance, "What we believe," http://www.idoalliance.org.
18 See, for example, Search and reunion services established under section 71 of the Adoption Act, R.S.B.C. 1996, c. 5.

19 See, for example, D. Le Lannou Secret et anonymat du don *de gamètes*, Journal de Gynécologie Obstétrique et Fertilité 2010 May; 38(5):324-31; Ole Schou, Founder, Cryos Sperm Bank, Denmark, http://www.kristeligt-dagblad.dk/artikel/300338:Etik–Paa-jagt-efter-donor-137 Posted on the Donor Sibling Registry: http://www.donorsiblingregistry.com/DSRblog/?cat=6 217-226 of Naomi Cahn's book "Test Tube Families," Newill R. Personal view. Br Med J (Clin Res Ed). 1982 Nov 13; 285(6352):1419.
20 *Human Assisted Reproductive Technology Act 2004* (N.Z.), 2004/92.
21 *Ibid.*, s. 4.
22 See, for example, Search and reunion services established under section 71 of the Adoption Act, R.S.B.C. 1996, c. 5.
23 http://www.ulcc.ca/en/us/index.cfm?sec=1&sub=1u9
24 Adoption Regulation, B.C. Reg. 291/96, s. 4.
25 Nishat Hyder, Lawsuit Against US Clinic Reignites Sperm Donor Debate, quoting Sean Tipton of the American Society of Reproductive Medicine. *BioNews*, 12 October 2009.
26 In *Cheskes v. Ontario (Attorney General),* the court struck down Ontario legislation that would have granted adoptees or birth parents almost unfettered access to adoption records. To prevent access, the relevant party would have to appear before a provincial board to explain why a disclosure veto should be granted to prevent sexual harm or significant physical or emotional harm to the applicants. The court ruled that the impugned law violated the parties' liberty interest not in accordance with section 7 of the Charter. New legislation was eventually passed permitting retroactive disclosure of adoption records provided the party had not filed a disclosure veto him or herself. 2007 CanLII 38387 (ON S.C.), *Child and Family Services Act*, R. S. O. 1990, c. C. 11, as amended 2010, c. 10, s. 23.
27 M.A. Crawshaw, E.D. Blyth and K.D. Daniels, "Past Semen Donors' Views About the Use of a Voluntary Contact Register," *Reproductive Biomed Online*, April 2007, 14(4):411-7.
28 K. Daniels, "Anonymity and Openness and the Recruitment of Gamete Donors. Part I: Semen Donors," *Human Fertility* (Cambridge, England), September 2007, 10(3):151-8.
29 *Proceed with Care*, Final Report of The Royal Commission on New Reproductive Technologies, (Ottawa: Canada Communications Group, 1993).
30 Patricia A. Baird, Reproductive Technology and the Evolution of Family Law, *Canadian Family Law Quarterly*, vol. 15 (1997): 103.
31 Uniform Law Conference of Canada, Uniform Child Status Act, April 1992, online: Uniform Law Conference of Canada, <http://www.ulcc.ca/en/us/index.cfm?sec=1&sub=1u9> [Uniform C.S.A.].
32 *Children's Act*, R.S.Y. 2002, c. 31., s. 13(6).
33 *Family Law Act*, S.A. 2003, c. F-4.5., s. 13.
34 *Children's Law Act*, R.S.N.L. 1990, chapter C-13 as amended, s.12.
35 *Civil Code of Quebec*, S.Q. 1991, c. 64 (C.C.Q.).
36 *Family Law Act*, S.A. 2003, c. F-4.5, s. 12.
37 *Civil Code of Quebec*, S.Q. 1991, c. 64 (C.C.Q.), s. 538.
38 E. Sloss and R. Mykitiuk, "The Challenge of the New Reproductive Technologies to Family Law," *Royal Commission on New Reproductive Technologies (RCNRT), Research Volume 4*, c. 3. (Ottawa: Canada Communications Group, 1993).
39 Constitution Act, 1982 (being Schedule B to the Canada Act 1982 (U.K.), 1982, c. 11) ss. 92(12, 13, 16).
40 http://www.ulcc.ca/en/us/index.cfm?sec=1&sub=1u9.
41 Daniel Wikler, "Policy Issues in Donor Insemination," *Stanford Law and Policy Review*, 6:2 1995: 47 at 52.
42 Subsection 22(4)(c) of the *Freedom of Information and Protection of Privacy Act*, R.S.B.C. 1996, c. 165, reads:
" (4) A disclosure of personal information is not an unreasonable invasion of a third party's personal privacy if.
(c) an enactment of British Columbia or Canada authorizes the disclosure,"
43 For example, such amendment might state something like: "Nothing in this Act shall be construed so as to abrogate or derogate from the rights, responsibilities and requirements recognized and affirmed in the [name of the provincially enacted assisted human reproduction

act] and the [name of the provincially enacted assisted human reproduction act] prevails over any enactment that it conflicts or is inconsistent with, and a regulation under the [name of the provincially enacted human reproduction act] prevails over any other bylaw, rule, order or regulation with which it conflicts."

44 British Columbia College of Physicians and Surgeons, Medical Records in Private Physicians Offices, online: https://www.cpsbc.ca/publications-resources/resource-manual.

45 Ken R. Daniels, Eric Blyth, Darrel Hall, and Kathy M. Hanson, "The Best Interests of the Child in Assisted Human Reproduction: The Interplay between the State, Professionals, and Parents," *Politics and the Life Sciences* 19, 1 (March 2000): 33-45.

46 *Supra*, note 36.

PART SEVEN

WHAT CAN WE CONCLUDE?

This book concludes where it began: with the words of a donor-conceived person. David Gollancz, a solicitor in the City of London, England, learned that he was donor-conceived when he was 12 years old. It is fitting that his is the last chapter of this book because he addresses the subject incisively from more than one perspective. From personal experience, he attests to the fact that donor anonymity can cause great pain. As a legal professional, Gollancz focuses on the moral obligations of the state to the donor-conceived. In a book dedicated to helping policy and law makers regulate the current practice of anonymous gamete donation, Gollancz, knowing that these are matters of the heart, goes to the heart of the matter. He argues that the state should not be party to the creation of fraudulent birth certificates and that, at the age of majority, individuals should have access to their accurate birth record. Gollancz concedes that there will be problems of implementation, but asserts the importance of the principle: the stories of our origins are an entitlement and among our most precious goods; while we cannot prevent individuals from lying to us, the state must refuse to be party to a lie.

Chapter Twenty-Two

Time to Stop Lying[1]

David Gollancz

One summer evening in 1965, when I was 12, my father said he had something to tell me. We went into my bedroom and, as I sat on the bed and he stood, he explained that he was not my biological father: I (and my sister) had been conceived using the sperm of an anonymous donor.

That was the start of a long journey. I am in my sixth decade now; I started speaking publicly about donor conception in 1994 and since then I have learned much about the questions I think donor conception raises, about what family is and about where rights reside. I have had the extraordinary experience of finding a number of half-siblings, ranging in age from their early 80s to their early 40s and living in the United Kingdom, the United States and Canada, all children of the same man – one of whom, Barry Stevens, is a co-contributor to this book. I have visited our donor's birthplace in Austria; and I have had the privilege of meeting and sharing the stories of many people whose lives have been touched and shaped by their involvement in donor conception.

In 1994, I and others started to campaign for an end to the United Kingdom law that protected anonymity of donors. In 2002, Jo Rose, another donor offspring, brought a claim against the UK government asserting that by denying her the possibility of identifying her donor, she had been deprived of her human rights. Although her case did not proceed to final judgment, the court found that there was a question to be determined – the *Human Rights Act* was "engaged" – and the government agreed to support the setting up of a voluntary register that could help donors and their offspring find each other.

As a result, in 2004, regulations were passed in the United Kingdom abolishing donor anonymity for the future. But the great problem remained: the overwhelming majority of parents in heterosexual relationships never tell their children that they were conceived from donor sperm or eggs, so many people are unlikely ever to inquire as to the identity of their donor, even if it is available. The voluntary register, UK Donor Link, has achieved some great successes, but is under-resourced and has relatively few registrants.

Another milestone was reached in 2007 when a United Kingdom parliamentary committee, which had been scrutinising the government's draft human tissue and embryos bill, recommended that the birth certificates of the donor-conceived should record the fact that they had been conceived using donor gametes (eggs or sperm).

So why is it important that donors be identified on their offspring's birth certificates?

Human beings are storytellers. We use stories to remember our past and to help us plan for the future by recording shared experience. We use them to account for our experience: to explain, exonerate, atone and celebrate. We use them, on every level, as a means of explaining and exploring who we are. I have come to believe that this storytelling is at the heart of our humanity: that it is at the heart of our ability to feel part of the world. Without it, we are flotsam: mere accidental concatenations of unaccountable desires and meaningless memories floating in the random currents of experience without context.

But for the donor-conceived, their story can be a lie. When my father told me the truth back in 1965, I felt as though someone was standing in front of me, tearing up my autobiography page by page. Of course, all the things in my story had happened – but the "me" to whom they had happened was not the me who had been telling himself the story. Not the descendant of Polish Jewish rabbis and scholars; not, in fact, cousin to my cousins or even, it seemed, properly entitled to my name. Of course, the sentimentalists say, "But of course you are entitled to your name, of course the culture and background of your paternal family belongs to you" – and of course they are not entirely wrong; those things can be claimed (and recently I went for the first time to Golancz, in Poland, in precisely such an act of reclamation) – but it is not the same. Being entitled to choose to claim a family heritage is not the same as simply owning it.

I believe that no one is entitled to tell that lie. No one is entitled deliberately to deceive other people, or deprive them of essential information, about their personal history. Our stories belong to us and we are entitled to the truth. This is not just some abstract right, it is a practical issue: people may need to know their family medical history, for example, or to understand what may otherwise be inexplicable physical or personality traits. But I do not think that it needs to be justified: we do not have to explain why or prove that we are entitled to know the truth about our own lives.

There are a number of reasons why parents lie to their children about the circumstances of their births: people want to believe that their infertility problem has been cured – that they are the family they would have been without infertility. Acknowledging the donor as a real person makes that more difficult. Infertile parents, particularly men, often feel profound shame and grief about their inability to beget their own children; again, denying that the donor exists may make it easier to avoid those painful feelings. My own father, and others I have known, have been afraid that if the truth were revealed, their children would not love them. And our understanding of the real importance of genetics in both physical health and personal development is extremely recent and still growing. Until relatively recently, sperm was seen as just fertiliser, rather than what it really is: the carrier of DNA, the book in which half the recipe for a new human being is written.

I think it will always be challenging for recipient parents to tell their children the truth; I think that, regrettably, many or most will tend to avoid doing so. And I would not pretend that it is easy. My father and I were, I think, closer and better with each other, eventually, than we would have been had the lie been sustained – but our relationship was forever subject to a sort of conditionality, a sense of choice that does not exist between my daughters and me. No one can legislate for parents, any more than any other group of people, to behave with impeccable moral probity; people will always lie to their children for all sorts of reasons, some of them no doubt benevolent.

But the state should not be party to such deceptions: the birth certificate of the donor-conceived person is a state fraud and that is wrong. There are practical difficulties: it will not be possible to provide 100% policing of compliance with a requirement to record the names of donors on certificates; there are genuine considerations of privacy which mean that the fact of donor conception ought perhaps not to be available to anyone who searches the register of births. But these are problems of implementation, not principle. It would be very simple to institute a system of three-part certification, and a model for such a system has been in use in the United Kingdom since the 1970s. In the United Kingdom everyone has a "short form" birth certificate which sets out their name and date of birth but does not identify their parents, and a "long form" certificate which does identify their parents. But adopted people have a short form certificate, exactly the same as everyone else', and a Certificate of Adoption, which tells them that they are adopted and provides a unique reference which links that certificate with their original long form birth certificate. When they reach the age of majority – 18 in the United Kingdom – they can gain access to that original long form certificate, which identifies their birth parents. This system does not breach the privacy of the people involved because the short form certificate is all that is required for almost all public purposes (applying for a passport and so forth). All that is required to implement this system for the donor-conceived is the political will.

The Government of Canada chose in 2004 to prevent donor-conceived people from knowing the names of their progenitors without the progenitors' consent. Although that relevant part of that legislation has been repealed, there is no provincial or territorial registry system to create, preserve and disclose donor information. The fertility industry makes it difficult for progenitors to have the choice to be contacted to seek their consent to because the industry often will not inform donors of the fact that their offspring seek contact. If Canada and its provinces ban donor anonymity and introduce a system of accurate birth certificates, donor offspring will still, as we always have, face the massed ranks of the fertility industry, who always fear that openness about donor conception will hurt their business. But there is a growing, and increasingly vocal, group of adult offspring of donors, and we are not about to stop making ourselves heard and telling our stories.

I believe that the underlying principle that access to one's personal history is a human right has much wider application than donor conception. If the principle were given legal status as a human right it might have protected the British children sent abroad to the colonies in the 50s and 60s by Barnardos on the false premise that their parents were dead or had rejected them, the children of the Argentinian "disappeared", adopted by their parents' murderers; the Australian Aboriginal children adopted forcibly into white Australian families and the Canadian native children from being forced into residential schools to be cut off from their ancestral culture.

I think all people have the right not to be deliberately deceived, or deprived of significant information, about their essential personal history. Our stories are ours, among our most precious goods, and while we cannot prevent individuals from lying to us, the state must not connive.

Note

1 A version of this article was originally published by The Guardian, Thursday 2 August 2007.

Chapter Twenty-Three
Conclusion

Juliet Guichon, Ian Mitchell, Michelle Giroux

This book was conceived as an attempt to advance the debate on whether secrecy concerning donor conception should be discouraged and donor anonymity should be retained or banned in Canada. Policy discussion about donor anonymity tended to exclude the insights, feelings and biographies of those most affected by the practice and for the longest time: the donor-conceived. Yet, despite the original limited aims of the book, the power of the stories of the donor-conceived, the size of the obstacles they face to learn what most of us take for granted, and the preliminary health science evidence available caused this work to become more ambitious. Rather than attempting merely to "level the playing field", the book now argues for, and proposes solutions to help give legislative effect to, what we believe is the right answer.

This collection of stories, studies and analyses together seek to present the case that secrecy should be discouraged and the law ought to ban donor anonymity. Many donor-conceived people wish to have the opportunity and right to know their identities. The evidence for this desire lies also on the World Wide Web. While the recipients of gametes and the donors themselves have important interests, banning anonymity is not certain to affect such interests negatively. The history of the practice and the development of medical ethics codes suggest that insufficient attention has been paid to the interests of the donor-conceived, a lesson that we might have learned from adoption history. Community health science research conducted to date cannot be used as definitive evidence that anonymity causes harm, but research on identity development and the value of having a full genetic history all suggest that donor anonymity harms the donor-conceived. Neither the threat of a decline in supply of gametes nor the 2004 Parliamentary focus on the interests of adults should be a barrier to banning anonymity, especially given that no plausible account of ethics can justify keeping donor identities secret, and Canada has international obligations and a constitutional duty equally to protect a person's right to know their progenitors. Adoption law and the law related to the registration of purebred animals demonstrate that it is possible to collect, preserve and disclose important records of identity and medical, social and cultural history for offspring. To facilitate a ban on anonymity, Quebec civil law and other provinces' and territories' common law ought to be amended to make clear the legal rights and responsibilities of donors. Donor-conceived people, like the rest of us, need to be able to tell their stories. It is time for the state to recognize the rights of the donor-conceived; time to stop conniving in concealment and lies. It is time for the truth.

List of Contributors, Advisors and Editors

Jean Benward, B.A. (Barnard) MSW (Columbia) LCSW, is a psychotherapist in San Ramon, California, who specializes in adoption and infertility, and serves also as a consultant to staff and patients in third party reproduction programs. As a member of the Mental Health Professional group of the American Society of Reproductive Medicine since 1994, she served on its executive committee for seven years, and as the former MHPG chair and former co chair of its donor registry task force. She has presented numerous lectures, workshops and papers to patients and professionals on topics including national donor registries, ethics issues in gamete donation, regulation of assisted reproductive technologies, parallels between adoption and donor conception, and the psychological issues in donor conception. She served nine years as co president of the Board of Directors of the Sperm Bank of California, which pioneered the use of identity release sperm donors.

Bill Cordray is a retired architect from Salt Lake City, Utah. He was conceived through sperm donation in Utah during World War II and was born three weeks before Hiroshima. Although he suspected his paternity for most of his life, he didn't learn the truth until he was 37. His search for his donor father has taken him into an ever-increasing set of labyrinths.

Mariana De Lorenzi LL.L. and LL.M. (Rosario, Argentina); Dip. Advanced Studies and PhD candidate (Barcelona, Spain) is a member of a Research Team of the University of Barcelona (School of Law, Department of Civil Law). She is interested in the fields of identity, parenthood and assisted human reproduction technologies. Her dissertation for the Diploma in Advanced Studies concerns the right to know one's genetic origins in assisted human reproduction. Ms. De Lorenzi has undertaken research in Argentina, Spain, Canada and England, which has been presented at national and international conferences and published in many journals and books (e.g. the Canadian Journal of Family Law, Personalized Medicine, Family Law in Latin-America, Revista de Derecho de Familia, For The Rights of Children and Adolescents: A Global Commitment from the Right of Participation in the 20th Anniversary of the Convention on the Rights of the Child).

W. Ben Gibbard, MD (UBC), MCS (Regent College), MSc (Calgary) is an Assistant Professor of Paediatrics at the University of Calgary and a Developmental Pediatrician at the Alberta Children's Hospital/Child Development Centre. His previous master's training in ethics and theology focused on issues in medical genetics. Present research interests include ethical issues related to the diagnosis and care of children with developmental disorders such as autism spectrum disorders and fetal alcohol spectrum disorders. Other research interests focus on social paediatrics, and cumulative risk in children with complex neurodevelopmental and neuropsychiatric conditions.

David Gollancz is a barrister practising in London, UK. He is a donor offspring. Since 1994 he has written and spoken publicly as an advocate of the right of offspring of assisted reproduction to know the truth about their conception, including the identity of gamete donors. He was a member of the Project Group on Assisted Reproduction (PROGAR), which played a major part in promoting the change in UK law set out in the Human Fertilisation and Embryology Authority (Disclosure of Donor Information) Regulations 2004.

Rhonda E. Harris, RN, MN, received a Diploma of Nursing from the Misericordia School of Nursing in Edmonton, and both a Bachelor's and Master's degree in Nursing from the University of Alberta. For her Master's thesis, Rhonda investigated women's experiences of infertility in a qualitative study, the findings of which are published in the edited book, *Uncertain Motherhood*. Rhonda has participated in a variety of research projects including a Canadian follow-up qualitative study that focused on oocyte recipients and their known donors. Based on an extensive literature review about the experiences of Donor Offspring, she presented, "Secret Fathers: Anonymity in Donor Insemination," at the 6th Western Canadian Conference on Sexual Health in Edmonton. Rhonda regularly shares her personal story of chronic illness with health-care students and professionals. She is also interested in Thanatology (i.e., Death and Dying). Rhonda's primary area of clinical practice is the Neonatal Intensive Care Unit (NICU).

Julie L. Lauzon, BSc, MDv(Ottawa); MHSC (Toronto), FRCPC, FCCMG, is a Clinical Assistant Professor in the Department of Medical Genetics at the University of Calgary. She works as a Clinical Geneticist at the Alberta Children's Hospital. She is the Chair of the Education, Ethics and Public Policy Committee of the Canadian College of Medical Genetics. She also serves on the Conjoint Health Research Ethics Board. Her research and clinical interests include consent and confidentiality in genetic testing as well as ethical issues in prenatal genetics.

List of Contributors, Advisors and Editors

Alison Motluk, BA (Toronto), MSc (London School of Economics, UK) is a freelance journalist who works for *CBC Radio, The Walrus, New Scientist, The Economist* and *The Globe and Mail*. She has reported widely on fertility issues, including the story of the boy who found his anonymous sperm donor using only his saliva and the internet, a story about the Donor Semen Archive, which analyzes DNA from semen vials, syringes and offspring so that offspring have access to information about their donors and siblings, and a two-part radio documentary for CBC Ideas about the new relationships that have come about as a result of sperm donation. She has also written and broadcast about egg donation and held a Canadian Institute for Health Research journalism grant to study and report on the experience of donating eggs in Canada.

Stacey A. Page BSc, MSc, PhD (Calgary) is Assistant Professor, Department of Community Health Sciences, Faculty of Medicine, University of Calgary. She is the Chair of the Conjoint Health Research Ethics Board at the University of Calgary and a member of the Mental Health and Addictions Ethics Committee, Calgary Zone, Alberta Health Services. Dr. Page served on the Executive of the Canadian Bioethics Society from 2004-2011. She has published in the areas of privacy, complementary and alternative medicine, and ethics in mental health.

Verónica B. Piñero LL.L., M.C.A., LL.M. JD is an articling student with a national law firm in Toronto. Ms. Piñero holds a civil law degree from the Universidad Nacional del Sur (Argentina), where she was awarded the Excellence Bourse for academic achievement. While living in Argentina, Ms. Piñero worked in the Federal Court's Criminal Law Division, specializing in illegal drug offences. She completed graduate education in criminology and law at the University of Ottawa. Her doctoral dissertation explored the legal history of the Canadian youth criminal law system. She has published her research broadly, and was a co-editor of *Droits de l'enfant. Actes de la conférence internationale, Ottawa, mars 2007* (Montreal: Wilson-Lafleur). In her undergraduate legal studies at the University of Calgary, she specialized in tax and natural resources law.

Olivia Pratten BA (UBC), MSc.(Columbia) is a professional journalist and an advocate for change in the area of reproductive technologies. Prior to the passage of the *Assisted Human Reproduction Act* (Canada, 2004), she was a speaker and panellist at numerous conferences and government consultations including the Commons Standing Committee on Health and the Senate Committee on Social Affairs, Science and Technology. Her advocacy continues through both the litigation she has brought before the Supreme Court of British Columbia, and her addresses to researchers and the media about the rights and interests of children conceived with reproductive technology.

Joanna Rose PhD (Queensland Univ. of Technology) is the first donor-conceived person in the common law world to bring litigation against a health authority regarding donor conception. The United Kingdom court held that a child conceived by donor gametes "is entitled to establish a picture of his [her] identity as much as anyone else."

Laura Shanner BA (Hons-Biology) Knox College; MA, PhD (Georgetown – Philosophy/Bioethics) is the founder of Nanaimo Health Ethics Consulting in British Columbia, and is an Adjunct Professor at the John Dossetor Health Ethics Centre, University of Alberta. Awards from the Canadian Institutes of Health Research and the Alberta Heritage Foundation for Medical Research supported her research in reproductive ethics, law and policy (2000-2005), and she served as an expert consultant to CIHR's Stem Cell Oversight Committee (2006-2011) and multiple Health Canada working groups on reproductive health policy. Dr. Shanner has worked in the U.S., Australia and the U.K in addition to Canada, and published in books and journals in medicine, law, philosophy and women's studies.

Barry Stevens is a Toronto writer and filmmaker. A film called *Offspring* about his search for the man from whose sperm he was made was seen in 61 countries and was nominated for an Emmy and a Grierson, and won the Donald Brittain Award as well as being voted the most popular film at IDFA, the world's largest documentary festival. He subsequently made another film that combined a personal story with an exploration of the future of reproductive and genetic technologies, called *Bio-Dad*. Barry is a founding member of the International Donor Offspring Alliance.

Project Advisor

Diane Allen is Executive Director of the Infertility Network (IN), a Canadian charity she helped to found in 1990 after a personal experience with infertility. Under her leadership, IN has provided information, support and referral to more than 50,000 Canadians; organized over 70 educational seminars and several international conferences; run a monthly support group; published a daily email news bulletin; developed an extensive national and international network of contacts involved in various aspects of Assisted Human Reproduction (AHR); and advocated for legislation and regulation to protect the interests of infertility patients, as well as children conceived through AHR. Her work has been recognized by awards from the Adoption Council of Ontario and the Donor Conception Support Group of Australia.

Editors

Juliet Guichon BA (Yale); BA, BCL, MA (Oxon.); SJD (Toronto) is Assistant Professor in the Department of Community Health Sciences. Called to the Bar of Ontario, she has served on the Calgary Conjoint Health Research Ethics Board and is an award-winning lecturer. Her publications focus on the intersection of law and medicine, in particular, consent to medical treatment and reproductive technology. She wrote the background report on preconception arrangements ('surrogate' motherhood) for the Royal Commission on New Reproductive Technologies. The video for which she wrote the screenplay *I Lease Wombs, I Don't Sell Babies: An Inquiry into 'Surrogate Motherhood'* was awarded the Silver Apple at the U.S. National Educational Film and Video Festival.

Ian Mitchell MB, ChB (Edin), MA, MRCP (UK), FRCPC. He is a Professor of Paediatrics at the University of Calgary where he has won numerous teaching awards, and a Paediatric Respirologist at the Alberta Children's Hospital. He earned a MA Bioethics, Medical College of Wisconsin, and is involved in bioethics teaching and in bioethics at a national level. He served as President of the Canadian Bioethics Society (2002-04) and is currently a member of Canadian Medical Association Committee on Ethics and Canadian Paediatric Society's Bioethics Committee. Formerly medical director of the Alberta Children's Hospital and Chair of the Conjoint Health Research Ethics Board of the Calgary Health Region and the University of Calgary, Dr. Mitchell's research and clinical interests include ethics in children, end-of-life decision making and ethical issues in the home care of children with complex life-threatening conditions.

Michelle Giroux, LL.L. (Ottawa), M.A. Medical Law and Ethics (London, UK) is Full Professor at the Faculty of Law, Civil Law Section, at the University of Ottawa. She is a Member of the Québec Bar and of the Interdisciplinary Research Laboratory on the Rights of the Child (LRIDE). In 2012, she was appointed by the Government of Québec to the Committee of Experts for the implementation of the recommendations of the Select Committee on Dying with Dignity. Professor

Giroux teaches family law, bioethics and public health law. She also collaborates in the multidisciplinary PHD Program in Population Health at the University of Ottawa. She published and presented on the right to know one's origins in Canada and abroad. Her research interests also focus on issues of parentage of children, namely those born of assisted human reproductive technologies, on surrogacy and on patient safety in the home care environment.